NONPROFIT
MARKETING

NONPROFIT
MARKETING

Marketing Management for Charitable and Nongovernmental Organizations

Walter WYMER, Jr.
Christopher Newport University

Patricia KNOWLES
Clemson University

Roger GOMES
Clemson University

SAGE Publications
Thousand Oaks ▪ London ▪ New Delhi

For information:

 Sage Publications, Inc.
2455 Teller Road
Thousand Oaks, California 91320
E-mail: order@sagepub.com

Sage Publications Ltd.
1 Oliver's Yard
55 City Road
London EC1Y 1SP
United Kingdom

Sage Publications India Pvt. Ltd.
B-42, Panchsheel Enclave
Post Box 4109
New Delhi 110 017 India

Printed in the United States of America

Library of Congress Cataloging-in-Publication Data

Nonprofit marketing: Marketing management for charitable and nongovernmental organizations / Walter Wymer, Jr. . . . [et al.].
     p. cm.
Includes bibliographical references and index.
ISBN 1-4129-0923-6 (cloth)
   1. Nonprofit organizations—Marketing. I. Wymer, Walter W.
HF5415.N65 2006
658.8—dc22   2005027277

This book is printed on acid-free paper.

06 07 08 09 10   8 7 6 5 4 3 2 1

Acquisitions Editor:	Al Bruckner
Editorial Assistant:	MaryAnn Vail
Production Editor:	Diane S. Foster
Copy Editor:	Bonnie Freeman
Typesetter:	C&M Digitals (P) Ltd.
Proofreader:	Dennis Webb
Indexer:	Molly Hall
Cover Designer:	Candice Harman

Contents

Acknowledgments

With thanks and love to our families for their understanding and support during this process. With special thanks to Mom (Knowles), who, at times, kept us fed and who makes the best pineapple upside-down cake in the world.

And, last but certainly not least, thanks be to God.

—Pat Knowles and Roger Gomes

I would like to thank my coauthors for their support and encouragement in the project, especially Walter.

—Mike Polonsky

One of life's great lessons that I learned is that we all need help from time to time. As a doctoral student, I had the privilege of receiving help from some of the finest, most generous people I've ever met. Joe Miller, thanks for your kindness. Dwight Burlingame, thanks for opening doors for me, providing opportunities. To Don Self, your mentorship and the opportunities you've provided have been invaluable to me. Joe, Dwight, and Don, you've been a cornerstone of whatever success I've had as a professor and scholar.

I would also like to acknowledge two colleagues for their creativity, energy, brilliance, and friendship. Sridhar Samu, having known you since we were doctoral students together has been an honor. Adrian Sargeant, you are a contemporary whom I admire and respect and whom I am privileged to call a colleague and a friend.

—Walter Wymer

Part I

Marketing Management

1

Introduction to Nonprofit Marketing

Content

Learning Objectives

On completion of this chapter, the reader will

- Understand the definition and aims of nonprofit marketing
- Understand the variety of purposes of nonprofit marketing
- Understand the importance of the nonprofit sector to our society
- Understand the various types of nonprofit organizations
- Understand the challenges faced by the nonprofit sector
- Understand how the nonprofit sector has adopted a marketing approach
- Understand some of the emerging issues faced by nonprofit marketers

Opening Vignette: Ty Hafan

Ty Hafan, founded in 1999, is a small nonprofit organization located near the town of Barry, in Wales, United Kingdom. This nonprofit is a 10-bed children's hospice. It offers comfort and support for dying children and bereavement counseling for family members. Its services are free. Ty Hafan's costs are about £2 million per year. Funding is provided by charitable contributions.

Ty Hafan actively raises funds in order to cover its operating expenses. Currently, it is offering a wristband for sale (£2 each) that bears the slogan "Live the Moment." It offers a variety of ways people who wish to support its mission can contribute or volunteer. Ty Hafan also actively uses its website to communicate with the outside world.

Like many nonprofit organizations, Ty Hafan has had to adopt a marketing approach to its administrative system. The need to build its public image, raise funds, and recruit volunteers demanded a systematic process to focus its various activities on prioritized goals.

Managers in many nonprofit organizations have adopted a marketing approach. In nonprofit organizations, marketing tactics are used to build the organization's image and reputation in society and help the public remember the organization and its cause. Marketing tactics help differentiate one nonprofit from another nonprofit that is offering similar programs. Marketing tactics are used to attract and retain donors and volunteers.

We define **nonprofit marketing** as the use of marketing tactics to further the goals and objectives of nonprofit organizations. Although advertising, public relations, and fund-raising are examples of nonprofit marketing tactics, nonprofit marketing also includes a broad array of other activities. Gathering and processing information for decision making are considered components of nonprofit marketing. Relations with governments, board members, donors, and volunteers are part of nonprofit marketing.

In a broader view, nonprofit marketing is a management orientation that helps the nonprofit organization expand its horizon beyond its internal operations and programs to also encompass the external world that affects the organization. A nonprofit organization that has a marketing orientation is able to focus its various activities and external communications to project a consistent image of itself and influence the way the external world perceives it.

In this book, we use the term *nonprofit organization* broadly to refer to a variety of related nonbusiness and nongovernmental organizations (NGOs). As illustrated in Figure 1.1, using employment figures, we distinguish between the nonprofit, government, and business sectors of society. The relative size of each sector will vary from country to country. It is also possible to have hybrid organizations resulting from intersectoral collaborations. We will also use the term **nonprofit sector** to refer to that portion of a society that includes all nonprofit, charitable, and nongovernmental organizations. The nonprofit sector thus includes religious congregations, universities, hospitals, environmental groups, art museums, youth recreation associations, civil rights groups, community development organizations, labor unions, political parties, social clubs, and others (Boris and Steuerle, 1999). The nonprofit sector is sometimes called the voluntary sector, the civil society, or the independent sector in various countries.

❖ **Figure 1.1**   Three Sectors of a Civil Society

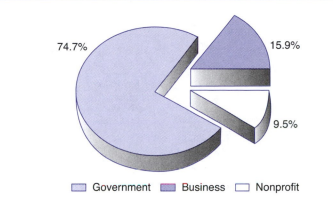

74.7%   15.9%

9.5%

☐ Government   ▥ Business   ☐ Nonprofit

SOURCE: Independent Sector Facts and Findings online at www.independentsector.org/PDFs/
npemployment.pdf

While nonprofit organizations have different names in different parts of the world, and while they encompass many different types of these organizations, from activist groups to zoological societies, we will standardize our terminology to a degree, sometimes abbreviating *nonprofit organization* as NPO in this book. We may also drop *organization* and simply refer to a nonprofit organization as a nonprofit. These uses are all commonly accepted among nonprofit professionals.

Dimensions of Nonprofit Marketing

In the previous section, we provided an overview of the nonprofit marketing concept. In this section, we will be more specific in delineating some of the various dimensions of nonprofit marketing. We will discuss planning, positioning, communicating, and attracting resources.

Planning. Marketing professionals in nonprofit organizations, or nonprofit marketers, develop plans to help the nonprofit achieve its strategic goals; that is, to fulfill its mission.

Positioning. Nonprofit organizations usually benefit from being widely known in society. There are many nonprofit organizations and many opportunities for people to contribute to a worthy cause. A nonprofit's first task in competing for donations is becoming well-known to the community it serves. People are bombarded with commercial marketing messages throughout the day. Nonprofit marketers must define their organizations in this clutter of information.

Once the NPO is known, the next task is to influence the public's perception of the organization. Do people have a favorable, unfavorable, or neutral attitude toward the

❖ **Figure 1.2** Positioning Tasks

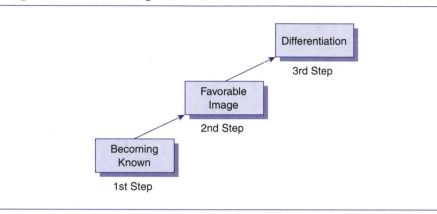

NPO? Do people know what the organization does? How do people think of the NPO in relation to other NPOs? **Positioning** refers to implementing marketing activities aimed at influencing the public's perception of the NPO, that is, developing a specific image of the NPO in the mind of the public. **Brand** refers to the name, logo, and symbols that uniquely identify an NPO and distinguish it from other organizations. Figure 1.2 shows the three progressive positioning tasks for a nonprofit. The foundation begins with getting the organization known. Then the image and the public perception of the organization become a greater concern. Last, the emphasis shifts to framing how the public perceives the organization in relation to other similar organizations, the task known as differentiation.

Communication. Communication is a key marketing activity that enables the organization to achieve many of its marketing goals. The NPO directs its communications to its various stakeholders. **Stakeholders** are groups that have a meaningful interest in the nonprofit organization. Generally, these include the organization's clients, board members, employees, volunteers, donors, granting organizations, government, other nonprofits, and the communities served by the NPO.

A nonprofit's clients are the people to whom it provides services. There must be effective communication for the exchange between client and organization to be successful. Board members must be recruited and retained. Employees need to understand the NPO's goals and objectives. They need to have a voice in the development of plans. Volunteers must be recruited and retained. Donors must be acquired and nurtured. Nonprofits often communicate with government officials to represent their causes and interests. The communities served by a nonprofit need to know about its services.

Successful nonprofit organizations establish bonds with their stakeholders and develop relationships with them. Nonprofits' communication programs are an important resource for reaching out and maintaining contact with stakeholders.

Resource Attraction. Nonprofit marketers have a very important **resource attraction function**. This generally refers to attracting donations of time and funds, as depicted

❖ **Figure 1.3**   Resource Attraction Function

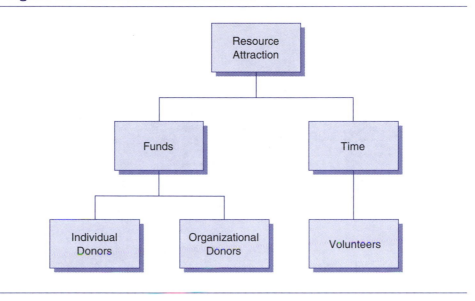

in Figure 1.3. *Donations of time* refers to the recruitment and retention of volunteers. *Donations of funds* refers to contributions from organizations and individuals. These contributions can be in-kind donations, such as products a company manufacturers, or monetary donations. Attracting contributions requires more discussion because it covers several topics. For example, individual donors are categorized in terms of contributed amount (large vs. regular donors), frequency (regular donors, annual campaign donors), events (special events or capital campaigns), and longevity (which includes bequest giving). Collaboration with the business sector is varied also.

Importance of Nonprofit Sector

The nonprofit sector exists to benefit society. Within the nonprofit sector, there is a rich and dynamic diversity of causes and organizations. Without the many thousands of nonprofits, with their many millions of volunteers, society would lack valuable services, diversity, and civic participation.

The nonprofit sector is important because it provides services that would not be performed by the business sector. Many services needed by a society do not generate a profit and are, therefore, unattractive to the business sector. Boys and Girls Clubs of America, for example, offers a variety of beneficial programs for youth. Examples include programs that foster conflict resolution skills, communication skills, improved homework performance, recreation and team sports, gang prevention, drug prevention, and prevention of teen pregnancy. Businesses are not interested in providing these services because, in most cases, the clients cannot afford to pay for them. Nevertheless, because nonprofits are available, these services are provided, and many individuals benefit, as well as society in general.

❖ **Table 1.1**   Charitable Giving in the United States, 2003

Segment	Giving Level ($ billions)	% Change From 2002 Giving	% of Total
Individuals	179.36	+2.5	74.5
Bequests	21.60	+12.8	8.2
Foundations	26.30	−2.5	10.9
Corporations	13.46	+4.2	5.6
Total	240.72		99.2

SOURCE: Adapted from Giving USA Foundation, 2004.

Nonprofits are important because they allow citizens to participate in their communities collectively. One of the hallmarks of a free, vibrant society is a strong nonprofit sector that activates citizen participation.

In 2002, there were about 1.8 million nonprofits in the United States (Lee, 2004). In terms of charitable giving in the United States, individuals, estates, foundations, and corporations gave an estimated $240.72 billion to charitable causes in 2003, according to "Giving USA 2004," a study released by the Giving USA Foundation. Table 1.1 shows how various segments contributed to this sum. In addition to charitable contributions, Americans generously donate their time. The Independent Sector (2004) estimates that Americans donated $266 billion of volunteer service to the U.S. nonprofit sector.

Statistics Canada sponsored a study of Canadian nonprofits in 2003. (The full report is available via www.nonprofitscan.ca). Canada had 161,000 nonprofits that year, and Canadians donated $8 billion to their nonprofit sector.

According to the Charity Commission for England and Wales, England had 166,129 nonprofits and revenues of £34.567 billion (U.S. $ system) in 2004. In addition, approximately 27,000 nonprofits exist in Scotland and 7,500 in Northern Ireland.

According to the Australian Bureau of Statistics, Australia had approximately 380,000 nonprofits of various types in 2000. About 35,000 of them had paid staff.

Although just a sampling of the scope of the nonprofit sector in various parts of the world, these figures illustrate that the nonprofit sector is substantial. It provides a variety of services and benefits to large portions of society.

Types of Nonprofit Organizations

Formal Versus Informal. Nonprofit organizations can be formal or informal. An **informal nonprofit** organizes for an event or project and disbands on completion. Informal nonprofits are volunteer operated, having no paid staff.

Formal nonprofit organizations usually, but not always, have one or more paid staff. They are usually chartered or registered with the government in their country.

In terms of relative size, formal organizations are usually larger than informal organizations. As a nonprofit grows, it hires more staff, separates its managerial tasks into functional areas, and hires professional staff to manage the functional areas. A small nonprofit may have only one marketing professional, who manages all the nonprofit's marketing activities. A large nonprofit is more likely to have marketing professionals directing the activities in subspecialty areas. For example, in a large nonprofit, there might be a marketing professional responsible for major donors, another responsible for corporate relationships, another for public affairs, another for advertising, another for volunteers, and so forth.

Categorization of NPOs. Countries may provide slightly different labels for some of the nonprofit categories, but nonprofits generally fall into the following groups:

- Religious organizations
- Education and research organizations
- Health-related organizations
- Social welfare organizations
- Art and culture organizations
- Business, professional, and membership organizations
- Youth development organizations
- Other types of nonprofits

The proportion of a population's charitable giving going to each category of nonprofit will vary by country, a reflection of cultural and governmental differences. For example, in the United States, religious organizations received the greatest share of charitable contributions (Giving USA Foundation, 2005). In Canada, arts organizations get about 20 percent of contributions, the most of any nonprofit category (Statistics Canada, 2004).

Challenges Faced by the Nonprofit Sector

Nonprofit organizations exist in a dynamic, continually changing culture. Nonprofit managers, to be effective, must anticipate changes. They must be aware of social, economic, technological, and political influences in society that also impact the nonprofit sector. NPOs must change and adapt along with society. In this section, we will discuss some challenges nonprofit managers currently face.

Governmental Shifting of Responsibility to Nonprofit Sector

Government has been shifting a growing proportion of human services to the nonprofit sector (O'Connell, 1996; Snavely and Desai, 2001). In many nations, a growing political conservatism seeks to reduce social welfare provided by government. For example, in countries as diverse as the United Kingdom and Chile, government has shifted social security from the government sector to the private sector. In instances in which providing social services is not profitable, society is looking to the nonprofit sector to take responsibility (Brock, 2005).

In intergovernmental service delivery, such as in international aid, governments typically rely on nonprofits. International aid is often provided to an international NGO, which will use the aid to deliver services to the targeted areas.

Reduced Government Financial Support of Nonprofit Sector

Ironically, while governments are relying more on the nonprofit sector, they are providing less funding to nonprofits (Johns Hopkins University News Releases, 2003). For example, U.S. President George W. Bush, in his proposed 2006 budget, has drastically cut government funding of nonprofits, as well as tax incentives to encourage individual donations (OMB Watch, 2005). The federal government, under a politically conservative majority, has proposed legislation to reduce tax incentives for individual charitable giving and to increase NPO taxation (Association of Fundraising Professionals, 2005). This phenomenon is also occurring at the state level. For example, in a manner parallel to the federal government, the state of Virginia (a) reduced taxes, which (b) reduced government income, which (c) created a budget deficit, which (d) necessitated budget cuts, which (e) resulted in sharply reduced government allocations to the nonprofit sector, across all types of NPOs, as well as to government social welfare programs (Venture Philanthropy Partners, 2003).

The trend toward governmental shifting of social responsibility to the nonprofit sector while concurrently reducing public funding is not limited to the United States. For example, the same phenomenon is occurring in Canada. Although on a smaller scale than in the United States, the Canadian government is undergoing an ideological shift, placing less emphasis on providing social services and funds for the nonprofit sector and greater emphasis on individual responsibility (Phillips, 2005). Government funding for the nonprofit sector has been reduced in Australia as well (Moore, 2004).

In the United Kingdom, the level of government funding of NPOs has remained about the same, but another change has occurred. U.K. NPOs more often receive funding on contract from local and central governments to provide public services rather than as grants for the nonprofits to do as they wish. Furthermore, members of Parliament have attempted to provide more scrutiny and tighter regulation of the nonprofit sector through measures such as the Charities Bill, the first such measure against U.K. charities in 400 years (Smithers and Carvel, 2004).

Reduction and Elimination of Estate and Inheritance Taxes

One goal of the conservative movement in federal and state government in the United States has been the redistribution of wealth in favor of very wealthy individuals. In 2001, President Bush and a conservative Republican Congress passed into law massive tax cuts, amounting to almost $2 trillion, that favored the most wealthy in society (Citizens for Tax Justice, 2002). In addition, the government reduced and then eliminated the estate tax, which was levied only on wealthy estates. Formerly, many wealthy individuals preferred to bequeath money to their favorite nonprofits rather than pay the entire tax to the government. The nonprofit community is waiting to learn what effect the elimination of the estate tax by the federal and some state governments will have on their bequest contributions (American Voice, 2004). North

❖ **Table 1.2**   Growth of U.S. Nonprofits

Year	Number
1940	12,500
1950	50,000
1967	309,000
1977	700,000
1989	1,000,000
1995	1,600,000
2002	1,800,000

America, Western Europe, and Australia have large populations who are at a stage in their life when they are drafting a will and considering how their estate will someday be distributed. Their decisions represent a major challenge for the nonprofit sector, which is increasingly dependent on bequest giving (Havens and Schervish, 2003).

Increasing Number of Nonprofits

The international nonprofit sector has been steadily growing (Salamon, 1996). This growth is occurring in areas of the world like eastern Europe (Yancey et al., 2002). Indeed, the growth of the nonprofit sector appears to be nearly a global phenomenon (Anheier, Kaldor, & Glasius, 2004). Although different countries may emphasize different dimensions of the nonprofit sector (for example, education and health in one country, social welfare in another), the sector is a growing, dynamic force (Homewood, 1998). Table 1.2 provides an example of the continuous growth of the nonprofit sector in the United States.

Increased Reliance on Business Sector

As the reader can anticipate from the preceding discussion, many nonprofits are facing substantial challenges. The number of nonprofits is growing, both internationally and domestically. Many governments are shifting the provision of social services to the nonprofit sector, all the while reducing governmental funding to nonprofits. NPOs are being asked to do more for society while competing with a growing number of other nonprofits for funding.

Nonprofits are looking to the business sector for additional funding. Businesses, on the other hand, are facing increased competition in their own industries and are supporting worthy causes as a means of enhancing their images and differentiating themselves from competitors. Business relationships with nonprofits is the topic of the final chapter of this book.

Collaboration for Capacity Building

As the number of nonprofits grows, foundations and other funding bodies, including umbrella organizations such as the United Way, are faced with requests from many more NPOs than they can possibly fund. If a foundation's mission is to alleviate child deprivation, it must decide which NPOs having relevant programs should be funded. The growing trend among funding bodies is to take a broader approach. Instead of working to improve child welfare by funding multiple nonprofits in a piecemeal fashion, foundations and other funding organizations are requiring related nonprofits to collaborate so as to manage their programs in a coordinated and more efficient manner.

Economic Cycles

National economies cycle through upswings and downturns, good times and bad times. The good times (economic growth and prosperity) usually benefit nonprofits. Individuals give more because they are more secure in their employment and because their investments are increasing in value. Foundations' endowments are earning healthy returns, providing greater amounts to be distributed to nonprofits. Businesses are profitable and sales are increasing, making collaboration with nonprofits more attractive.

Economic downturns are generally not good for nonprofits. Individuals are less secure about their employment, and their investments do not do well, so they are less generous in their contributions to charities. Foundations' endowments earn less income, providing a smaller pool of funding for the nonprofits requesting grants. Corporations' sales and earnings are weak, making corporate support of NPOs more difficult to justify.

Nevertheless, when economic times are troubled, nonprofits still need funding. If fact, for social service nonprofits, the need for funding very well may increase as the negative social effects of a weakened economy increase the demand for social services. Nonprofit managers are challenged to find stable sources of revenue to provide a predictable, consistent resource stream to maintain their nonprofit's operations. Because attracting resources is such an important challenge in the modern environment in which nonprofits exist, the second half of this text is largely devoted to ways of attracting funding and volunteers.

Getting Through Communications Clutter

The business sector bombards individuals with marketing messages incessantly. The number of advertising messages the average American is exposed to increased from 560 each day in 1971 to more than 3,000 each day by 1997 (Shenk, 1997). American businesses spend more than $200 billion annually to put their brands before individuals (Kilbourne, 1999). Globally, the amount spent on advertising is expected to grow from $358 billion in 2004 to $477 billion in 2009 (Newcomb, 2005).

CHAPTER INSIGHT	**Getting Through the Noise**

- Some 700 new products are introduced every day.
- In 2004, 26,893 new food and household products were introduced, including 115 deodorants, 187 breakfast cereals, and 303 women's fragrances.
- There are about 2 million brands in the world.
- The average American adult is bombarded with as many as 3,000 advertising messages a day, up more than fivefold in less than 30 years.
- Children are presented with about 40,000 commercials annually.
- By the age of 10, children have memorized 300 to 400 brands.
- The average adult can recognize thousands of brands.

SOURCE: Hotz (2005)

Because individuals are exposed to numerous marketing messages every day and because the media are saturated with commercial advertising, the nonprofit marketer's task of communicating to various target audiences is made ever more challenging.

Ethical Issue	The Next Competitive Battlefield: The Brain

The U.S. Food and Drug Administration has recently given its approval for Cyberkinetics to test its BrainGate system on humans. A small hole is cut into the skull. A tiny computer chip is inserted onto the brain. Its electrodes are inserted into various parts of the brain. BrainGate is designed to read electronic signals from the brain, understand what thoughts the signals represent, and take the appropriate actions. At this early stage, a person using BrainGate can operate a computer and its applications by thought. The system is designed to allow people who have lost the use of their hands to use a computer. A computer interface detects brain signals and activates the appropriate robotic controls, substituting for the impaired human brain-to-nerve-to-muscle system. Research is currently under way to develop a system, called electroencephalography, that will use a device that attaches to the skull instead of the brain. People with spinal cord injuries could benefit from this developing technology (Pollack, 2004).

At the same time the BrainGate study is progressing, two researchers from the California Institute of Technology's social cognitive neuroscience laboratory have received millions of dollars in grants to also study the human brain. A 12-ton magnetic imaging scanner is studying the effects of marketing messages and images on the brain. The researchers are learning which marketing signals are most effective and how the brain assembles belief. Advertisers who can manipulate the human brain into forming beliefs favorable to their company's brands and products will have a strong competitive advantage (Hotz, 2005).

❖ **Table 1.3** Nonprofit Marketing Functions

Function	Examples
Attracting funding	Submitting grant proposals to government agencies and foundations, conducting annual campaigns and capital campaigns, organizing planned giving, seeking corporate donations, holding special events, etc.
Attracting volunteers	Understanding where to reach potential volunteers, what message will appeal to them, how to deliver appeal, etc.
Building relationships	Developing and maintaining relationships with board members, corporations, volunteers, clients, donors, funding agencies, government, media, public, etc.
Communicating	Advertising, publicizing, conducting public relations, reaching clients, maintaining government relations, carrying out advocacy and education

Adoption of Marketing Approach

To respond effectively to all the challenges facing nonprofits, nonprofit administrators (especially in larger organizations) have adopted a marketing orientation to managing their NPOs. This section discusses what is meant by a marketing orientation and how nonprofits use marketing tactics to achieve their goals and objectives.

Nonprofit Marketing Orientation

A nonprofit organization has a **marketing orientation** when it relies on marketing tactics to achieve its goals and objectives. An NPO that has a marketing orientation employs the array of marketing functions to attract resources and build vital relationships. Table 1.3 presents nonprofit marketing functions.

When an NPO has a marketing orientation, its various operational units and programs work in a coordinated fashion to (a) further the organization's mission, (b) achieve the organization's goals, and (c) communicate a consistent and focused message to groups of interest (clients, volunteers, donors, public, etc.).

When all parts of the organization are working toward common goals, all members of the organization can work with purpose, unity, and focus. This results in greater efficiency and consistency, reducing divergences of purpose all the while. Furthermore, when all parts of the organization are working together and communicating a consistent message outwardly, important constituencies obtain a clearer understanding of the organization's distinctiveness and value.

A marketing orientation helps the nonprofit focus outwardly. Staff persons naturally tend to concentrate on their functional areas of responsibility or on their programs. A marketing orientation helps to broaden their ability to take into account how their decisions affect other parts of the organization and how their statements and other messages influence the outside world's perception of the organization and its purpose.

A marketing orientation provides systematic means of coordinating activities designed to attract resources. When different areas of a nonprofit are focused on its direction and priorities, efforts to attract contributions, grants, volunteers, corporate support, and the like reflect organizational priorities rather than those of a program director or individual board member, for example. The energies of valuable staff are concentrated in areas likely to offer the greatest benefit to the organization.

Finally, a marketing orientation provides an organized approach to planning. The overarching strategic goals and objectives of the organization, guided by the nonprofit's vision and mission, reflect a consensus of the board and executive staff on the direction for the nonprofit. When strategic goals and objectives at the organizational level are clear, consistent, and focused, staff members in operational units have guidance in arriving at their own planning. Tactical planning in lower levels of the organization will help the organization achieve its strategic goals.

Current Issues in Nonprofit Marketing

Branding

Branding is a topic of major importance for nonprofit managers. Nonprofit managers think of a nonprofit's brand as its image or reputation: the way the organization is perceived by the public. A strong, favorable brand provides advantages for the nonprofit. The most widely known organizations have greater credibility because people already know about the organization and its mission.

When the tsunami disaster struck Asia in December 2004, the American Red Cross was able to raise millions of dollars of relief aid because people knew of the organization (brand awareness). Americans felt sending their donations to the American Red Cross was safe, and they believed the funds would be used responsibly (brand image). The American Red Cross is perceived by Americans to be a well-established, highly regarded, trustworthy disaster relief organization (brand personality).

Nonprofits that are most widely known (brand awareness) have a larger pool of potential donors. Through positioning activities, mentioned previously, a nonprofit helps the public understand its purpose and how it differs from other nonprofits (differentiation) and how the nonprofit is remarkable (brand personality). Through consistent public relations communications to various audiences, nonprofits establish favorable reputations (brand image).

Social Marketing

Social marketing refers to the use of marketing tactics in the creation, execution, and control of programs designed to influence social change. Many nonprofits desire to improve public health or social conditions. In doing so, they must find ways to increase public awareness of an issue and help a society or a subgroup of society change to a more healthful set of behaviors.

Changing human behavior is challenging, even when the change is beneficial. Teenagers receive immediate social rewards from smoking and discount the long-term consequences. The same can be said of drug use, teen pregnancy, sexually transmitted diseases, and drug or alcohol use.

In some important areas, corporations' interest in selling products and earning profits works against social marketers. Corporations spend billions of dollars encouraging unhealthy behaviors like smoking, drinking alcohol, eating processed and fast foods, and following sedentary lifestyles. Social marketers' resources for bringing their messages to groups of interest are often dwarfed by corporate advertising budgets.

Use of the Internet

Nonprofits use the Internet. The ways the Internet can be used are limited only by the prevailing technologies and the creativity of nonprofit managers. Websites are used to communicate with external groups. A professionally designed website reflects the professionalism of the nonprofit. Nonprofits use their websites to communicate a consistent message of the organization's purpose, mission, and cause.

Nonprofits raise funds online. They recruit volunteers online. E-newsletters and e-mails are sent to supporters. Online surveys obtain marketing information. Educational materials are distributed online. Products are sold online.

Organization of This Book

This text is organized to address the fundamentals of marketing in nonprofit organizations as well to address more advanced topics of special interest. The first half of this text (Chapters 1 through 6) surveys the breadth of nonprofit marketing. It is intended to familiarize the reader with the basic principles of nonprofit marketing. The second half (Chapters 7 through 12) deepens the reader's knowledge of important nonprofit marketing topics.

In Chapter 2, we will look more closely at the nonprofit and its cause, that is, the product part of the marketing mix. Chapter 2 will discuss in detail the nonprofit's mission and the importance of mission-focused management. We will examine how a nonprofit distinguishes itself (positioning) and communicates its value (unique value proposition).

Marketing managers, in order to make effective decisions, must have useful and timely information. Chapter 3 will discuss how nonprofit marketing managers obtain and use information to help them make marketing decisions.

With good information, nonprofits can develop their marketing plans. Marketing plans are descriptions of annual marketing activities and accompanying budgets. Developing marketing plans is the topic of Chapter 4.

In developing their plans, nonprofit marketing managers make numerous decisions. These may involve adjustments to programs, changes in public relations, advertising, collaboration with partners, and so forth. Marketers make decisions on those elements within their control (such as the amount of their budgets to allocate to advertising). These elements are called controllable variables (i.e., elements that can be changed by a marketing manager). Many other forces operate outside a manager's control, however (such as a new law, the economy, and so forth). These are known as uncontrollable variables. In marketing planning, managers decide which controllable variables to manipulate to achieve organizational goals.

Controllable variables are generally referred to as the **marketing mix**, the assortment of variables marketers use in achieving organizational goals and objectives. The controllable variables, or the marketing mix, are classified into one of four categories: product, place, promotion, and price. These four categories are known as the 4 P's of marketing and are the topics of Chapters 5 and 6.

With nonprofit marketing fundamentals presented in Chapters 2 through 6, a more in-depth coverage of specific topics begins in Chapter 7. The resource attraction function of nonprofit marketing, discussed earlier in this chapter, is the focus of Chapters 7 through 10. Direct marketing, the topic of Chapter 7, deals with marketing appeals targeted to specific individuals. For example, many nonprofit organizations have annual fund-raising campaigns in which letters are sent to current and prospective donors asking for their support. A large number of smaller donations are typically obtained by this means.

Special attention is usually given to individuals having the potential for giving disproportionately large donations. Whereas a large number of small donations are obtained through direct marketing techniques, a small number of large donations are usually obtained through personal marketing techniques. Chapter 8 addresses topics involved in attracting large donations.

To supplement the activities of direct marketing and marketing efforts to attract large donations, many nonprofits also conduct special events to raise funds, to increase public awareness of the nonprofit, and so forth. A special event may be the centerpiece of some nonprofits' fund-raising activities. Because of the importance of these events, this text includes a chapter on special events (Chapter 9).

The reader may recall that the resource attraction function of nonprofit marketing included both fund-raising activities and volunteer recruitment activities. Many nonprofits rely on volunteers. Recruiting and retaining volunteers is the topic of Chapter 10 and concludes our coverage of important resource attraction activities.

The final unit in this text devotes special attention to important emerging topics in the nonprofit sector. Chapter 11 discusses social and issues marketing, that is, bringing important issues to public attention and potentially changing public policy or public behavior. People are often reluctant to change their individual behaviors, even when the change would result in positive outcomes for them or for society in general. There are many such desirable changes, such as recycling, environmentally friendly gardening, quitting smoking and substance abuse, practicing safe sex, controlling one's weight, building physical fitness, and so forth.

This text concludes with a chapter devoted to cause marketing. Cause marketing, which is business sector support of nonprofits and their causes, has become common in many countries. It began to emerge in the United States in the 1980s, and its use has grown steadily since. Chapter 12 discusses cause marketing and how nonprofit managers can use it effectively.

Summary

Scope of Nonprofit Marketing. Our concept of nonprofit marketing includes the broad array of marketing tactics and activities that nonprofit organizations use to reach their goals and objectives. We will use the term *nonprofit organization* in this text to refer to all types of voluntary-sector organizations.

Dimensions of Nonprofit Marketing. Marketing professionals rely heavily on communicating with outside groups, or **publics**, in conducting marketing activities. A nonprofit organization becomes better known, helps others understand its mission, and influences public attitudes toward it through marketing activities like publicity, public relations, advertising, or special events. Nonprofit marketing professionals recruit volunteers, board members, and other supporters through communication vehicles like public service announcements, flyers posted in public spaces, and personal recruitment appeals. Funding is attracted through communication vehicles like the nonprofit's website, direct mail, telephone soliciting, e-mail appeals, and interpersonal contacts.

Nonprofit Sector. The nonprofit sector is an important component of a civil society. Nonprofit organizations provide important services that are not suitable for the government or business sectors to provide to a society. The number of countries with growing nonprofit sectors is large and getting larger. The regions with the largest nonprofit sectors include North America, western Europe, Australia, and New Zealand. Less-developed countries undergoing economic growth are also experiencing growth in their nonprofit sector.

Types of NPOs. There is a large variety of nonnprofit organizations that comprise the nonprofit sector of a civil society. Nonprofits can be **formal**, having paid staff and officially registered with the government. Nonprofits can also be **informal**, existing to serve a very specific or temporary purpose, and these are usually comprised of volunteers. Some nonprofits provide services to an international community, whereas others serve in their host countries. There are many different types of nonprofit organizations.

Nonprofit Sector Challenges. The sector faces several challenges. Some governments (such as the U.S. government) are adopting a more conservative ideology, shifting the responsibility for providing some public services to the nonprofit sector. These governments are also reducing grant funding to nonprofits and reducing tax incentives for citizens to donate to charities; the gradual elimination of the inheritance tax in the United States is one example. The number of nonprofits available to meet societal needs is growing. However, this also means that nonprofits must pay greater attention to attracting and retaining contributors who have a growing number of alternatives vying for their donations.

Marketing Orientation. Nonprofit administrators are responding to many of their challenges by becoming marketing oriented. They are adopting a marketing perspective and applying marketing tactics to their communication activities, attracting funding, recruiting volunteers, and managing relations with individuals and publics outside the organization.

Glossary

4 Ps of marketing. See *marketing mix.*

Brand. The name, logo, and symbols that uniquely identify an NPO and distinguish it from other organizations. A brand reflects a nonprofit's image or reputation, in other words, the way the organization is perceived by the public.

Formal nonprofit. A type of nonprofit organization that usually, but not always, has one or more paid staff members. Formal nonprofits are usually chartered or registered with their government. Formal organizations are usually larger than informal nonprofits.

Informal nonprofit. A type of nonprofit organization often created for an event or project and disbanded on completion. Informal nonprofits are operated by volunteers.

Marketing mix. The assortment of controllable variables marketers use in achieving organizational goals and objectives. The controllable variables that make up the marketing mix are classified into one of four categories: product, place, promotion, and price. These four categories are known as the 4 P's of marketing.

Marketing orientation. An approach to managing an organization that relies on marketing tactics to achieve the organization's goals and objectives. An NPO that has a marketing orientation employs the array of marketing functions to attract resources and build vital relationships.

Nonprofit marketing. The use of marketing tactics to further the goals and objectives of nonprofit organizations. In this book, we use the term *nonprofit organization* broadly to refer to a variety of related nonbusiness and nongovernmental organizations (NGOs).

Nonprofit sector. That portion of a civil society that includes all nonprofit, charitable, and nongovernmental organizations. Outside the United States, the nonprofit sector is sometimes called the voluntary sector, the civil society, or the independent sector.

Positioning. Implementing marketing activities aimed at influencing public perception of the NPO.

Publics. External groups of individuals of interest to nonprofit organizations.

Resource attraction function. Attracting donations of time and funds. Attracting donations of time refers to the recruitment and retention of volunteers. Donations of funds refers to contributions from organizations and individuals. These contributions can be in-kind donations, such as products a company manufacturers, or monetary donations.

Social marketing. The use of marketing tactics in the creation, execution, and control of programs designed to influence social change.

Stakeholders. Groups that have a meaningful interest in the nonprofit organization. Generally, these include the organization's clients, board members, employees, volunteers, donors, granting organizations, government, other nonprofits, and the communities served by the NPO.

QUESTIONS FOR REVIEW

1. What is nonprofit marketing and what are its functions?
2. What are the different types of nonprofit organizations?
3. What is the nonprofit sector?
4. What is the relationship between positioning and branding?
5. What are the challenges faced by nonprofit organizations?

QUESTIONS FOR DISCUSSION

1. How can marketing professionals in nonprofits effectively respond to the challenges presented in this chapter?

2. What types of nonprofit organizations are most likely to adopt a marketing orientation?

3. How are nonprofit organizations using the Internet and related information technologies?

4. What types of nonprofits are most likely to attract corporate support? What types of nonprofits are likely to be avoided by the business sector? Why?

5. How are the fields of communications and marketing related and differentiated?

INTERNET EXERCISES

1. Visit the website of a large nonprofit organization. How is the nonprofit using its website? Which marketing functions are being addressed? What are other marketing activities the nonprofit could use on its website?

2. Conduct an Internet search to learn more about the nonprofit sector in a given country. How many nonprofits are in the country? What are the sources and levels of nonprofit funding in the country?

3. Visit the websites of some well-known corporations. Which are publicizing their support for a nonprofit on their websites? Why do you think the corporations chose the nonprofits they did?

4. Visit the websites of some well-known nonprofits. Which are publicizing their corporate supporters? What are the advantages and disadvantages of corporate sponsorship?

5. Visit the website of two or three nonprofits in your local area. Do the websites encourage you to donate? Do they allow you to donate online? Do the websites encourage you to volunteer? Do they provide details about available volunteer opportunities?

TEAM EXERCISES AND ROLE PLAYING

1. Have a class debate in which one side takes the conservative position on government funding of nonprofits and another side takes the progressive or liberal position.

2. In teams, interview nonprofit managers in your community. Each team should report the answers to the following questions: Does the nonprofit have a marketing orientation? Does the nonprofit develop annual marketing plans? What proportion of the nonprofit's budget is allocated for marketing activities?

3. In teams, choose a type of nonprofit organization (e.g., political organization, youth development, health). Choose two or three corporations that you believe would be a good fit as a corporate supporter and explain your choices.

MINICASE: The Society for the Prevention of Cruelty to Animals

The Society for the Prevention of Cruelty to Animals (SPCA) is a nonprofit organization working to reduce abusive treatment of animals. It investigates reports of animal cruelty and operates rescue shelters where abandoned pets can be temporarily housed pending adoption or euthanasia. The SPCA operates in the United States, the United Kingdom, Australia, and New Zealand. In each country, there is a national SPCA, which is primarily an advocacy and administrative organization, and local SPCAs, which operate animal shelters.

All SPCAs accept donations from supporters. In New Zealand, no government funding is provided to the SPCA. In the United States, local government funding is provided to some local SPCAs. One local SPCA in the United States attracts individual donations and local government grants. It generates additional funding through adoption fees, retail sales, and admission to its petting zoo.

During the past year, the city government disputed the SPCA's accounting procedures. A conflict ensued. Articles about the city's concern over the SPCA's accounting practices appeared regularly in the local newspaper. The city contracted with the local SPCA to operate the city's animal control services, providing the SPCA with its largest source of revenue. As a result of the failure of the city and the SPCA to resolve their conflict, the city failed to renew its contract with the SPCA.

The SPCA now finds itself in need of new funding sources. It must rely more heavily on donations from individual contributors. Once concerned chiefly with operating an animal shelter, the executive director now has to focus on fund-raising activities. Before the loss of city funding, very little attention was given to marketing.

As a result, even after its years of operation in the community, people know little about the SPCA. They think of it as "the shelter," a place people take unwanted or abandoned pets. Residents are generally aware of the dispute over the SPCA's accounting practices.

The executive director finds herself leading an organization that is not well-known but is in immediate need of donations from area residents. She must decide how to get the SPCA's name before the public more often, how to counter bad publicity from the dispute with the city, and how to find potential donors.

People who care about the treatment of animals have numerous donation alternatives. There is a range of animal activist organizations, from People for the Ethical Treatment of Animals to activists who protest the treatment of circus animals to activists who protest the use of animals in the testing of consumer products. There are animal rights organizations concerned about specific species and breeds. Animals of concern are chimpanzees, parrots, cats and various cat breeds, dogs and various dog breeds, and so forth.

Questions for the Case

1. If you were the executive director of this SPCA, what are the short-term (1- to 4-month) and longer-term (5- to 12-month) marketing tactics you would perform?

2. To whom would you direct your fund-raising appeal?

3. Would you take actions to improve the name recognition and image of the SPCA? What would you do?

References and Bibliography

American Voice. (2004). Issues and allegations: Estate tax. *American Voice 2004: A pocket guide to issues and allegations.* Retrieved September 28, 2005, from americanvoice2004.org/taxes/estatetax.html

Anheier, H. K., Kaldor, M. H., and Glasius, M. (2004). *Global civil society: 2004/5.* Thousand Oaks, CA: Sage.

Association of Fundraising Professionals. (2005, Feb. 14). *A new report by the Joint Committee on Taxation in Congress includes proposals to limit or eliminate certain types of deductions for charitable giving.* Retrieved October 4, 2005, from www.nsfre.org/tier3_cd.cfm?folder_id=2466&content_item_id=19830. Full report available online at www.house.gov/jct/s-2-05.pdf

Boris, E. T., & Steuerle, C. E. (1999). *Nonprofits and government: Collaboration and conflict.* Washington, DC: Urban Institute Press.

Brock, J. (2005). *The evolution of a government/non-profit relationship: Nonprofits, government & public policy* (summary report). Retrieved October 4, 2005, from www.nonprofitresearch.org/newsletter1531/newsletter_show.htm?doc_id=16028

Bruneau, C. L., & Campbell, M. (2001). Expanding the use of focus groups in the nonprofit sector. In *Proceedings of the Allied Academies Internet Conference, Vol. 3. Importance of nonprofit sector, increasing competitiveness of sector* (pp. 6–10). Cullowhee, NC: Allied Academics.

Citizens for Tax Justice. (2002). *Year-by-year analysis of the Bush tax cuts shows growing tilt to the very rich.* Retrieved September 28, 2005, from www.ctj.org/html/gwb0602.htm

Giving USA Foundation. (2005). Charitable giving rises 5 percent to nearly $250 billion in 2004. Retrieved October 3, 2005, fromaafrc.org/gusa/GUSA05_Press_Release.pdf

Giving USA Foundation. (2004), "Americans give $241 billion to charity in 2003," AAFRC Foundation Press Release. Available online 3 October 2005 at /www.aafrc.org/press_releases/trustreleases/americansgive.html

Havens, J. J., & Schervish, P. G. (2003). Why the $41 trillion wealth transfer estimate is still valid: A review of challenges and questions. Planned Giving Design Center. Retrieved September 28, 2005, from http://www.pgdc.com/usa/item/?itemID=29102

Homewood, G. S. (1998, Nov. 9). Nonprofit sector is a burgeoning economic force. *Gazette Online: The Newspaper of the Johns Hopkins University.* Retrieved October 4, 2005, from www.jhu.edu/~gazette/octdec98/nov0998/09nonpr.html

Hotz, R. L. (2005, Feb. 27). Searching for the why of buy. *Los Angeles Times.* Retrieved November 16, 2005, from www.latimes.com/news/science/la-sci-brain27feb27,0,3899978.story?coll=la-home-headlines

Independent Sector. (2004). *INDEPENDENT SECTOR determines new estimate for value of volunteer time.* Retrieved October 3, 2005, at www.independentsector.org/media/voltime04PR.html

International Federation of Library Associations and Institutions. (1998). Section on Management and Marketing, Glossary of marketing definitions. Retrieved September 28, 2005, from www.ifla.org/VII/s34/pubs/glossary.htm#N

Johns Hopkins University News Releases. (2003). U.S. nonprofit sector feeling squeeze of government budget cuts: "Listening Post" Project takes the pulse of nonprofit sector. Retrieved September 28, 2005, from www.jhu.edu/news_info/news/home03/jul03/listen.html

Kilbourne, J. (1999). *Deadly persuasion: Why women and girls must fight the addictive power of advertising.* New York: Free Press.

Lee, M. (2004). The coming nonprofit crash. *PA Times, 27*(9), 5, 9.

Moore, C. (2004). Services on the edge: Paying the price. *Impact*, Summer, 4–5.

Newcomb, K. (2005). Global advertising on the upswing. *ClickZNews* (22 June). Retrieved October 3, 2005, at www.clickz.com/news/article.php/3514771

O'Connell, B. (1996). A major transfer of government responsibility to voluntary organizations. *Public Administration Review, 56*(3), 222–225.

OMB Watch. (2005, Feb. 14). *The Bush FY2006 from a nonprofit perspective.* Retrieved October 4, 2005, from www.ombwatch.org/budget/FY06budgetimpactonnonprofits.pdf

Phillips, S. D. (2005). Redefining government relationships with the voluntary sector: On great expectations and sense and sensibility. Retrieved September 28, 2005, from vsr-trsb.net/publications/phillips-e.html

Pollack, A. (2004, April 13). With tiny brain implants, just thinking may make it so. *New York Times*, F5.

Richie, J. B. R., Swami, S., & Weinberg, C. B. (1999). A brand new world for nonprofits. *International Journal of Nonprofit & Voluntary Sector Marketing 4*(1), 26–42.

Salamon, L. M. (1996, Oct. 30). The international rise of the nonprofit sector, a global "associational revolution." *Canadian FundRaiser.* Retrieved September 28, 2005, from www.charityvillage.com/cv/research/rint7.html

Salamon, L., Sokolowski, S. W., et al. (2004). *Global civil society: Dimensions of the nonprofit sector* (Vol. 2). Bloomfield, CT: Kumarian Press.

Shenk, D. (1997). *Data smog surviving the information glut.* San Francisco: HarperEdge.

Smithers, R., & Carvel, J. (2004, December 22). Charities bill gets a warm welcome. *Guardian.* Retrieved October 4, 2005, from society.guardian.co.uk/charityreform/story/0,11494,1378453,00.html

Snavely, K., & Desai, U. (2001). Municipal government–nonprofit sector collaboration in Bulgaria: An attitudinal analysis. *American Review of Public Administration, 31*(1), 49–65.

Statistics Canada. (2004, September 20). *News release: New study on nonprofit and voluntary sector first of its kind.* Retrieved October 4, 2005, from publicdocs.volunteer.ca/news/NSNVO%20News%20release% 20-%20FINALENGLISH.htm

Venture Philanthropy Partners. (2003). *The changing nonprofit funding environment: Implications and opportunities.* Retrieved October 4, 2005, from www.vppartners.org/learning/perspectives/workshop/full_report.html

Yancey, J., Dehoog, R., Racanska, L., Kuti, E., Stark, D., & Bach, J. (2002, March/April). Nonprofit sector growth in eastern Europe: Emerging trends and tips for American mentors and funders. *Snapshots: Research Highlights from the Nonprofit Sector Research Fund.* Retrieved October 2, 2005, from www.nonprofitresearch .org/usr_doc/mar_apr_02_Snapshots2.pdf

Setting the Path of the Nonprofit Organization ❖

Mission Focus, Strategic Objectives, Differentiation, Positioning, Unique Value Proposition, Branding, Segmentation

Learning Objectives

On completion of this chapter, the reader will

- Understand the importance of developing a concise mission statement and what the components of that statement should be

- Understand how a nonprofit's strategic objectives depend on the mission

- Understand why nonprofits should give careful consideration to differentiation

- Understand what positioning is and be able to explain a perceptual map and the various positioning strategies

Learning Objectives (Continued)

- Understand what the unique value proposition is and why it is important to nonprofit organizations

- Understand why branding, brand perception, differentiation of a brand, brand extensions, licensing, brand elements, brand characters, brand equity and strength, and brand image can be important to nonprofit organizations

- Understand what segmentation is and why it is important, even for nonprofit organizations

Opening Vignette: The Atlanta Homeless Project

Kaitlyn Bowen was settling into her new office as executive director of the Atlanta Homeless Project (AHP). She was excited and worried at the same time. She was excited to be suddenly in charge of an organization and to be able to help homeless people find a better life. She was worried that she had given up a secure job in advertising (which she had loved) and that AHP needed to change significantly if it was to continue offering client services. The organization's financial situation was not good, and Kaitlyn had been brought in by the executive board to turn the organization around. She knew that unless AHP made a dramatic turnaround, her days as an executive director would be numbered.

The board's feeling was that the nonprofit environment had changed dramatically and that the previous executive director had done little to help AHP change with the times. A decade ago, AHP was Atlanta's main local conduit for United Way and state funding to help those temporarily and chronically homeless. Its clients often included individuals who were evicted or victims of spousal abuse and those who could not afford rent for a wide variety of reasons. In addition to directly feeding, housing, or giving money to clients, AHP had helped organize, fund, and coordinate a number of groups to directly provide additional services (such as food kitchens and treatment for substance abuse and for medical and mental illness). Some of these groups had now developed into nonprofits that were more specialized and successful than AHP.

Each night, APH counselors drive vans through city streets to bring the homeless to one of the organization's three centers. Each center provides warm clothing, hot food, and a clean and safe place to sleep for the night. On an average day, the centers serve 300–500 individuals. In the winter, the numbers double. Depending on the season, the vans also carry sandwiches or blankets and hot soup to the homeless who do not wish to be brought to a center. It is believed that about 70% of the homeless are adult males, 20% are adult females, and 10% are children. In AHP interviews with the adults, about 30% of those served reported miscellaneous economic setbacks as the main reason for their homelessness, 40% listed alcohol and drugs, 25% medical conditions, and 5% other.

AHP also operates a longer-term residential program designed to return clients to the mainstream by treating the underlying cause of their homelessness. Counseling, training, jobs, and medical treatment are provided to individuals and families in need. Although the residential program has been successful with 4- to 6-week interventions, the waiting list is long, and the program capacity desperately needs to be increased from the current 20 beds.

Recent years brought a nationwide economic slowdown, and that has meant less money from traditional funding sources. To make matters worse for AHP, a number of other nonprofits have sprung up or expanded in the area to also provide services to homeless clients, and faith-based groups have become more active. The result is that AHP is receiving a diminishing share of the already-reduced available funding. However, the numbers of those in need seem to be increasing. A manual census identified 7,000 Atlanta homeless on an average day (although some agencies believe the actual number is 2 to 3 times as many).

From her marketing background, Kaitlyn knows that she has to find a special role for her organization. It might be a service niche or some unique position in the minds of AHP funding agencies and donors. It might involve what, when, or how clients are identified or the types of services provided. AHP needs something that differentiates it from other service providers, and it needs to bring some unique value to those in need. She may have to consider increasing the scope of client services or expanding to statewide or regional operations. She may need to consider whether AHP's mission to "help the homeless" is too broad and whether it has led the organization into too many service areas.

Kaitlyn turns to you to help her develop a mission statement, including its focus and scope; set strategic objectives; and consider how to differentiate her program and determine an appropriate market position, unique value proposition, and positioning. She also needs help with branding and market segmentation. Once you have read this chapter, begin by using the Internet to review AHP's main potential competitors for funding to see what they offer clients and how they raise funds. Then develop a written plan showing where and how a reorganized AHP could successfully fit into this environment. Unfortunately, AHP's small website is being revised, so you will not be able to review it.

AHP is aware of the nonprofits listed below that serve homeless causes in its area. Some may not be large enough to have websites; others are national and have local operations in the Atlanta area. You will want to do an Internet search for additional Atlanta homeless service providers that AHP may not be aware of and others that may have found attractive niches in other major cities (which AHP can learn from).

Atlanta S.O.S.

Atlanta Homeless Outreach

Atlanta Union Mission

Atlanta Homeless Commission

Night Shelter at Druid Hills

National Low Income Housing Coalition

National Coalition for the Homeless (note "Fun Ways to Support NCH")

Bringing America Home Campaign (note "The Organizer's Toolkit")

Also investigate organizations serving Atlanta and the surrounding area such as Our Daily Bread, Community Care, Meals on Wheels, Homebound Missions, Food Bank Ministries, Crossroads, Samaritan House, and Intown Community Assistance.

Mission—Defining a Focus and Scope

An organization's **mission statement**, or the stated purpose of the nonprofit organization, is a carefully crafted definition of its long-term focus and scope. Properly done, the statement provides the basis for setting objectives and all the strategic planning that follows. Even in day-to-day operations, the mission should provide guidance for all levels of organizational decision makers. It ensures that all a nonprofit's target publics (its employees, clients, volunteers, and donors) understand the nonprofit's reason for existing.

Some early strategic planners thought that mission statements should inspire, challenge, convey values, and provide an understanding of future direction for an organization. Such statements often resulted in lengthy, complicated statements such as this early mission statement for a large, private, nonprofit educational institution:

> The University of _____ exists that human knowledge be treasured, preserved, expanded and disseminated and that the human mind, body and spirit be nurtured and strengthened through learning. The University is committed to meet these great obligations: That our students learn well, guided, stimulated and helped by scholarly, dedicated teachers so that each may grow according to his or her own talents; That its students broaden and deepen their knowledge of life and thought and values, encouraged to understand what has gone before, to wonder what may yet come, and to dream; That its undergraduate study include rigorous, disciplined exploration of the accumulated core of human knowledge, and that graduate and professional study include mastery of that mix of knowledge, expertise and skills that provides the foundation for effective, ethical service to others; That there be fostered respect for the differences among people, the nurturing of curiosity, the insistence upon high standards of thought, study, communication and the skills that should characterize the educated person; That its graduates be broadly educated men and women, prepared to bear that special responsibility in a free, pluralistic society of those privileged to have a higher education; That the University firmly maintain its independence; That there be and be defended an atmosphere of tolerance and the freedom to explore, to question, to argue, to create, to accept or reject. . . .

A major problem with such lengthy, value-laden statements is that they are difficult to read and remember, not only by target publics of an organization but by employees and volunteers as well. Particularly in larger nonprofits, it is easy to imagine the problems that can occur with no common understanding of mission. By way of illustration, a number of years ago, when working with a historic home foundation, students in a nonprofit marketing class were given the assignment of calling individuals within various units of the same organization (e.g., the gift shop, grounds division, and educational services) and asking them what the mission was for the organization as a whole and how they contributed to achieving that mission. Whereas the mission of that nonprofit centered on historic education, research, and garden and house tours, almost no one knew that. Responses ranged from "Be all we can be" to "Something to do with education, I think." A quote from Yogi Berra sums up the basic problem of such a situation: "If you do not know where you're heading, you're likely to end up somewhere else."

More recently, marketing consultants have stressed that mission statements should be concise and to the point. Those consultants can then help their clients develop separate vision statements and values statements to go along with the mission statement and to be used by the organization when it makes important decisions. Now, consider the newer, more concise mission statement of the same private, nonprofit educational institution:

> The University of _____'s mission is to educate and nurture students, to create knowledge, and to provide service to our community and beyond. Committed to excellence and proud of the diversity of our University family, we strive to develop future leaders of our nation and the world.

Mission Scope, Feasibility, Ability to Motivate, and Distinctiveness

In addition to being concise and to the point, an organization's mission statement should specify the organization's scope and should be feasible, motivating, and distinctive.

Scope. A nonprofit's mission statement should specify three dimensions of an organization's scope, namely (a) target publics (*Who* will be served by the nonprofit), (b) target publics' needs (*What* needs of the target publics will be met), and (c) technologies (*How* the nonprofit will go about meeting the specified needs of the target publics it will serve). In Exhibit 2.1, consider the mission statement for Comic Relief UK, a registered charity in the United Kingdom, followed by the same statement with the three aspects of scope indicated. As one can see in the Exhibit, the target publics (who?) identified in the mission statement consist of people in the United Kingdom as well as those in the poorest countries in the world. The target publics' needs (what?) that will be served by Comic Relief UK include an end to poverty and social injustice. Finally, when it comes to technologies (how?), Comic Relief UK intends to go about ending poverty and social injustice for people in the United Kingdom and in the poorest countries in the world by raising money, informing, educating, raising awareness, promoting social change, allocating funds both responsibly and ethically, and ensuring that fund-raising costs are covered by cash and in-kind sponsorships.

Feasibility, Ability to Motivate, and Distinctiveness. In addition to specifying the scope, a nonprofit organization's mission should be feasible, motivating, and distinctive. Feasibility (or practicability) means that the nonprofit should actually be able to achieve its mission given its available resources. For an organization such as Comic Relief UK, a mission such as ending world hunger would be a "mission impossible." In addition, the mission statement of a nonprofit should be motivating for the nonprofit's employees and volunteers, inspiring them through hard work and setbacks that may occur. Finally, the mission statement should be distinctive or unique to the nonprofit that owns it. A state park system in South Carolina should not write a mission statement that, simply by changing names, could be relevant for Virginia or any other state in the union.

❖ **Exhibit 2.1**   **Mission Statement for Comic Relief UK (Registered Charity 326568) and Specification of the Three Elements of the Scope**

Comic Relief is seriously committed to helping end poverty and social injustice in the UK and poorest countries in the world. We do this by:

Raising money from the general public by actively involving them in events and projects that are innovative and fun.

Informing, educating, raising awareness and promoting social change.

Allocating the funds we raise in a responsible and effective way to a wide range of charities which we select after careful research.

Ensuring that our Red Nose Day fundraising costs are covered by sponsorship in cash or in kind so that every penny raised goes to charity.

| **Target publics – Who?** | | **Target publics' needs – What?** |

Comic Relief is seriously committed to | helping end poverty and social injustice | in

| the UK and poorest countries in the world. | We do this by:

raising money from the general public by actively involving them in events and projects that are innovative and fun.

informing, educating, raising awareness and promoting social change.

allocating the funds we raise in a responsible and effective way to a wide range of charities which we select after careful research.

ensuring that our Red Nose Day fundraising costs are covered by sponsorship in cash or in kind so that every penny raised goes to charity.

Technologies – How?

Sharing the Mission With Target Publics

While the mission statement retains its planning importance to an organization, today it is often not displayed prominently in market communications. While "organizational purpose" (i.e., mission) is required on IRS Form 990, finding it on the websites of many large nonprofits often requires quite a search (if it can be found there at all). For strategic planning purposes, the concise mission statement is preferred, but for other communication with a nonprofit's various target publics (e.g., stakeholders and potential donors), the more traditional, inspirational, and value-laden version has many advantages.

In modern nonprofits' website communications, an expression of "Who We Are" or "How We Work" or "About Us" (as a main element in the home page or print brochure) often brings together elements of mission, vision, and values and is delivered in everyday language, as if the nonprofit is speaking directly to the reader. It is easy to understand why marketers prefer this down-to-earth communication over concise, formal, planning-type statements. But marketers should still appreciate the mission as an organizational statement of purpose that keeps new initiatives and programs in line with why the organization exists and that forms the foundation for all strategic objectives. Otherwise, the nonprofit risks evolving, over time, into an organization that will be indefinite to publics both inside and outside it.

A Sampling of Mission Statements

Here are mission statements from several types of nonprofits:

American Heart Association (www.americanheart.org)

Our mission is to reduce disability and death from cardiovascular diseases and stroke.

CARE Australia (www.careaustralia.org.au/)

CARE's mission is to serve individuals and families in the poorest communities in the world. Drawing strength from our global diversity, resources and experience, we promote innovative solutions and are advocates for global responsibility. We facilitate lasting change by strengthening capacity for self-help; providing economic opportunity; delivering relief in emergencies; influencing policy decisions at all levels; and addressing discrimination in all its forms. Guided by the aspirations of local communities, we pursue our mission with both excellence and compassion because the people whom we serve deserve nothing less.

Green Cross International (www.gci.ch/en/about/mission.htm)

The mission of Green Cross International is to help ensure a just, sustainable and secure future for all by fostering a value shift and cultivating a new sense of global interdependence and shared responsibility in humanity's relationship with nature.

St. Jude Children's Research Hospital (www.stjude.org)

Our mission is to find cures for children with catastrophic illnesses through research and treatment.

The Nature Conservancy (www.nature.org)

The Nature Conservancy's mission is to preserve the plants, animals and natural communities that represent the diversity of life on Earth by protecting the lands and waters they need to survive.

A nonprofit's overall mission and any later proposed changes to mission are issues that should be dealt with at the highest levels of organization management and by the board of directors. The mission is not something that should be open to frequent change, and it should be written such that market, environmental, and technological change will not necessitate any drastic rewriting. However, there are times when a change in the mission is required to maintain a nonprofit's relevance and credibility.

Strategic Objectives to Achieve the Organization's Mission

When nonprofit executives are challenged to manage resources, attract funding, and create programs to achieve a mission (such as to reduce disability, save lives, find cures, distribute food, or preserve nature), they must start with a strategic market analysis to develop a clear understanding of market needs, perceptions, preferences, values, and competitive forces. (Chapter 3 covers marketing research in detail, and the reader is directed to that chapter in order to appreciate the value and importance of engaging in research to learn about its target publics. Chapter 4 covers strategic market analysis and planning.) Based on the in-depth understanding that a market analysis brings, the organization's main strategic objectives can be set.

A nonprofit's **strategic objectives** state the broad direction of the organization. They should lead logically to clearly stated marketing and other objectives at lower units of the organization. Although all of them are important, they should be stated in a hierarchical order from most to least crucial. They should be quantified so that progress toward their achievement can be measured impartially. And they should be internally consistent and feasible in light of the organization's resources. Once the nonprofit's overall objectives are set, each operating unit within the organization should set its own objectives to meet a portion of the total organization objectives according to its function and capability. This process is repeated at all the levels in an organization. This approach aligns the goals of individuals to those of their department; the goals of the departments to the goals of the operating units; and finally, the goals of the operating units to those of the organization as a whole.

For example, the Legal Services Society (LSS) of British Columbia (www.lss.bc.ca/__shared/assets/Strategic_Objectives571.pdf) has as a mission "To assist low income individuals to resolve their legal problems by providing a spectrum of services that promotes their effective participation in the justice system." To achieve its organizational mission, and in light of a recent market analysis, the LSS has set the following strategic objectives:

1. Develop and continually improve an integrated legal aid system that provides a range of high quality legal services that are responsive to the needs of low income individuals.

2. Identify and assess the legal needs of low income individuals in British Columbia, and increase awareness of the services provided by LSS.

3. Secure sufficient funding from diverse sources for LSS to fulfill its mandate and be accountable for the use of that funding.

4. Develop and retain staff who work to their potential to meet the society's objectives, and expand the capacity of legal professionals and other service providers to assist low income individuals to resolve their legal problems.

5. Build and maintain relationships with communities to enhance our mutual ability to meet the needs of people with low incomes.

6. Have a presence in all regions of British Columbia through people and technology.

7. Develop, implement, and evaluate innovative approaches to improve delivery of legal services.

8. Work with others for justice system reform, and, in doing so, advocate for the interests of low-income individuals. (Legal Services Society, 2005)

Differentiation

Although Chapter 4 describes the sequential steps involved in nonprofit strategic planning, the issues of differentiation, positioning, and unique value proposition are introduced here because they are closely related, fundamental, and tied directly to mission and objectives.

In your mind, pick some product that you care about and are knowledgeable about (e.g., clothing, motorcycles, snowboards, music). Think about the differences between the major brands. On what basis did you come to prefer the brand you use today? Is there a brand or model that you would love to own if you could only afford it? Do you think that these products and the way they are offered have been custom crafted by marketers to create these preferences?

People who care about nonprofits and causes also come to have preferences. There are thousands of worthy nonprofits, and many of them address similar causes. At each, marketers strive to create programs that satisfy unmet needs of target publics and to communicate with them that their efforts are worthy and special. They do that by differentiating their offering mix.

At its most basic, **differentiation** involves developing two or more marketing mixes that create a perception by the target publics that an organization's offer(s) are distinct from those otherwise available in ways the target publics would value. A **marketing mix** consists of the controllable variables in the specifics of a nonprofit's offers to the market: the *product* or *offer* (e.g., services and programs), the *place* (location where the product or service is available), the *price* (the perceived value of a program or service), and the *promotion* (communicating the organization's purpose and activities to various publics by tactics such as advertising, publicity, word-of-mouth referrals, and so forth). When you do the Internet Exercise at the end of this chapter, you may be struck by how many different ways nonprofit cancer-fighting organizations approach cancer. It is unlikely they could be effective and successful by providing the same offers and then attempting to compete for the same target publics. Instead, each tries to focus on a different aspect of the cause, a different technology or approach, or tries to appeal to a different stakeholder segment. As you explore the various cancer websites, you can clearly see how the marketing mix has been used to try to make each organization distinctive and different from the others in its environment.

If you were placed in charge of marketing planning for the LSS of British Columbia, you would need to create a way to achieve the organization objectives (listed earlier) in a manner that accords with the organization's mission and in a way that target publics perceive as special and worthwhile. Creating distinctive value must then be followed with a plan that integrates elements of the marketing mix to communicate that value.

Nonprofit differentiation can be achieved by any or all the 4 P's of marketing—the product (offer), the place (location and distribution of the offer), the promotion, and the price (monetary and nonmonetary)—as well as by the nonprofit's people. Therefore, a nonprofit organization that wants to differentiate itself from the competition may do so through actual *offer differentiation,* such as by having an offer that is better than the competition's. Or it may be that its offer is simply more conveniently located or involves more pleasing surroundings—*place differentiation.* Or through its promotional mix (e.g., advertising, public relations, personal persuasion), it may emphasize its positive image—*promotional differentiation.* It also may have prices (monetary and nonmonetary) that are more in line with the expectations of its target public—*price differentiation.* Further, a nonprofit may be able to differentiate itself from the competition on the basis of its people (e.g., a hospital may emphasize the number of award-winning physicians and nurses on its staff)—*personnel differentiation.*

One might argue that in providing pro bono legal services to the poor, a nonprofit would need to pay little attention to differentiation because there is little competition in providing legal services for free. There is, however, considerable competition for financial support from local, state, and federal governments; private donors; and foundations. A wide variety of causes, public agencies, and private charities competes constantly for scarce financial resources. Those that succeed in differentiating themselves and showing themselves to be particularly worthy of support usually do so by creating a special position in the mind of their target publics.

Positioning

Positioning involves designing and implementing an offering mix to create and maintain a particular image of an organization and its offers relative to its competition in the minds of target publics. This definition probably sounds similar to the definition of differentiation, and it is. The two concepts are closely related and easy to confuse. It may help to consider that differentiation occurs *through* positioning.

An example with a familiar consumer product will illustrate the difference. To college students interested in motorcycles, a top-of-the-line Harley-Davidson is clearly differentiated in their mind (in ways that are important) from a top-of-the-line Honda. If what is important to them has more than one dimension, each offer could be rated on those dimensions and plotted on two- or three-dimensional maps called perceptual maps. A perceptual map (Exhibit 2.2) is a graphic representation of the importance of different dimensions and the perceptions of various alternatives along those dimensions for one or more target publics. Say a researcher finds that style and operating cost are two pertinent considerations, or dimensions, for particular target

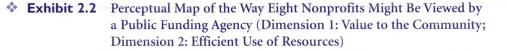

❖ **Exhibit 2.2**   Perceptual Map of the Way Eight Nonprofits Might Be Viewed by a Public Funding Agency (Dimension 1: Value to the Community; Dimension 2: Efficient Use of Resources)

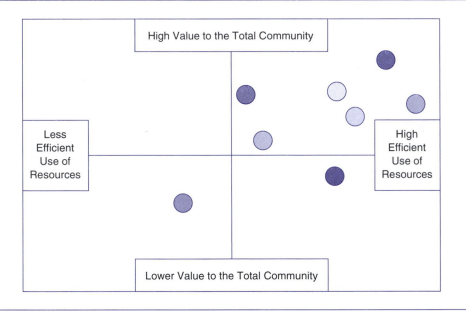

publics. A marketer would first ask the target publics to rate the importance of those dimensions. Then, the same target publics would be asked to evaluate alternative motorcycle brands, including the particular model of Harley-Davidson, along those dimensions (e.g., "How likely is it that motorcycle "C" has dimension 1? dimension 2?") Then data from both parts of the research would be plotted on a perceptual map—in this case, a two-dimensional map. The perceptual map (plot) would thus show the position that each offer holds versus the competition (at least as far as those two dimensions are concerned). In addition to determining how your target publics perceive your offer, you may find potential opportunities: a particular combination of attributes that target publics value but no current offer covers.

Nonprofits and their offers (products, programs, and services) are positioned by a similar process in the minds of their target publics even if a nonprofit does not purposely develop a position. Sometimes, nonprofits do not try to develop a position because they fear that having a position may alienate potential target publics. Generally speaking, however, unplanned positions are undesirable. Furthermore, if an organization does not have a clear position, it is unlikely the organization will ever be a target public's first choice among alternatives. Because organizations will have a position, even if it is unplanned or purposely vague, it makes sense for organizations to carefully develop their position.

For a new nonprofit, probably the only type of nonprofit that truly has no position, marketing may be challenged to position the organization in a strategically beneficial way. Existing nonprofits present their marketers with the need to defend and maintain their current positions or, alternatively, develop new ones. Positions become particularly important when nonprofits compete for funding.

Most basically, marketers must determine how their organizations are currently perceived relative to competitors and how their offers are perceived. Positioning brings together market, competitive, and internal analyses. The positioning process includes eight steps to develop an offering mix that correctly resonates with the target publics it was designed to reach:

1. Use market research techniques to analyze the needs, perceptions, and preferences of the target market(s). Uncover what issues drive value and satisfaction.

2. Segment the market to determine which are the most important segments, what factors are important to each segment, and what positions on those factors would result in the most effective appeal.

3. Survey the market to uncover current positions of each competitive offering (including your own).

4. Create a perceptual map for each segment of interest and analyze your present or planned positioning compared with the competition's.

5. Analyze the alternative attractive positions (opportunities) available and what marketing resources would be required to move to them.

6. Decide what position is strategically beneficial to your nonprofit (the upcoming chapter on strategic planning will address this step).

7. Create an integrated marketing program to achieve the positioning.

8. Monitor your target publics to ensure that your nonprofit is perceived the way you intended, and monitor competitors' reactions to your positioning activities that could alter your current position in the minds of your target group.

Central to the concept of positioning is the belief that a nonprofit offer competes on a number of levels, including its own physical attributes, its economic costs, its social position or impact, its target publics, its competitors, and its quality, as well as other aspects relevant to its target public. A second belief is that it is unlikely that any nonprofit can position its offers to excel in all areas that are relevant to its target publics. Offers are usually trade-offs, favoring one set of aspects at the expense of others, which creates the opportunity for competing nonprofits to design their offers to favor distinct combinations of the 4 P's and, thereby, appeal to different target publics. A third fundamental belief of positioning is that market research must be able to uncover the dimensions that the nonprofit's target publics use to evaluate alternative providers, the importance or weight they place on each dimension, and the exact way target publics process that information in making a decision.

Exhibit 2.3 shows the type of information that marketers at Sisters Community Hospital (a fictitious organization) would like to know about themselves and their competitors. From this information, a series of perceptual maps could be created and presented, and alternative future positioning could be evaluated. A marketer might

❖ **Exhibit 2.3**   Perceived Importance (PI) and Perceived Quality (PQ) Rating of Fictitious Sisters Community Hospital by Client Segment Served

	Main Client Segments Served									
	Low Income		Middle Income		Upper Income		Older		Indigent	
	(PI)	(PQ)	(PI)	(PQ)	(PI)	(PQ)	(PI)	(PQ)	(PI)	(PQ)
Surgery										
ER care										
Cardiac care										
Room and facility aesthetics										
Physician capability										
Nurse capability										
Teaching										
Research										
Community programs										
Efficiency										
Segment served										

want to appeal to multiple segments and position offerings highly on the aspects most important to each segment, but done incorrectly, this strategy can lead to brand image confusion. This dangerous possibility shows how complex positioning is and how much marketer creativity, skill, and persistence it requires. In actual practice, a marketer would survey a sample from the target publics of interest using an instrument similar to Exhibit 2.3. Individuals from a target public (e.g., low income, older) would rate each attribute (e.g., surgery, cardiac care) on a scale of low to high, perhaps circling a number from one to seven. The average of each public's score would be placed in the appropriate cell in Exhibit 2.3.

Common Positioning Strategies

Name the first nonprofit that comes to mind for each area listed below.

1. The fight against cancer

2. Preserving the environment

3. Helping sick children

4. Helping low-income families by providing homes

5. An organization through which the nation's colleges and universities govern their athletics programs

6. Help in an emergency

The organization that comes to mind in each situation is likely to have used long-term, integrated marketing communications to associate its name with its particular cause or function. While every area has its market leaders, there are usually many other organizations addressing different aspects of the same issues. Rather than use a "me too" positioning strategy, most competitors wisely seek to compete via alternative positions. Positioning typically has multiple aspects, but the following marketing promotion themes illustrate common options.

Positioning by Offer Features and Attributes. A nonprofit might consider simply indicating the features or attributes of its offers. For example, a local homeless program run by a religious institution might emphasize that it not only feeds the hungry but also nourishes the spirit and trains clients in marketable skills.

Positioning by Benefits or Needs Addressed. Another positioning option is for a nonprofit to specify the benefits of its offers for its target publics. For example, Beta Gamma Sigma, an international business honor society, indicates on one of its Web pages (www.betagammasigma.org/benefits.htm) that "membership provides recognition for a lifetime. As the highest national recognition a business student can earn, it is appropriate to include Beta Gamma Sigma membership on one's resume."

Positioning by Offer or Cause. In for-profit marketing, this positioning strategy is referred to as "positioning by product/offer class," but in the nonprofit sector, the term *offer* or *cause* is more appropriate. An example is Amtrak, a public, nonprofit organization that uses a strategy of positioning its offer (rail service between cities) against other sorts of travel between cities, such as bus, plane, or car travel. Another example is the Autism Society of America (www.autism-society.org), which positions itself with the following statement: "to promote lifelong access and opportunity for all individuals within the autism spectrum."

Positioning by Use. Another way to position a nonprofit is based on how or when an offer is to be used. Nonprofit marketers need to discover how their offers can solve problems for target publics. See, for example, how the Public Broadcasting Service (PBS) positions itself as a source of information that is available on television, radio, and the Internet, as follows: "A trusted community resource, PBS uses the power of noncommercial television, the Internet and other media to enrich the lives of all Americans through quality programs and education services that inform, inspire and delight (PBS, 2005).

Positioning by Offer Class. Positioning by offer class involves a nonprofit's comparing its offer to a competitive offer that is in a different but related offer class. For example, the College of William and Mary (www.wm.edu/) positions itself relative to private colleges as follows:

> The College of William and Mary is the second oldest college in the country and has been rated the number one small public university in the U.S. It is known as one of the "public Ivy" colleges (institutions in the United States that offer the same education as an Ivy League school just at a lower cost). (Harter, 2005)

Positioning by User Group. In this strategy, a nonprofit positions its offer for a particular group of users. For example, the Association for Women in Sports Media (www.awsmonline.org) positions itself this way: "The Association for Women in Sports Media is an organization of women who work in the sports media, and women and men who support them in their work."

Positioning Relative to Competitors. Whereas a new nonprofit may want to position itself as similar to a competitor that is a market leader by emphasizing points of parity, it is more common for organizations to attempt to position themselves in relation to competitors by emphasizing points of difference between themselves and other organizations. An example is the Alzheimer's Association (www.alz.org/), which positions itself as "the world leader in Alzheimer research and support, . . . a voluntary health organization dedicated to finding preventions, treatments and, eventually, a cure for Alzheimer dementia" (Biotechnology Industry Organization, 2004). Nonprofits can position their offers to set themselves apart from the competition, show superiority, and so on. Gifts In Kind International positions itself as superior to other organizations involved in product philanthropy: "Driven by a mission of providing an effective conduit for the donation of products, goods and services from the private sector to the charitable sector, Gifts In Kind International is the recognized leader in the field of product philanthropy" (Gifts in Kind International, 2005).

Positioning by Price and Quality. In this strategy, the price-quality relationship is stressed. For example, some organizations may set themselves apart from others by assuming a very high price-quality association, while others may choose to be positioned as having the lowest price offers. An example of a nonprofit's assuming a high price-quality association is a city's symphony sponsoring a "Symphony Ball": "Invitations to this season's Symphony Gala Ball are being mailed to a list of more than 3,000 of the Valley's elite residents and corporate officers. Tickets begin at $500 per person . . ." On the other hand, a local Boys and Girls Club may offer tickets for $5.00 each to the club's spaghetti dinner in a church basement.

Positioning by Cultural Symbol. Nonprofits may also use symbols to position themselves in the eyes of target publics. Some examples include the World Wildlife Fund's giant panda and the U.S. Forest Service's Smokey Bear.

In her book *Beyond Fundraising,* Kay S. Grace (1997) says nonprofits must position themselves as organizations that do the following:

1. Meet needs, not as organizations that have needs.

2. Focus on program results, not just on financial goals.

3. Understand that the process of asking and giving is based in shared values. (Board Matters, 2005)

To design a successful offer mix that is attractive is not enough. A nonprofit's prospective target publics must know about it, be able to assess it, and find that it contains more value than their alternatives.

The Unique Value Proposition

Many for-profit businesses view their "value proposition" as their single most important organizing principle. **A unique value proposition** is a set of specific, tangible, and measurable factual statements describing the real value (benefits) that target publics can expect to receive from an organization's offerings. For a nonprofit, it defines what the nonprofit does better than anyone else and why that is important to its target publics.

An effective value proposition should clearly differentiate the organization's offers from those of competitors. To do that, it needs to be unique in some way that matters. Vague generalities and subjective puffery do not have a place in a proper value proposition. The unique value proposition is similar to the definition of differentiation in that the exercise of creating a formal value proposition forces an organization to list those things that are going to differentiate it in the marketplace. It is a list that nonprofit management can prominently post and emphasize to ensure that everyone in the organization works to achieve and maintain the same things.

In the day-to-day scramble to provide offers (goods, services, and programs) and maintain funding, nonprofit leaders typically have little extra time to contemplate what has made them successful in the first place, how market and environmental needs may be changing, and the potential impact of other nonprofits that are moving in to serve the same area. But for nonprofit marketers, these issues are critical to maintaining a nonprofit's unique value proposition.

It is important for nonprofits to communicate their unique value propositions to important publics. People have many alternatives for their discretionary income, free time, and emotional involvement. Not all benefits of nonprofit offers are automatically apparent to target publics, so nonprofit marketers need to present and communicate them. For example, wealthy individuals may enjoy a night at the symphony but not be fully aware of the real benefits the symphony provides to them, their family, and the community. If they become aware that the benefits are real and special, they are much more likely to become a patron.

Branding

Creating a successful unique value proposition, positioning the offer, and differentiating it all come together to create a successful and sustainable brand. A **brand** for a nonprofit organization is basically the collection of perceptions in the minds of its target publics that is based on how they value and relate to the organization's mission, offers, and reputation. A target public's perception is created and constantly updated based on interactions with brand representatives, marketing communication, and publicity (to name a few areas the organization can influence). Each interaction can support, increase, or decrease the target public's perception of brand equity and worth. The positive sum of all the thousands or millions of target public perceptions of value and trust creates brand strength. In a real way, a brand is a promise that target publics can count on and trust. It is a promise of what a nonprofit organization stands for, its operational values and integrity, and the promise of the benefit it will deliver to society. Positive brand value and strength need to be earned by commitment, action, and communication.

Brand Perception Examples

- Imagine that you suddenly need a complicated surgical procedure that is beyond the capability of your local hospital. What well-known hospital comes to mind that would provide you with the best chance of having a favorable outcome? If you ask your family doctor to recommend a hospital for your surgery, on what would the doctor base a recommendation?
- Suppose you were a wealthy person who would like to make a charitable donation to an organization that would make good use of the funds. What organizations come to mind as worthy charities?
- Say you are a college student deciding what to wear in the morning. If your options included T-shirts with the names of companies, company products, or public or private nonprofit organizations or their programs, what are some examples you would feel good about wearing?
- Can you think of a living religious figure or organization that you admire, that you would be willing to support, and that has developed large-scale fund-raising, outreach, and mission programs all commonly identified with its name?

All these examples involve one's personal perceptions and evaluation. Think about how your own perceptions were formed. What was the basis for your evaluation? How did a particular person, group, organization, offer, or cause earn your trust or admiration? All these issues are of interest to marketers, even nonprofit marketers, when designing brand strategies. Not only does an effective marketing communications program play a critical role in developing a positive brand presence in the market; one must also appreciate how *everything* an organization says or does can directly impact brand perception. That idea is worth emphasizing—*creating a strong brand involves more than just creating a powerful promotion campaign.* The Greenpeace organization provides an example. It is generally known as a nonprofit organization that advocates rebellious but nonviolent action against environmental polluters and the like. The Greenpeace "brand" of active ecological advocacy is promoted and distributed via the organization's ecological travel offers as well as its advertisements and public relations. However, Greenpeace emphasizes its brand not just through market communications; its brand is also supported by the activities of its volunteers: avid ecologists who often engage in prominent and media-savvy activities in the name of Greenpeace.

Particularly when it comes to marketing nonprofit services, new brand experiences that do not meet one's expectations can quickly erode positive perceptions, even where there has been past satisfaction. The Parasuraman, Zeithaml, and Berry (1985) Service Quality Gap Model suggests that clients' service expectations are influenced not only by marketers' promotion campaigns but also by a client's personal needs for the service, word-of-mouth input from users, and the client's own past experience. A problem can arise if there is a gap between an "expected service" and a "perceived service." A nonprofit's market strategy can influence both the expected and the perceived aspects of service. It is important that market strategy be based on the reality of client expectations and the reality of client service perceptions, not what an organization wishes they were, thinks they are, or believes they should be.

The Importance of Differentiating a Brand

Clients and other target publics have choices about how they spend their money, time, efforts, and loyalties. Facing strong competition, strategic marketers weigh the benefits of a less expensive but perhaps less effective undifferentiated strategy versus a more expensive but perhaps more effective differentiated strategy. Using an **undifferentiated strategy,** the nonprofit would develop just one marketing mix (e.g., one offer, one sort of distribution for that offer, one promotion campaign for that offer, and one price—monetary or nonmonetary—for that offer) and then provide that mix to all potential target publics. On the other hand, as noted earlier in this chapter, a **differentiated strategy** would involve two or more marketing mixes that create a perception by the target public that an organization's offer(s) is distinctive from those otherwise available in ways that target publics would value. It is easy to see the advantage of a differentiated strategy (e.g., the relative advantage of marketing the Peace Corps relative to a little-known nonprofit dedicated to helping people in drought-stricken areas of the world or the advantage of being the Red Cross rather than an in-hospital blood collection department).

You may have attended a university with a generic business school. Imagine how being branded might improve a business school's success at raising funds, attracting the best students, qualifying for grants, and involving Fortune 100 companies in research programs. There are many branded business schools, but most business executives would agree that the strong brands are Northwestern University's Kellogg School of Management, The University of Virginia's Darden Graduate School of Business Administration, and the University of Pennsylvania's Wharton School. Harvard and other Ivy League schools would tend to extend their already strong university brand name to their business schools and all their other programs.

For clients, donating to, or involving themselves with, a strong brand reduces search costs, signals quality (and therefore probable satisfaction), and reduces overall risk. Reducing risk includes reducing social risk (embarrassment), psychological risk (negative self-views), and financial risk (poor use of funds). In general, target publics prefer brands that are consistent with their personal values and norms. But if a nonprofit has not undertaken the steps necessary to create a strong brand, target publics may never even know it exists.

For nonprofits, brand strength and organizational success go hand in hand. Having a strong brand or strong brands creates competitive advantage, inspires trust from target publics, and attracts and retains valuable donors, executives, and board members. Typically, strong brands also earn higher income in excess of costs than weak brands do.

Brand Extension

Importantly, a strong brand also supports brand extensions (as in the Harvard example). **Brand extension** involves an organization's using an existing brand name to assist in the launch and acceptance of new offers. Brand extension also provides brand value to all the offers clustered under the brand designation. A good for-profit example would be Microsoft Windows, Microsoft Office, and Microsoft Internet Explorer, all trademarked products under the Microsoft brand. Likewise, in a nonprofit, a strong brand (e.g., Red Cross Blood Collection) can similarly transfer the target public's trust to new endeavors and impart credibility to existing auxiliary programs (e.g., Red Cross Community Services and Red Cross Volunteer Services). Indeed, brand extension often becomes critical to growing a brand and keeping the brand relevant and up to date.

The National Geographic Society has grown aggressively, adding magazine extensions, television programs, and books; in fact, it has grown so much that most target publics are now more aware of its for-profit activities than its original efforts in exploration and education. And therein lies the trap of unchecked brand extension. Without careful planning and attention to mission, brand strength can lure a nonprofit into becoming what is predominantly a for-profit business (justifying ever more overhead and executive energy for commercial growth). This may or may not be true of the National Geographic Society, but aggressive brand extension is something to approach with caution and strict attention to the nonprofit's mission.

A strong nonprofit brand can also attract brand alliances with strong brands of other organizations, both for-profit and nonprofit. An ad featuring an IBM computer with an Intel processor is intended to combine the brand power of both companies in the consumer's mind. The Martha Stewart brand was strong enough to extend to several magazines, television programs, and books, but at some point during Ms. Stewart's legal problems, Kmart may have questioned the wisdom of its brand alliance with Martha Stewart. In the nonprofit arena, the Arthritis Foundation linked its name with the McNeil Consumer Products, maker of a type of pain reliever that was effective in reducing the pain of arthritis. The alliance of the two companies came under fire for a number of reasons, including the ethicality of the Arthritis Foundation's favoring one brand of analgesic over alternatives that were just as effective. Ultimately, both sides of the alliance experienced negative consequences. Another example of a brand alliance gone wrong was the 1997 agreement between the American Medical Association (AMA) and Sunbeam. The AMA permitted Sunbeam to put the AMA's name on such products as blood pressure monitors and heating pads, which resulted in so much protest from AMA members themselves that the AMA's upper management ended up paying Sunbeam $10 million to settle a breach-of-contract lawsuit. For a final example, the American Cancer Society allowed SmithKline Beecham to use the society's seal on one of the pharmaceutical company's smoking-cessation products. Attorneys general from 12 states forced the drug company to pay a fine and to clearly indicate in its ads that it donates a large sum of money to the American Cancer Society in return for the permission to use its seal. These examples emphasize that brand alliances should be undertaken carefully after much thought and consideration.

The for-profit sector seems to make more use of both brand extensions and alliances than nonprofits do—probably because of their highly competitive markets, great emphasis on marketing, large promotional budgets, and structural organization for brand management. However, given that the numbers of nonprofits are growing rapidly, nonprofit professionals will likely need to increase their strategic skills in this area. This topic is covered in more detail in Chapter 12, about cause-related marketing.

Licensing

It is also possible that a nonprofit with a strong brand identity could benefit financially by licensing the use of its name to manufacturers or program providers whose offerings are consistent with the brand image of the nonprofit. Licensing is one type of brand alliance between organizations. Products or even entire stores that bear a nonprofit's name may in fact be offered or owned by licensees. For example, in 1992, Save the Children licensed an exclusive line of neckties. Currently, Save the Children has licensing agreements with Checks in the Mail, Elmer Candy Corporation, Jo-Ann Stores, LC Creations, and Whisper Soft Mills, among others (at www.savethechildren.org, look under "Corporations" and then "Licensing" for more information). As for how licensing works, if a major toy company offers a toy panda bearing the World Wildlife Fund (WWF) logo and includes a statement on the box that, for each panda purchased, $1.00 will be donated to the WWF, it would be likely that the toy company has negotiated a license arrangement providing for an up-front payment and a royalty payment of $1.00 per unit sold. Such agreements can benefit both parties. The nonprofit receives an additional revenue stream, and the toy company expects higher profits than if it did not use the WWF-affiliation approach. Currently, WWF has alliances and licensing agreements with Build-A-Bear Workshop, Organicbouquet.com, and Barnes and Noble, among others (at www.worldwildlife.org, look under "Get Involved" and then "Shop Online" for more information).

Strategically Choosing Brand Elements

Several marketing textbooks (e.g., Kotler & Keller, *Marketing Management,* p. 282) suggest that brand elements (including the brand name, logo, symbol, character, packaging, and slogan) should be chosen on the basis of a number of dimensions. For example, one authority has suggested that each brand element should have the following characteristics:

1) memorable—easy to recognize and recall, 2) meaningful—have meaning that is consistent with the mission of the organization, 3) likable—evoke a positive response, 4) transferable—can be used in brand extensions, 5) adaptable—can be easily updated as needs and aesthetics change over time, and 6) protectable—unique enough to be registered and copyrighted. (Vanauken, 2004)

Brand Characters

A **brand character** can be defined as a cartoon or other mascot that comes to symbolize or at least remind target publics of a brand. Since 1944, Smokey Bear (also considered to be part of a positioning strategy, positioning by cultural symbol) has represented the U.S. Forest Service, reminding us that "Only You Can Prevent Forest Fires." The character was based on an injured baby bear found after a major forest fire and brought to the National Zoo. The relevance of the character to the message and organizational mission has helped it last more than 60 years. In comparison, most people would not be able to recall the brand character(s) from even the last Olympics. Perhaps such an inability results from a character's lack of relevance or a feeling that such characters are sometimes created more to sell as stuffed animals than to symbolize the true spirit of a nonprofit.

Brand Equity—A Measure of Brand Strength

Brand strength and brand equity are related terms, and each is multidimensional. For example, **brand strength** is equal to the degree of differentiation and relevance of the brand to target publics. Differentiation and relevance of a brand are dependent on such dimensions as positioning, competition, and past performance, among others. **Brand equity** is defined as the marketing effects or outcomes that add value to an organization's offer relative to offers without the brand name. For some, it is tempting to try to limit the measure of brand equity to the profit obtained from a branded versus an unbranded offer, but equity is more than the simple profit or financial value represented by a brand. Target publics, their preferences, and competitive offerings are always dynamic, and today's value will be different from tomorrow's, and market responses will depend on individual perceptions, assumptions, and reactions. If an organization launches an initiative, competitors may or may not follow, so it is exceedingly difficult to determine the initiative's value at a particular time or how much of that value is due to the offer's particular brand designation.

Fortunately, monetary brand equity is somewhat less an issue in the nonprofit sector than it is among for-profits. Nonprofits are very interested in the intangible and perceptive value dimensions of brand equity, however. One can see some examples of these nonmonetary dimensions (and how difficult they are to quantify) by looking at popular models for measuring or visualizing brand equity. Included in such models are the following dimensions of brand equity:

1. Loyalty, awareness, perceived quality, and image associations

2. Differentiation, relevance, esteem, and knowledge

3. Quality and salience

4. Personal bonding, advantage, performance, relevance, and presence

Nonprofit marketing strategists would typically want to see how their brand compares with other well-known nonprofit brands that can serve as benchmarks and to track how these relationships change over time. For example, a particular brand equity ranking scheme might rank one nonprofit's brand below that of a certain market leader, but that ranking has strategic significance if the brand seems to be closing the gap with the market leader's over time. It would also be strategically significant if one found that different segments of an organization's target publics could be identified by grouping similar responses.

Building and Measuring Brand Image

A positive brand image is built on the foundation of strong favorable impressions and associations in the minds and memories of target publics. Favorable impressions and associations can derive from many sources. Some are under the marketer's direct control (e.g., marketing communications, service interactions) while others come from less-controllable sources (e.g., word-of-mouth, publicity, personal experience). The sum of these influences creates personal perceptions of value, uniqueness, integrity, and reliability. The accumulation of these influences and impressions is an ongoing process for target publics, so brand image can be quite dynamic and will definitely change during a brand's life cycle.

An effective brand image is not built just by introducing an offer into a market. Brand image should be strategically planned for and built into the 4P marketing mix, including marketing campaigns, design, and operations policies. Little should be left to chance when marketers plan programs and invest resources to assure that target publics are aware of brand attributes (features) as well as how these attributes provide brand benefits with personal meaning and value.

Collecting data on measures of brand image within various target publics is a bit easier than collecting data on brand equity. To assess brand image, marketers can use the marketing research process to directly ask target publics to rate a brand. Brands can be rated on indicators of good brand image, such as value, uniqueness, integrity, and reliability, and by responses to questions such as "How does the brand make me feel?" "What does using the brand say about me?" "What does the brand stand for?" and "How loyal am I to this brand?"

An understanding of how target publics perceive, evaluate, and feel about a brand becomes the basis for a future marketing strategy to maintain or improve brand image. The brand image held by target publics of one brand versus competitive offers forms the basis for the offer positioning analysis previously discussed. For marketing purposes, marketers might group target publics that possess similar levels of favorable brand image, or they might group target publics who similarly emphasize the importance of particular brand benefits. If these groups are differentiated from one another along demographic lines (the individuals within groups have identifiable similarities, and there are differences between groups), marketers may be able to design customized 4P marketing approaches for each group. This analysis is the basis for strategic segmentation.

Segmentation

The relevance of all the topics covered so far in this chapter is more likely than not to vary across the target publics of a nonprofit organization. Indeed, brand strength is partially defined by the brand's relevance to existing and potential target publics. Specifically, target publics may differ in how they perceive a nonprofit's offers, brand equity, offer value, and offer positioning, as well as how they view a brand's differential advantage compared with alternative uses of their time and resources. It would be a huge mistake for a marketing strategist to assume that a nonprofit's target publics are one-dimensional or that they see the world through the strategist's own eyes. Some target publics are millionaires and some are not; some are conservative and some are not; some are old; some are young; some like country music; and others like classical, rock, rap, or heavy metal. The point is that marketers need to recognize that different opinions, interests, and resources are to be expected, even within seemingly similar target publics.

Adopting a strategy of market segmentation allows nonprofit marketers to balance the need to be concerned with the needs and wants of individuals with the constraints of running an economical operation. Segmentation allows an organization to identify prospective publics within a large mass market and then develop a cost-effective way of reaching those publics. Segmentation of the market for a nonprofit's offers allows marketers to design offers that serve specific needs of important subgroups, or segments, and to create the most effective marketing plan that their resources will allow. In segmentation, marketers divide the market into subsets that share common needs, characteristics, or responses. The definition of **market segmentation** is the development and pursuit of marketing programs directed at specific groups within the population that the organization could potentially serve.

Recently, an international market study asked respondents if they would consider having a favorite brand logo permanently tattooed on their upper arm. Most respondents said no, but almost 19% stated that they would agree to have the tattoo. But before concluding that this group would be *a* market segment for a tattoo parlor or an organization that is considering promoting itself or one of its offers via "human billboards," the researchers found that those pro-tattoo respondents were not homogeneous but differed in terms of their individual demographics, psychographic characteristics, lifestyles, life stage, benefits sought, and belief and value systems. Some indicated that they would be willing to have a Harley-Davidson tattoo, others wanted Disney, and still others Coca-Cola.

Although nonprofits are not likely to be interested in tattooing anybody, it is potentially valuable for them to recognize that there can be groups with exceptional brand loyalty and commitment. Where advantageous, populations can be segmented, and 4P offering mixes can be custom designed to meet the particular interests of target groups.

As discussed under "The Importance of Differentiating a Brand," nonprofits do not have to engage in segmentation at all but can choose to put together one undifferentiated or marketwide marketing approach wherein they would serve up the same marketing mix to all their target publics. That would be appropriate if the nonprofit knew that, for a particular type of offer (a) everyone's needs are more alike than different and (b) it would not be cost effective to have more than one approach to its target publics. At the other extreme would be the creation of an individual marketing mix for each person in the target population, or **mass customization**. For most nonprofits, mass customization would generally be cost prohibitive. Most organizations choose a strategy somewhere between the two extremes and target specific groups. Differentiation that is done by nonprofits is often referred to as **niche** or **focused marketing** because, unlike very large for-profits, which may find it cost effective to develop many 4P marketing mixes targeted to specific segments, most nonprofits choose to focus on relatively few target segments, with unique marketing strategies for each segment.

Two Examples of Segmentation

An example can illustrate how a segmentation approach can be useful to nonprofits. Several examples from the for-profit sector can be found in many current textbooks, such as Keller's *Strategic Brand Management: Building, Measuring, and Managing Brand Equity (1998)*. Presented here is a fictitious example of a nonprofit animal welfare organization. Say that in the "small donor" market (those who give $50 or less annually) for animal-care organizations, a research study uncovered four segments:

1. Habit givers—those who give out of habit (20%)

2. Self-esteem givers—those who give to build their self-esteem (40%)

3. Nuisance stoppers—those who give in order to stop people from asking (25%)

4. Other givers—those who give for other reasons (15%)

It should be easy to see how and why an organization would do well to design different 4P marketing mixes for each segment. The marketer would want to know as much as possible about the demographics, behavior, and size of each of these segments.

The sum of the percentages of the market in each segment should equal 100%. That allows the construction of a pie chart, which is a very effective visual aid in understanding the makeup of the market.

A second example of nonprofit market segmentation, drawn from Roper's Worldwide Global Consumer Surveys and presented in Johansson's *Global Marketing: Foreign Entry, Local Marketing, and Global Marketing* (2000), is culture related and based on personal values. In this approach, six market segments were identified:

Segment 1 emphasized religion and tradition.

Segment 2 emphasized social and welfare issues.

Segment 3 emphasized family and personal relationships.

Segment 4 emphasized pleasure and fun.

Segment 5 was primarily motivated by learning, knowledge accumulation, and mastery over technology.

Segment 6 emphasized accumulating material possessions and was driven by professional goals.

Such values-based segmentation is said to be useful across cultures and types of offers and remains fairly stable over time. But because a host of variables may combine in unique ways to describe various segments, nonprofit marketers should determine the most effective market segmentation for their organization's offers and competitive environment.

Why Segment?

The marketing concept suggests that nonprofit organizations should take an approach centered on customer needs when they decide which offers to provide to which market groups at what price, with what promotion, and with what distribution. Except for donors who give major gifts, offering a customized marketing mix to each potential donor would be prohibitive in terms of cost and resources. It is more economical to group individuals who share similar needs and show similar market responses and then address the needs of a group of individuals—a segment—with one marketing mix. Nonprofits can frame their messages in the words and values of particular segments and avoid the waste inherent in sending those messages to the wrong people. Segmentation also allows the marketing strategist to identify and serve the particular needs of attractive niche target segments. Such a niche-serving approach to the market may very well become an organization's key marketing strategy and differentiate it from competitive offerings to a major degree.

In short, organizations segment to be more efficient and effective at serving their target markets.

Evaluating Segments

When it comes to a decision about the "right" number of segments, the answer depends on the judgment of a nonprofit's marketing strategist. Too few, and the organization and target publics are not receiving all the potential benefits of segmentation. Too many, and the organization is investing in too many costly individual marketing programs targeted at groups whose needs are not that different from others'. Typical numbers would be between 5 and 20 segments.

The process of segmentation itself can help nonprofits determine an appropriate number of segments for them. Basically, the number of segments on which to focus depends on several factors. Target segments should be

- Measurable—Can the nonprofit ascertain the size, the potential for use of the nonprofit's offers, and other characteristics of potential segments?
- Substantial—Are the segments large enough and cost-efficient enough for the nonprofit to pursue? Whereas for-profits tend to make decisions to develop specific marketing mixes largely on the basis of the size of a segment, nonprofits may not want to use size as their criterion. Some nonprofits are required by their mission to serve particular target publics regardless of their numbers.
- Compatible—Is the make-up of a segment consistent with the institutional mission? This factor is much more significant for nonprofits than is size. For most nonprofits, in fact, the compatibility of a segment with their mission is of primary importance.
- Accessible—Can segment members be reached easily with marketing communications? If not, the nonprofit may not be able to pursue the segment. The question then becomes whether a nonprofit should engage in controlled coverage or self-selection. **Controlled**

coverage, or marketing communications that are placed to appear in or on media relevant to a target segment, can be used if a nonprofit knows what a particular target segment reads, listens to, or watches. If a nonprofit finds that an otherwise significant target segment simply cannot be reached with a marketing mix, it may try what is called **self-selection,** or placing marketing communications in or on mass media and hoping that the target segment will be among the people who are exposed to those media. Although the U.S. Army engages in self-selection when it places advertisements in televised college football games, such a strategy would be well beyond the monetary resources of most nonprofits.

- Differentiable—Are individuals within a segment homogeneous within segments (i.e., do they show important similarities within the segment) and heterogeneous between segments (i.e., do all members of one segment differ in important ways from members of other segments)?
- Actionable—Is the nonprofit able to develop a marketing mix that would meet the needs of the segment?

Strategists who favor statistical approaches tend to be partial to the elegance of factor and cluster analysis. Strategists who are uncomfortable with mathematical approaches often see statistical analysis as unnecessary and prefer using their business judgment and creativity to design segments. Perhaps segmentation comes down to art versus science. With so much at stake, a marketer may well decide to use both approaches and compare the results. Eventually, marketers gain the confidence to define the methods that work best for their organization's particular situation.

Ideally, segments will be created that minimize the criteria and response differences between "in group" members and maximize the differences between "out of group" members. Once segments are selected, the marketer must again decide how to best present the brand offers to each segment. This often involves customizing marketing mixes for each segment and may involve developing specific brands for major segments. This is an ongoing process since the market and, typically, most everything about it is dynamic. Because the idea of segmentation and target markets pervades every area of marketing, there will be considerably more discussion of the topic in the upcoming chapters.

Managerial Issues

The following issues are relevant for nonprofit managers:

1. Mission, or defining a focus and scope. Traditionally, a characteristic of nonprofits has been a tendency to believe that target publics will forgive them for lengthy, complicated mission statements. Such mission statements, however, are at best difficult to read and remember and at worst likely to drive away target publics that want to know more about a nonprofit before consuming offers or donating money. Worse, employees and volunteers of nonprofits may also be confused about the mission and, therefore, make decisions and take courses of action that have little or nothing to do with the nonprofit's purpose. In order to keep everyone on the same page, effective mission statements should be concise and to the point.

2. **Differentiation, positioning, and unique value proposition.** Nonprofits may differentiate their offers from those of the competition by a number of methods, such as stressing a better offer, a more convenient location, better promotional materials, better prices, and better personnel. Even nonprofits with little or no direct competition face considerable competition from a wide variety of causes, public agencies, and private charities when it comes to scarce financial resources. Those that succeed in differentiating themselves and showing themselves to be particularly worthy of support usually do so by creating a special position in the mind of their target publics as well as a unique value proposition.

3. **Branding.** A successful unique value proposition, successful offer positioning, and successful differentiation all come together to create a successful and sustainable brand. Establishing a brand can make life easier for a nonprofit by making it easier to differentiate itself from other brands, attract brand alliances with other organizations, and introduce brand extensions. Further, nonprofits may find that licensing their brands becomes easier with stronger brands. Brand elements and brand characters can strengthen the brand if they are thoughtfully chosen.

4. **Segmentation.** Even nonprofits should engage in market segmentation because it allows them to balance the needs and wants of individuals and the constraints of running an economical operation. Segmentation allows nonprofits to identify prospective publics within a large mass market and then develop a cost-effective way of reaching those publics so that they make the best possible use of their monetary and human resources.

Summary

The nonprofit marketing issues presented in this chapter are summarized here according to the chapter learning objectives they meet.

Understand the importance of developing a concise mission statement and what the components of that statement should be. Lengthy, complicated mission statements are difficult for a nonprofit's target publics, employees, and volunteers to read and remember. Further, they can easily lead to a situation in which there is no common understanding of mission. Concise mission statements, however, are by their nature easier to understand and, therefore, can be used in decision making. Nonprofit mission statements should specify the organization's scope, and they should be feasible, motivating, and distinctive.

Understand how a nonprofit's strategic objectives depend on the mission. Since an organization's mission defines its long-term focus and scope, it can be used to provide the basis for setting objectives and all the strategic planning that follows. Even in day-to-day operations, objectives that are derived from a well-crafted mission will provide guidance at all levels of the organization.

Understand why nonprofits should give careful consideration to differentiation. Nonprofits that succeed in distinguishing themselves and showing themselves to be particularly worthy of support usually do so by creating a special position in the mind of their target publics.

Understand what positioning is and be able to explain a perceptual map and the various positioning strategies. Differentiation is effected via a positioning strategy. A positioning strategy involves creating and maintaining a particular image of an organization and its offers relative to its competition in the minds of target publics. If that image consists of more than one attribute, each offer could be rated on those attributes and plotted on two- or three-dimensional maps called perceptual maps. A perceptual map shows the position that each offer holds relative to the competition (at least as far as those attributes are concerned). Positioning strategies include positioning by offer features and attributes, benefits or needs addressed, offer or cause, use, offer class, user group, relation to competitors, price or quality, and cultural symbol.

Understand what the unique value proposition is and why it is important to nonprofit organizations. A unique value proposition is a set of unique, specific, tangible, and measurable factual statements describing the real value (i.e., the benefits) that target publics can expect to receive from an organization's offerings. A good unique value proposition should clearly differentiate the nonprofit's offers from those of competitors.

Understand why branding, brand perception, differentiation of a brand, brand extensions, licensing, brand elements, brand characters, brand equity and strength, and brand image can be important to nonprofit organizations. Establishing a brand, which can be the organization itself, an offer, or both, in the minds of one's target publics can, generally speaking, make life easier for nonprofits. The brand becomes a shorthand way for target publics to think about the nonprofit and, with time, may make the nonprofit's work easier. Most basically, a brand is a promise of what a nonprofit organization stands for, its operational values and integrity, and the promise of what benefit it will deliver to society. Once a positive brand perception is achieved, the nonprofit will likely find it easier to differentiate itself from other brands, attract brand alliances with other organizations, and introduce brand extensions that are likely to be more successful than new offers that are not branded. Nonprofits can earn income from licensing their brand(s) to appropriate relevant organizations, and licensing becomes easier when nonprofits have developed strong brands. Brand elements (e.g., the brand name, logo, symbol, character, packaging, and slogan) and brand characters can strengthen the brand if they are thoughtfully chosen. Brand strength and brand equity refer to the degree of differentiation and relevance of the brand to target publics, and brand image should be measured from time to time to monitor how nonprofits are doing when it comes to the perception of their offers.

Understand what segmentation is and why it is important, even for nonprofit organizations. Market segmentation allows nonprofit marketers to balance their concern for the needs and wants of individuals and the constraints of running an economical operation. Segmentation allows an organization to identify prospective publics within a large mass market and then develop a cost-effective way of reaching those publics.

Glossary

Brand. Basically the collection of perceptions in the minds of its target publics based on how they value and relate to the organization's mission, offers, and reputation; a promise that target publics can count on and trust.

Brand character. A cartoon or other mascot that comes to symbolize or at least remind target publics of a brand.

Brand equity. The marketing effects or outcomes that add value to an organization's offer relative to offers without the brand name.

Brand extension. An organization's using an existing brand name to assist in the launch and acceptance of new offers.

Brand strength. Equal to the degree of differentiation and relevance of the brand to target publics.

Controlled coverage. Marketing by placing materials in or on media relevant to a target segment.

Differentiated strategy. Use of two or more marketing mixes that create a target public perception that an organization's offer(s) are distinctive from those otherwise available in ways that target publics would value.

Differentiation. Development of two or more marketing mixes that create a target public perception that an organization's offer(s) are distinctive from those otherwise available in ways that target publics would value.

Focused marketing. See **niche marketing.**

Marketing mix. The controllable variables in the specifics of a nonprofit's offers to the market, that is, the *product* or *offer* (e.g., goods, services, social programs, etc.), the *place* (e.g., the location and accessibility of offers), the *price* (in terms of such things as money, psychic energy, social risks, time, effort, perceived risk), and the *promotion* (e.g., advertising, personal selling, publicity, and sales promotion).

Market segmentation. The development and pursuit of marketing programs directed at specific groups within the population that the organization could potentially serve.

Mass customization. The creation of an individual marketing mix for each person in the target population.

Mission statement. A carefully crafted definition of an organization's long-term focus and scope; the stated purpose of the nonprofit organization.

Niche marketing. A focus on a few target segments, with unique marketing strategies for each segment.

Perceptual map. A graphic representation of the importance of different dimensions and the perceptions of various alternatives along those dimensions for one or more target publics.

Positioning. Designing and implementing an offering mix to create and maintain a particular image of an organization and its offers relative to its competition in the minds of target publics.

Self-selection. Marketing by placing marketing communications in or on mass media and hoping that the target segment will be among the people exposed to those media.

Strategic objectives. Statement of the broad direction of the organization.

Undifferentiated strategy. The strategy in use when a nonprofit develops just one marketing mix and then offers that mix to all potential target publics.

Unique value proposition. A set of specific, tangible, and measurable factual statements describing the real value (benefits) that target publics can expect to receive from an organization's offerings.

QUESTIONS FOR REVIEW

1. Define *mission statement* and explain the three dimensions of mission scope.

2. Describe *strategic objectives* and explain how they should be related to the nonprofit mission.

3. Explain how a nonprofit could differentiate itself and its offers.

4. Define *positioning* and explain each of the options.

5. Define *unique value proposition*.

6. Define *branding, brand perception, brand extension, licensing, brand elements, brand character, brand equity* and *strength*, and *brand image*.

7. Define *market segmentation*.

QUESTIONS FOR DISCUSSION

1. What are some problems with traditional (long and complicated) mission statements?

2. How and why does specifying the who, what, and how of a mission improve it?

3. Why and how might nonprofits differentiate their offers from the competition's?

4. What is involved in a positioning strategy?

5. What are the various positioning strategies a nonprofit could use for its offers?

6. How does a unique value proposition relate to an offer's differentiation?

7. How might a strong brand relate to brand differentiation, brand extensions, and licensing?

8. What are examples of brand elements? What are the important dimensions of brand elements when it comes to deciding which to use and which to avoid?

9. Why is segmentation important for nonprofits?

INTERNET EXERCISES

1. Use your search engine to search for nonprofits that work with the homeless. Choose one and develop a possible segmentation approach for potential donors to that organization. Estimate the size of the total market and the number in each segment.

2. Enter www.marchofdimes.com/, the website for the March of Dimes, a nonprofit founded in 1938 by President Franklin D. Roosevelt to conquer polio (he was a polio victim himself). FDR's portrait appears on the U.S. dime to commemorate his ardent support for the

March of Dimes. (Your grandparents may remember collecting dimes in elementary school for this famous and important organization.) Consider what happened to the March of Dimes when, by the 1960s, medical advances that they helped to fund essentially wiped out the disease in all but the least developed countries. Imagine the marketing challenge to reposition the organization. Any change in an organization's mission requires an in-depth understanding of the nonprofit's target publics. From studying the organization's current home page, assess the logic of the cause it adopted after polio. Evaluate the quality of its Web presence in light of probable stakeholders and market segments.

3. Consider the case of multiple nonprofit organizations dealing with some dimension of curing cancer. It would be likely that each would be created (or would evolve) to serve a particular niche. For each of the following cancer organizations, compare the apparent (a) target publics served, (b) target publics' needs to be met, and (c) technologies to be used to meet those needs:

American Cancer Society (www.cancer.org)

National Cancer Institute (www.cancer.gov)

Cancer Care (www.cancercare.org)

American Association for Cancer Research (www.aacr.org)

Memorial Sloan-Kettering Cancer Center (www.mskcc.org)

National Breast Cancer Association (www.nationalbreastcancer.org)

National Ovarian Cancer Coalition (www.ovarian.org)

Women's Cancer network (www.wcn.org)

Skin Cancer Foundation (www.skincancer.org)

Leukemia and Lymphoma Society (www.leukemia-lymphoma.org)

Y-Me (www.y-me.org).

What are the major challenges to each organization's marketing function in this type of environment?

Visit the websites of 8–10 major nonprofits and look for examples of brand elements, e.g., registered brand names, logos, and slogans. Also, look for examples of brand characters and evidence of brand alliances. Share your findings with the class.

TEAM EXERCISES AND ROLE PLAYING

1. This team exercise involves finding and perhaps rewriting mission statements for each of the following types of nonprofits: (a) a nearby hospital, (b) a nearby university or college, (c) a nearby cultural museum (e.g., art, historic artifacts), and (d) a national charity with local offices. Search on the Internet for examples that interest the group. Find the mission statement on the website. If a mission statement already specifies the scope, put together a presentation (similar in appearance to Exhibit 2.1) showing the who, what, and how of the statement. If a mission statement does not specify the scope, rewrite it so that it does. Again, put together an example of the original mission statement and your new and improved version.

2. In teams, look for examples of nonprofits that seem to be engaging in the various types of positioning—positioning by offer features and attributes, positioning by benefits or needs addressed, positioning by offer or cause, positioning by use, positioning by offer class, positioning by user group, positioning relative to competitors, positioning by price or quality, positioning by cultural symbol. Be sure to look for examples that are not already given in the text. Prepare a brief presentation for the class. The class will vote on the best examples.

MINICASE: The XYZ Regional Hospital Foundation

It was Jessica Kennedy's first day as executive director of the XYZ Regional Hospital Foundation. She was excited and worried at the same time. She was sure that the Foundation's board of directors would be watching her carefully to see if she was capable of moving up to the executive director position. Her previous positions were all in fund-raising, and she had no experience at all with a medical nonprofit.

What Jessica did have (and what had convinced the board to hire her) was a real passion for developing programs and a talent for getting potential major donors involved and contributing. As far as the board was concerned, her first job would be to come up with a formal plan to at least double donations and incoming grants and to develop new sources of income. According to the board's explanation during her employment interview, the previous executive director had founded the Foundation 3 years earlier with the objective of raising funds to be donated to the regional hospital. The hospital would use the funds to enhance its community health programs and to support its medical care mission. Since accepting the executive director position, Jessica has discussed the Foundation's role with senior executives at the Regional Hospital and discovered that they were not at all pleased with the Foundation's efforts. At this point, she was pretty sure that the top management at the hospital was pressuring the Foundation's board to increase financial support and that this pressure had led to her being hired. Now that she was on board, the pressure to perform was being passed on to her.

Jessica felt sure that her experience winning major grants, gifts, and bequests and succeeding at creative fund-raising would serve her well in her new position. Still, the more she learned about her new organization, the more she became convinced that the previous director's idea of mission focus, positioning, market analysis, and overall strategic planning left a great deal to be desired. In fact, it seemed as if it might be necessary to start from scratch and (from a marketing perspective) reinvent the entire Foundation.

Looking through the past year's expenses, Jessica noted the following: office rent, $18,500; office cleaning, $3,500; office equipment, $8,250; utilities, $1,200; employee dues, $550; recruiting, $900; fund-raising, $15,400; event catering, $990; and outside services, $35,130; among others. A historical chart of funds raised versus funds donated to the hospital indicated the following:

	Funds Raised by the Foundation	Foundation Donations to the Hospital
Year 1	$97,000	0
Year 2	$237,000	0
Year 3	$283,000	$2,500

It appeared that over the past 3 years, the Foundation's expenditures for salaries, employee benefits, overhead, fund-raising, office equipment, and other expenses had pretty much used up all its financial support (with essentially nothing left over to donate to the hospital). Jessica suspected that if things didn't change, expenses would continue to increase to match what was being raised. It appeared that the Foundation had been evolving to support its own existence rather than being true to its stated mission, "to raise funds for the hospital." She also figured that it was only a matter of time until the media and donors caught on to what was going on.

Jessica knew that she had to "set a new path" for the Foundation and do it quick. She took a pad of paper and noted the following:

1. Need very visible change.

2. Need new mission focus.

3. Need new strategic objectives.

4. Need clear differentiation and positioning in donors' mind.

5. Need unique value proposition.

6. Need to become a "brand" with image of integrity.

7. Need to segment market opportunities and analyze donor motivation and behavior.

8. Need to create a new set of offering mixes by target segment, consistent with our mission and image of integrity.

9. Need to earn the respect of top management at the hospital, my own board members, and the leaders in the community.

Turning the page, she wrote:

Community description—Rural, lower income, weak school system, but with significant business communities in several small cities and towns.

Foundation board of directors description—Business people, lawyers, medical doctors, very conservative religiously and financially. Probably think the answer to the Foundation's problems is to raise more money.

Foundation organization description—Mostly volunteers, few full-time staff, more used to being told what to do than to thinking for themselves or working as a team.

My description—Willing to make best effort. Willing to try a marketing concept approach rather than a straight sales-and-fund-raising approach. Driven to make a difference for good. Willing to stand up to the Foundation board, hospital top management, and the community with a plan for real change.

Case Assignment

Pick a smaller local suburban or rural hospital to become the XYZ Regional Hospital in the above case. It will bring more reality to the case if you can explore the website of the hospital your foundation is supposed to be serving. You are Jessica. Plan your "new path" for the Foundation, addressing the nine issues she listed above and including additional issues she probably should have listed. The board is going to require you to be specific about what you propose to do in each area. For example, for item 2 on her list, tell the board exactly what the new mission focus will be and how you will create and implement it.

Good luck. If you are successful in putting this organization on the right track, there is little doubt that you will go on to become the executive director of bigger and bigger nonprofits. You will be able to make more and more of a positive impact on the lives of those who need it most. If you fail, you will most likely end up back in a fund-raising position of a smaller organization.

Bibliography

Amon, F. S. (2004). *Organizational change communication, identity, image, and culture: The case of CARE International.* Retrieved October 6, 2005, from purl.fcla.edu/fcla/etd/UFE0004702

Andreasen, A. R. (2001). Firm responses to consumer information policy. In P. N. Bloom & G. T. Gundlach (Eds.), *Handbook of marketing and society.* Thousand Oaks, CA: Sage.

Andreasen, A. R. & Kotler, P. (2003). *Strategic marketing for nonprofit organizations* (6th ed.). Upper Saddle River, NJ: Prentice Hall.

Angelica, E. (2001). *The Wilder nonprofit field guide to crafting effective mission and vision statements.* Saint Paul, MN: Amherst H. Wilder Foundation.

Arsenault, J. (1998). *Forging nonprofit alliances: A comprehensive guide to enhancing your mission through joint ventures and partnerships, management service organizations, parent corporations, and mergers.* San Francisco: Jossey-Bass.

Austin, J. E. (2000). *The collaboration challenge: How nonprofits and businesses succeed through strategic alliances.* San Francisco: Jossey-Bass.

Bernstein, P. (1997). *Best practices of effective nonprofit organizations: A practitioner's guide.* New York: Foundation Center.

Biotechnology Industry Organization. (2004). *Patient and medical health advocacy display participants.* Retrieved October 6, 2005, from http://www.bio.org/events/2005/programs/patientlist.asp?p=yes

Board Matters. (2005). *Business-community funding.* Retrieved October 6, 2005, from www.governance.com.au/BoardMatters/brdmattersarticleNew19.pdf

Brinckerhoff, P. C. (2000a). *Mission-based management: Leading your not-for-profit in the 21st century.* New York: Wiley.

Brinckerhoff, P. C. (2000b). *Social entrepreneurship: The art of mission-based venture development.* New York: Wiley.

Brinckerhoff, P. C. (2003). *Mission-based marketing: Positioning your not-for-profit in an increasingly competitive world* (2nd ed.). Hoboken, NJ: Wiley.

Bryson, J. M. (2004). *Strategic planning for public and nonprofit organizations: A guide to strengthening and sustaining organizational achievement* (3rd ed.). San Francisco: Jossey-Bass.

Carver, J. (1997). *Boards that make a difference: A new design for leadership in nonprofit and public organizations* (2nd ed.). San Francisco: Jossey-Bass.

Cochran, A. C. (2004). *Roberta's rules of order: Sail through meetings for stellar results without the gavel: A guide for nonprofits and other teams.* San Francisco: Jossey-Bass.

Cogan, S. (2001). *Branding for nonprofit organizations.* Master's thesis, Rowan University, Glassboro, NJ.

Deutsch, J., & Real, T. (2002). *Just who do your customers think you are?—A guide to branding your organization.* Lansing: Michigan Museums Association.

Fine, S. H. (2004). *Marketing the public sector: Promoting the causes of public and nonprofit agencies.* Retrieved July 23, 2005, from search.epnet.com/direct.asp?db=buh&jid=%22 PXE%22&scope=site

Gifts in Kind International. (2005). About Gifts in Kind International. Retrieved October 6, 2005, from www.giftsinkind.org/newhome/aboutus.asp

Grace, K. S. (1997). *Beyond fundraising.* Indianapolis, IN: Wiley.

Hanzlik, K. D. (2002). *The name game: Branding a social service nonprofit.* Master's thesis, Graduate School of Business, University of St. Thomas, Saint Paul, MN.

Harter, G. (2005). College of William and Mary. Retrieved October 6, 2005, from silverchips.mbhs.edu/siteFeatures/college/profile.php?cid=5115

Herman, M. L. (2004). *Managing risk in nonprofit organizations: A comprehensive guide.* Hoboken, NJ: Wiley.

Hesselbein, F., Goldsmith, M., & Beckhard, R. (1997). *The organization of the future.* San Francisco: Jossey-Bass.

Hummel, J. M. (1996). *Starting and running a nonprofit organization* (2nd ed.). Minneapolis: University of Minnesota Press.

Johansson, J. K. (2000). *Global marketing: Foreign entry, local marketing, and global management* (4th ed.). Boston: Irwin McGraw-Hill.

Keller, K. L. (1998). *Strategic brand management: Building, measuring and managing brand equity.* Upper Saddle River, NJ: Prentice Hall.

Kotler, P., & Keller, K. L. (2005). *Marketing management* (12th ed.). Upper Saddle River, NJ: Prentice Hall.

Legal Services Society. (2005). *Mission, vision, strategic objectives, and values statement.* Retrieved October 5, 2005, from www.lss.bc.ca/__shared/assets/Strategic_Objectives571.pdf

Medina-Borja, N. A. (2002). *A non-parametric approach to evaluate the performance of social service organizations.* Doctoral dissertation, Virginia Polytechnic Institute and State University, Blacksburg. Retrieved June 15, 2005, from scholar.lib.vt.edu/theses/available/etd-04262002–234501

Miller, J., & Muir, D. (2004). *The business of brands.* Chichester, UK: Wiley.

Nissim, W. H. (2003). *Orange County rescue missions search for relevance: Branding methodologies employed by a nonprofit organization.* Master's thesis, California State University, Fullerton.

O'Neil, C. V. S. (2002). *Who you are and what you stand for: Nonprofit branding and the Women's Center.* Master's thesis, University of North Carolina at Chapel Hill.

Parasuraman, A., Zeithaml, V. A., & Berry, L. L. (1985). A conceptual model of service quality and its implications for future research. *Journal of Marketing, 49,* 41–50.

PBS. (2005). *About PBS: Welcome.* Retrieved October 6, 2005, from www.pbs.org/aboutpbs/

Self, D. R., & Wymer, W. W. (1999). *Volunteerism marketing: New vistas for nonprofit and public sector management.* New York: Haworth Press.

South Carolina Center for Grassroots and Nonprofit Leadership, South Carolina Rural Communities Compassion Project, and South Carolina—Educational Television Commission. (2003). *Creating a road map for success: Developing a business plan* [videocassette].

Stewart, B. K. (1998). *Interagency relationships among nonprofit social service organizations: A means for achieving organizational objectives.* Doctoral dissertation, University of Texas at Austin.

Stride, H. (2003). *An investigation into the value dimensions of branding: Implications for the charity sector.* Henley-on-Thames, UK: Henley Management College.

Tweeten, B. L. (2002). *Transformational boards: A practical guide to engaging your board and embracing change.* San Francisco: Jossey-Bass.

Vanauken, B. (2004). *The brand management checklist: Proven tools and techniques for creating winning brands.* Eastbourne, England, UK: Gardners Books.

Warwick, M. (2000). *The five strategies for fundraising success: A mission-based guide to achieving your goals.* San Francisco: Jossey-Bass.

Weisbrod, B. A. (1998). *To profit or not to profit: The commercial transformation of the nonprofit sector.* New York: Cambridge University Press.

3

Research in Nonprofit Organizations

Learning Objectives

On completion of this chapter, the reader will

- Understand who the important publics of nonprofits are

- Understand the various orientations that nonprofits may have

- Understand why it is important for nonprofits to spend time, effort, and money on research

- Understand why nonprofits should have a marketing information system (MIS)

- Understand where research fits into the nonprofit's MIS

- Understand the research process

Opening Vignette: Marketing Research in the Lupus Advocacy Foundation*

It was not long after Jessica Bowen started her internship at the Lupus Advocacy Foundation that she started to wonder whether something was amiss. Either real-world nonprofits did not act at all like her marketing classes had said they would, or the nice people who ran the organization were not very knowledgeable about modern marketing research. After several discussions with the organization's executive director, senior fund-raising officer, and senior outreach program officer, Jessica had the feeling that much of what the nonprofit was doing was based pretty much on what similar advocacy associations were doing for other diseases. As part of her internship, Jessica was assigned to help with several outreach programs, where she interacted face-to-face with quite a few clients who suffered from the most serious form of lupus. Through these interactions, Jessica came to believe that lupus patients had needs that were not being met by the medical and nonprofit communities.

Background

The scientific name for lupus is systemic lupus erythematosus. It is an immune system disorder in which the system that is supposed to attack only invading bacteria and viruses instead starts to attack the patient's own tissues. In serious cases, the patient's immune system attempts to destroy joints, heart, kidney, and other vital organs. Even when lupus is under partial control through medication, the patient may suffer constant pain; fatigue; a variety of other symptoms, depending on what area of the body is under attack; and often serious side effects from the prescribed medications. The Lupus Advocacy Foundation offers local and online self-help courses for living with lupus, including topics like pain management, moderate exercise programs, and a popular Internet chat room. The organization has also sponsored events intended to raise funds for operating costs and research, but these efforts have never been very successful. Although the events made money, their costs were so high that little was left over for operations or research.

Jessica's Situation

There was no doubt in Jessica's mind that the staff and volunteers at the Foundation were sincere in their caring for the sufferers of this disease and their desire to make a positive contribution. She just had a feeling that the nonprofit was applying the approaches of the past even though marketing and the world of patient needs had been changing dramatically. Today, she felt, outreach programs should be designed on the basis of a steady flow of market-environment research and research into the needs of clients in various target segments. Jessica wondered how outreach programs could be planned without in-depth knowledge of current technological research, pending legislation, and most of all, the lifestyles of lupus sufferers of all ages, genders, income levels, and disease stages. As often happens to individuals who make suggestions, as soon as Jessica expressed her opinions, she was put in charge of doing the marketing research she felt was so important. Now, instead of just the "idea of research," she has to come up with the actual ways to complete this research, the time frame, a budget, and the measurable beneficial outcomes that can be expected.

*This case was written to generate class discussion on topics that will be covered in depth in this chapter. "The Lupus Advocacy Foundation" is intended to be a fictional name and does not represent any of the fine nonprofit organizations that work in the area of lupus advocacy or any related areas.

❖ **Exhibit 3.1**   Some Publics of a Nonprofit Council on Teen Pregnancy Prevention (CTPP)

Publics of Nonprofits

Most nonprofits have at least two important target publics: their clients and their donors. In addition, many nonprofits have to deal with other important publics, such as the media, towns and cities, regulators, and the like. **Publics** of nonprofits can be characterized as people, groups, and organizations in four separate categories: **input publics,** such as donors, suppliers, and regulatory officials, who supply original resources and constraints to the organization; **internal publics,** including management, board of directors, staff, and volunteers, who convert inputs into useful goods and services and define and carry out the organization's strategies; **partner or intermediary publics,** such as merchants, agents, facilitators, and marketing firms, who carry, promote, and distribute the goods and services; and **consuming publics,** clients, local publics, activist publics, general publics, and media publics, for example, who use the goods and services and have an interest in the output of the organization. An example of some of the publics of a Council on Teen Pregnancy Prevention (CTPP) is presented in Exhibit 3.1. An example of an input public for the CTPP is the Foothills United Way, and an example of an internal public for it is its board of directors. Examples of partner and consuming publics are also given.

Jessica, in her work for the Lupus Advocacy Foundation (LAF) described in the opening vignette, should first identify all LAF's relevant publics. For example, among potential input publics, she might find donors such as corporations and individuals; one or more well-known artists who contribute a design for Christmas, Hanukkah, and other cards; and pharmaceutical regulators (for the drugs many lupus patients need to take). She already knows the executive director, senior fund-raising officer, and senior outreach program officer but would also need to identify other paid employees, the various board members, as well as volunteers for LAF. Partner or intermediary publics may be found online and in the community. For example, the state of Georgia has the Georgia Center for Nonprofits (www.gcn.org), which serves and supports nonprofit organizations; Utah has the Utah Nonprofits Association (www.utahnonprofits.org); and Virginia has the Commonwealth of Virginia Campaign (www.cvc.vipnet.org). States that do not have nonprofit centers may have local chapters of national lupus organizations; South Carolina, for example, has the Lupus Foundation of America, Inc., South Carolina Chapter (www.midnet .sc.edu/lupus/). The Arthritis Foundation (www.arthritis.org) may also be a partner public in that it serves as a resource for any lupus organization in the United States (arthritis and lupus are both diseases that affect the immune system). Finally, among consuming publics, Jessica might identify lupus patients, families and friends of lupus patients, family physicians, corporations, medical and nursing students, and the like.

Orientations of Nonprofits

When it comes to allocating resources, nonprofits, like for-profits, need to make decisions about what is most important to them: the organization itself, their target publics, or society in general. The orientation of for-profit organizations traditionally evolves from production to product to selling and finally to marketing. In the non-profit arena, the counterpart to a production orientation is a **cause orientation**, a complete focus on the cause the nonprofit was formed to address. Nonprofits that operate under a cause orientation tend to believe that target publics will come to them or support them because the cause is so interesting, important, or worthwhile. Often they develop a sort of myopia toward their cause and take for granted that their clients and donors, as well as other target publics, love or will come to love the cause too (and that donations will come rolling in once that happens). The counterpart to a for-profit product orientation is an **offer orientation**, a complete focus on the offers of the non-profit. Nonprofits that operate under an offer orientation tend to believe that target publics will come to them or support them because they offer important, worthwhile goods, services, or social programs, for example. They tend to focus so much on the importance of what they offer that they fail to consider other factors important to their target publics, such as the availability of offers, the information in marketing commu-nications, and their offers' cost (monetary or nonmonetary). So nonprofits with an offer orientation tend not to engage in marketing communications that are relevant to target publics but, instead, are likely to develop advertisements or public relations that tout the existence of the offer rather than how the offer benefits target publics. With time, perhaps after experiencing disappointment in the numbers of target publics served, nonprofits may develop a **fund-raising orientation**, a focus on raising funds to support the organization and its offers. A for-profit counterpart to this orientation is a sales orientation. Nonprofits that operate under a fund-raising orientation tend to believe that they must be aggressive in seeking funding and target publics whether or not they are consistent with the mission and values of the nonprofit. Such nonprofits often pursue funding instead of developing offers that are needed or wanted by their target publics; delivering those offers at times, places, and costs (monetary and nonmonetary) that benefit those target publics; and communicating the offers' benefits to those target publics.

Eventually, the shortcomings of the cause, offer, and fund-raising orientations become clearly evident. For example, a nonprofit may realize the general public does not share its view of how compelling the cause is, or the nonprofit may become exhausted by constantly working to raise funds or entice target publics to use its offers. At this juncture, the nonprofit should strongly consider adopting a **needs-centered orientation**, which means having a strong vision of its mission (its cause) and at the same time taking the point of view of its publics' needs and wants. A needs-centered orientation in a nonprofit is similar to a marketing orientation in the for-profit arena. Nonprofits with a needs-centered orientation would realize the importance of developing offers that benefit their target publics. Unlike for-profits, nonprofits do not have to pander to their target publics—they do not have to take a short-term view that the customer is supreme—but they do have to consider what they can offer that can benefit target publics in the long term. They also realize that although they may be devoted to their offers, others may not even be aware of them. They realize that they need to make their offers available when and where target publics need and want them and at a price (monetary or nonmonetary) that is considered appropriate by those publics. Last, they know that they need to communicate information needed by their target publics instead of a list of offer features.

To continue the example from the opening vignette, Jessica's next step would be to determine which kind of orientation the LAF has. Exhibit 3.2 offers a comparison of the four orientations in regard to seven indicators of nonprofit orientation. For example, whereas nonprofits with a needs-centered orientation tend to focus on the needs of their target publics and tend to hire employees or seek volunteers to do marketing who have marketing knowledge, nonprofits with a cause orientation tend to focus almost exclusively on their reason for being—their cause—and tend to hire employees or seek volunteers to do marketing who are committed to the nonprofit's cause regardless of whether they know anything about marketing. Having a cause orientation will not necessarily doom a nonprofit to failure, but if such a nonprofit is operating below expectations, in terms of either donations or use of its offers, it is likely to be so self-focused that it cannot understand why it is experiencing problems. You can use Exhibit 3.2 to analyze any nonprofit by considering each indicator carefully and selecting the orientation that seems to best reflect how the nonprofit operates. After assigning numbers to each orientation, you could sum the numbers and average them such that the nonprofit could earn a score that would reveal its overall orientation. For example, say a cause orientation = 1, an offer orientation = 2, a fund-raising orientation = 3, and a needs-centered orientation = 4. If a nonprofit

❖ **Exhibit 3.2**   Comparison of Seven Indicators of a Nonprofit Orientation

	Nonprofits With a			
	Cause Orientation	Offer Orientation	Fund-Raising Orientation	Needs-Centered Orientation
Have an organizational focus on	the cause	the offers	raising funds	needs of target publics
Hire employees or seek volunteers to do marketing who	are committed to the cause or mission	are knowledgeable about the offers	are knowledgeable about communication or fund-raising	have marketing knowledge
Believe that competition comes	only from other nonprofits with the same cause or mission	only from nonprofits with similar offers	from any nonprofit that seeks money	from any of a number of avenues and from many types of organizations
Answer questions by	looking to their nonprofit's mission	looking to their nonprofit's offers	looking to what the competition does	relying on research
Believe that when it comes to market segmentation,	everyone should understand the importance of their nonprofit's cause, so there is no need for segmentation	everyone should understand the importance of their nonprofit's offers, so there is no need for segmentation	anyone might be a target for fund-raising, so they do little or no segmentation	targeting segments is important, so they look for best market segments
Believe that when it comes to marketing strategies,	there is no need for them; people will be drawn to their nonprofit's cause	the focus should be on their offer (product), not the other aspects of the marketing mix	the focus should be on persuading anyone who may be a target for fund-raising through promotion	it is important to develop marketing strategies (using all elements of the marketing mix) for each target segment
Believe that when marketing strategies fail,	it is because customers are ignorant or lazy if they seem not to value the nonprofit's cause	it is because customers are ignorant or lazy if they seem not to value the nonprofit's offers	it is because fund-raisers are not doing their jobs	it is the nonprofit's fault for not putting together a better strategy

ended up with a score of 7, it would have a strong cause orientation, whereas a score of 28 would indicate a strong needs-centered orientation. Finding that the LAF has a cause, offer, or fund-raising orientation would allow Jessica to work with upper management to move the nonprofit toward a needs-centered orientation.

Why Nonprofits Must Do Research

Once a nonprofit has a needs-centered orientation, a logical next step is to engage in research to better understand its publics. Note that understanding the point of view of the nonprofit's publics does not mean that the nonprofit should pander to the wishes of those publics. Instead, it means that the nonprofit can understand its own offers from the point of view of those publics and, if appropriate, change one or more aspects of an offer, such as the time of day a program is offered, so that the offer better meets a public's needs. According to the American Marketing Association, marketing research can be used (a) to identify and define marketing opportunities and problems, (b) to generate, refine, and evaluate marketing actions that have been or will be implemented, and (c) to monitor marketing strategies (American Marketing Association, 2005). **Marketing research** is defined as the methodical design, collection, analysis, and reporting of reliable marketing information that is relevant to a particular problem faced by an organization in order to reduce uncertainty to tolerable levels at a reasonable cost.

When managers or directors of small organizations—for-profit as well as nonprofit—first hear the term *marketing research,* their immediate thought is often a negative one, followed closely with reasons marketing research cannot be done in their particular organization. For example, nonprofit directors might suggest that they do not have enough time or money to do research. They may believe that they cannot do research because no one in the nonprofit knows how to do it. Or they may believe that they do not need to do research because they are too small or have only minor decisions to make.

Some nonprofit marketing scholars suggest that those reasons are, for the most part, excuses born of lack of knowledge and that research does not have to take a lot of time or cost a lot of money. Furthermore, although research can be complicated, it is not true that only a research expert can do it. Indeed, a needs-centered nonprofit would be able to use its marketing person to determine its research needs. Finally, every organization needs to engage in ongoing research in order to stay abreast of changes or trends in its environments. At the very least, even very small and extremely focused nonprofits need to know about their various publics.

Fortunately, nonprofits are often able to use their nonprofit status to get help from a number of outside sources, such as local colleges or universities or specific academic departments that enthusiastically embrace the concept of **service learning**, a method of teaching and learning whereby participants learn and develop through active participation in thoughtfully organized service. Service learning melds education with social responsibility. Students and their instructors bring their knowledge to bear on solving a nonprofit's problem, and the nonprofit and the academics work together so that both benefit; the students gain experience applying their knowledge in the real world, while the nonprofit receives much-needed help. If a nonprofit cannot leverage its status through service learning, it may be able to find a board member or other volunteer to help direct a research project or program. It could also work with other nonprofits and pool their resources to gather data, or it could even piggyback some research questions onto another organization's surveys. Finally, it could work with external research organizations, for instance the Center for the Advancement of Marketing and Social Science (business.clemson.edu/camss/Index.htm), which may offer reduced prices for their work for nonprofits.

Why Nonprofits Should Have a Marketing Information System (MIS)

Not only should nonprofits engage in marketing research to better understand their various publics, they would also benefit from a marketing information system, which combines information learned from research with information gleaned from other sources. A **marketing information system** (MIS) uses people, equipment, and procedures to collect, sort, integrate, analyze, evaluate, and distribute necessary, timely, and accurate information to key marketing decision makers. Compared to marketing research, then, an MIS is a much more general system, and it should be a planned, routine, and ongoing process. An MIS involves three subsystems—an internal reports system, a marketing intelligence system, and an analytical marketing system—in addition to the marketing research system. Hence, marketing research should be part of a larger MIS for a nonprofit. It is vital for nonprofits to manage and disseminate marketing information as quickly and effectively as possible in order to better serve their clients and better deal with their various other important publics. If implemented well, an MIS can provide instant information while continuously monitoring the nonprofit environment so that management can adjust activities as conditions change. An optimal MIS is designed to gather important data from every activity and every section of the nonprofit and then translate that data into useful information for anyone in the nonprofit who needs it.

Where Research Fits Into a Nonprofit's MIS

Exhibit 3.3 illustrates the relationship between the marketing environment, sources of marketing information, and nonprofit marketing managers and other key decision makers. The whole process, from gathering information regarding both external and internal marketing environments to bringing it to the key decision makers, comprises the MIS. To begin, data, which would be in the form of facts, figures, and numbers, are derived from various sources within the internal and external marketing environments of the nonprofit. Sources of information within the internal marketing environment include employees, financial analyses, and operating data. Data from external marketing sources might arise from the nonprofit's clients, donors, competition, government regulators, or suppliers. Data from these environments would then be collected and entered into appropriate data-handling areas of the MIS for storage, interpretation, and analysis and ultimately used to answer specific questions.

There are four systems of data management: marketing intelligence, internal reports, marketing research, and analytical marketing. For a nonprofit organization, **marketing intelligence** refers to the collection and analysis of everyday, publicly available information that pertains to important developments related to that particular

❖ **Exhibit 3.3**   A Schematic View of a Marketing Information System

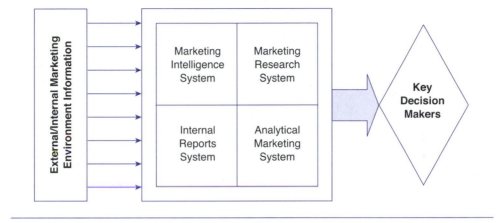

Sources of Marketing Information

| External/Internal Marketing Environment Information | Marketing Intelligence System | Marketing Research System | Key Decision Makers |
| Internal Reports System | Analytical Marketing System | |

nonprofit. Anyone associated with the nonprofit may find and submit marketing intelligence simply by engaging in such everyday activities as reading newspapers and magazines, watching television, and listening to clients, donors, the radio, and the like.

The **internal reports system** involves the collection of information from data sources within the company. It may be collected, measured, and submitted by the people and groups within a nonprofit that handle marketing activities and accounting and financial data as well as the people who regularly make presentations to individuals or groups outside the nonprofit. The nonprofit may also have information about program and service usage as well as information about past attendance at outreach programs or other results that should be made a part of internal reports.

The **marketing research system** is charged with design, collection, analysis, and reporting of data about a specific problem or situation faced by the organization. Marketing research may be done within the organization or may be bought as needed and performed by marketing research firms.

The **analytical marketing system** is charged with organizing general data, performing any needed data analysis, and generating reports—usually for data other than those collected via marketing research. The task of organizing available data and presenting it in understandable reports is especially important given the amount of information now available to nonprofit organizations.

Once information has been processed through the MIS, it would then be presented in a usable form and should be made available to key nonprofit executives and decision makers so that they can make informed decisions concerning the nonprofit's various publics. This information increases the likelihood of making good decisions.

Just as some nonprofits believe they do not need to do marketing research, some believe they do not need an MIS. Even nonprofits that understand the importance of marketing research may believe that they do not need an MIS because they think research alone will provide adequate information for effective decision making. However, because marketing research is typically focused on a specific problem or project and therefore has a definite beginning, middle, and end, even small nonprofits should consider developing an MIS because an MIS is much wider in scope than marketing research and is an ongoing process. An effective MIS will enable managers, staff, board members, and volunteers, even in small nonprofits, to have access to information from internal reports, marketing intelligence files, and marketing research reports and even to use the MIS's decision-support system to make informed, effective decisions about everything from choice of marketing strategy to the prices to charge for programs. Further, an MIS would be an invaluable source of information for fund-raisers working to develop relationships with various kinds of donors. Making marketing decisions, even in nonprofits, without input from the marketplace is unnecessarily imprudent, especially considering the degree of competition encountered by most U.S. nonprofits when it comes to major gifts and perhaps even when it comes to serving clients. The nonprofit MIS should be used to process and provide information about client and donor problems and dissatisfactions, actual or potential problems arising from partnering relationships, and competition for either a nonprofit's clients or its donors, as well as about other external and internal factors, *before* crises develop. Therefore, a properly formulated MIS can be preventative as well as curative for problems or potential problems commonly faced by nonprofits.

As noted in the opening vignette, Jessica believed (a) lupus patients had needs that were not being met by the medical and nonprofit communities, (b) outreach program design needs to be based solidly on a steady flow of market-environment research and research into client needs across various target segments, and (c) LAF needed in-depth knowledge of technological research and pending legislation and most of all, a real understanding of the lifestyle of lupus sufferers of all ages, genders, income levels, and stages of the disease. Given her beliefs, she no doubt would see the need for an MIS and should advocate adopting it at LAF. Like any nonprofit, LAF would likely already have some of the principal components of an MIS already operating, such as an informal marketing intelligence system and internal support system. Other components, such as the analytical marketing system, would likely need to be added before LAF would be able to formalize the process. Everything, from face-to-face interactions of staff with lupus patients to the outcome of various outreach programs and to information about up-to-date technological research and pending legislation, needs to be included in LAF's analysis of its external and internal marketing environments and entered into the appropriate part of the MIS. In order to set up an MIS, LAF would likely need to call on experts in marketing management as well as someone with computer knowledge (either current employees, volunteers, or board members or others via service learning projects) to ensure that all relevant information is included in the system and will be made available to decision makers in formats they can understand.

The Research Process

The marketing research process should be orderly and proceed in a logical manner. At any step of the process, the researcher may find that the answer to the original research

❖ **Exhibit 3.4**

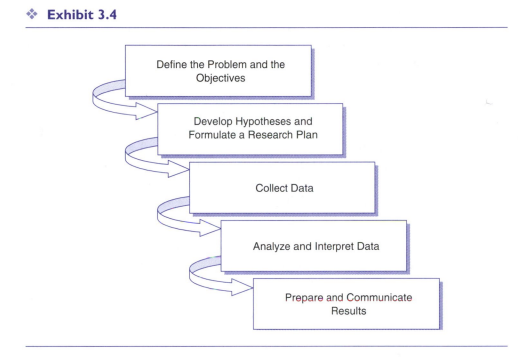

problem has become clear and that the process should not continue past that point. As seen in Exhibit 3.4, marketing research can be envisioned as a process of five steps. Those steps are discussed in the following subsections.

Define the research problem and objectives. The first step, to define the research problem and objectives, is critical. If the research problem is not clearly defined, the information obtained via the research process is unlikely to have any value. Defining the research problem may seem to be an easy task, but it is possible to confuse symptoms of a problem with the problem itself. As an example, say that a nonprofit historic home foundation believes that its problem is that it attracts too few people relative to other historic homes in the area. However, that knowledge involves only **descriptive understanding**—the lowest level of understanding, which consists simply of knowing that something is happening at a particular time. A nonprofit may know how many people took house tours on Monday or how many men and women gave blood during a single week, but simply counting the number of occurrences in the past or present does not necessarily mean that the nonprofit can expect the same number and makeup of visitors in the future. The fact that relatively few people come to tour the home may be a symptom of something wrong with the marketing environment, the marketing mix, or both. Or it may not be a symptom of a problem at all. It may even be that, given the location of the home, the number of tour visitors is actually quite good.

In order to identify the problem, nonprofit researchers should begin by asking questions to determine if the relatively small number of people taking house tours is a new phenomenon or if it has been an ongoing occurrence. If there was a time when there were many more tour visitors than there are now, researchers may want to look for any recent changes in the marketing mix, the marketing environment, and the tour personnel. If the number of tour visitors has always been low, the problem could be that the house tours are not very good or that there are too few of them or that the price of admission is higher (or lower!) than that of other homes. It could be that the nonprofit is not communicating with its target markets about tour times, hours of admission, or prices. Or it may be that the home is located in an out-of-the-way area of a state. In any case, if the research addresses only symptoms and not the real problem, the nonprofit will likely be very frustrated at the end of the research process because it will not have found information that is actionable.

At this point in the process, nonprofit researchers may wish to engage in **exploratory research**, which involves gathering preliminary information that may help define the problem and suggest hypotheses. It is informal, involves only a few respondents, is not strictly controlled, and is relatively unstructured. Researchers may want to run one or more focus groups, use projective techniques, or do some in-depth interviewing to discover attitudes, opinions, or beliefs that may illuminate possible problems with the nonprofit or its offers. A difficulty with exploratory research is that nonprofit management, employees, volunteers, and even board members may not understand that the information obtained from it cannot be generalized to any population.

In addition to exploratory and descriptive research, researchers should search for any pertinent background issues that may affect the problem or the information sought. They should also determine how the information obtained by research might be used, such as to establish the research objectives. If they were to discover that no matter what the outcome of the research, the nonprofit's decision makers would not make any changes to the marketing mix (i.e., product or offer, place or distribution, promotion or communication, and monetary or nonmonetary price), there really is no point in continuing.

Also in this stage, researchers may find that a nonprofit has a cause orientation. For example, employees, staff, volunteers, and even board members may offer "evidence" that they are doing everything right. In our historic home example, some may proclaim that they have asked friends, relatives, or people in a nearby town about the quality of the tours and have been told "The tours are great!" Another symptom of a cause orientation is a tendency to "blame the customer or client" for not coming. If researchers determine that a nonprofit does not yet have a needs-centered orientation, they may have to begin the research by introducing needs-centered thinking, or in other words, they may have to market marketing.

To continue the historic home foundation example, let us say that information obtained from one or two focus groups, along with information from some in-depth interviewing and use of the MIS, indicates that (a) at least five cars per day turn around and leave the gate when informed of the price of admission, (b) actual tour visitors claim that they were not aware of the admission price the first time they came to the house, and (c) potential tour visitors said they were not aware of the cost to tour the home. Given those points, researchers might then be able to define the research problem: The nonprofit seems not to be communicating effectively with its target markets; more specifically, it has not addressed several aspects of its marketing mix, including price information, when it comes to house tours. The research objective might now be phrased as gathering information that can help the nonprofit make decisions about how to improve its marketing mix.

Develop hypotheses and formulate a research plan. Once researchers have clarified the problem(s) and determined the research objective(s), they should formulate hypotheses, determine the information that is needed to solve the problem, and put together a research plan.

First, using the information revealed by exploratory research and other information they discovered, the researchers should develop one or more **hypotheses**—or conjectural statements about the relationship between independent and dependent variables—that can be tested. An example of a hypothesis for our example would be the following:

H_1: Price information appearing in the nonprofit's promotional material will result in fewer cars turning away at the gate.

Before the research hypothesis can be tested, researchers must determine what information would be needed to test it successfully. For the nonprofit historic home foundation, researchers would need to collect some preliminary data; the gate attendants should count the number of vehicles that turn away at the gate during a specific period of time, as well as the number of vehicles that enter the grounds. Also, the gate attendants should collect information from the license plates of the cars that turn away to determine if the lost tour visitors were from the local area or from farther away. The "turning away" data should be compiled daily, weekly, and perhaps even monthly.

Before collecting even one bit of primary data, researchers should begin analyzing **secondary data**, or information that has been collected previously, for some reason other than the current research question or project, to see if answers already exist. One can find secondary data in any number of places, including internal sources, external sources, and the Internet. Internal sources of secondary data include marketing plans, organization reports, and the MIS. Organizations (even nonprofit ones) produce, assemble, distribute, and store a variety of internal literature and statistics. Internal information ranges from simple, informational memorandums to substantial reports describing some direction that the nonprofit anticipates taking. It includes accounting information and summaries and data about successful and unsuccessful past programs. If an MIS has been established at the nonprofit, researchers should begin there to see if information already exists that may solve the problem.

More general and more diverse secondary data may be found in external sources. Nonprofit researchers may wish to look for pertinent governmental, commercial, and professional secondary data in various places, including the Internet and the World Wide Web, which have eliminated much of the drudgery associated with searching for external secondary data. Exhibit 3.5 contains a partial list of websites that nonprofit researchers may visit to gather secondary information.

❖ **Exhibit 3.5** Some Useful Web Sources of Secondary Data

Organization	URL	Description
American Marketing Association	www.ama.org	One can search AMA publications and search for other information
Aspen Institute	www.aspeninstitute.org/	Offers reports online or through its online bookstore
Gianneschi Center for Nonprofit Research	www.fullerton.edu/gcnr/	Has a helpful "Publications" section
Google Scholar Search Engine	scholar.google.com/	Type in "nonprofit research" to locate more sites
GuideStar	www.guidestar.org/	A national database of nonprofit organizations
The Nonprofit Resource Center	www.not-for-profit.org/	Under Support Organizations, click on "Publications"
Nonprofit Sector Research Fund	www.nonprofitresearch.org/	Disseminates research findings; click on "Projects and Findings
U.S. Census Bureau	www.census.gov	A good source for general information

Although secondary data may already exist and may clarify the nonprofit's current problem, researchers must always keep in mind that such data are historical and have been gathered by people either inside or outside the organization to meet their own needs. If those needs are similar to the nonprofit's current needs, there is no reason to collect primary data. Secondary data are usually cheaper and quicker to collect than are primary data, but researchers must always consider their relevance (How relevant are these data to the present research problem?), accuracy (Were these data contaminated by poor research methods or untrained researchers?), credibility (How and who were the respondents chosen for the research?), and timeliness (When were these data collected?).

If enough pertinent information cannot be found in internal or external secondary data to solve the nonprofit's problem, the researchers then proceed to design a study wherein they will collect **primary data**: information collected for a particular research question or project. Primary data are more expensive and time consuming to collect than secondary data are, so the cost of obtaining primary data must be weighed against its value to nonprofit researchers.

Depending on the research problem, objectives, and hypotheses, researchers may choose to engage in observational, survey, or experimental research. **Observational**

studies monitor respondents' behavior, sometimes without the respondents' knowledge. There are many ways to conduct observational research. The researcher may be overt or covert, and the data collection may be structured or unstructured and done by humans or machines. Finally, observational data collection may be direct (measuring actual behavior) or indirect (measuring surrogates of behavior, e.g., counting the number of items in a subject's recycling bin as a measure of environmentalism). In our nonprofit historic home foundation example, researchers may observe and record the number of tour visitors to other historic home sites that either do or do not communicate price information in their marketing communications. With enough observation, researchers may eventually uncover similarities among their target historic home tour numbers and those of other historic homes that do not communicate admission price in their marketing communications. This example points to the major advantage of observational studies: researchers are able to note what people really do rather than what they may report on a questionnaire. Thus, observational research requires that the behavior in question either be obvious and measurable or be easily inferred from related behavior.

A second type of research is **survey research,** which uses paper-and-pencil instruments to understand behavior. Surveys help researchers understand why particular decisions are made, how they are made, and who makes them. Four common survey methods are (a) personal interviews, (b) telephone surveys, (c) mail surveys, and (d) Web-based surveys. In a personal interview, researchers have respondents complete a survey while the two are face to face. Either the respondent completes the survey with the researcher present to clarify questions and answers if necessary, or the researcher can read each survey question to the respondent and then mark the answer. The personal interview method is the most flexible survey method and allows a variety of question types. If the respondent does not understand a question, the interviewer may be able to rephrase it. In a personal interview, researchers aim to uncover both the direction and the intensity of feelings and motivations. Sometimes, tape recordings are used to record the natural give-and-take of the survey interview. Taping interviews entails time to complete, transcribe, and read the interviews, and an experienced practitioner, who knows both the technique and the nonprofit organization under study, must analyze the results.

Telephone surveys are the most convenient means of reaching respondents, although they are not as flexible and versatile as the personal interview. A major drawback of telephone surveys is that respondents cannot see the questions and have to answer questions while mentally recalling them. On the other hand, using telephones means that distance is not a serious obstacle to getting information.

A third survey method, mail surveys, is used extensively in marketing research because of some advantages. Mail surveys are relatively inexpensive to send and, as with telephone surveys, distance is not a problem. Also, researchers can reach a large sample simultaneously. Further, because they allow respondents time to read the questions and think about their answers, mail questionnaires tend to be more accurate and may even be more revealing because respondents may divulge confidential information if they can remain anonymous. Despite their advantages, mail surveys do have drawbacks. For example, no one is available to ask or rephrase the questions, explain the purpose of the study, induce cooperation, record the answers, or cope with any problems that develop. An additional drawback is that mail surveys take more time than personal interviews or telephone research because they involve sending the surveys and waiting for them to be returned.

A fourth survey method, Web-based surveys, is the newest form of survey delivery. Respondents can be invited to participate in a survey by methods ranging from e-mail to advertising placed on search engines (e.g., www.google.com and www.yahoo.com). A nonprofit wishing to develop a Web-based survey will have no trouble finding a website that can help; it just needs to go to its favorite search engine and type in "Web-based surveys." Some Web-based survey development companies offer free survey building with a cost of about $30 if the nonprofit wants to view its data for longer than 15 days. Other companies charge higher fees (e.g., $670 per year at www.keysurvey.com) but offer help building a sophisticated online survey and many more services. Whereas the average cost of mailed surveys is just over $2.00 per respondent, the average cost of Web-based surveys is about $0.88 per respondent. Web-based surveys, like the other types of surveys, have advantages and disadvantages, which a nonprofit would need to evaluate before using them. One advantage is that they are easier to send, and a nonprofit may be able to receive information within hours or days. A disadvantage is that a nonprofit's target market may not have access to computers on a daily basis.

Let us return now to our nonprofit historic home foundation example. Say that researchers developed a survey that asked respondents about their attitudes, opinions, and beliefs about various aspects of the house tours. If research results indicated that local residents were more negative about admission prices than other respondents, the most that could be said—if analysis indicated that the difference between locals and others was significant—is that there is a correlation between place of residence and perception of admission prices. It may be that local tour visitors know more about the historic home and do not believe that the house tour is worth the admission price. Or perhaps local visitors have a lower average income compared with visitors from farther away.

Although observations and surveys help researchers collect data in an orderly and structured manner, they allow only understanding of association (correlation), which is only somewhat better than descriptive understanding. **Correlational research** involves collecting information (via observation or surveys) and running correlational statistical analyses to determine the relationship between two or more variables. However, although researchers may learn through correlational research that two variables are related to one another, they have no way to know whether one of those variables causes the other or whether some other variable is causally related.

Searching for a causal relationship between two or more variables requires using the third type of research: **experimental research.** In this type of research, all variables surrounding the research subject are held constant except one, called the **independent variable**, which is varied in a systematic way. Researchers then measure the effect of that variation on some other variable of interest, called the **dependent variable**, which is the measure of performance. In our example, suppose researchers want to know whether including admission fee information in the foundation's direct mail communications would result in fewer cars turning away at the gate. Thus, the presence or absence of admission fee information is the independent variable, and the number of cars turning away at the gate is the dependent variable.

Now the researchers can test the research hypothesis (H_1) against what is called a "null" hypothesis (H_0). The null hypothesis predicts that varying the independent variable will have no effect on the dependent variable. In our example, the research hypothesis and the null hypothesis could be stated like this:

H_1: Price information appearing in the nonprofit's promotional media will result in fewer cars turning away at the gate.

H_0: Price information appearing in the nonprofit's promotional media will have no effect on the number of cars turning away at the gate.

Let's say our researchers decided to prepare two direct mail pieces: one containing information about home tours and including admission price information and one containing information about home tours but no mention of admission price. The historic home foundation believes that some potential visitors may be staying away because of the lack of information, so the researchers may suggest that, for now, the foundation focus on people who are not currently on the foundation's mailing list. One half of a selected sample would receive the direct mail piece with admission price information, and the other half would receive the direct mail piece without admission price information. Selecting the sample and putting sample members into the two groups is important to having valid results, so the researchers must attend to all the important issues surrounding drawing respondent samples, including sample size (see www.statlets.com/sample_size.htm), sampling with and without replacement, and the like.

Once the researchers have determined whether to engage in observational, survey, or experimental research, they specify exactly what is to be measured; who will be observed, surveyed, or selected as subjects; how data will be analyzed; and the projected cost of the research. All this information is combined into a research plan, a document that lays out the course of research. The nonprofit's key decision makers and researchers should examine it to make sure that needed information will be collected and that the benefits of the research outweigh its costs. If top management approves the research plan, the research process continues. In Exhibit 3.6, one can see that a research plan consists of three major parts: the introduction section, the methodology section, and the data analysis section. The introduction includes the main topic of the research, along with the hypothesis or hypotheses. The methodology section describes the number and source of the respondents who will be used, the instruments (e.g., survey or measurement forms), any materials that will be used, the general design of the experiment or survey, and the procedure that the researcher will follow. The data analysis section spells out how collected data will be analyzed.

Execute the research design. Depending on the research method selected—observation, surveying, or experiment—this activity involves engaging in observation, administering questionnaires, or manipulating variables and measuring results.

❖ **Exhibit 3.6** General Layout of a Research Plan

Introduction

Main topic
Hypothesis (or hypotheses)

Methodology

Participants: The number of participants, how they will be selected, and what population they represent.

Instruments/Materials/Design: Clear description and justification of all instruments; discussion of reliability and validity measures; detailed description of experimental design, if needed.

Procedures: Clear description of procedures. The rule of thumb here is that enough information must be provided to allow another researcher to replicate the research.

Data analysis

Description of the analysis
Justification of the analysis: Reasons it is the proper choice for the situation, taking into account the way the groups are going to be assigned, the number of groups involved, the number of variables, and the kind of data collected.

Prepare and analyze data. After a predetermined period allocated for data collection, perhaps 2 months, the researcher prepares the data for analysis. Data may be coded, meaning numerical values or alphanumeric symbols are assigned to represent a specific response to a question. Data analysis is used to interpret what happened in the study, so analysis attempts to turn numbers into data and then to turn data into marketing information. An important guideline is to use as simple a technique as possible for understanding, whether that is simple frequency analysis or complex multivariate techniques. In our foundation example, a simple t test would likely be sufficient to determine whether the data confirm or falsify the research hypothesis. There are many websites devoted to statistics, many of which have programs that researchers can simply enter data into for testing (e.g., www.statsoftinc.com/textbook/stathome.html). In our example, suppose the group that received the new direct mail piece with fee information visited more than the group that received the mailing without fee information. Because the experimental method was used, the nonprofit may now say that the direct mail piece with fee information was more effective in bringing tour visitors than the less informative piece. It has reached **cause-and-effect understanding**.

The researchers have to interpret the results of the data analysis; in other words, they have to ask themselves questions like the following: What has been learned? Now that we have these numbers, figures, and results, what does all this mean for the manager who must make decisions? Does communicating pricing information appear to improve attendance? Do the research findings offer any insights into variables other than price that may also improve attendance? The researcher's interpretation of the data is an important component in communicating the research results.

Prepare and communicate results. Even though the technical research work ends with the interpretation of the data, the researchers' work is not yet finished. Now the research report needs to be written. Favorable reception of research results depends on the way in which they are presented. The research report typically involves a written report, an oral presentation of the research process and findings, and at least the offer of follow-up, either in person or via telephone or e-mail. The writer should focus on the "actionability" of the results while justifying the dollar outlay for the research study. The follow-up may involve a survey or personal interview so that both the researcher and the nonprofit can attempt to measure the efficiency of the research project as a whole. The aim is to improve the entire research process in order to improve decision making.

Although there are no official guidelines when it comes to report writing, it helps to keep the readers in mind, using terms and language that are meaningful to them. Rather than presenting each research finding point by point and explaining each detail of a statistical test, present the research clearly and succinctly. And, of course, check spelling and grammar and be sure that the overall look of the report is professional.

Example. Returning now to Jessica and the opening vignette, suppose that LAF believes it has a problem: Its self-help courses for people living with lupus attract too few people when compared with classes offered by other nonprofits, for instance cardiopulmonary resuscitation classes offered by the American Red Cross. Since Jessica knows that awareness of relatively low attendance at previous self-help classes involves only descriptive understanding, she would understand that she might be observing a symptom of something wrong with the marketing environment or the marketing mix or both. Furthermore, there may be no problem at all, or it might even be that, given the location of the courses, the number of people who attended previous classes was actually quite good.

As a marketer, Jessica should determine whether the relatively small number of people attending LAF's self-help courses is a new phenomenon or an ongoing occurrence. If many more people attended at some time in the past than do now, researchers may want to look for any recent changes in the marketing mix, the marketing environment, or the course personnel. If the number of attendees has always been low, it could be because the courses are not very good or held at undesirable times or places or because the price of the courses is too high (or too low!). It might be that the nonprofit is not communicating with its target markets about course locations, times, or prices.

Jessica would likely want to engage in exploratory research and gather preliminary information that may help her define the problem and hypotheses. She may run a few focus groups to search for any pertinent background issues that may affect the problem or the information sought. She should also determine how the information obtained by research might be used, in other words, establish the research objectives.

Given what she finds during her exploratory research, she would be ready to define the research problem, craft the research objective, and develop one or more hypotheses. She would need to take some time to figure out what information would be needed to successfully test the hypotheses and, before collecting any primary data, she would gather any relevant secondary data. If LAF had an MIS, she could begin there and would also look in external sources. If Jessica still was not able to answer the research question, then she would develop a study to gather primary data. Depending on the data she has been able to pull together, she may choose to run an observational study, conduct some type of survey, or engage in experimentation.

Managerial Issues

The following issues are relevant for nonprofit managers:

1. **Nonprofits' publics.** Generally speaking, nonprofits always have one more public to focus on compared with for-profit organizations. This extra public usually consists of donors, grantors, or legislators. Too often, nonprofits have looked at their resource suppliers with frustration instead of focusing on them as simply one more target public. Once a nonprofit understands that it has to develop a marketing mix that will appeal to its resource suppliers, it will likely have far more success. Resource suppliers, however, do not use the nonprofit's regular offers, that is, they are not clients. Instead, they look for such benefits as feelings of goodwill in return for their gifts of money, time, or effort.

2. **A needs-centered orientation.** It may be possible for nonprofits lacking a needs-centered orientation to be successful. However, by having a needs-centered orientation, nonprofit managers and administrators are more likely to focus on the needs of their target publics; hire or sign up people to do marketing who know what they are doing; understand that competition comes from many avenues and from many types of organizations; rely on research rather than intuition to answer questions; develop marketing mixes, using all four elements, that are important to specific target segments; and understand that it is the nonprofit's responsibility to serve its publics and not the other way around.

3. **Research and an MIS.** Once a nonprofit has accepted the importance of having a needs-centered orientation, it will need to spend time and money developing an MIS. A good MIS, which includes market research as one of its components, will provide nonprofit managers with enough information to make better-informed decisions about target publics, allocation of resources, and their marketing mixes.

4. **The research process.** The marketing research process should be orderly and proceed in a logical manner through five steps: Define the research problem and objectives, develop hypotheses and formulate the research plan, collect data, analyze and interpret the data, and prepare and communicate the results.

Summary

The nonprofit marketing issues presented in this chapter are summarized here according to the chapter learning objectives they meet.

Understand the important publics of the nonprofit. Publics of nonprofits can be characterized as people, groups, and organizations in four separate categories: input publics, who supply original resources and constraints to the organization; internal publics, who convert inputs into useful goods and services and define and carry out the organization's strategies; partner or intermediary publics, who carry, promote, and distribute the goods and services; and consuming publics, who use the goods and services and have interest in the output of the organization.

Understand the various orientations that nonprofits may have. Nonprofits evolve, beginning with a cause orientation, when they are so focused on the cause that they almost forget about serving clients or donors. Next, they may attain an offer orientation, believing that "everyone can see how important our offers are." When they need more resources to keep things going, they are likely to evolve into a fund-raising orientation and work to obtain any likely avenue of funding. Finally, when they adopt the marketing concept, they evolve into a needs-centered orientation, in which they maintain a strong vision of their mission (cause) and at the same time take the viewpoint of their publics' needs and wants. This customer-oriented point of view makes it more likely that the nonprofit will stay competitive while serving its target publics effectively and efficiently.

Understand why it is important for nonprofits to do research. Nonprofits that have accepted the importance of having a needs-centered orientation should also realize that marketing research is absolutely essential when it comes to understanding a nonprofit's various publics. To really understand clients' and donors' needs and wants, there is no way around engaging in systematic, orderly collection of information.

Understand why nonprofits should have an MIS. Not only should nonprofits engage in research; it would be even better for them to develop an MIS. An MIS is a system that collects, sorts, integrates, analyzes, evaluates, and distributes information to key marketing decision makers. It gathers information from both external and internal marketing environments; integrates the information with information in an internal reports system, a marketing intelligence system, an analytical marketing system, and a marketing research system; and makes the analyzed, interpreted information available to the key decision makers in the nonprofit.

Understand where research fits into the nonprofit's MIS. Marketing managers in nonprofits require useful and timely information to make effective decisions. The MIS is an organized approach for gathering and organizing this information. In some instances, the information needed is available inside or outside the organization. However, if the needed information does not exist, then research will have to be conducted to create this information. Therefore, research provides information for the manager that would not otherwise be available. Information obtained from marketing research becomes part of the MIS.

Understand the research process. The marketing research process should be an orderly process that consists of five steps: Define the research problem and objectives, develop hypotheses and formulate the research plan, collect data, analyze and interpret data, and prepare and communicate the results.

Glossary

Analytical marketing system. The part of a marketing information system charged with organizing general data, performing any needed data analysis, and generating reports, usually for data other than those collected via marketing research.

Cause-and-effect understanding. The level of understanding at which one knows that one variable affects another in a systematic way.

Cause orientation. A complete focus on the cause the nonprofit was formed to address; the nonprofit equivalent of a production orientation in the for-profit sector.

Consuming publics. Those who use the goods and services of an organization and have an interest in its output.

Correlational research. Collecting information (via observation or surveys) and conducting correlational statistical analyses to determine whether a relationship exists between two or more variables (but not whether one of the variables causes the other or whether some other variable is causally related).

Dependent variables. Measures of performance; the behavior or event that happens as a result of an independent variable.

Descriptive understanding. The lowest level of understanding, which consists simply of knowing that something is happening at a particular time.

Experimental research. The type of research employed when researchers want to understand cause-and-effect relationships among variables.

Exploratory research. Gathering preliminary information that may help define the problem and suggest hypotheses.

Fund-raising orientation. A focus on raising funds to support the organization and its offer; the nonprofit equivalent of a sales orientation in the for-profit sector.

Hypothesis. Conjectural statement about the relationship between independent and dependent variables.

Independent variables. Factors in experimental research that are varied in a systematic way.

Input publics. Those that supply original resources and constraints to the organization; examples include donors, suppliers, and regulatory officials.

Internal publics. Those that convert inputs into useful goods and services and define and carry out the organization's strategies; examples are management, board of directors, staff, and volunteers.

Internal reports system. The collection of information from data sources within the company.

Marketing information system (MIS). A system that uses people, equipment, and procedures to collect, sort, integrate, analyze, evaluate, and distribute necessary, timely, and accurate information to key marketing decision makers.

Marketing intelligence. The collection and analysis of everyday, publicly available information that pertains to developments important to a particular nonprofit.

Marketing research. The methodical design, collection, analysis, and reporting of reliable marketing information that is relevant to a particular problem faced by an organization in order to reduce uncertainty to tolerable levels at a reasonable cost.

Marketing research system. The part of a marketing information system charged with design, collection, analysis, and reporting of data about a specific problem or situation faced by an organization.

Needs-centered orientation. A nonprofit's maintaining a strong vision of its mission (its cause) and at the same time taking the point of view of its publics' needs and wants; the nonprofit counterpart to a customer or marketing orientation in the for-profit sector.

Observational studies. Studies that monitor respondents' behavior, sometimes without the respondents' knowledge.

Offer orientation. A complete focus on the offers of the nonprofit; the nonprofit equivalent of a product orientation in the for-profit sector.

Partner or intermediary publics. Those who carry, promote, and distribute a nonprofit's goods and services; examples include merchants, agents, facilitators, and marketing firms.

Primary data. Information collected for a particular research question or project.

Publics. People, groups, and organizations that are important to a nonprofit; they can be classified into four separate categories, input publics, internal publics, partner or intermediary publics, and consuming publics; see separate entries in this Glossary.

Research plan. A document that lays out the course of a particular research project.

Secondary data. Information that has been collected for some reason other than the current research question or project.

Service learning. A method of teaching and learning whereby participants learn and develop through active participation in thoughtfully organized service.

Survey research. The type of research that uses paper-and-pencil instruments to understand behavior.

QUESTIONS FOR REVIEW

1. Explain the four orientations through which nonprofits seem to evolve.

2. List the various publics of nonprofits.

3. Define *marketing research*.

4. Define *marketing information system*.

5. Explain the difference between secondary and primary data.

6. Explain the four types of surveys.

7. Know the steps in the research process.

QUESTIONS FOR DISCUSSION

1. Describe the four types of orientations through which nonprofits seem to evolve and explain why having a cause or a funding orientation may hurt a nonprofit organization.

2. What are examples of each of the four publics of nonprofits?

3. What is an MIS, and how does marketing research fit into it?

4. Why should a nonprofit try to find secondary information prior to collecting primary data?

5. Explain the four types of surveys. What are the advantages and disadvantages of each?

6. Explain the five steps in the research process. Why is the first step especially important?

INTERNET EXERCISES

1. Enter thomas.loc.gov and search for pending legislation that involves lupus. Report how these measures could impact nonprofits that provide services to lupus patients and non-profits that raise funds for lupus research.

2. Enter www.census.gov and search for available information and trends involving poverty and the aging of the population.

3. Enter www.stat-usa.gov and search for economic trends that may reduce the number and size of individual and corporate donations.

4. Enter www.google.com and search for {"marketing research" nonprofits}. Use this and other searches you devise to uncover (a) marketing research companies that specialize in services for nonprofits and (b) other important marketing research for nonprofit issues you feel are important.

5. Enter users.cnu.edu/~jnpsm/, review the Table of Contents of the *Journal of Nonprofit & Public Sector Marketing* for the past five issues, and report on the types of marketing research being published.

TEAM EXERCISES AND ROLE PLAYING

1. A large foundation has $200 million dollars in new funds and has invited your nonprofit to present your case for receiving part of this funding. The instructor and the rest of the class will represent the foundation. In teams, pick a nonprofit to represent, research the nonprofit and its offerings, and then develop and present the most powerful presentation that you can. After evaluating the presentations, the class will vote on how to distribute the funds. Suggested nonprofits: Metropolitan Opera Association, American Cancer Society, Food for the Poor, Art Institute of Chicago, The Nature Conservancy, March of Dimes, America's Second Harvest, Gifts in Kind International, World Vision, Salvation Army.

2. Form groups, and then split each group into two teams. In each group, one team will be the hiring team and the other will be the job seeker team. Go to www.philanthropy.com/jobs/jobs2 .htm. Each group of two teams will pick a job announcement from this list. The hiring team will prepare its list of requirements for this job and the questions it will ask in an interview. The job seeker team will prepare for the interview based on the contents of the ad and the team's marketing research of the nonprofit, its staff, and its clients. The groups will take turns conducting the interviews in front of the class. If time permits, the group can pick another ad and the teams can switch roles. If there is a problem with this website, use a general search engine to search on the term *nonprofit jobs* and try to find sites that list jobs in the nonprofit sector.

MINICASE: The Arthritis Outreach Foundation

It was early in the day at the Arthritis Outreach Foundation in Chicago. In her office overlooking Michigan Avenue, Katie Sanchez was going over her files on past successful charitable events. She had documents on the financial performance of her own organization's past events and many newspaper clippings covering the events of other charities. In going through these files, she was hoping for an inspiration. In a city the size of Chicago, there were always many competing events, and the rich and powerful tended to attend only the best. Katie needed a blockbuster event idea that would attract the right people and generate serious media attention. The right event could attract a great deal of media attention, and that type of exposure could attract funding for the foundation's many programs, which provided information, classes, and meetings and funded research to help arthritis sufferers.

Katie had received the assignment earlier in the week, when she had met with the foundation's executive director and director of major gifts. They had liked her suggestion of an event to recognize several major donor couples, and they had put her in charge of organizing the event. Initially, Katie was overwhelmed with the enormity of the responsibility, but she soon moved past that phase and was now full of excitement and had most of the steps organized on a time planning chart. Katie was most excited about her idea that the event should be a blockbuster instead of the usual dreary black-tie dinner recognizing multimillionaire donors. A blockbuster event would attract the city's political and social elite, and their being in the audience for the donor recognition would make it very special indeed. As a bonus, the income from the big event would almost certainly far exceed that from a regular dinner.

Katie planned to spend this afternoon exploring the websites of two event production companies (remvideoevent.com/mtgintro.html and www.chicagoevents.com/csem.html). She also planned to explore the websites of two companies that book celebrity speakers (www.allamericans peakers.com/guide.php and www.speakerbooking .com/categories.html). At some point, Katie knew, she would need some help figuring out what kind of event would best attract the right people. She knew what she would like to see, but she was 20 to 50 years younger than the rich and powerful people she wanted to attract.

Assignment: Help Katie evaluate which production company and which speaker's agency to use by researching each company's offerings, past successes, and reputation. Once you have picked companies to work with, decide on several alternative event formats and themes and pick several alternative celebrity speakers from your speaker agency's offerings. If you have difficulty accessing these companies' websites, use a search engine to uncover others.

Once you have some alternatives, design a primary research study to capture what will best attract Katie's target segment to the event. Design what will be used to gather the information, specify a sample size, and describe how the sample will be picked. Specify how the data will be analyzed and how you will recommend Katie make the final decision. Estimate how long the research study will take to complete and how much it will cost.

References and Bibliography

American Marketing Association. (2005). Marketing Research. Retrieved October 8, 2005, from www.marketing power.com/mg-dictionary-view1884.php?

Andreasen, A. R. (2002). *Marketing research that won't break the bank: A practical guide to getting the information you need.* San Francisco: Jossey-Bass.

Anheier, H. K., & Ben-Ner, A. (2003). *The study of the nonprofit enterprise: Theories and approaches.* New York: Kluwer Academic/Plenum Publishers.

Bergan, H. (1996). *Where the information is: A guide to electronic research for nonprofit organizations.* Alexandria, VA: BioGuide Press.

Blankenship, A. B., Breen, G. E., & Dutka, A. F. (1998). *State of the art marketing research* (2nd ed.). Lincolnwood, IL: NTC Business Books.

Booth, W. C., Colomb, G. G., & Williams, J. M. (2003). *The craft of research* (2nd ed.). Chicago: University of Chicago Press.

Campbell, B. (2000). *Listening to your donors: The nonprofit's practical guide to designing and conducting surveys that improve communication with donors, refine marketing methods, make fundraising appeals more effective, increase your income.* San Francisco: Jossey-Bass.

Cherny, J., Gordon, A. R., & Herson, R. J. L. (1992). *Accounting—A social institution: A unified theory for the measurement of the profit and nonprofit sectors.* New York: Quorum Books.

Czinkota, M. R., Ronkaninen, I. A., & Tarrant, J. J. (1995). *The global marketing imperative.* Lincolnwood, IL: NTC Business Books.

Denzin, N. K., & Lincoln, Y. S. (2000). *Handbook of qualitative research* (2nd ed.). Thousand Oaks, CA: Sage.

Feig, B. (1997). *Marketing straight to the heart.* New York: AMACOM.

Flynn, P., & Hodgkinson, V. A. (2001). *Measuring the impact of the nonprofit sector.* New York: Kluwer Academic/Plenum Publishers.

Frumkin, P., & Galaskiewicz, J. (2004). Institutional isomorphism and public sector organizations. *Journal of Public Administration Research and Theory, 14*(July), 283–308.

Gainer, B., & Padanyi, P. (2005). The relationship between market-oriented activities and market-oriented culture: Implications for the development of market orientation in nonprofit service organizations. *Journal of Business Research, 58*(June), 854–862.

Gibaldi, J. (2003). *MLA handbook for writers of research papers* (6th ed.). New York: Modern Language Association of America.

Goel, R. K. (2004). Research by not-for-profit enterprises. *Journal of Technology Transfer, 29*(April), 211–216.

Hellebust, L. (1996). *Think tank directory: A guide to nonprofit public policy research organizations.* Topeka, KS: Government Research Service.

Herman, R. D. (1990). Methodological issues in studying the effectiveness of nongovernmental and nonprofit organizations. *Nonprofit Voluntary Sector Quarterly, 19*(Fall), 293–307.

Herndon, S., & Kreps, G. L. (2001). *Qualitative research: Applications in organizational life.* Cresskill, NJ: Hampton Press.

Hogan, C. (2004). *Prospect research: A primer for growing nonprofits.* Boston: Jones and Bartlett Publishers.

Jephcott, J., & Bock, T. (1998). The application and validation of data fusion. *Journal of the Market Research Society, 40*(July), 185–205.

Kanter, R. S., & Summers, D. V. (1987). Doing well while doing good: Dilemmas of performance measurement in nonprofit organizations and the need for a multiple constituency approach. In W.W. Powell (Ed.), *The nonprofit sector: A research handbook* (pp. 54–166). New Haven, CT: Yale University Press.

Kilpatrick, A., & Silverman, L. (2005). The power of vision. *Strategy and Leadership, 33*(Feb), 24–26.

Lane, C. A. (2002). *Naked in cyberspace: How to find personal information online* (2nd ed.). Medford, NJ: CyberAge Books.

Lettieri, E., Borga, B., & Savoldelli, A. (2004). Knowledge management in non-profit organizations. *Journal of Knowledge Management, 8*(June), 16–30.

Levy, D. C. (1996). *Building the third sector: Latin America's private research centers and nonprofit development.* Pittsburgh, PA: University of Pittsburgh Press.

Linn, S. (2004). *Consuming kids: The hostile takeover of childhood.* New York: New Press—W. W. Norton & Co.

Macpherson, M. (2001). Measuring business excellence. *Performance Measurement in Not-for-Profit and Public-Sector Organisations, 5*(June), 13–17.

Mann, T. (1998). *The Oxford guide to library research.* New York: Oxford University Press.

McNabb, D. E. (2002). *Research methods in public administration and nonprofit management: Quantitative and qualitative approaches.* Armonk, NY: M. E. Sharpe.

Morris, V. B., & Pankratz, D. B. (2003). *The arts in a new millennium: Research and the arts sector.* Westport, CT: Praeger.

Pava, M. L., & Primeaux, P. (1999). *Research in ethical issues in organizations.* Stamford, CT: JAI Press.

Powell, W. W. (1987). *The nonprofit sector: A research handbook.* New Haven, CT: Yale University Press.

Pyc, G. J. (2001). Research of an organizational trend. *Leadership in Health Services, 14*(Feb), 1–6.

Underhill, P. (1999). *Why we buy: The science of shopping.* New York: Simon & Shuster.

Weitzman, M. S. (2002). *The new nonprofit almanac and desk reference: The essential facts and figures for managers, researchers, and volunteers.* San Francisco: Jossey-Bass.

Strategic Marketing Analysis and Planning

❖

Learning Objectives

On completion of this chapter, the
reader will

- Define and understand strategic
  marketing and strategic planning

- Understand the importance of
  marketing analysis and planning

- Explain the interrelatedness of marketing
  topics

- Understand the basic strategic market
  analysis process

- Explain the areas of potential change
  that may affect strategic planning

- Understand the three situations in the
  nonprofit sector in which an individual is
  most likely to engage in strategic
  planning

Content (Continued)

Learning Objectives (Continued)

- Understand why strategic planning is based in marketing theory
- Understand how organizational culture, values, and approach to management may affect planning
- Explain when market-based strategic planning is most important

Opening Vignette: Bringing Strategic Planning Into a Church

In many of their previous classes, university and college students may have analyzed cases involving a wide variety of industrial and service corporations. Additionally, many current non-profit professionals may have had experience in for-profit organizations. Because many non-profits are run similarly to for-profit businesses, the skills that one has learned in business or business courses can often be applied to nonprofits. However, to add to one's existing knowledge base and confidence, this case examines a situation that is common in the nonprofit sector but which, on the surface, may seem to involve issues that are quite removed from the usual topics covered in marketing classes and books.

Case Background

Recently, the leaders of an independent regional church association of 65 congregations with a total of 27,000 members decided on a new vision statement. The new vision was expressed to the congregations as follows:

> Imagine your congregation transformed. Imagine it as a place of profound community, of spiritual growth, of miraculous expectation, and of personal transformation; a place in which faithful pilgrims journey together with a shared vision that leads them to embrace the unchurched and each other and, in the process, to find immense fulfillment and meaning for their lives. (Payne and Beazley, 2000)

Probably there are many church associations that feel they already live this type of vision, but for this particular association, it will involve a major cultural change. Individual congregations operate fairly autonomously under the direction of their own pastor and lay board. Interestingly, in this denomination, the regional associations and the national association (with which the regionals, in turn, are affiliated) tend to be more liberal than most of the individual congregations. In most congregations, worship is traditional, and spiritual growth is a personal issue. Appointed committees address a variety of local community and social needs, but these projects are usually done at arm's length (i.e., with funding support and the personal involvement of only a few individuals). In general, the denomination is not known for trying to attract new members. It may be that the vast majority of members will not initially see the new vision as desirable. Some older members will probably actively object to any significant change. "After all," they might say, "the old way is what has defined this denomination for hundreds of years." "This has never been a denomination for the masses," some might think to themselves.

A regional church organization of this size would have an executive staff responsible for the business functions that are common to all organizations (e.g., accounting, marketing, operations management, etc.). As one might expect, the actual names given the functions would probably be quite different, and one would probably find individuals within each church expected to fulfill overlapping or multiple assignments. Regardless of the job titles, some group is going to have to develop a strategic plan to bring the association and its congregations from where they are to where they want to be. Clearly, there are many issues here beyond marketing, but real-world marketing is never separate from all the other aspects of an organization or corporation.

Defining Strategic Marketing and Planning

First, we should distinguish between what is meant by the terms *strategic* and *strategy*. They are quite different concepts. When the term *strategic* is used, it means something is important and affects an entire organization. *Strategy*, however, refers to a method.

When the top management team of a nonprofit organization, working with its board of directors, makes decisions regarding the future direction, goals, and objectives for the entire organization, it is engaging in **strategic planning**. In Chapter 1, nonprofit marketing was defined as the use of marketing tactics to further the goals and objectives of nonprofit organizations. Marketing tactics include activities such as advertising, fund-raising, event planning, public relations, publicity, volunteer recruitment, marketing research, and so forth. **Strategic marketing** refers to the integrated and coordinated use of marketing tactics to help the NPO achieve its strategic objectives. The strategic marketing plan refers to a detailed program of marketing activities to implement over a specified time to help the NPO achieve its strategic goals and objectives. Strategic marketing planning, then, refers to the process of gathering information and establishing procedures to develop the strategic marketing plan.

When the term *strategy* is used, it generally refers to a chosen method of doing something. For example, it may refer to a type of advertising strategy the NPO is using or its chosen fund-raising strategy.

The Importance of Marketing Analysis and Planning

Strategic market analysis refers to a systematic study of an organization's internal and external environments to inform strategic marketing planning. Historically, nonprofit managers have tended not to engage in strategic analysis or planning for a number of reasons. First, probably because many nonprofit managers have traditionally not had much formal business training, they simply may have no knowledge of the need to engage in these activities. Or if they realize that they should engage in market analysis and planning, they may not do so because they believe they cannot do it without a degree in the subject. Second, because nonprofits often begin life with few employees and volunteers who must undertake the many tasks involved in starting up the nonprofit and who may be eager to begin really making a difference, nonprofit managers may believe that they simply have no time to engage in analysis and planning. Third, even if nonprofit managers know they should engage in strategic analysis and planning, they may fail to do so because they believe they would have to hire an expensive marketing consultant. Since many nonprofits begin life with very limited financial resources, hiring such a consultant would be out of the question. Fourth, they may fear what a strategic analysis might reveal, such as important target markets that don't prefer the nonprofit's offers. Fifth, nonprofit managers might believe that because the marketing environment is so dynamic, an analysis will be out of date before it is complete. Finally, some nonprofit managers might be very action oriented, they may have been victims of low-quality marketing analyses or plans in the past, or they may have experienced poorly implemented plans. Such experiences may lead those managers to believe that written documents such as analyses and plans will not be useful.

But strategic analysis and planning are important, even for small nonprofits. For example, even nonprofits need to worry about effectiveness and efficiency when it comes to choosing among various ways to expend their resources. Given the increasing competition and demands for accountability, having a plan based on a thorough market analysis is a must. Further, plans allow nonprofits to coordinate activities throughout their organization over time so that actions that need to be completed before others will be done on time. Therefore, plans allow nonprofits to set timetables for their different programs and activities. Good plans are not only based on thorough market analyses; they are also written down and disseminated throughout an organization. When everyone in the organization has access to a written plan, nonprofits should experience better communication throughout. Systematic, careful, forward-looking market analyses should identify expected developments, which can lead to good preparation, not only for expected developments, but for possible ones as well. High-quality plans may also serve as a basis for evaluating programs, resource allocation, and people within nonprofits. When everyone in the nonprofit has access to a written plan, individuals and departments will know what is expected of them and on what bases they will be evaluated. Finally, having plans based on an in-depth strategic analysis can keep nonprofits focused on their missions, maintaining their organizational integrity rather than drifting away because of short-term factors.

The Interrelatedness of Marketing Topics

Students who are busy mastering the fundamentals of modern business and organizational theory, as well as nonprofit managers who might be setting up or managing a nonprofit organization, often perceive each marketing topic as somehow standing alone. Business schools, marketing departments, professors, and even marketing books often add to this perception by teaching or approaching broad topics and specific subjects as if they were independent. For example, objective setting may be discussed separately from new offer development and advertising, or public relations, sales promotion, interactive marketing, and personal persuasion might all be covered separately with no effort to show how interrelated they should be. Although this segmentation is often done for good reason—to simplify marketing material—students as well as nonprofit managers may be presented with little, if any, integration across topics and subjects that must together form the foundation for an organization's determination of who it is, whom it serves, where it is now, where it wants to be, and what the best way is to get there.

Whereas it makes perfect sense to master the basics before tackling the integrated whole, expecting one capstone course to tie everything together at the end of the fourth year is almost certainly unrealistic. Even worse is to expect that intelligent nonprofit managers, many of whom have had little or no business education, will be able, on their own, to integrate what they have learned from a myriad of marketing books. Therefore, it is important to understand that all other marketing information—including material covered in the other chapters of *this* book as well as marketing content learned in other marketing and business classes or books—comes together here in the interconnected building blocks of strategic analysis, strategic planning, and strategic implementation. What makes strategic planning and analysis particularly exciting is that, in addition to textbook knowledge, they require a great many practical skills and qualities, such as courage, instinct, energy, logic, and creativity. Strategists need theory-based knowledge *plus* the personal determination to take on the challenge of providing organizational leadership and creating a viable path to the organization vision.

The Strategic Market Analysis Process

The strategic market analysis process (**SMAP**), shown in Exhibit 4.1, is comparable to the process used in the for-profit business world. In classes offered by one of us (Patricia A. Knowles), student groups have successfully applied this process in service learning projects for a wide variety of nonprofit organizations, including local chapters of the American Red Cross and the Boys and Girls Clubs of America as well as a state park commission and many others. In these projects, the nonprofit organizations benefited by having teams of energetic "soon to be professionals" apply effective marketing approaches to their specific situations. At the same time, the students benefited from "learning by doing" in a real-world situation and from being able to include the marketing analysis in their educational portfolios. Indeed, having local college or university marketing classes take on strategic market analyses for local nonprofits is a way that nonprofits can overcome the second and third reasons they often fail to engage in strategic analysis, no time and no money.

There are several barriers to mastering the SMAP, however. One barrier is overlooking the fact that the sections of the SMAP are interdependent. For example, analysis of, say, sustainable differential advantage depends on the various interrelated sections that come before it, such as the needs-centered orientation analysis. At the same time, an analysis of sustainable differential advantage affects sections that come after it, such as the positioning analysis, for example. And depending on what is learned when analyzing an important topic appearing later in the situation analysis, such as positioning, an analyst may need to go back and reanalyze one or more of the earlier sections.

Another barrier to mastering the SMAP stems from the use of different terms in different nonprofits as well as in the for-profit and nonprofit sectors. For example, whereas for-profits have customers and stakeholders, nonprofits have many constituencies,

❖ **Exhibit 4.1**   **Strategic Market Analysis Process (SMAP)**

Situation analysis:

> Introduction
> Needs-centered orientation analysis
> Managerial analysis
> Board analysis
> Sustainable differential advantage
> Demand analysis
> Market segmentation
> Consumer or buyer behavior by segment
> Individual or organizational decision process by segment
> Marketing mix analysis
> New offer development process analysis
> Positioning analysis
> Competitive analysis
> Financial analysis
> Client needs assessment
> Environmental analysis
> Offer life cycle
> SWOT (strengths, weaknesses, opportunities, threats)
> Problem definition

Strategic alternatives

Evaluation of alternatives

Decision(s)

Implementation

Monitoring

SOURCE: Adapted from "Strategic Planning for Public and Nonprofit Organizations: Rethinking the Strategic Market Analysis Sections," by R. Gomes and P. A. Knowles, 1998, *Journal of Nonprofit and Public Sector Marketing, 6*, pp. 3–22. With permission.

including the four publics noted in Chapter 3—input, internal, partner or intermediary, and consuming publics. After much discussion, we agreed to use the term *target publics* to refer to a nonprofit's customers, patrons, donors, users, clients, and so on.

A more obvious barrier is superficial analysis and planning, which may be produced by well-meaning but untrained or inexperienced managers of nonprofits. They may see the sections or steps in the SMAP as simply calling for various lists of facts. For example, in the marketing mix analysis step, untrained individuals might suppose that they need only list the nonprofit's current marketing mix (product or offer, place, promotion, and price). However, that section actually requires analysts to evaluate the appropriateness of the nonprofit's current marketing mix based on the nonprofit's objectives, target publics, any pertinent marketing research the nonprofit has done, and any relevant marketing theory. When performing the financial analysis step, untrained analysts might believe they need only attach financial statements provided by a nonprofit's outside accountants instead of analyzing the implications of those statements. It is easy to list facts, but it takes trained professionals to apply theory, uncover hidden forces and causal relationships, project results, evaluate alternatives, and properly create and implement a plan.

Given the work involved in a full SMAP, one can well understand why many managers believe the process is too time-consuming and complex. One way for busy managers to ease the burden is to assign different analysis topics to different people and distribute completed analyses among employees and volunteers so that the full picture of the nonprofit can be understood. Another way to overcome problems of time and complexity is to recruit a volunteer or board member with experience in strategic market analysis to do parts of the SMAP. A nonprofit may also ask for free or low-cost help from local universities or marketing firms.

The remainder of this section focuses on a basic SMAP. The 19 subsections under "Situation Analysis" make up the theory-based analysis of the organization's current reality—the situation analysis. "Theory-based analysis" refers simply to what is actually included in those 19 subsections. For example, given the state of current marketing theory, marketers tend to believe that appropriate sections of a situation analysis should include such topics as the extent of a nonprofit's marketing orientation, the level of market demand for a nonprofit's offers, and an analysis of a nonprofit's current marketing mix, among others. Although Christian Grönroos and others have argued that traditional, goods-focused marketing models are skewed toward buying and selling and have shortcomings when it comes to services (and, we would argue, when it comes to social behavior programs and social causes), those models can still set a baseline or foundation for nonprofits working to understand their dynamic environments both inside and outside the organization. Marketing theories concerning "consumption" may help nonprofits understand which target publics use their offers and how often they do so. Other theories, say concerning branding, may be useful for nonprofits when it comes to getting noticed by their target publics.

To understand the idea of marketing theories setting a baseline or foundation for nonprofits, it might be helpful to use a building as a metaphor: The foundation is marketing theory, the lower floors are the situation analysis, and the top floor is the strategic plan based on the situation analysis (see Exhibit 4.2). As a building planner or a strategic planner, one would want to assure that the top floor was supported by the lower floors and that the lower floors were, in turn, well supported by the foundation. All "floors" are interdependent and interconnected. A weak theory foundation or missing or weak elements of the strategic analysis would mean the resulting strategic plan would contain structural weaknesses that could limit its usefulness and even result in a catastrophic collapse of the plan or the entire organization.

Readers who have already mastered the basics of marketing will find the following discussion familiar. If this is your first exposure to topics like market segmentation, market positioning, financial analysis, and the like, then it would serve you to have a textbook on the principles of marketing by your side, perhaps checked out from a local university's library. However, because even senior marketing majors and the occasional

❖ **Exhibit 4.2**   The SMAP as a building with marketing theory as the foundation, the situation analysis comprising the lower floors and the strategic plan supported by both

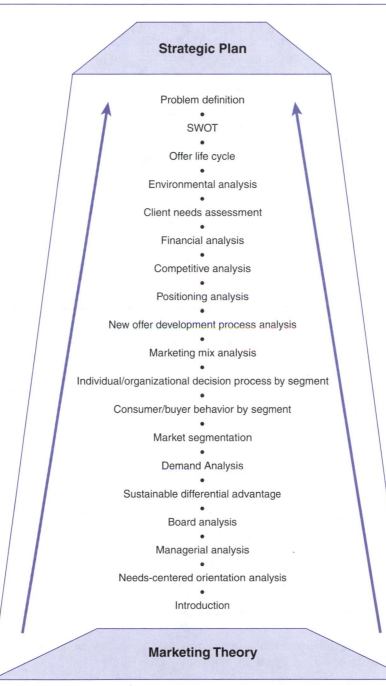

MBA student may forget a term here or there, terms and topic headings are explained or defined throughout. Before undertaking an actual SMAP, nonprofit managers will of course need to devote some time to understanding marketing terminology as well as what a thorough job at each step entails. Even if a nonprofit is able to secure low-cost or free help with its SMAP, nonprofit personnel must understand the process in order to use it properly in strategic planning. Truly, there are no shortcuts to learning business theory, but if novice planners read and understand the materials cited within each section, they will get a significant boost in applying theory to their particular organization and situation.

The topics that follow are pretty much in an order that will allow an analyst to take advantage of information from previous sections. Still, it is important to reiterate that they are all interdependent, and information uncovered in a later section will sometimes make it necessary to rethink an earlier section. Experienced market analysts find that they sometimes need to add topics to the situation analysis that are pertinent to a particular organization or situation. And sometimes they find that some sections are not relevant. Novice analysts may also see a need for additional topics and may feel that some discussed here are not needed. However, before eliminating a topic from consideration, they should be sure that they completely understand it because until they understand the "language," many of the most important topics might seem irrelevant.

Although much of the following discussion of strategic analysis is expressed in terms of an analyst functioning alone, the reality of the process is that it can be done by either individuals or groups. How much an executive director or department head involves staff in the process is a cultural and management issue. Certainly, in a team-oriented environment, nonprofit managers would encourage individuals to be involved in the development of policy and strategy. In any nonprofit organizational culture or environment, though, it is common for managers to find themselves in roles similar to product or brand managers. When managers have this role, there is little question about who holds the primary responsibility for the development and implementation of marketing strategy.

The objective for analysis is not only to apply the theory behind each topic to a particular organization but also to analyze and interpret the implications of theory for the particular situation of that organization. This is so important that it is worth repeating. One cannot simply analyze buyer behavior by segment, for example, and then go on to the next step. One must first analyze the implications of the analysis for the particular buyer segments. At each step, the results and implications of the analysis must be addressed.

Situation Analysis

Most of the following sections discuss the steps in a situation analysis. When a manager needs to decide how much effort to put into each topic, it is important to appreciate the importance of the overall analysis to the future of an organization. Think about the expectations of team members who are assigned to do a strategic market analysis—an assignment that could very well determine the success or failure of the entire organization. Also keep in mind that nonprofits influence real people's lives and well-being. Savvy nonprofit managers who assign senior staff members to do a topic analysis would expect a very complete and well-done result that is well thought out and applies all relevant theory to achieve the best possible understanding of the issues.

Introduction. Rather than just repeating the name and type of organization, try getting to the heart of the matter using strategic theory terminology. For example, say XYZ (a private, nonprofit religious organization) currently offers church services at 8:00 a.m. and 10:30 a.m. on Sundays, noon on Tuesdays, and 6:00 p.m. on Wednesdays and is experiencing very low attendance at its Tuesday and Wednesday services. (The services of XYZ are one type of offer it provides to its target publics, in this case its church family.) Say that XYZ is thinking about repositioning some of its services to attract new target publics (nearby college students) or discontinuing some. An introductory statement for XYZ might be the following:

> This analysis concerns two possible offer strategies for XYZ, an "offer repositioning strategy" and an "offer elimination strategy" in a saturated market where the present target market (both local residents who belong to XYZ church and unchurched residents) regards the offer as a high-involvement specialty offer.

Here is another example of an introductory statement:

> We are a health-related private nonprofit organization with heavy local competition. We currently have poor coordination of service offerings in our organization, and we think we need to make a decision between launching one of two new services.

Finally:

> We face dynamic markets and are depending on this strategic plan to provide direction into the next 5 years.

While some of this terminology may be off-putting to some nonprofits, it may seem less of a problem if one sees it for what it is—shorthand representations of concepts that are shared by many different types of organizations. The terminology works whether a nonprofit offers goods, services, or social programs and whether it seeks to encourage target publics to buy a good, attend a performance or event, discontinue harmful behaviors, or adopt positive behaviors and norms.

Needs-Centered Orientation Analysis. In this step, the strategist needs to uncover the effect of the nonprofit's current orientation. In Chapter 3, four types of nonprofit orientations were discussed: cause, offer, fund-raising, and needs-centered. Further, those orientations were compared to the traditional production, product, selling, and marketing orientations, respectively, that distinguish the priorities of for-profits. So, whereas in for-profit strategic analysis, this step would be concerned with the level of marketing orientation, the SMAP for nonprofits has been modified to examine the extent to which a nonprofit realizes the importance of having a needs-centered orientation and developing offers that benefit their target publics.

Information about a nonprofit's level of needs-centered orientation can be gleaned from interviews of nonprofit managers, employees, and volunteers and by reading past reports and other materials. With enough input, an analyst should be able to come to some conclusions about a nonprofit's overall orientation as well as what influence that orientation is likely to have on the success or failure of its mission. For example, an expensive private nonprofit university with a very large endowment may have a very strong student-needs-centered orientation and show behavior similar to a for-profit with a marketing orientation. On the other hand, a large state university (which relies on state tax monies as well as donations and grants) may focus more on the importance of what it offers (an offer orientation) than on what might benefit its target publics; in other words, it shows behavior similar to a for-profit with a product orientation.

Whereas one nonprofit may be essentially a machine for raising funds and have a strong fund-raising orientation, another nonprofit, concerned with the same cause and with a similar name, may be much more focused on serving client needs and have a strong needs-centered orientation. Both raise funds and deliver services, but the question here is, "Where is their heart and organizational culture?"

Managerial Analysis. This section addresses managerial structure or style issues that may impact the nonprofit's marketing strategy. Include the organization's mission, objectives, organizational chart, and the senior executives' backgrounds and style of management (e.g., are they autocratic? participative? do they manage by objectives? are they team facilitators?). Of course, one must be tactful in reporting this information, but analysts must (at least in the privacy of their own mind or notes) be sure to explore issues that may directly impact marketing strategy implementation. Be on the lookout for internal **culture conflicts** that might occur if, for example, one level or section of the nonprofit is business oriented and operates under a corporate culture while another level or section operates under a social service culture.

Board Analysis. Similar to the managerial analysis, in this step an analyst needs to consider the makeup of the nonprofit's board and the role it plays. It could be that the board itself could be a valuable resource in ways that have not yet been explored. The board might be called a board of directors, board of visitors, board of trustees, or some other term. According to the National Center for Nonprofit Boards, a nonprofit board of trustees is legally and morally responsible to its particular nonprofit in 10 functional areas. Boards may also play political roles within the nonprofit. Generally speaking, a board has responsibilities to its nonprofit when it comes to governance, use of funds, and accountability. Exhibit 4.3 shows a list of functional and legal responsibilities of boards. Board responsibilities are likely to differ somewhat from one nonprofit to the next, so the analyst should consider the extent to which the nonprofit's current board meets relevant responsibilities.

Boards can also be characterized according to their level of engagement. In Exhibit 4.4, one can see that boards may show one of five different levels of engagement, ranging from the least engaged board (a traditional, passive board) to the most engaged board (an operating board). A passive board has what has been called a ratifying style (a "board of nondirectors" that rubber-stamps whatever nonprofit managers send its way). A certifying board mainly certifies to a nonprofit's stakeholders that the nonprofit's CEO is doing what the board expects. An engaged board sets overall strategy for the nonprofit and then delegates the execution of the strategy to the CEO and through the CEO to the staff and volunteers. An intervening board tends to appear during crises in the nonprofit and is characterized by frequent, intense meetings that may be called on

❖ **Exhibit 4.3**   Functional and Legal Responsibilities of Boards

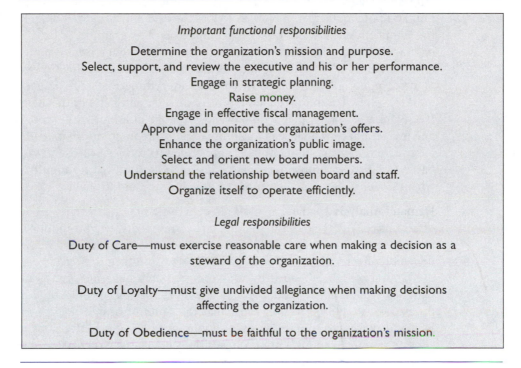

Important functional responsibilities

Determine the organization's mission and purpose.
Select, support, and review the executive and his or her performance.
Engage in strategic planning.
Raise money.
Engage in effective fiscal management.
Approve and monitor the organization's offers.
Enhance the organization's public image.
Select and orient new board members.
Understand the relationship between board and staff.
Organize itself to operate efficiently.

Legal responsibilities

Duty of Care—must exercise reasonable care when making a decision as a steward of the organization.

Duty of Loyalty—must give undivided allegiance when making decisions affecting the organization.

Duty of Obedience—must be faithful to the organization's mission.

SOURCE: Adapted with permission from www.boardsource.org. For more information about Board Source, formerly the National Center for Nonprofit Boards, visit www.boardsource.org or call 800-883-6262. BoardSource © 2005. Text may not be reproduced without written permission from BoardSource.

❖ **Exhibit 4.4**   Five Different Levels of Board Engagement

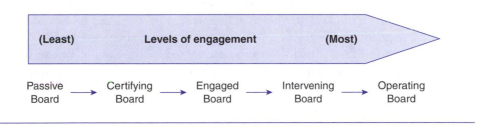

| (Least) | Levels of engagement | (Most) |

Passive Board → Certifying Board → Engaged Board → Intervening Board → Operating Board

short notice. Finally, the operating board is one that makes key decisions, which the nonprofit's management then puts into action. Which board style is best for which nonprofit is a matter best determined by the nonprofit and its own board; however, the analyst has the responsibility to determine if the relationship is a good one or not.

Sustainable Differential Advantage. In this step, the analyst must identify the aspects of the nonprofit and its offers, be they goods, services, or social programs, along with the offers' price, place, and promotion, that either deliver or create the perception of long-term value. It is also important to determine how much value is perceived by current and potential target publics, as well as the extent of perceived difference between the nonprofit's offers and offers by competitors. For example, potential donors are beset with requests for support from many nonprofits, so it is important to understand how these donors perceive the value of the nonprofit's offers compared with the value of its competitors'. Analysts must consider everything that may be part of a target market's value perception, including the basic offer and parts of the augmented offer (see Exhibit 5.1 in Chapter 5) and even things like offer quality, nonprofit personnel and image, and convenience of location. An old story in nonprofit marketing concerns a day care center that thought its clients valued its service because it was a religious-based facility. On completing a marketing analysis, however, it found that, in reality, what its client-base valued far more was the location of the facility.

Demand Analysis. Demand analysis refers to the level of demand for an organization's offers (along with the other marketing mix components, e.g., promotion) by its target publics. If the nonprofit has a history and has collected data, one may analyze past demand for its various offers to gain valuable insight into which have been most used, purchased, or attended by which target publics at which times and locations, with what patterns, at what cost, and so on. Each offer should be examined, and projections should be made about what the nonprofit might expect in the future. Demand analysis has important implications when it comes to decisions about how to allocate resources among a nonprofit's various offers, the level of service to offer (e.g., how often to run a program), the monetary and nonmonetary prices associated with offers, and the operational levels that may be needed. Later in the SMAP, the analyst will need to project what has been learned in this step in order to evaluate the likely outcomes of alternative market strategies. Demand forecasting and statistical analysis (e.g., time series and regression) are tools that can be used to do that.

Market Segmentation. A critical first step in nonprofit marketing is the identification of relevant target markets, which are often selected following a segmentation process. Segmentation was presented in Chapter 2, where you can review a definition of market segmentation and an explanation of the way segmentation might be done. Because a nonprofit's eventual success is determined by how well it can serve the needs of its target markets with offers that are perceived to have sustainable, differential value, this step is very important. Nonprofits should engage in market segmentation for each type of target public: users, donors, supporters, and intermediaries.

There are various approaches to segmentation, such as formal quantitative and qualitative methods, and the choice of approach itself can influence a nonprofit's market strategy. As in every step, analysts must be sure to include the implications of any choices they make in order to ensure the best segmentation strategy. Generally speaking, nonprofits may benefit from looking at **enabling characteristics**, or those characteristics, such as age, state of health, or where someone lives, that make target publics eligible to use a nonprofit's offers, as well as **distinguishing characteristics**, or those characteristics, such as lifestyle, attitudes, and level of motivation, that distinguish those who can use a nonprofit's offers but don't from those who can and do. If a nonprofit has to consider organizational or corporate markets in addition to individuals, the analyst will need to segment those markets so that appropriate target segments can be selected. Organizational segmentation variables might include organization size, location, and the like. Further, the choice of segmentation approach by nonprofit analysts should be influenced by all the other sections of the SMAP as well as by the nonprofit's resources and ability to deliver differential advantage. That means that analysts may have to revisit this section as they progress through the process.

Consumer or Buyer Behavior by Segment. It is easy to appreciate that this topic is closely tied to the segmentation topic. You may have taken a course in consumer behavior or read about buyer or organizational behavior, but it may not have been clear at the time that strategic analysis and planning are some of the major areas where such insight is applied. Analysts need to understand as much as possible about each target segment, particularly what motivates its members and what drives their preferences and actions. Why, when, how, what, and where individuals' and organizations' wants or needs are felt, expressed, or acted on determine how nonprofits can and should market to them, whether the segments include volunteers, donors, or some other public. The literature addressing consumer and buyer motivation and behavior is extensive and easily found, and making good use of it can contribute in an important way to an organization's perceived offer advantage.

Individual or Organizational Decision Process by Segment. The decision processes of consumers and buyers are such an important part of strategy determination that they are addressed separately from consumer or buyer behavior. In this stage, analysts need to uncover the details of each target public's step-by-step decision process and remember that factors such as the type of offer (good, service, or social program), the risk involved in using it, the involvement with the offer, or the decision itself can change the steps in the process. As shown in Exhibit 4.5, a high-involvement decision process for individuals involves a five-stage model that begins with problem recognition and ends with postpurchase behavior. For organizations, eight stages of decision making, labeled **buyphases,** have been identified. Similar to individual decision making, these buyphases begin with problem recognition and end with performance review. Analysts would need to determine where particular target publics are in the decision process as well as how the nonprofit stands in relation to the publics' alternatives. Research is often required to learn those details; guessing at the components of a decision process and then custom-fitting a marketing strategy to those guesses can lead to a costly blunder if an analyst guesses wrong.

Marketing Mix Analysis. Nonprofit marketers and strategists are responsible for certain controllable variables in the specifics of their offers to the market: the marketing mix (see Chapter 2 for a definition of *marketing mix*). In the marketing mix analysis stage, analysts need to evaluate the appropriateness of their nonprofit's current marketing mixes in terms of their target publics, finding answers to such questions as "Is the promotional effort for this mix effective?" and "Are the offers available at the right time and place?" Doing this may seem like a formidable job—and it is. To an untrained person, it may be difficult to determine where to begin such an analysis.

❖ **Exhibit 4.5** Stages of Decision Making for Individuals and Organizations

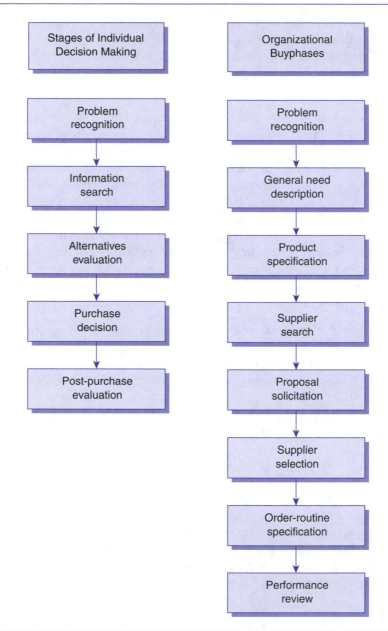

Stages of Individual Decision Making	Organizational Buyphases
Problem recognition	Problem recognition
Information search	General need description
Alternatives evaluation	Product specification
Purchase decision	Supplier search
Post-purchase evaluation	Proposal solicitation
	Supplier selection
	Order-routine specification
	Performance review

Note that this step and the preceding one (consumer or buyer behavior) will determine much of the final strategy in the marketing plan. Further, when market segmentation is included, analysts can gain great insight into their target publics. Tactics based on these steps will need to be developed (often with groups of tactics directed at each decision stage in Exhibit 4.5) to facilitate and accelerate the adoption process. Without this understanding, a strategist runs the risk of creating a mix that brings potential adopters only partway through the decision process. An extreme example would be spending a nonprofit's entire communications budget on a campaign that creates great awareness but little more.

However, to complete this step, nonprofit managers may be able to enlist help from volunteers or board members knowledgeable in marketing. Indeed, enlisting help here may be a way to overcome nonprofit managers' worry that they do not know enough to attempt this analysis.

New Offer Development Process Analysis. Many offers go through predictable life-cycle stages of growth and decline. With a formalized new offer development plan in place, an organization can automatically and continuously evaluate and work through the development of the best offers (goods, services, and social programs) to add or to replace those approaching decline. A formal approach assures that new ideas receive timely and appropriate consideration and that the responsibility for developing successful new offers is clear. It would not be unusual to find that a nonprofit has no such development program in place.

Positioning Analysis. Nonprofits, like for-profits, compete with other organizations. However, rather than competing for profits, sales, and employees, nonprofits compete for donations; grants and tax monies; program usage; and employees, volunteers, and perhaps board members. Understanding positioning, a basic marketing tool addressed in Chapter 2, is essential. Nonprofit analysts need to evaluate the current position of their nonprofit overall as well as the position of its offers as perceived by present and potential donors, clients, and other target publics. There are several ways to go about positioning, and they are covered in Chapter 2 of this textbook as well as in most basic marketing texts. Determining the position of the nonprofit and its offers in the marketplace as perceived by its various target publics will usually require an investment in primary research. Such research does not necessarily have to be costly; nonprofit analysts can appeal to university marketing departments or volunteers to collect the necessary background information. The objective of a positioning analysis is to produce a strategic interpretation of what a perceptual map shows. Analysts must put thought into which dimensions should be measured and why. It may be important to measure a number of dimensions and examine multiple plots of the data. The Customer Value/Mission matrix, covered in Chapter 5, may also be adapted as part of any nonprofit's positioning analysis.

Competitive Analysis. As we have stated before, even if a nonprofit has no direct competitive offers, it still must compete in many areas, including donations, grants, stakeholders' attention, and volunteers' time, to name just a few. If a nonprofit cannot know all there is to know about each competitor, a search for relevant information (e.g., advertising materials of competing organization) will provide at least some information and insight into how competitors' offers and actions may impact the nonprofit's plans. In an analyst's projections of the results of implementing a particular strategy, the nonprofit will need to be able to judge actual and potential competitive reaction and its results.

Financial Analysis. Good strategic planning analysis needs good financial analysis. Calculations of breakevens, cash flow, margins, and contributions provide useful insights for planning. Most nonprofits, even small ones, have accounting and financial specialists, perhaps on their board of directors, to assist with this section of the analysis and the final financial evaluation of the alternatives. It is important for the planner not only to utilize the financial experts' skills but also to make an effort to understand the process in depth.

Marketing strategists always need to remember where the revenue is coming from. It is not unusual to find marketers underestimating the negative financial effect a new policy can have on a donor group that a nonprofit has traditionally taken for granted. Recall the example of the church association with a new mission described in the opening vignette of this chapter; it is very possible that a large percentage of current donors will not support the new mission and may demonstrate their nonsupport in the form of decreased financial pledges. Perhaps the new mission can be marketed such that current church members do support it, but doing so would require changing some very deeply held beliefs. Support could drop off very quickly, and the strategist should be aware of issues involved in the introduction of a new idea or offer, especially if "new mission" supporters are expected to replace existing ones. Strategists and pastors have been fired for blindly introducing well-intended policies that had unforeseen negative financial repercussions. The moral here is to apply the best marketing analysis and planning tools, and then have the courage to follow through with good business judgment and convictions.

Client Needs Assessment. As you might expect in a marketing culture that stresses the importance of a needs-centered orientation, defining what client needs are and where, when, and how they can best be served is a critically important function. Clients of nonprofits may be the people who use a nonprofit's offers, or they may be donors. They may be parents or high school guidance counselors or art patrons. Complicating attempts to understand clients' needs is the fact that clients' own perceptions of their needs often differ from experts' perceptions. In fact, it is not unusual to have recommendations from experts that contradict each other as well as what clients say they want, and this discord has to be balanced with what is consistent with the nonprofit's mission and ability to deliver. For example, a mental health nonprofit may find a segment of mental health professionals that believe in treatment A and another segment of mental health professionals that believe only in treatment B. At the same time, the patient clients may indicate they want something else, say help with living expenses, so that they can live independently (without treatment A or B). Obviously, nonprofits have some amount of moral responsibility for the outcome of their choices about which needs to serve and not serve. Their reputation and, indeed, their whole reason for being are called into question if they choose incorrectly. A real-life example will illustrate how high the stakes can be: Several years ago, different groups that train and monitor lifeguards had differences of opinion about correct lifesaving techniques. One group argued that CPR was the best way to revive a swimmer that had drowned; this group advocated American Red Cross lifeguarding classes. Another group argued that lifeguards should instead begin their lifesaving efforts with the Heimlich maneuver. One group believed that it was okay for lifeguards to sit atop traditional lifesaving towers, but another argued that lifeguards should be watching swimmers from ground level and should always carry their lifesaving flotation buoy. One can easily understand the vital and moral choices involved in setting a curriculum for training lifeguards.

Environmental Analysis. When one looks up *environmental analysis* or *environmental scanning* (the terms used in marketing strategy), one finds chapter sections like political, regulatory, sociocultural, legal, economic, and technological environments. The objective in this step is to analyze how issues in these environments present opportunities or risks for nonprofits. For example, which political party is in office may affect many programs, grants, and other funding for nonprofits with politically sensitive offers, such as local councils for teen pregnancy prevention or public television stations. For nonprofits that engage in blood collection, a less restrictive regulatory environment, such as a relaxation of prohibitions on blood from persons who visited England during mad cow disease outbreaks as far back as the 1980s, can make it easier to find qualified blood donors. As for the sociocultural environment, over time, the general U.S. public has become more and more strongly opposed to drinking and driving, a trend that helps nonprofits such as Mothers Against Drunk Driving (MADD) and Students Against Drunk Driving (SADD) communicate their messages to their target publics. In the United Kingdom and many other parts of the world, more and more people are concerned with preventing cruelty to animals. Organizations such as the Scottish Society for the Prevention of Cruelty to Animals (www.scottishspca.org/), organized in 1839 to ensure the welfare of carthorses, and A.P.M.A. Belgian Animal Welfare (www.apma.be/) now enjoy a sociocultural environment wherein their messages are taken seriously. A great deal of important material that will impact strategic decision making can be uncovered in this step, so it is very important for nonprofit analysts to carefully consider each environment and learn where things are at present and what is likely to happen in the future. It is very common in "postimplementation reviews" of failed strategies to find the seeds of failure in this section, where important issues were ignored or misunderstood.

Offer Life Cycle. Offers customers perceive as having value typically progress through stages referred to as introduction, growth, maturity, and decline. In the for-profit arena, sales and profits of offers are plotted over time, and generally speaking, one would find that sales generally rise from a low during the introduction stage to a high during the maturity stage, after which they plateau and eventually decline. Profits move from a negative amount during introduction (when a lot of money is being spent to promote the offer) to a high during the late maturity stage, before profits too plateau and eventually decline. Although nonprofits often do not sell offers for money, the concept of the offer life cycle may still be relevant and may still help nonprofit managers when it comes to making decisions. Instead of sales, a nonprofit may wish to plot usage, and instead of profits, a nonprofit may choose to plot donations or grants.

Recognizing the tendency of offers to reach a plateau in terms of their ability to serve client needs, nonprofit strategists may enhance or otherwise adjust an offer to match a new situation or, alternatively, have a new-offer-development process online should the board or upper management make a decision to remove an offer. The basis for a decision to eliminate should be the *target public's* perception of an offer rather than upper management's instincts. Although an offer may be new for a nonprofit, the target public for that offer may perceive it as "the same as old mature offer that has long been available through other sources." Basic marketing theory includes standard ways to extend offer life cycles when appropriate. As in each step, analysts should remember to include an analysis of the implications of offer life cycle for all offers of their nonprofit.

SWOT. SWOT stands for strengths, weaknesses, opportunities, and threats. In the **SWOT analysis** step, nonprofit analysts need to step back, take an overall view of the nonprofit's situation, and list all the perceivable and predictable strengths and weakness inside the nonprofit as well as all the perceivable and predictable opportunities and threats outside it. This is a very traditional and powerful section in strategic analysis. Issues uncovered here may very well send analysts to rethink their approach in previous steps, and these issues (or lack of them) will certainly impact the nonprofit's final strategy. This step is considered toward the end of the situation analysis so as to best utilize issues uncovered in earlier analysis steps.

In the resultant strategic plan, nonprofits will want to apply their strengths toward creating differential value and taking advantage of appropriate opportunities. Weaknesses and threats will have to be addressed also. It is important to note that this analysis requires an unbiased, somewhat hard-nosed assessment. This is not a place for ignoring problem issues, playing politics, or developing the best spin possible to impress the board. If problems develop later, the board can very easily return to this section to see what was underplayed or ignored (and by whom).

A SWOT analysis can be a wonderful opportunity for participation across the organization. Anyone can understand SWOT, and contributions from other departments, units, functional areas (e.g., service delivery, volunteer organization, community relations), or sections that may have different points of view are very important. It does not take any particular marketing training to uncover organizational strengths, weaknesses, opportunities, and threats, and such issues often are most apparent to those who work with them every day.

In addition to completing a SWOT, an analyst should seriously consider assigning a few staff members to create a strategy for a hypothetical, aggressive nonprofit or for-profit competitor who has resources and is out to increase its funding or deploy its offers at your nonprofit's expense. Done effectively, this effort can point out SWOT issues that more conventional thinking probably would not uncover.

Problem Definition. In this step, nonprofit analysts should look for any underlying source(s) of any major problem(s) the nonprofit is facing. These problems may have arisen in the analysis of any of the previous steps. A way to get to the underlying source of problems is to ask a series of "and what is that a symptom of" questions. Note that environmental and market realities are not problems in this sense of the term. All marketers need to deal with such realities, and having to fulfill one's responsibilities is not a problem. However, it could be that some of the nonprofit's staff are not effective in their roles, which would be a symptom of something. Or it could be that the nonprofit's charitable activities are not widely known or are known but not well thought of among its target publics, and that also would be a symptom of something. It should not come as much of a surprise that when previous strategy has been developed by individuals with little or no business or marketing background, the underlying source of problems will often be as simple as poorly executed marketing, planning, leadership, or plan implementation. The challenge is to identify any problems and figure out why they happened. Just furnishing a nonprofit organization a good strategy, without considering and effectively handling any underlying problem(s), will most likely mean that the organization will soon be back in a problematical situation.

Strategic Alternatives

Once the analyst or strategy team has completed the situation analysis for the nonprofit, then it is time to develop strategic alternatives for the organization to pursue. Novice strategists often have considerable difficulty with this stage. First of all, strategic alternatives need to be complete 4P (product, price, place, promotion) marketing plans with enough detail to cost out (i.e., with enough tactical specifics so that all costs can be estimated). Alternatives also need to be somewhat mutually exclusive (hence the term *alternative*).

Each strategic alternative that is developed should be the organization's best approach to that strategic direction. For example, one alternative for a health care organization might be to expand an offer into a different county, and another might be to redefine an offer's target public in the original county. Yet another might be to reorganize branch offices into independent, affiliate nonprofits. Alternatives are high-level strategic directions.

Analysts should not develop alternatives that are identical except for one area. For example, if alternative 1 is a complete 4P marketing plan with direct mail promotion sent out four times a year, alternative 2 should not be the same 4P plan with the direct mail promotion sent out three times a year. In a situation such as this one, conventional marketing theory and administrative judgment should be used to determine the best promotional content, timing, and frequency.

It is of critical importance that the strategic alternatives all be derived from the situation analysis. It would be a glaring mistake to come up with some snappy new alternative at this point instead of one that is supported by the complete situation analysis. An example of a flawed alternative would be a dramatic promotional campaign that does not support movement through the decision processes of the target publics. This would invite failure and would likely utilize the wrong appeal, aimed toward an inappropriate segment, with illogical media choices. This point brings us back to why strategists need to master marketing theory basics before attempting to integrate them into a strategic plan.

Evaluation of Alternatives

In this section, one needs to project costs and the performance results of each complete 4P marketing approach. This requires a quantitative evaluation (pro forma projection of performance, including all costs and financial statements, breakevens, cash flow, etc.) and a qualitative evaluation (estimates of risk, resources needed, fit, client response, etc.).

At this point in the analysis, if nonprofit managers find themselves seriously considering adopting multiple alternatives rather than one, it may be that the alternatives have been poorly developed, with part of a 4P marketing mix appearing in one solution alternative and the other part of the marketing mix appearing in another.

Although it is possible to adopt multiple alternatives, it is probably not appropriate for strategists-in-training.

One thing to avoid is considering only what upper management has already planned to adopt. If that happens, there really was no evaluation of alternatives. Sometimes adopting all possible alternatives is a version of that. This is particularly bad if the entire situation analysis was unconsciously biased to fit a preferred final strategy. Another version of a "no real alternative analysis" would be a straw man option, in which one alternative is actually set up to fail the evaluation. Obviously, there is no point going through the evaluation process for such an alternative. An important test of whether appropriate alternatives have been developed is that the most desirable alternative should not be clear until this evaluation and comparison step is completed.

The Decision

Now, with the complete costs, benefits, risks, resources, fit with organizational mission, and the rest clearly analyzed and compared, the strategy team can simply make the best decision for the organization. Arguably, this decision can be far from simple, but for most executives, this type of managerial judgment, based on all the information uncovered by the market analysis and evaluation sections, is much easier than making blind strategic decisions. At this point, the nonprofit has a marketing plan that can be written up, copied, and disseminated to department heads, area coordinators, and other relevant employees and volunteers.

Implementation

When it comes to strategy implementation, it might be helpful to take the point of view of a nonprofit executive director, president, or managing director. Such individuals would need to have a plan that is very specific and that clearly indicates who will be expected to do what and when in order to implement the nonprofit's strategy.

Keep in mind that many good plans fail due to poor implementation or outright internal resistance to change. In fact, one of the biggest challenges for strategists is to gain the cooperation of all those who will be involved in implementing the new strategy. Cooperation in implementing a plan benefits from wide participation in its development, which generally leads to increased feelings of involvement and ownership. These benefits make a good case for strategy training classes throughout the organization, and in the case of a nonprofit with help from a marketing class or other outside group, the nonprofit's staff should be involved in the analysis and planning process. In the case of this chapter's opening vignette, this step will likely make or break the church's success with its new mission.

Monitoring

The success of a major new strategic plan should be very important to an organization. Since the analyst and the nonprofit have invested many hours in completing the process, it would not make sense to merely produce a plan and then move on to the next activity. The implementation of strategic plans must be monitored. Some points in the implementation of a plan are more important than others, and nonprofits should set

❖ **Exhibit 4.6**   Potential Areas of Change That May Affect Strategic Planning

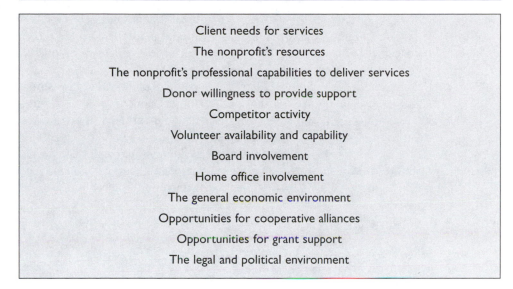

Client needs for services

The nonprofit's resources

The nonprofit's professional capabilities to deliver services

Donor willingness to provide support

Competitor activity

Volunteer availability and capability

Board involvement

Home office involvement

The general economic environment

Opportunities for cooperative alliances

Opportunities for grant support

The legal and political environment

up a way to gather timely data on those activities or responses to plan implementation. Some aspects of a plan may produce outcomes that could be measured whereas others may indicate future performance or problems. Managers may find that, at some points, a strategic course of action was based on weak situation analysis steps (i.e., steps where data were lacking).

In any case, a set plan of monitoring important indicators will allow time to intervene before too much damage is done. It would be unusual if a strategic implementation and its results went exactly as planned. An organization is always inviting disaster when it monitors the success of an implementation by looking only at final results. Then it is too late to make any changes.

Potential Areas of Change That May Affect Strategic Planning

There are a great many nonprofit organizations (hundreds of thousands), and they operate in very dynamic environments. (The interested reader may wish to refer to www.guidestar.org/, a website with a searchable database of more than 850,000 nonprofits recognized by the U.S. Internal Revenue Service. The British Charities website, www.britishcharities.com/, lists more than 300 charities in the United Kingdom.) Exhibit 4.6 lists several areas in which changes could influence a nonprofit's plan. Better-managed nonprofits make an organized effort to proactively monitor the environment to identify early signs of change and chart an effective course to their objective. This takes a great deal of knowledge and a driving personal desire to learn more. The fact that nonprofits usually have worthy goals helps immensely; something is involved in operating an organization seeking a cure for children's cancer that makes it very different from operating an organization seeking more profits from selling widgets.

Those with the point of view that "anyone with a little common sense can easily put together a strategic plan" and those with the view that "strategic management only requires a strong-willed leader" have a nonmarketing point of view. The first point of view usually involves informal management and planning, and the second, autocratic management and planning. Dealing with such viewpoints can be one of a nonprofit manager's biggest challenges. Usually the best way to deal with them is to demonstrate the steps and the value of the strategic planning process. Because strategic planning is theory based, it involves setting specific and measurable goals that often are not a part of either informal or autocratic management and planning. Happily, nonprofit management teams, whether marketing oriented or not, are usually very receptive to approaches that work better than what they are currently doing. If marketers find they must win over resistant individuals, focusing on those individuals as simply another target public that needs to understand the benefits of a marketing point of view may help.

Three Planning Situations

New (Start-Up) Nonprofit Organization Planning

Individuals may be required to engage in strategic planning in the nonprofit sector in three particular situations. The first situation is a new (start-up) nonprofit organization. An example would be an individual who founds an organization and receives a grant to help local homeless people. Typical characteristics of new nonprofit organizations include the following:

1. Very few employees and volunteers.
2. Energy and direction that flows from the founder.
3. Specific roles for most employees and volunteers (although assigned roles may not fully reflect level of responsibility, as in the case of a secretary who actually functions as deputy director).
4. Very limited financial resources.
5. Few established policies and procedures (although what needs to be done gets done).
6. Operational and target public offer delivery processes that have been set up with little application of nonprofit or marketing theory, required financial practices, or future donor development.

Entry-level employees who are recent college graduates may feel overwhelmed joining this type of start-up nonprofit, but there would be great need for their knowledge and skills, and significant responsibility would likely come very quickly.

Planning New Offers in an Established Nonprofit Organization

A second situation is developing a new offer for an established nonprofit, such as an SPCA chapter in Boston seeking corporate support for a new direct mail program. Typical characteristics of strategic planning in this situation include the following:

1. Few employees and volunteers.
2. A need for each employee and volunteer to be multifunctional (do more than one job).

3. Little or no formal organizational structure, with leadership either coming from the program director or being shared collaboratively.

4. Limited financial resources.

5. Established organizational policies and procedures.

This sort of situation is a more typical entry-level position for new graduates and constitutes a learning opportunity in which future leaders can discover how to bring people and resources together to accomplish mission-supporting objectives of the operating unit.

Unit or Departmental Operational Planning in an Existing Nonprofit Organization

A third situation is developing a new unit or departmental operational plan for an established nonprofit. An example of this situation would be an assignment to develop a new local chapter of an organization such as the Boys and Girls Clubs of America. Typical characteristics of this situation include the following:

1. Employees and volunteers who operate under established policies and procedures.

2. Employees and volunteers with assigned duties and responsibilities.

3. An ongoing need to maintain and increase financial support.

4. An established organizational culture (e.g., collaborative, bureaucratic, or authoritarian).

Why Is Strategic Planning Based in Marketing Theory?

Planning can be undertaken without an integrated marketing foundation, but the results are often disappointing. Imagine a very slick promotional campaign that appeals to its creators but falls flat in the marketplace or an offer that is not appropriate for or does not appeal to its intended target public. Many people view the output of promotional campaigns without understanding the psychological, behavioral, and other theoretical and professional skills that went into their creation, and they come to believe that they need to learn only about promotional techniques, not about underlying theory.

Take an everyday example: There are many individuals, even those with health insurance, who self-treat their medical conditions, either because they do not want to visit a physician or because they think they already know what the physician will say or do. They might say, "I have a headache, and the doctor will prescribe acetaminophen." Or they might say, "I have pain in my legs, and the doctor is going to suggest that I lose weight." These patients would be underestimating the importance of the process a medical professional goes through to arrive at a diagnosis and plan. The self-treatment may be harmless, but it could also harm the individual in that it does not treat the real illness—possibly tumor, stroke, or a heart attack. To underscore the point here, Exhibit 4.7 shows the typical responsibilities and "results of work" of three types of professionals: marketers, physicians, and attorneys. (Of course, many other

❖ **Exhibit 4.7**   Comparison of Work Done by Various Professionals

Profession	Typical Responsibilities	Result of Work
Marketer	Analyzes situations, diagnoses needs, applies marketing, accounting, and economic theory with creativity and sound professional judgment	Marketing mix, offer mix
Physician	Analyzes symptoms, diagnoses symptoms, and applies medical theory with creativity and sound professional judgment	Treatment program
Attorney	Analyzes situations and extenuating circumstances and applies legal theory with creativity and sound legal judgment	A legal brief, proper court preparation, and trial strategy

professions' typical responsibilities are often overlooked by laypeople unfamiliar with the level of education involved.)

Although some may contend that nonprofit objectives are not as important as medical treatments or legal aid, some nonprofits do have life-and-death impacts on their target publics; the American Red Cross (www.redcross.org) and the American Cancer Society (www.cancer.org) come readily to mind. Others, like the Alliance for Aging Research (www.agingresearch.org), are important in the long-term well-being of their clients. Still more, such as the Fund for Peace (www.fundforpeace.org), deal with other important issues. All in all, most nonprofits have important missions and influence people's lives. It would be a form of malpractice to have individuals leading them who do not know what they are doing.

Organizational Culture, Values, and Approach to Management Affect Planning

Faith-Based Strategic Planning

The story is told that soon after Christianity spread to what is now Ireland and the United Kingdom, abbey-trained monks would sometimes set out alone in crude, homemade, animal-skin boats to spread knowledge of their religion. A monk would allow himself to be swept out to sea on the faith that he would be delivered to where he needed to be. The North Sea and the Atlantic Ocean can be cruel to tiny craft drifting in the current and wind. Some (perhaps many) were never heard from again, but it could be that they reached distant lands and arrived where they could do the most good. The reader is invited to take a moment to think about the monks' plan.

History respects their faith, and tradition has it that they had some great successes, so one might argue that faith-based planning has its merits. Similar to the monks who left their fate to faith, nonprofits and their leaders clearly have the right to avoid the application of modern business planning in their operations if they wish. Outsiders cannot really fault them for having faith. Sometimes they have the right offering at the right time and place and positively touch a great many lives. It could be divine intervention or the power of their convictions or a combination. They have the right to set their own mission, scope, objectives, and approach, as they wish. Marketers, however, are, like physicians, trained in a particular skill set. Some see their profession as pure application of scientific principals, and others have no problem incorporating their own spiritual belief that they were placed in a particular place and time with tools to help achieve a worthy mission.

So we may find worthy nonprofit organizations led by sincere people who choose faith-based, rather than marketing-based, strategy and tactical implementation. We can also find worthy nonprofit organizations led by sincere people who employ marketing-based strategy to achieve faith-based objectives. As marketers, we are more familiar with the latter, but we should have respect for the former. There have been a great many thoroughly researched new offers that should have been successful but were not. Conversely, there have been dramatic offers that should not have worked, but did. Success or failure may involve divine intervention, faith, luck, excellent strategic marketing, or pure coincidence, among other possibilities. This is a personal matter that mature professionals understand they have to decide for themselves.

Incremental Improvement-Based Planning

Many nonprofit organizations have adopted traditional management by objectives (MBO) and continuous improvement (CI) approaches common in the for-profit sector. In MBO, top management derives overall objectives from the mission, and each unit or department is assigned some of those objectives; individuals within each unit take responsibility for a part of the department's objectives. When the individuals in a department meet their objectives, the sum accomplishes the department's objectives. When all the organization's departments reach their objectives, then the objectives set by top management and based on the nonprofit mission are met.

Typically, in order for individuals and departments to be fairly evaluated in terms of their ability to accomplish these objectives, they would be expected to be involved in defining them. Often the objective is incremental in nature (e.g., a 15% increase in donations, target public responses, or reduction in expenses).

In CI, the management process first identifies areas of opportunity for improvement via detailed consultation with staff. Second, the areas in which improvements can be made in the next planning cycle are noted. Third, an action plan is developed and implemented. Fourth, staff members who achieve desired improvements are rewarded. Fifth, changes are monitored periodically and compared with objectives and targets.

The MBO and CI approaches can be good approaches to management; many for-profit companies have found they work best in slow-moving or static environments. However, surrounded by market change, increasing at an increasing rate (some nonprofit examples would be dynamic issues such as fast-changing technology, client needs, Internet reach, competitive responses, and oversolicited donors), leading-edge organizations that switch from incremental improvement to outside-the-box thinking can create order-of-magnitude improvements.

Zero-Based Planning, Order-of-Magnitude Improvement, and Outside-the-Box Thinking

This approach to planning starts with a blank sheet of paper ("base zero"), as opposed to starting with where the organization is, what it does, and how it does it. For example, a goal of creating a direct mail solicitation campaign that will increase first-time donors by 15% over last year is a very traditional approach. Modern nonprofit executive directors and their staff, however, may be better off challenging themselves to use outside-the-box thinking to come up with, say, a 5,000% increase in first-time donors. Perhaps they will change over to totally Internet-based donor solicitation and client-service delivery. Perhaps they will completely redefine who they are and what groups they serve. They may have been utilizing marketing approaches to create public awareness and facilitate donations from private individuals, then using those donations to sponsor various researchers working on curing a disease. They may believe they can do better with a strictly Internet approach, even though it may entail abandoning both a well-known program that asked target publics to "adopt a sick child" (financially) and a snail mail database of donors. Both these programs involve a considerable number of people.

A nonprofit's mission does not usually dictate how many people it will employ or what those people will do. Nonprofits evolve under the influence of their environmental realities and capabilities, and continuing environmental and other changes may mean their mission could best be served in a new way. If the mission involves helping cure a disease, for example, perhaps the nonprofit could do that best by creating an alliance of drug companies and acting as their industry association arm to lobby the government. Or perhaps, because of new understanding of the disease, the nonprofit should shift its efforts to another part of the world, where the real battle needs to be fought. Perhaps a merger, alliance, or acquisition should be considered.

Not surprisingly, outside-the-box thinking can sound pretty extreme initially, and it can understandably scare and upset staff who suspect their skills may no longer be needed. And nonprofit managers may avoid analysis and planning out of fear that many employees, including themselves, may prove to be unnecessary. However, if a nonprofit board decides to go in a completely new direction, employees and volunteers often can be reshuffled or retrained and the nonprofit downsized through attrition rather than firings.

When Market-Based Strategic Planning Is Most Important

With the possible exception of some faith-based organizations, most strategists would agree that a competitive environment makes market-based strategic planning a critical requirement for success. Generally we worry that organizations without a formal approach to strategy formulation can become stagnant or drift in directions that professionals would avoid. If an organization has no limits on resources, no competition for donors, no competition for target publics, and an abundance of cooperative clients, then it is an exception, and its choice of approach probably matters little. In the real world, nonprofits' budgets, the number of target publics they can serve, and the number of offers they can provide are limited. Few organizations of any type would argue with the concept that they need to apply their limited resources in the most effective manner possible. Doing so typically means (a) analyzing market needs and potential, (b) applying nonprofit, business, and marketing theory to develop an offer mix, working model, and plan, (c) planning the specific tactical steps and details of implementation, (d) monitoring the implementation of the plan with ongoing evaluation, and (e) intervening early if results start to trend off target.

Managerial Issues

The following issues are relevant for nonprofit managers:

1. **The impact of constant environmental change.** With environmental change accelerating, the price of an organization's survival is constant awareness and continuing evolution, supported by constant learning and a burning desire to serve the mission. In your generation, that will likely mean working long hours and facing client needs that seem to grow and grow.

2. **Organizational culture, values, and approach to management.** It is important to understand your organization's culture, your values, and your approach to management because these factors affect nearly every decision you and you organization will make. If you work for or with someone with different values and different management approaches, it is important to resolve your differences in some way so that all of you will be consistent in your approach to important decisions.

3. **Barriers to applying the SMAP process.** When it comes to applying the SMAP process, barriers to proper application derive from not realizing that the process is interdependent. Each part of SMAP depends on the other parts; a decision made about one aspect, such as demand analysis, affects all other parts.

4. **Different organizations' need for different steps in the SMAP process.** Organizations may need to add or subtract topics in their situation analysis.

Summary

The nonprofit marketing issues presented in this chapter are summarized here according to the chapter learning objectives they meet.

Define and understand strategic marketing and strategic planning. The concepts are interrelated: Strategic marketing is the process of planning and implementing the offer, pricing, promotion, and distribution to meet the needs or wants of individuals and organizations; strategic planning refers to the ongoing process by which a nonprofit assesses the needs and behavior of the donor, client, and other stakeholder environments, evaluates alternative program content, and determines the specific professional activities and programs it will undertake to reach the organization's mission-based objectives.

Understand the importance of marketing analysis and planning. Nonprofit managers have tended to omit strategic analysis or planning because of fear; a lack of knowledge, experience, time, or money; or beliefs that analysis and planning would be a waste of time or that written analyses and plans will not be useful. However, nonprofits should engage in both analysis and planning for a number of reasons: (a) effectiveness and efficiency; (b) accountability; (c) coordination of activities throughout an organization over time; (d) scheduling; (e) better communication; (f) ability to identify expected and possible developments; (g) criteria for evaluating programs, resource allocation, and people within nonprofits; and (h) focus and integrity.

Explain the interrelatedness of marketing topics. Marketing information, including material covered in the other chapters of this book as well as marketing content learned in other marketing and business classes or books, comes together here as the interconnected building blocks of strategic analysis, strategic planning, and strategic implementation. Strategists need theory-based knowledge *plus* the personal determination to take on the challenge of providing organizational leadership and creating a viable path to the organization's vision.

Understand the basic SMAP. The SMAP consists of an extensive situation analysis, followed by presentation of strategic alternatives, evaluation of alternatives, decision, plan implementation, and planned evaluation to monitor the decision.

Explain the areas of potential change that may affect strategic planning. Among areas of change that may affect strategic planning are client needs for services, the nonprofit's resources, its professional capabilities to deliver services, donor willingness to provide support, competitor activity, volunteer availability and capability, board involvement, home office involvement, the general economic environment, opportunities for cooperative alliances, opportunities for grant support, and the legal and political environment.

Understand the three situations in the nonprofit sector in which an individual is most likely to engage in strategic planning. Someone might be involved in (a) a new (start-up) nonprofit organization's planning, (b) new program planning in an established nonprofit organization, or (c) unit or departmental operational planning in an existing nonprofit organization.

Understand why strategic planning is based in marketing theory. Strategic planning springs from marketing theory, and marketing training provides the skills needed to analyze situations; diagnose needs; and apply marketing, accounting, and economic theory with creativity and sound professional judgment.

Understand how organizational culture, values, and approach to management may affect planning. Via example, you learned about the difference between faith-based planning, traditional management, and outside-the-box thinking. Such differences, arising from one's organization culture, values, and approaches to management, have a huge impact on the end result. Clearly, the starting point for an organization has an important effect on where that organization ends up.

Explain when market-based strategic planning is most important. Market-based strategic planning is important in real-world situations when nonprofit budgets are limited, the number of clients that can be served and the number of services that can be provided are limited, and the organization wishes to apply its limited resources in the most effective manner possible.

Glossary

Buyphases. The stages of an organization's decision-making process.

Culture conflicts. Tension that occurs between those in a nonprofit who operate according to a social service orientation and those who operate (or wish to operate) according to a business orientation.

Distinguishing characteristics. Those characteristics, such as lifestyle, attitudes, and level of motivation, that distinguish those who can use a nonprofit's offers but don't from those who can and do.

Enabling characteristics. Those characteristics, such as age, state of health, or where someone lives, that make target publics eligible to use a nonprofit's offers.

Marketing. The process of planning and implementing offer, pricing, promotion, and distribution to meet the needs or wants of individuals or organizations.

SMAP. Strategic market analysis process.

Strategic market analysis. A systematic study of important facets of an organization's internal and external environments as they relate to an effective strategy or plan of action.

Strategic marketing. A series of integrated actions leading to a sustainable competitive advantage.

Strategic planning. The ongoing process by which a nonprofit assesses the needs and behavior of target publics, evaluates alternative courses of action, and determines the specific professional activities and programs that will be undertaken to reach the organization's mission-based objectives.

SWOT analysis. Step in the SMAP in which an organization's strengths, weaknesses, opportunities, and threats are analyzed.

❖

QUESTIONS FOR REVIEW

1. Define *strategic marketing* and *strategic planning*.

2. List reasons nonprofit managers may not want to engage in strategic market analysis.

3. List reasons analysis and planning are important to nonprofit managers.

4. Give an overview of the SMAP.

5. What are the potential areas of change that may affect strategic planning?

6. What are the three situations in which someone is most likely to be asked to engage in strategic planning?

7. Why is strategic planning discussed in marketing theory?

8. How can organizational culture, values, and approach to management affect planning?

9. When is market-based strategic planning most important?

QUESTIONS FOR DISCUSSION

1. How are strategic marketing and strategic planning related?

2. Why might nonprofit managers not want to engage in strategic market analysis? Accompany each of those reasons with examples from the chapter.

3. Why should a nonprofit manager want to engage in strategic market analysis?

4. What does it mean to say that "marketing topics are interrelated?"

5. What is the purpose of the SMAP?

6. How might the potential areas of change actually affect a nonprofit's strategic plan?

7. Of the three situations in which an individual is most likely to engage in strategic planning, which would you most prefer to be involved with and why?

8. Why is strategic planning based in marketing theory?

9. How might organizational culture, values, and management approach affect planning?

10. When is market-based strategic planning most important?

INTERNET EXERCISES

1. Visit the websites and locate the mission statements of (a) the University of Miami (Florida), (b) the largest public university in your state, and (c) your own university or college. (If you attend the largest public university in your state, look for the website and mission statement of a different university or college in your state.) Compare their mission statements, and consider how their orientation impacts their strategy. Share the results with the class. It is important to complete this assignment even if it is not assigned by your professor. In learning, there are many things that you have to think through for yourself. There is just no other way.

2. Visit the Claritas website (www.clusterbigip1.claritas.com/claritas/Default.jsp) and search in "Industries we serve" for a nonprofit organization. Summarize for the class how segmentation analysis has helped that organization.

3. Search online for the various companies or services that nonprofits can use when locating information to use in a SMAP. Begin with Blackbaud Corporation (www.blackbaud.com) and Kintera (www.kintera.org). Find at least six organizations that nonprofits might want to use, and explain what each organization offers and what its services may cost.

TEAM EXERCISES AND ROLE PLAYING

1. (This assignment uses the chapter's opening vignette as its input information. It asks you to apply skills you have learned in a basic marketing class but requires you to be creative in how to apply them in a nonbusiness situation. This will likely take considerable time and

thought, but the process will form an excellent base for further understanding of the nonprofit strategic planning process.) As communications director on the church's executive staff, you find that you are the only staff member with a marketing or business undergraduate degree. There is a critical need for the development of a strategic plan to address the new vision, and you are the only one who actually knows what strategic planning involves. Other staff members have backgrounds in liberal arts, education, ministry, and the like. The spiritual leader of the association and all the pastors of the 65 individual congregations were trained in seminaries that never covered marketing or strategic planning.

According to modern team theory, the leadership role shifts to the one who can do it. Obviously, the association's spiritual leader will still be in charge, but you are the one most capable of applying business theory to this situation, so you will take the lead.

Begin by identifying where and how you could "market" the vision to the congregations, being specific as to what the message would be, how it would be delivered, and how you would measure its effectiveness. This marketing effort will involve a campaign rather than a one-time communication.

Next, identify where and how you could use your skills in market research, segmentation, product positioning, consumer behavior, the consumer decision making process, forecasting, the marketing concept, environmental analysis, economic analysis, product or offering life cycle, personal selling, and sales management. Be specific as to what you could do and how you could do it.

Finally, be sure to consider how you will identify and treat the various views likely to be found, and be particularly careful to identify key sources of revenue for a church and how the change may affect them. Be specific.

2. Your college or department probably has an advisory board of business executives. Uncover how this board is currently utilized and consider ways it might be better utilized. Share your findings with the class, and if you find the board has not been utilized well, explain why you think that. Note: It would be easier if the list of board members were just given to you, but strategists need to get used to the idea that they must search out who has the data they need and be willing to interview individuals at a variety of executive levels to gain insight into internal operations and relationships.

3. You have been appointed the Habitat for Humanity coordinator for volunteer sign-up and fund-raising for your school. Segment the student body. Think about how potential target segments might differ if you segment the student body by year (freshmen, sophomores, etc.), grade point average, gender, Greek affiliation, family income, major, or other factors. Come up with your own recommendation for a segmentation strategy that will be most useful for your objectives. Share your segmentation and the reasons for it with the class. You will undoubtedly find that other students, faced with the same information and objectives, have arrived at different segmentation results. Their segments would lead to selection of target markets and overall strategies different from yours. That is to be expected. Organizations should try to identify the segmentation strategy that will create target segments for whom they can provide differential value.

4. As executive director of America's largest charity addressing a terrible disease, you have 5,000 employees in cities across the country. Your organization uses direct mail, annual regional telethons, and local events such as "walks for life," through which you raise many millions of dollars. Of the amount raised, 30% goes for fund-raising and administration. The 10-year trend for donations and the projections for the foreseeable future show a slow, steady increase of 7% per year. As usual, you have your staff and several outside consultants exploring ways to

increase donations. Extending appeals to segments that have not traditionally been generous in charitable giving seems like a possibility because their incomes have been increasing, and in several other aspects these groups have begun to take their place among the country's large middle class. Unfortunately, the funds supporting research for a cure have shown few results of late. In fact, for the past 10 years, there has been less and less to show for the funds invested, but the cost of the research keeps going up and up. This disease might be something that is simply beyond the reach of science for the foreseeable future. As executive director, you are wondering whether the organization should be doing something different instead of continuing the same old marketing approaches to get more and more funds from more and more donors.

Assignment: Form groups and decide whether your organization's role should continue to be fund-raising or whether you owe something more to society. Should you inform donors that their donations are not producing much in the way of results, or should you emphasize that "we have come a long way from where we started. It is possible that with enough support, a cure could soon be forthcoming." If you decide you should change your nonprofit's approach, outline a strategic plan, including who will do what with what results and how soon.

MINICASE (suitable for term project assignment)

In this chapter, you have been exposed to the SMAP process, which can be used by nonprofit organizations to quantitatively and qualitatively analyze their current situation, evaluate their alternatives, and map out an implementation plan that will allow them to reach their strategic goals. The ability to take an organization through this process while generating feelings of participation and ownership in the executive team that will be involved is a skill set critical for all future managers. It is certainly important to learn the idea of the process, but that is only a first step. There is really no substitute for the experience you will gain from analyzing real data and working with a real-world organization. In this case assignment, you will be part of a team of students creating a SMAP document for a real nonprofit organization.

SMAP documents are usually in the 100-plus page range. While the typing can be split up, it is strongly recommended that the content development not be split up among students. The objective is for each student to gain experience with the entire process, not to become a specialist in one aspect. It must be clearly understood that the sections are interdependent and cannot be completed independently from the others. It is also critical to understand that each student is responsible for the entire result, not just one part of it. That is the way a team operates in the real world, and that is the way you should be trained in the classroom. That means, for example, that before the client receives the completed document, the entire contents have been completely read and approved by each team member (i.e., in a four-member team, the final document will have been read carefully from beginning to end a minimum of four times).

If your professor has not selected a nonprofit organization for this assignment, you may want to review the section in Chapter 1 that covered the different types of nonprofits. The telephone book or the local chamber of commerce can also be a good source of candidate organizations. When you first meet with your nonprofit's representatives, be sure to verify that it is a nonprofit and is willing to share the operating information you will need to complete the assignment. Your professor will also be in contact with the nonprofit and will have access to its existing planning documents. Remember, your objective is to provide a service for the organization, not just duplicate what it already has. You will often find yourselves analyzing its markets and environments in ways it has never considered and coming up with offering mixes that are truly innovative. Always remember that the final mix needs to flow from the situation analysis sections; there must be a clear connection. You cannot complete the situation analysis and then ignore it to come up with a slick strategy. Keep in mind that the document you create should be a valuable addition to the portfolio you show recruiters at employment interviews.

For new strategists, it is often helpful to review a completed strategic analysis and plan before developing your own. University student teams have been applying the SMAP model in their service learning projects for many years. Note: It is very important to keep in mind that you cannot simply change the wording of the sample for your assigned client. The sample is only to show the idea and depth of a SMAP. Obviously, the situation analysis sections and final strategy developed for different organizations should have little in common except format.

Bibliography

Anderson, P. F. (1982). Marketing, strategic planning and the theory of the firm. *Journal of Marketing, 46* (Spring), 15–26.

Ben Ner, A., & Hoomison, T. V. (1989). *The governance of nonprofit organizations: Law and public policy.* Paper no. 143, Program on Non-Profit Organizations, Yale University, New Haven, CT. Retrieved October 16, 2005, from ponpo.som.yale.edu/paper.php?ArticleID=-1307

Brown, W. A., & Iverson, J. O. (2004). Exploring strategy and board structure in nonprofit organizations. *Nonprofit and Voluntary Sector Quarterly, 33*(3), 377–400.

Burton, D. (2005). Marketing theory matters. *British Journal of Management, 16*(March), 5–18.

Chait, R. P., Ryan, W. P., & Taylor, B. (2005). *Governance as leadership: Reframing the work of nonprofit boards.* Hoboken, NJ: John Wiley & Sons.

Corning, J., & Levy, A. (2002). Demand for live theater with market segmentation and seasonality. *Journal of Cultural Economics, 26*(3), 217–235.

Day, G. (1994). The capabilities of market-driven organizations. *Journal of Marketing, 58*(October), 37–52.

Dickinson, R., Herbst, A., & O'Shaughnessy, J. (1986). Marketing concept and consumer orientation. *European Journal of Marketing, 20*(10), 18–23.

Dierickx, I., & Cool, K. (1987). Asset stock accumulation and sustainability of competitive advantage. *Management Science, 35,* 1504–1511.

Doyle, P. (2000). Valuing marketing's contribution. *European Management Journal, 18*(3), 233–245.

Fisher, M. (1998, March 17–20). *MSE growth: The importance of market analysis and technology development.* Paper presented at the meeting of the Supporting Growing Businesses in Africa Conference, Nairobi, Kenya. Retrieved October 16, 2005, from www.nbs.ntu.ac.uk/cgb/CONFER/1998-03-a/Fisher.html

Grant, R. M. (1991). The resource-based theory of competitive advantage: Implications for strategy formulation. *California Management Review,* (Spring), 18.

Grönroos, C. (2004). *What can a service logic offer marketing theory. No. 508, Working Papers from Swedish School of Economics and Business Administration.* Retrieved October 12, 2005, from econpapers.repec.org/paper/hhbhanken/0508.htm

Grönroos, C. (1984). Internal marketing—Theory and practice. In *The American Marketing Association 3rd conference on services marketing, services marketing in a changing environment: Vol. III.* Chicago, IL: American Marketing Association.

Hambrick, D. C., & Fredrickson, J. W. (2001). Are you sure you have a strategy? *Academy of Management Executive, 15*(4), 48–59.

Ingram, R. T. (2003). *Ten basic responsibilities of nonprofit boards.* Washington, DC: BoardSource.

Kotler, P. (2002). *Marketing management: Analysis planning and control* (8th ed.). Englewood Cliffs, NJ: Prentice Hall.

LeBaron, M. (2003). *Bridging cultural conflicts: A new approach for a changing world.* San Francisco: Jossey-Bass.

Littrell, M. A., & Dickson, M. A. (1999). *Social responsibility in the global market: Fair trade of cultural products.* Thousand Oaks, CA: Sage.

McAlister, D. T., & Ferrell, L. (2002). The role of strategic philanthropy in marketing strategy. *European Journal of Marketing, 36*(5–6), 689–705.

McClusky, J. E. (2002). Re-thinking nonprofit organization governance: Implications for management and leadership. *International Journal of Public Administration, 25*(4), 539–559.

McKittrick, J. B. (1957). What is the marketing management concept?. In F. M. Bass (Ed.), *The frontiers of marketing thought and science.* Chicago, IL: American Marketing Association.

Mercer Delta Consulting Limited. (2003). Beyond compliance: The challenge of board building. Retrieved October 16, 2005, from www.cscs.org/news/challengeofboardbuilding.pdf

Middleton, M. Nonprofit boards of directors: Beyond the governance function. In W.W. Powell (Ed.), *The nonprofit sector: A research handbook* (pp. 141–153). New Haven, CT: Yale University Press.

Miller, C. (1999). Stages of change theory and the nicotine-dependent client: Direction for decision making in nursing practice. *Clinical Nurse Specialist, 13*(1), 18–22.

Mitchell, C. (2002). Selling the brand inside. *Harvard Business Review, 80*(1), 99–105.

Moore, J. F. (1993). Predators and prey. *Harvard Business Review,* (May–June), 75–86.

Parry, M., & Parry, A. E. (1992). Strategy and marketing tactics in nonprofit hospitals. *Health Care Management Review, 17*(1), 51–61.

Payne, C., and Beazley, H. (2000). *Relcaiming the Great Commission: A practical model for transforming denomina-tions and congregations.* San Francisco: Jossey-Bass.

Peteraf, M. A. (1993). The cornerstones of competitive advantage: A resource based view. *Strategic Management Journal, 14,* 179–191.

Prahalad, C. K., & Hamel, G. (1990). The core competence of the corporation. *Harvard Business Review, 68,* 79–91.

Prentice, R., Davies, A., & Beeho, A. (1997). Seeking generic motivations for visiting and not visiting museums and like cultural attractions. *Museum Management and Curatorship, 16*(1), 45-70.

Ritchie, R. J. B., & Weinberg, C. B. (2000). Competition in the nonprofit sector: A strategic marketing framework. Retrieved October 17, 2005, from people.sauder.ubc.ca/phd/ritchie/Papers/NP-COMP.pdf

Sargeant, A. (1999). Marketing management for nonprofit organisations. Oxford, UK: Oxford University Press.

Stone, M. M., Bigelow, B., & Crittenden, W. (1999). Research on strategic management in nonprofit organizations: Synthesis, analysis, and future. *Administration & Society, 31*(3), 378–423.

Teece, D. J., Pisano, G., & Shuen, A. (1996). *Dynamic capabilities and strategic management,* Working paper 53. Berkeley, CA: University of California Press.

Thompson, A. A., Jr., & Strickland, A. J., III. (1996). *Strategic management* (9th ed.). Chicago, IL: Irwin.

Todd, S., & Lawson, R. (2001). Lifestyle segmentation and museum/gallery visiting behaviour. *International Journal of Nonprofit and Voluntary Sector, 6*(3), 269–277.

Weinreich, N. K. (1999). *Hands-on social marketing: A step-by-step guide.* Thousand Oaks, CA: Sage.

Wiedman, H. K. (1990). Volunteers' life-styles: Market segmentation based on volunteers' role choices. *Nonprofit and Voluntary Sector Quarterly, 19*(1), 21–31.

Wilensky, A. S., & Hansen, C. D. (2002). Understanding the work beliefs of nonprofit executives through organi-zational stories. *Human Resource Development Quarterly, 12*(3), 223–239.

Willig, R. D. (1976). Consumer's surplus without apology. *American Economic Review, 66*(4), 589–597.

5

Offers in Nonprofit Organizations

Product and Place

Learning Objectives

On completion of this chapter, the
reader will

- Understand the makeup of the nonprofit
  marketing mix

- Define the term *offer* and identify offers
  in different kinds of nonprofits

- Understand the five levels of an offer

- Understand the three different
  classification schemes for offers

- Understand what is involved in managing
  nonprofit offers

- Understand the new offer development
  process

- Understand what is involved in managing
  nonprofit distribution

Opening Vignette: Offers in Nonprofit Organizations

Consider the following descriptions of three nonprofit organizations:

On a designated day each spring, Hands on DC coordinates thousands of volunteers in renovating the U.S. capital's schools and in raising funds for scholarships for local students. During 9 years, the organization has provided a total of approximately 100,000 volunteer hours cleaning, repairing, landscaping, and improving more than 100 Washington, DC, public schools. In addition to generously giving their time, these volunteers have raised more than $400,000 for college scholarships. Deserving students receive money for college, volunteers have fun and are able to network with people throughout the community, and local and national businesses and other organizations are able to give back to the community. The interested reader is invited to visit the website of Hands on DC at www.handsondc.org.

The High Museum of Art is the leading art museum in the southeastern United States. The Museum's collections include African art, American art, decorative arts, European art, folk art, modern and contemporary art, and photography. The museum offers exhibitions, special events, films, and educational programs. It also offers membership programs, workshops, tours, rentals of various spaces within the museum, and a museum shop. The interested reader is invited to visit the website of the High Museum at www.high.org.

The mission of Musicians on Call is to use music and entertainment to promote and complement the healing process in health care facilities. The organization has accomplished this through its performance program (in-room hospital performances by both local musicians and national celebrities), music lessons, loans of musical instruments, a CD library, and ticket donations. Groups and performers who have supported Musicians on Call include Bruce Springsteen and the E Street Band, Def Leppard, Britney Spears, The Who, Bon Jovi, Donald Fagan of Steely Dan, and Dave Koz. The interested reader is invited to visit the website of Musicians on Call at www.musiciansoncall.org.

These are three very different nonprofit organizations, and yet they all have offers (goods, services, and social marketing programs), and each provides its offers at different places and times.

The Nonprofit Marketing Mix

Nonprofit marketers have at their disposal the **marketing mix**—four controllable variables, product, place, promotion, and price—that may be combined to shape market demand and facilitate transactions and that should be considered when it comes to meeting the needs of target publics. These four controllable variables are often labeled the **4 P's**–the product (the offer), the place (distribution, location, and availability of offers), the promotion (marketing communication with target audiences), and the price (monetary and nonmonetary costs). Understanding that nonprofits have control over these elements is important when it comes to making decisions about where to allocate scarce resources. Two of these variables, product and place (the times and places the offer is available to target audiences), are discussed in this chapter. Promotion and price are discussed in Chapter 6.

Identifying the Offer in Nonprofit Organizations

What is the offer of the Red Cross and Red Crescent organization? How about the American Red Cross or a historic home site like Robert E. Lee's birthplace, Stratford Hall? How about a national, state, or local park? When faced with these questions, many students jump to answer them and then, when called on, hesitate and end up with the remark, "I don't know." Perhaps a definition of the term *offer* is required.

> An offer is defined as any combination of benefits existing in a good, a service, or a social marketing program that can satisfy a need or want of an organization's target markets.

Offers of nonprofit organizations are often difficult to identify because they are only rarely goods and are, most often, services or social marketing programs. **Goods** are offers that are tangible (can be handled or sensed), nonperishable, separable (from the provider or manufacturer), tend to be nonvariable (consistent from one to the next), and can be inventoried (stored for later use). **Services** tend to be intangible, perishable, inseparable from the "manufacturer," variable from one instance to the next because they often depend on the service provider for their quality, and unable to be inventoried. **Social marketing programs** are even more difficult to define in that they are even more intangible, perishable, variable, and inseparable than services. Social marketing programs are also sometimes referred to as issues marketing, social norms marketing, health marketing, or behavior change marketing and include such organizations as the Foundation for a Smokefree America (www.anti-smoking.org/), the Partnership for a Drug-Free America (www.drugfree.org/), and Safe Kids World-wide (www.safekids.org), among many others that focus on health and social issues. Marketers of social marketing programs intend those programs to influence attitudes concerning health, social behavior, and lifestyle, for example, and ultimately the behavior of their target audiences. Therefore, in a very real sense, behaviors that result from social marketing programs do not exist independent of a target public (a client or donor). Therefore, services and social marketing programs may be relatively difficult to discuss or understand because they are more indefinite than physical goods.

Let's pose the question again: What is the offer of the Red Cross and Red Crescent? In the first place, there is not *an* offer of that organization; instead, there are offer*s* of the Red Cross and Red Crescent. Only in very, very small nonprofits would one find only one offer. According to the International Federation of Red Cross and Red Crescent Societies website (www.ifrc.org), its offers are categorized into disaster management programs, health activities, and capacity building. Further, disaster management programs include programs in disaster preparedness, disaster management, and disaster response. Disaster preparedness programs include vulnerability and capacity assessment, better programming initiatives, a well-prepared national society checklist, and an outreach project—a refugee protection training program. Disaster management and disaster response also involve several subprograms, some of which have subprograms of their own.

Say that one asks instead about the American Red Cross (ARC). Looking at the ARC website (www.redcross.org), one finds nine different types of services, including disaster services, biomedical services, armed forces emergency services, health and safety services, international services, community services, volunteer services, youth services, and nursing services. The categorizations, however, are not separate offers but are really more like a list of the ARC's "product lines." To find specific offers, one must look more closely at the categories. Looking at health and safety services, one discerns that the ARC offers first aid, cardiopulmonary resuscitation (CPR), and automated external defibrillator courses, swimming and lifeguarding courses, HIV/AIDS education, caregiving and babysitting courses, youth programs, and a "living well/living safely" module. Many chapters also handle blood and tissue donations.

Offers of a historic home such as Stratford Hall may consist of tours of the home and grounds, educational programs, rentals of the facilities for special events, research opportunities, workshops, and special exhibits, among others. The Stratford Hall website, www.stratfordhall.org, lists many offers, ranging from tours to gift shop items.

Finally, offers of a state park system may consist of hiking trails, fishing, boat and canoe rentals, swimming, hunting guides, mineral leases, items in park gift shops and park stores, archery ranges, bicycle trails, camping services, golf courses, laundry and meeting facilities, picnic areas, playgrounds, tennis courts, educational programs, and interpretive centers, among many other possible offers.

The Five Levels of an Offer

Now that you've been introduced to some examples of offers of nonprofit organizations, the next question is, What is an offer from the point of view of a target public? People tend to focus on the part of the definition that is relevant to them, namely, that an offer is a bundle of benefits. A marketer should consider several levels of an offer (see Exhibit 5.1). This approach can help nonprofit marketers when it comes to developing better offers, anticipating competition, developing marketing communications, and so on. As shown in Exhibit 5.1, these different levels of offers are referred to as the core benefit, the basic offer, the expected offer, the augmented offer, and the potential offer. For purposes of discussion, we will use an example from the American Red Cross, namely, taking a CPR course. A target public of a CPR course from the American Red Cross is not necessarily seeking to take a course from the Red Cross but, instead, is seeking knowledge about CPR. Therefore, the knowledge of CPR is the **core benefit** that the target public seeks. Although the Red Cross may be tempted to believe that there is only one way to learn about CPR (i.e., taking one of its courses), there are in fact many ways a target public could get that knowledge. For example, people could find materials and learn about CPR on their own, or they could take a CPR course offered by a hospital or a different nonprofit organization. In fact, the news media have reported a young woman's learning how to do CPR by watching a television show. Knowing what core benefit a target public is seeking is useful to a nonprofit when it comes to identifying and dealing with competition. If, for example, the Red Cross believed that its CPR course was, in fact, the core benefit being sought by its target publics, then it might make the mistake of believing that only other CPR courses serve as competition. By redefining the core benefit as "knowledge about CPR," the Red Cross can more accurately understand that its competition, when it comes to CPR courses, comes from many different avenues, not just other classes.

❖ **Exhibit 5.1**   Five Levels of Nonprofit Offers

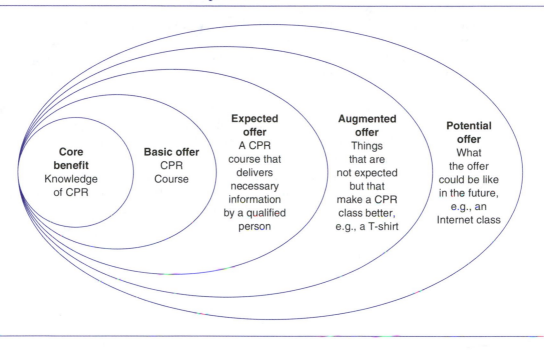

As shown in Exhibit 5.1, the next level of offer is the **basic offer**. In our example, the basic offer is the CPR class presented by the Red Cross. At this level, the CPR class should meet when scheduled, and information about CPR should be conveyed.

To continue our example, the **expected offer** is what an organization's target publics expect when taking a CPR class. For example, people in the target public of a CPR course are likely to expect a course that delivers necessary information by a qualified person. They also may be likely to expect that they will be able to practice CPR on a resusci-Annie and come away from the class with a feeling of competence in CPR skills and with a certificate.

The next level is that of the **augmented offer**, which is anything that comes with the expected offer that the target public does not expect. An example might be a T-shirt or a pin announcing their new skills for students who successfully completed the program. It is important to note that augmentations can become part of the expected offer over time, so organizations have to continually strive to provide low-cost augmentations that distinguish their offers from the competition's.

The final level of offer is the **potential offer**. For many nonprofits, marketing was probably not in vogue in the nonprofit sector at their inception. Therefore, many offers were presented with little or no thought of core benefits or expected or augmented offers. Also, little or no self-analysis or research was done to determine customer and donor needs and wants. So offers were developed and presented and changed and altered based not on what the customer or donor needed or wanted but on what the nonprofit management believed was important. If that is the case, then the fifth level of the potential offer is the level at which previous mistakes or omissions can be corrected. By clearly defining what the core benefit is for each offer of the nonprofit and then engaging in research and self-analysis, the nonprofit may be able to develop choices for directions of core benefits in the future. In our example, the Red Cross may find out that its target publics prefer some sort of Internet CPR instruction with only, say, one hour on-site for testing. Or students may prefer to check out a computer-linked CPR dummy and learn and be certified at home.

Although identification of the different offer levels for goods and services is relatively straightforward, offer levels are also pertinent when it comes to social marketing organizations such as Environmental Defense (www.environmentaldefense.org) and Adopt-A-Minefield (www.landmines.org.uk), which offer programs and campaigns primarily. A current campaign of Environmental Defense is the Discover Hetch Hetchy (DHH) program (www.discoverhetchhetchy.org), which is concerned with the Hetch Hetchy valley in Yosemite National Park. Until about a century ago, the Hetch Hetchy valley was a beautiful place that rivaled Yosemite Valley in the national park. Currently, however, it is filled with water and serves as a reservoir that supplies water and energy to several northern California communities. The objective of the DHH campaign is to restore the valley and move the water to other reservoirs. Target publics of Environmental Defense are not necessarily those that seek to participate in the DHH program specifically but may, instead, be those looking for a public service program of some type that is related to saving the environment. So the core benefit of DHH is that its purpose is to save a part of the Earth's environment. Among alternatives to participating in the DHH program would be joining the Sierra Club or engaging in any number of other programs and projects concerned with restoring or saving parts of the world's environment. The basic offer of this Environmental Defense campaign is the DHH program. The expected offer is that the DHH will have a website where target publics can find information about the problem as well as the solution. Publics may also expect that they will be asked to "take some sort of action and even to donate money, with the result that they can feel good about their activities in support of the environment." The augmented offer, anything that comes with the expected offer that target publics do not expect, might consist of a pen, T-shirt, download, or other small gift acknowledging a donation to the DHH campaign. The final level of an offer, the potential offer, would come about if DHH did some research and found that target publics would like to have some sort of "interactive chat on or through the website about issues surrounding the DHH program."

The Adopt-A-Minefield organization sponsors a "No More Landmines Day"; asks individuals, groups, and organizations to host fund-raising meals to clear landmines and help landmine survivors in their "1000 Dinners" program; and even has ideas for kids who would like to help, such as e-mailing friends with one of the program's flashing messages, reading other kids' stories on the website, performing the program's one-act play at a school assembly, or studying lesson plans about land mines. For each of Adopt-A-Minefield's programs, one could identify its core benefit, basic offer, expected offer, augmented offer, and potential offer.

❖ **Exhibit 5.2**   Different Methods of Classifying Offers of a State Park System

Goods/Services/ Social Marketing Programs	Core/Supplementary/ Resource Attraction Offers	Unsought//Convenience/ Shopping/Specialty Offers

Goods
Items in the gift shops, park
  stores, and tackle shops
 	
Services
Archery ranges
Bicycle trails
Boat and canoe rentals
Camping services
Golf courses
Hiking trails
Laundry facilities
Meeting facilities
Picnic areas
Playgrounds
Swimming
Tennis courts
 	
Social marketing programs
Educational programs
Interpretive centers
	Core offers
	Camping services
	Hiking trails
	Interpretive centers
	
	Supplementary offers
	Archery ranges
	Bicycle trails
	Picnic areas
	Playgrounds
	Swimming
	Tennis courts
	
	Resource-attraction offers
	Boat and canoe rentals
	Golf courses
	Items in the gift shops, park
	  stores, and tackle shops
	Laundry facilities
	Meeting facilities
		Unsought offers
		Archery ranges
		Laundry facilities
		
		Convenience offers
		Items in the gift shops, park
		  stores, and tackle shops
		
		Shopping offers
		Bicycle trails
		Boat and canoe rentals
		Educational programs
		Hiking trails
		Interpretive centers
		Meeting facilities
		Picnic areas
		Playgrounds
		Swimming
		Tennis courts
		
		Specialty offers
		Camping services
		Golf courses

Offer Classification

As shown in Exhibit 5.2, nonprofit offers may be classified along a number of dimensions in various classification systems. We will discuss three different classification systems.

Goods, Services, and Social Marketing Programs

One can place offers into categories according to whether they are goods, services, or social marketing programs. Classifying offers into goods, services, and social marketing programs is important when it comes to the three other marketing mix variables—price, place, and promotion. For example, because goods tend to be tangible, nonperishable, separable, nonvariable, and able to be inventoried, they tend to be easier for an organization to handle, store, and promote compared with services and social marketing programs. In the state park system example, items in park gift shops and park stores would be classified as goods. Bicycle trails, boat and canoe rentals, camping services, hiking trails, laundry and meeting facilities, picnic areas, playgrounds, swimming pools, tennis courts, and golf courses would all be services. Of course, social marketing organizations are unlikely to offer any sort of good. However, if they decided to offer premiums, such as tote bags and the like, then those particular items would be considered goods.

Services are more difficult to manage than goods in that (a) they are intangible (the target market cannot handle or inspect them before purchase), (b) they are perishable (if a service is not used when it is offered, it is wasted because it cannot be saved for later), (c) they are inseparable (the target market and the service provider often have to be in the same place at the same time for the service to be provided; in education, for instance, students and professors traditionally meet face to face in order for course content to be delivered); and (d) they are variable (service quality often depends on the quality of the service provider).

Finally, in this classification scheme, educational programs and interpretive centers would be examples of social marketing programs for the state park because they are intended to change target public behavior. Social marketing programs involve target publics' learning and applying what they have learned from programs. Such programs are usually meant for societal change rather than individual change but, at the same time, seek to initiate societal changes through individuals or small groups of people. Some programs even ask individuals to change their behavior or take action for the betterment of a third party. For example, Environmental Defense, as a part of its DHH campaign, not only asks members and visitors who live in California to send a letter about the lost valley to various California leaders; it also asks members and visitors who live outside California to send letters to their congresspersons as well.

An example of large-scale societal change that grew out of grass-roots social marketing aimed at individuals (many with no disability), companies, and Congress is the Americans with Disabilities Act (ADA), passed in 1990. The ADA grew out of a network of small organizations that advocated for legislative and policy changes in the treatment of handicapped individuals.

Core, Supplementary, and Resource-Attraction Offers

An alternative classification system places offers into categories according to their purposes. **Core offers** are intended to advance the mission of the nonprofit organization. In our state park system example, core offers would include camping services, hiking trails, and interpretive centers because those offers advance the educational, preservational, and research mission of the state parks. Offers are considered to be **supplementary offers** if they are intended to facilitate or enhance the customer's use of the core products. Supplementary offers for a state park system might include archery ranges, bicycle trails, picnic areas, playgrounds, swimming pools, and tennis courts because those offers make the core offers seem stronger, better, or perhaps more enjoyable. **Resource-attraction offers** are intended to develop additional funds and volunteers. For our state park system, resource-attraction offers would include boat and canoe rentals; golf courses; items in the park gift shops, stores, and tackle shops; laundry facilities; and meeting facilities because those offers can be used to tap additional sources of funds, volunteers, and donated resources.

Nonprofits can classify their offers using this system whether they offer goods, services, or social marketing programs, and it may help nonprofits make decisions about developing new offers. Following an examination of their various core offers, for example, a nonprofit's decision makers may realize that supplementary offers such as a parking lot or a child care program could be added to the offer mix to better meet the needs of the nonprofit's target audiences.

Unsought, Convenience, Shopping, and Specialty Offers

A third way to classify the offers of a nonprofit is to use the classic consumer-goods categories of convenience, shopping, specialty, and unsought offers. Particular items in the various stores of a state park system may be considered unsought offers. **Unsought offers** are offers that target publics either do not know about or do not think about using. An example in a state park system might be archery ranges. Such offers may be unsought if the activity has fallen out of favor with the general public. For social marketers, unsought offers may be very new programs. Offers may also be classified as **convenience offers** (e.g., soft drinks, chips) because they tend to be used frequently, immediately, and with little effort. Offers such as hiking trails, on the other hand, may be considered **shopping offers**, which the target public usually compares on the basis of their suitability to its needs and wants and their quality, price, and style. Trails at one park or recreation site may be easier or harder to hike than those at another (an issue of suitability to need), or they may be better or more poorly maintained than others (an issue of quality). Some recreational sites have no charge or only a small fee, and other sites may require a monthly or yearly membership (an issue of price). So hikers may compare possible trails in a way similar to a consumer comparing appliances or furniture. Finally, consider a state park with a golf course that is so unique that golfers will willingly travel some distance to play it. It would be classified with **specialty offers**, or offers that have unique characteristics such that a sufficient number of the target public will make an effort to use them.

Understanding unsought, convenience, shopping, and specialty offers is especially important when it comes to the "place" variable in the marketing mix. In a later section in this chapter, you will see that unsought and convenience offers need to be extensively distributed (and promoted; see Chapter 6), whereas shopping offers may be distributed through selective distribution channels, and specialty offers may be distributed in an exclusive network of channel members.

Each type of classification has its strong and weak points, covered in myriad other marketing textbooks. For our purposes, however, some classifications developed for for-profit organizations may not be too helpful in managing nonprofits' offer portfolios. Further, it is important to point out that not every nonprofit will have all these sorts of offers. For example, social marketing organizations may offer *only* social marketing programs and no goods or services. Further, although every nonprofit must have one or more core offers, not all nonprofits have to include supplementary offers or even resource-attraction offers (in the event that a nonprofit has no need for money, volunteers, or other resources). Finally, not every nonprofit will have unsought, convenience, shopping, or specialty offers.

The three classification systems discussed here are not the only ones available. One may want to classify nonprofits and their offers more generally, either according to the Nonprofit Program Classification system, which classifies nonprofits according to the activities they offer, or in the United States, according to the National Taxonomy of Exempt Entities, which looks at nonprofits' organizational purpose. Or one might want to consider the durability of offers. Durable offers are, generally speaking, goods that last through several uses. A durable offer, then, from our example, would be a good such as a fishing pole bought in a park shop. Nondurable offers, on the other hand, may be goods that are used up in one or a few uses. They would include food or other items bought at a park shop and consumed. Nondurable offers may also include services. As was discussed earlier, services tend to be intangible, perishable, inseparable, and variable.

Managing Nonprofit Offers

Many of the activities involved in managing nonprofit offers are similar to those performed by for-profit managers. In both situations, the marketing manager must make decisions about resource allocation for different offers. However, differences in organizations lead to differences in models helpful for nonprofit marketers.

The Gomes/Knowles CV/M Matrix—A Nonprofit Model

Even though models developed for for-profits may not be appropriate for nonprofits, nonprofit managers still have to decide on the most appropriate mix of offers to put forward. Their organization's offer portfolio needs to be analyzed. The Gomes/Knowles Customer Value/Mission (CV/M) model allows nonprofit marketing managers to analyze their offers along two dimensions that are directly pertinent to the nonprofit: faithfulness to the organizational mission and perceived customer value. The CV/M matrix addresses the needs of nonprofit managers to meet the nonfinancial goals inherent in their missions and, at the same time, be customer centered by taking into account current and potential target publics' perceptions of the organization's offers. The matrix uses the core, supplementary, and resource-attraction classification, and nonprofit managers can use the matrix to analyze a strategic marketing unit (SMU), a group of offers (offer lines), or individual offers themselves. An **SMU** is a part of an organization that can be planned separately from the rest of the organization and that has its own set of competitors and a manager who is responsible for strategic planning and performance success.

Faithfulness to mission. The vertical axis of the matrix concerns the contribution of each offer (or offer category or SMU) to advancing the organizational mission. There are a number of ways to determine the extent to which each offer advances the mission; one way is to charge top administration or even the board of directors with this task. They may begin by analyzing each offer from a strict, dispassionate standpoint to determine whether it is consistent with the mission. To illustrate how nonprofits may benefit from the CV/M matrix, we will use data from a real state park system. A number of useful scales exist; we chose a 7-point Likert-type scale, on which

7 meant an offer *strongly advanced the mission* of the state park system and 1 meant an offer *strongly detracted from the mission.* Managers can use single-item or multi-item measures for each offer.

The state park's mission statement reads as follows:

> To promote, publicize and advertise the state's tourist attractions. To promote the general health and welfare of the people of the State by developing and expanding new and exist-ing recreational areas, including the existing state park system. To develop a coordinated plan utilizing to best advantage the natural facilities and resources of the State as a tourist attraction. To preserve and perpetuate our State's rich historical heritage by acquiring and owning, recognizing, marking and publicizing areas, sites, buildings and other landmarks and items of national and statewide historical interest and significance to the history of our State.

For each offer of the park (see Exhibit 5.2), we asked, "To what extent does this offer advance the organization's mission?"

Not too surprisingly, all the core offers of the state park system identified in Exhibit 5.2 (e.g., camping services) were rated as strongly advancing its mission. Supplementary and resource-attraction offers ranged from having a medium rela-tionship to the mission of the state park (e.g., picnic areas, boat/canoe rentals) to detracting from its mission (e.g., tennis courts, archery ranges, golf courses).

Customer Value. Perceived customer value of each offer, offer category, or SMU is also assessed in this model. Various target markets should be surveyed to determine their perceptions of the offers of a nonprofit. An organization should identify and survey both existing and potential markets to understand which offers the different markets value. One can use any of a number of scales, just as in measuring faithfulness to mission; we again used a 7-point Likert-type scale, where 7 meant an offer was *well-liked by the nonprofit customer* and 1 meant the offer was *strongly disliked.* Such surveying may cost some money, but the information it yields is invaluable to any organization. As with the mission dimension, one can use single-item or multi-item scales to measure value.

The Matrix. Once the manager has the mission data and the customer value data, it is a simple enough matter to plug the values into the CV/M matrix (see Exhibit 5.3). One might use different bubble sizes to indicate the relative size of each offer in terms of the total costs incurred for it by the nonprofit. In the example, perceived customer values of core offers range from high-medium ratings (hiking trails) to medium-low ratings (e.g., house tours, museums). Given that some core offers have low customer-value ratings (e.g., historic house tours), the state park may consider modifying those offers so that they have more customer relevance. Because only one target public was surveyed in this example, it is unlikely the state park system would want to make any changes on the basis of Exhibit 5.3 alone.

The state park's supplementary offers range from having a high-medium per-ceived customer value (e.g., picnic areas) to having a medium-low value (e.g., archery

❖ **Exhibit 5.3**   The CV/M Matrix for the Offers of a State Park System

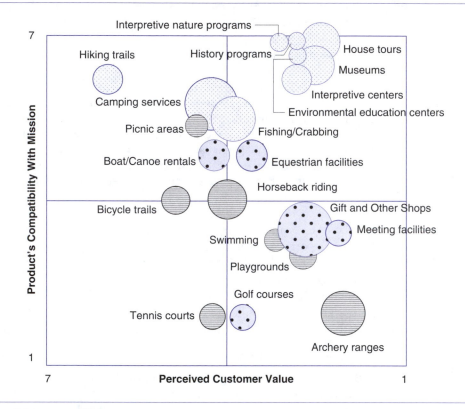

Small dots = core offerings
Horizontal lines = supplemental offerings
Large dots = resource attraction offerings
Circle size indicates relative size of each offer in terms of the total costs incurred for it by the nonprofit.

ranges). Again, the state park might attempt to alter those offers so that they more actively advance the mission and have higher customer value. Finally, the park's resource attraction offers range from medium to low perceived customer value (e.g., boat and canoe rentals, meeting facilities).

The overall goal for nonprofit organizations is to adjust the marketing mix of offers that appear in the lower right-hand part of the matrix so that they move toward the upper left section (highly related to the mission and high perceived customer value). Advancing the mission and increasing customer value at the same time are not always possible, however, because the two goals are not always compatible.

The value of the CV/M matrix is that it allows nonprofit marketers and administrators as well as boards to make informed decisions when it comes to planning and implementing more effective resource allocation, and it helps direct organizational attention toward offers that rate well in advancing the organization's mission. Note that we are *not* suggesting that a nonprofit load its offer portfolio with services or social marketing programs that customers value at the expense of the nonprofit's mission. Indeed, in many cases, nonprofit offers may not be valued by the nonprofit's target publics in the here and now. For example, the American Legacy Foundation (ALF; www.americanlegacy.org), which promotes "a world where young people reject tobacco and anyone can quit," and which has programs aimed at youth and adults, faces a lot of resistance from cigarette smokers who do not want to stop smoking today. But for a nonprofit to be viable, there has to be a certain amount of perceived customer value in the long run. And so today, even avid smokers may listen to or read materials from ALF that they think may help them in the future, when they decide to quit smoking. Programs of another nonprofit, Help the Aged (www.helptheaged.org.uk/default.htm), may be seen as relatively unimportant by 20-, 30-, and even 40-somethings, but with age or with experience with their own aging grandparents and parents, they may come to value the programs and the organization itself.

Nonprofit Offer Development

In time, many nonprofits are faced with the possibility of adding and/or deleting offers from their offer portfolio. Of course, not all nonprofits are able to add or delete offers. Some operate within strict parameters and restrictive missions. But for more-flexible nonprofits, there are several possible "beginnings" to new offer development. For example, perhaps a nonprofit has completed a CV/M matrix or other model and found that one or more offers are having a negative impact on its mission, so it decides to stop offering them and start to offer new ones. Universities may find that some courses or even degrees are hopelessly outdated, and other nonprofits may find that, like archery in Exhibit 5.3, offers that are not valued by their target publics and do not advance their mission are using up scarce resources and therefore should be discontinued. Another indicator that suggests a nonprofit should add new offers is market segmentation (discussed in Chapter 2) that turns up one or more relevant market opportunities for which the nonprofit has sufficient wherewithal to develop offers. Perhaps an observant and creative board member, employee, or volunteer has listened to one or more enthusiastic donor(s) and is inspired to propose a new offer. Or, as happens in many nonprofits, management may simply feel a need for ongoing grant applications so that the nonprofit can remain relevant to its target publics. Nonprofits may find or decide that they need (a) new core offers to meet the changing needs of their target markets, (b) new supplementary offers to facilitate or enhance core offers, or (c) new resource-attraction offers to bring in monetary or other resources that may be used to run the organization or help in providing or developing core or supplementary offers.

When it comes to developing new offers, nonprofit organizations would do well to consider using a process similar to that used by for-profits. The major steps in the new offer development process appear in Exhibit 5.4. Although this process may look overwhelming at first, the steps serve as a template that any nonprofit can use for developing new offers.

Review of Mission and Objectives of the Organization. A new offer development process should begin with a review of the mission and the objectives of the nonprofit

❖ **Exhibit 5.4**   New Offer Development Steps

- Review of mission and objectives of the organization
- Idea generation
- Idea screening and evaluation
- Feasibility analysis
- Offer development
- Market testing
- Commercialization and introduction

organization in order to avoid what has been called mission creep. **Mission creep** occurs when offers are added indiscriminately to the offer mix of a nonprofit as board or management whims dictate until the organization realizes it has moved far from its original mission. To avoid mission creep, a nonprofit should examine its various offers on a regular basis, comparing them to the mission and objectives of the organization.

Idea Generation. Ideas for new offers can come from just about anywhere, including target publics of the nonprofit, such as clients, donors, media, and the like. They may also come from other nonprofits, competitors as well as noncompetitors. New offers that arise in response to a market opportunity or need are much more likely to succeed than those from other sources, so the nonprofit should be sure to carefully analyze demographic, societal, economic, political, and other trends. An important point is that anyone in the nonprofit can have a great idea, not just board members or upper management, and nonprofit workers who have direct contact with target publics can be asked to report what those publics think about current offers as well as any difficulties using them. Another source for ideas is marketing research involving customer surveys or focus groups. It is imperative to be creative, even visionary, in this stage in order to increase the likelihood of finding an innovative and significant offer. Because the next step involves weeding out poor or inappropriate ideas, at this stage the nonprofit should strive to increase the number of ideas suggested. A relatively young nonprofit such as Handicap International (www.handicap-international.org/esperanza/site/onglet4/pyramide/menu.asp), which was launched in 1982 with projects in Thailand, would want to carefully consider which programs or campaigns it might add but would likely benefit from being very open to ideas and suggestions. For example, in the United Kingdom, some current supporters are taking part in marathons and runs to raise funds for the nonprofit. The larger organization may want to consider adding these activities to its list of ongoing projects.

Idea Screening and Evaluation. At this stage, suggested ideas are screened and evaluated in terms of their fit with the mission and objectives of the nonprofit. There are many different methods that can be used to screen and evaluate ideas. Some organizations use rating instruments in which screening criteria are developed, weights are assigned to each criterion, and then each idea is evaluated. A nonprofit might develop a number of criteria related to factors that impact acceptance of new offers. Generally speaking, new offers are more likely to succeed if the following conditions are met:

1. They have a relative advantage over competitors' offers.

2. They are compatible with the values and activities of target publics.

3. They are simple to understand and to use.

4. A target public can try the offers before committing to them.

5. They can be explained or communicated easily to the relevant markets.

6. There is a low risk associated with their use.

The manager or group charged with new offer development, then, could rate each idea on these or other criteria. Those ideas judged a good fit with the nonprofit's mission and likely to succeed pass into the feasibility analysis stage, and those ideas that do not show promise are no longer considered. In the past, most nonprofits have not accepted the necessity of a new offer development process, and those with cause or offer orientations (see Chapter 3) tend to add offers that the board or upper management advances. It is not until a nonprofit has a needs-centered orientation that it will routinely evaluate new ideas according to its target publics' needs.

Feasibility Analysis. Ideas not eliminated in the previous step enter the feasibility analysis stage. The new-idea committee may examine return-on-investment criteria, asking, "How likely is it that this idea would advance the nonprofit mission and objectives given the work that the nonprofit would have to do to offer it?" In addition, the committee should examine the new idea in comparison with offers (existing or potential) of competitive nonprofits. The committee would also want to consider the potential for successful market entry. In addition, during this stage, the committee would need to weigh estimated program costs against program outcome benefits. The likelihood (feasibility) of acquiring funding for the proposed idea is also taken into account.

Offer Development. This step takes the offer from an idea to an actual good, service, or social marketing program. In many cases, an idea that is favorably evaluated in prior steps while in the concept stage is found to be impossible to develop into a good, service, or social marketing program that is practical for the nonprofit to offer. In these cases, the new offer committee would discontinue developing the new idea further.

Market Testing. The nonprofit may decide to "market test" the new offer. A nonprofit could use market-testing firms for this step, or if the nonprofit is national in scope, it could present the new offer in one or more markets to test its acceptance. A caveat here is that market testing does have its risks, one being that once a new offer is in the marketplace, competitors may copy it and even get theirs to a national market before you can.

Commercialization and Introduction. This is the final stage of new offer development, the stage when the new offer becomes widely available. The nonprofit needs to carefully plan the introduction of a new offer so as to publicize it along with explanations of when and where it may be available.

Managing Nonprofit Distribution

In addition to determining and developing offer(s), nonprofit marketers also need to turn their attention to how those offers or information about them will reach their various publics. Typically, nonprofits must overcome time, place, and possession gaps that often exist between nonprofit offers and their publics; therefore, nonprofits must engage in activities that are part of the place (distribution, location, and accessibility) variable in the marketing mix.

When it comes to managing distribution of a nonprofit's offers, a number of strategic issues should be addressed to ensure that the nonprofit meets the needs of its publics. Among these issues, shown in Exhibit 5.5, are determining (a) whether the nonprofit should engage in direct or indirect distribution, (b) what channels of distribution should be used, (c) who should handle the various distribution functions, (d) how many locations there should be, (e) what the operating hours should be, and (f) how to secure help in distributing offers.

Should the nonprofit engage in direct or indirect distribution? At their inception, many nonprofits, unlike for-profits, engage in direct distribution of their offers for the simple reason that they do not know that there are other options. Direct distribution refers to any sort of direct contact with the various publics, such as via salespeople or personal persuaders, direct mail, e-mail, or an Internet website. Advantages to direct distribution include the nonprofit's retaining control over its offer(s) and being able to maintain contact with its own publics; hence, a nonprofit can better keep up with its publics' needs or wants as well as with any developing problems, changes, or competitive offers. In addition, if the nonprofit is selling offers for a price, it will be able to keep more of its money if it uses direct distribution. Direct distribution also means that the nonprofit can be more responsive to its publics and make changes quickly because outside distributors do not have to be considered.

On the other hand, many small nonprofits may not be able to engage in direct distribution and may have to make use of outsiders to get their offer(s) to their important publics. Or it just might make more sense to use an existing channel of distribution rather than build a new one from scratch. For example, many nonprofits have formed to raise awareness of the spread of HIV/AIDS worldwide or to sponsor research to fight it. One of those organizations, the Interfaith Center on Corporate Responsibility, plans to call on several multinational companies, including Procter & Gamble and Colgate-Palmolive, to use their existing distribution networks to educate people about the disease (see www.iccr.org).

What channels of distribution should be used? Channel of distribution refers to a conduit for bringing together a nonprofit marketer and a target customer or market at

❖ **Exhibit 5.5**   **Issues to Consider in Getting an Offer to Its Target Public(s)**

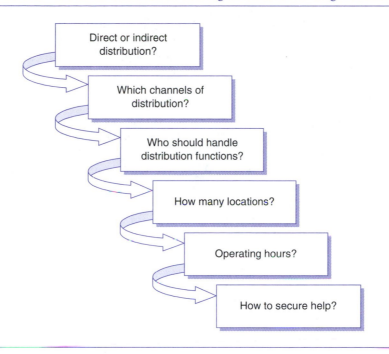

some place and time for the purpose of facilitating a transaction. The channel includes buildings and a combination of internal nonprofit resources (e.g., salespeople) and external intermediaries (e.g., ad agencies, marketing research firms, direct mail) to move an offer from a nonprofit to the appropriate public. Even if a nonprofit chooses to engage in indirect distribution and employ other organizations to help, it still needs to set up one or more channels on its own. For example, a nonprofit has to have a headquarters of some sort, or it may use direct mail to reach current or potential target markets. Social marketing organizations need to consider promotion channels rather than physical distribution channels at this point because social marketers usually do not make contact with their target publics directly but instead use promotion channels such as advertising, public relations, Internet marketing, and the like to make their programs known and accessible.

Who should handle the various distribution functions? Nonprofit marketers should carefully consider who will handle the various marketing distribution functions. Specific distribution functions include buying and selling, transportation and storage, sorting and assorting, financing, and assuming risk. If a nonprofit takes on direct distribution of its offer(s), it will likely take on most, if not all, of the various distribution functions. Whereas goods may require physical distribution channels, involving transportation, storage, and display, services may be delivered to the customer directly at the nonprofit headquarters site or transmitted electronically. Like for-profits, nonprofits need to consider each of the various functions involved in getting their offers to their publics. Finally, some functions may not be necessary at all; services, for example, cannot be stored. Which distribution channels and which functions a nonprofit chooses depend on the type and size of the nonprofit as well as its offers.

How many locations should there be? Location is the physical place an offer is available to target publics. If nonprofits provide goods or services, they should try to locate their offices near their particular target markets if at all possible.

Depending on the type of offer(s) produced by a nonprofit, publics may want or expect them to be offered in many different places or only in a few places. In Exhibit 5.2, we noted that one classification of offers involves unsought, convenience, shopping, or specialty offer categories. Generally speaking, convenience and unsought offers should be available to target publics where and when they want them or, in the case of unsought offers, where target publics may come into contact with them. For example, a nonprofit that focuses on individuals who might be at risk for high blood pressure and that provides free blood pressure checks may determine that its target publics do not want to be bothered by having to go to an office to have their blood pressure checked. (This is very likely to be the case because most people with high blood pressure do not feel ill.) Those nonprofits would be more successful if they offered blood pressure checks in many different locations. Therefore, distribution for unsought and convenience offers needs to be intensive (available in as many different locations as possible). In the case of social marketing, unsought programs may need to be widely promoted via advertising or public relations. Shopping offers are those that target publics are willing to shop for, and they compare shopping offers on the suitability of an offer to their needs and wants in terms of quality level, price, and style. Shopping offers may be available through selective distribution (use of more than a few but not all the intermediaries that would be willing to distribute an offer). Examples of shopping offers in the state park example shown in Exhibit 5.2 include swimming and interpretive centers. City people who like to be outdoors would likely compare swimming pools in the city to swimming facilities available at a nearby state park and perhaps choose the park facilities because they are in a natural setting and not surrounded by cement and parking lots.

Finally, nonprofit offers that are considered to be specialty offers, such as having a celebrity speak to members about an issue, need engage only in exclusive distribution, because target publics of these offers will go to great lengths to take advantage of the offer. Also, although the nonprofit should schedule the talk for a time and place to suit most of its target audience, it does not have to offer the talk in many different locations at many different times.

What operating hours should the nonprofit have? In addition to the number of locations available, nonprofits need to consider accessibility, which has to do with hours of operation. Generally speaking, nonprofit marketers need to carefully consider the needs and wants of their target publics when setting operating hours. Too often, organizations (for-profit organizations, too!) tend to consider only traditional hours of operation. Needs-centered nonprofits will focus on their target market's needs and set hours at times when most of the target audience can partake of their offers.

A clue to the operating hours that would be most effective comes from the classification of offers into unsought, convenience, shopping, and specialty offers. Convenience offers need to be available not only where target publics want them but also when target publics need them. The nonprofit that provides free blood pressure checks would be more successful not only if if offered blood pressure checks in many different locations but also if if did so during times that the most people could be served. Hours of operation are just slightly less important when it comes to a shopping offer like the swimming facilities at a state park. The park may not be able to allow swimming 24 hours per day (given federal and state regulations), but the facilities need to be open as much as possible if they are going to be competitive with other swimming facilities. If the park is not sensitive to the needs and wants of its target publics, those publics are likely to go elsewhere to swim. Finally, when it comes to a specialty offer like having a celebrity give a talk, hours may be much more restricted because target publics will be more willing to accept the celebrity's schedule.

How does a nonprofit go about securing help in distributing offers? A caveat here is that when a nonprofit decides to work with one or more outside distributors, and even if the nonprofit is lucky enough to have distributors willing to help it for free, relationships between the two organizations still need to be managed. So-called place decisions are among the hardest to change once they have been made because they involve agreements on both sides that must be honored.

This decision involves nonprofit marketers' selecting which, if any, intermediaries they will partner with to get their offers to their publics. Some types of intermediaries are agents, brokers, wholesalers, and retailers. Nonprofit marketers need to consider each of the various intermediaries that may help in getting their offers to their publics and view the process of securing help as a marketing problem. Nonprofit marketers should make clear to a potential intermediary the likely benefits that would accrue to the intermediary as a result of participating in distribution. For example, the nonprofit may allow the intermediary to publicize its involvement in helping or working with the nonprofit, in other words, use reward power to get help. Of course, a public nonprofit organization (a government agency) may choose to use coercive power to get help from large for-profit firms in distribution of pamphlets and the like; however, using threats goes against the marketing orientation recommended in this textbook.

Unlike for-profits, who are expected to pay for distribution of their offers, some organizations are willing to distribute materials for nonprofits for free (e.g., the King County Library System in Preston, Washington, will distribute literature about nonprofits in its individual library buildings). In some countries, nonprofits have learned to make use of existing for-profit and nonprofit channels to get their offers to their publics (see www.psi.org/resources/pubs/cent-asia-brochure.pdf). Other organizations, such as TechSoup (www.techsoup.org), are willing to connect nonprofits with donated and discounted technology products that may be used to deliver offers to publics.

When it comes to deciding which intermediaries to work with, a nonprofit marketer needs to consider a number of factors. For example, there should be a match between the nonprofit and the intermediary in terms of values and interests; the non-profit marketer should avoid linking up with just any organization. An intermediary with some experience working with nonprofits can also be desirable. Another important point is that it is better to have more than one channel of distribution. A nonprofit museum marketer may have a channel relationship with retailers and also a channel of distribution that handles direct mail to notify current and potential patrons of upcoming shows and events.

Managerial Issues

The following issues are relevant for nonprofit managers:

1. **The nonprofit marketing mix.** Like for-profit marketers, nonprofit marketers have at their disposal four controllable variables that should be considered when it comes to meeting the needs of their target audiences. The elements of the marketing mix are the product (the offer), the place (distribution, location, and availability of offers), the promotion (marketing communication with target audiences), and the price (monetary and nonmonetary costs). Understanding that even nonprofits have control over these elements is important when it comes to making decisions about where to allocate scarce resources.

2. **Identification of offers.** It is important for nonprofit managers to understand that offers are any combination of benefits existing in a good, a service, or a social marketing program that can satisfy a need or want of an organization's target publics. Because nonprofits tend to offer services and social marketing programs rather than goods, they may be difficult to explain to others because they tend to be more indefinite than physical goods offered by for-profit firms.

3. **The five levels of an offer.** Five levels of an offer should be considered by a marketer: core benefit, basic offer, expected offer, augmented offer, and potential offer. Paying attention to these levels can help nonprofit managers develop better offers, anticipate competition, develop marketing communications, and so on.

4. **Classification schemes for offers.** Three different classification schemes include (a) a distinction between goods, services, and social marketing programs; (b) a scheme based on the purpose of each offer, whether core, supplementary, or resource-attraction; and (c) a classification based on the expectations of target publics and whether offers are unsought, convenience, shopping, or specialty offers. Using *all* these classifications to think about a nonprofit's offers can help managers make better decisions about communicating the offers and deciding between keeping and discontinuing a particular offer.

5. **Managing nonprofit offers.** Many of the activities involved in managing nonprofit offers are similar to those performed by for-profit managers. In both situations, the marketing manager must make decisions about resource allocation for various offers.

However, nonprofit marketers are usually concerned with more than the bottom line and so need a model that allows them to determine both the degree to which existing offers advance the mission of the organization and the level of customer value for each offer.

6. The new offer development process. In time, many nonprofits are faced with the possibility of adding or deleting offers from their offer portfolio. New offer development may occur after a nonprofit has completed an internal analysis of its existing offers, after a nonprofit has engaged in market segmentation and has turned up one or more relevant market opportunities, or in response to observations on the part of nonprofit employees and volunteers. Nonprofit organizations would do well to consider using a process similar to that used by for-profits. The major steps in the new offer development process include reviewing the mission and objectives of the organization, generating ideas, screening and evaluating ideas, analyzing feasibility, developing an offer, market testing the offer, and commercializing and introducing the new offer.

7. Managing nonprofit distribution. In addition to determining and developing offer(s), nonprofit managers also need to turn their attention to how offers and information about them will reach their various publics. Typically, nonprofits must overcome time, place, and possession gaps that often exist between nonprofit offers and their publics and therefore must deal with distribution, location, and availability issues, which make up the place variable in the marketing mix.

Summary

The nonprofit marketing issues presented in this chapter are summarized here according to the chapter learning objectives they meet.

Understand the makeup of the nonprofit marketing mix. Like for-profit marketers, nonprofit marketers have at their disposal four controllable variables that should be considered when it comes to meeting the needs of their target audiences. The elements of the marketing mix are the product (the offer), the place (distribution, location, and availability of offers), the promotion (marketing communication with target audiences), and the price (monetary and nonmonetary costs). Understanding that even nonprofits have control over these elements is important when it comes to making decisions about where to allocate scarce resources.

Define the term *offer* and identify offers in different kinds of nonprofits. An offer is any combination of benefits existing in a good, a service, or a social behavior program that can satisfy a need or a want of an organization's target markets. A quick look at the websites for several nonprofits shows that many actually have several offer lines (several categories of offers that are available). Therefore, instead of talking about *the* offer of the American Red Cross, for example, we actually have to discuss the *many* offers that can be found in their several offer lines.

Understand the five levels of an offer. In order to really see their own offers from the point of view of their nonprofit's target publics, nonprofit marketers needs to look at each offer on each of five levels. At the most basic level is the core benefit, followed by the basic offer, the expected offer, the augmented offer, and the potential offer. Marketers are likely to find potential competition at each level and need to anticipate that competition in order to better serve their own clients and donors.

Understand the three different classification schemes for offers. Three different classification schemes are presented in this chapter. One is based on the characteristics of the offers themselves and consists of goods, services, and social behavior offers. As one moves along a continuum from a pure good to a pure social behavior offer, the offer becomes less tangible, more perishable, less separable, and more variable. Another classification scheme is based on what the nonprofit intends an offer to do for it. In this scheme, some offers are core offers and must actively advance the mission of the organization, some are supplementary and are meant to facilitate or enhance core offers, and some offers are resource-attraction offers and are expected to bring money or volunteers into the organization. The final classification is based on the amount of shopping that clients or donors are willing to engage in for an offer. Some offers are unsought and some are convenience offers, neither of which the target public would want to shop for. Other offers are shopping offers, and still others are specialty offers. On a continuum from shopping offers to specialty offers, target publics demonstrate more and more willingness to shop.

Understand what is involved in managing nonprofit offers. Although many of the activities involved in managing nonprofit offers are similar to those performed by for-profit managers, not all should be the same. In both situations, the marketing manager must make decisions about resource allocation for various offers. However, nonprofit marketers are usually concerned with more than the bottom line and so need a model that allows them to determine not only how customers perceive each offer's value but also whether existing offers strongly advance the mission of the organization.

Understand the new offer development process. Many nonprofits are faced with the possibility of adding or deleting offers from their offer portfolio. There are several reasons a nonprofit may decide to develop one or more new offers, but those reasons center on finding and exploiting marketing opportunities. Nonprofit organizations would do well to consider using a process for offer development that includes the steps of reviewing the mission and objectives of the organization, generating ideas, screening and evaluating those ideas, analyzing their feasibility, developing an offer, market testing it, and commercializing and introducing the new offer.

Understand what is involved in managing nonprofit distribution. In addition to determining and developing offers, nonprofit managers also must turn their attention to how offers and information about them will reach their various publics. Typically, nonprofits must overcome time, place, and possession gaps between nonprofit offers and their publics and, therefore, must deal with issues that are part of the place (distribution, location, and availability) variable in the marketing mix.

Glossary

4 Ps. The marketing mix, which consists of the product (the offer), the place (distribution, location, and availability of offers), the promotion (marketing communication with target audiences), and the price (including both monetary and nonmonetary costs).

Augmented offer. Anything that comes with the expected offer but that the target public does not expect.

Basic offer. The offer presented by an organization; it should do what it is supposed to do—a class provides information, a sandwich satisfies hunger, an after-school program offers safety.

Channel of distribution. A conduit for bringing together a nonprofit marketer and a target customer or market at some place and time for the purpose of facilitating a transaction.

Convenience offers. Offers that tend to be used frequently, immediately, and with little effort.

Core benefit. The most basic aspect or element of an offer that is sought by a target public, e.g., anything that meets a principal human need, such as hunger, thirst, safety, esteem, and the like.

Core offers. Offers intended to advance the mission of the nonprofit organization.

Expected offer. What a target public reasonably expects when using an offer.

Goods. Offers that are tangible (can be handled or sensed), nonperishable, separable (from their provider or manufacturer), nonvariable (consistent from one to the next), and able to be inventoried (stored for later use).

Marketing mix. The four controllable variables—product, place, promotion, and price—that may be combined to shape market demand and facilitate transactions.

Mission creep. Situation when offers are added indiscriminately to the offer mix of a nonprofit as whims of board or management dictate, until the organization has moved far from its original mission.

Offer. Any combination of benefits existing in a good, a service, or a social marketing program that can satisfy a need or want of an organization's target markets.

Potential offer. Any changes or improvements to a basic offer that may better serve the needs of the target publics.

Resource-attraction offers. A nonprofit's offers that are intended to develop additional funds and volunteers.

Services. Offers that tend to be intangible, perishable, inseparable from the "manufacturer," variable from one instance to the next, and unable to be inventoried.

Shopping offers. Offers the target public usually compares on the basis of suitability to its needs and wants, as well as quality level, price, and style.

Social marketing programs. Offers that are even more intangible, perishable, variable, and inseparable than services are; sometimes referred to as issues marketing, social norms marketing, health marketing, or behavior change marketing; tend to focus on health and social issues.

Specialty offers. Offers with unique characteristics such that a sufficient number of the target public will make an effort to use them.

Strategic marketing unit. A part of an organization that can carry out planning separately from the rest of the organization and that has its own set of competitors and a manager who is responsible for strategic planning and performance success.

Supplementary offers. Offers intended to facilitate or enhance the customer's use of a nonprofit's core products.

Unsought offers. Offers that target publics either do not know about or do not think about using.

❖

QUESTIONS FOR REVIEW

1. Define *marketing mix.*

2. Define the term *offer* from the point of view of a nonprofit employee or staff member and from the point of view of a client and a donor.

3. What are the differences between goods, services, and social marketing programs?

4. What are the five levels of an offer?

5. Explain the difference between core, supplementary, and resource-attraction offers.

6. Explain the difference between unsought, convenience, shopping, and specialty offers.

7. Define *mission creep.*

8. Define *channel of distribution.*

❖

QUESTIONS FOR DISCUSSION

1. Why is it important for a nonprofit to know and understand the 4 P's of the marketing mix?

2. What effect might the differences between goods, services, and social marketing programs have on how those types of offers are distributed?

3. Why is it important for nonprofit marketers to know the five levels of an offer?

4. What are the differences between core, supplementary, and resource-attraction offers?

5. How should unsought, convenience, shopping, and specialty offers be distributed?

6. Explain what the CV/M matrix shows and why it might be useful for nonprofits to apply?

7. What are some reasons nonprofits might have for developing new offers?

8. What are the factors that seem to be very important when it comes to the success of a new offer?

9. What are the steps of the new offer development process, and why is each step important in developing a successful offer?

10. What issues are involved in managing nonprofit offer distribution?

---❖---

INTERNET EXERCISES

1.   Enter www.startnonprofit.org/, the website of the Colorado Nonprofit Development Center (CNDC). After reading about the center, click on Current Projects, on the right. Click on some of the nonprofits that CNDC is mentoring. Consider how your department might do the same.

2.   Enter the term *Dell Foundation* in Google and search. Look for the link that has a URL starting with www1.us.dell.com/. Click on it, and then click on Open Grants, on the right. Look at the bottom of the page, where Dell tells prospective grant seekers that their offering must be catalytic, collaborative, sustainable, and outcome oriented. Note everything on this list, and incorporate these qualities into your offering designs.

3.   Enter www.onphilanthropy.com/, and in the upper right search box, enter the term *branding*. Read the articles about branding for nonprofits. Many are quite short but make important points.

4.   Use your search engine to search on the term *+nonprofit +"life cycle"*. Explore what is being said about the concept.

5.   Use your search engine to research the future of videoconferencing technology. Someday this technology will be as widely used as the telephone. List what types of nonprofit service delivery and offerings will be forever changed.

6.   Go to the Adopt-A-Minefield UK website (www.landmines.org.uk), choose one program explained there, and analyze that program using the template from Exhibit 5.1. That is, for your selected program, determine that offer's core benefit, basic offer, expected offer, augmented offer, and potential offer.

---❖---

TEAM EXERCISES AND ROLE PLAYING

1.   As a university student and client, you have in-depth knowledge of your school's service offerings and their delivery system. The offer and place are called "controllable" marketing mix variables because they are designed and set in place by marketers like you and us. Work in teams. Each team will pick one of the following issues regarding first-year college students (classes, registration, parking, housing, campus food, campus services). Develop a plan for new and improved service in the area you have chosen. The class will vote on the best new ideas.

2.   Go to www.switchboard.com; then, in the Find a Business section, enter your location, state, and the term *organization* for the Business Name or Category. Several types of organization categories should come up, but if they do not, pick a larger, nearby city. From the list, click on Charitable and Nonprofit Organizations and review those in your area. Then do the same for the listing Social Service & Welfare Organizations. Form teams; each team should pick a local nonprofit to advise. Review the nonprofit's offerings and client base in depth and suggest offering improvements and new offerings. Present your proposals to the class, and if it approves, send the suggestions to the nonprofit's executive director.

MINICASE: Working for the Director of State Parks—Part A

Working for the director of state parks was a big change for Nina Black. Right after college, she had gone to work for a major aeronautical company. She had enjoyed her assignments, which involved her in several of the company's major government projects. Soon it became clear that she was on the fast track for advancement, but it was a career path that would require frequent transfers to other company locations. She loved her job, but not the moving. The job with the parks department sounded as if it would be even more fun than working with airplane contracts, and she would finally be able to settle down in one place.

As soon as she started interacting with other state departments, Nina began to wonder seriously whether anyone in government service understood marketing. They were all wonderful people, but they seemed to have very conservative and traditional perspectives. For example, although the world had changed dramatically, park offerings were pretty much the same as when she was a girl. Nina did have fond memories of her parents' taking her to state parks for swimming, hikes, and picnics, but she did not think those offers would be very attractive to today's kids and their families. The steady decrease in state funding for parks seemed to support her worry that perhaps the public viewed parks as old fashioned.

Because Nina had taken marketing classes in college, she knew that tastes change and that service providers have to constantly differentiate themselves and keep up with the times. She thought about what was different about people's lives today compared with 20 years ago. She was particularly interested in what activities attract groups. Where did groups of kids go to play today, and what did they play? She asked herself the same question about tweens, teenagers, young adults, families, and senior citizens. She thought about today's amusement parks and attractions and the activities scheduled for visitors at popular resorts.

She wondered if state parks should rethink their offerings and become involved in more of today's leisure activities. She knew that people today did not hesitate to spend a lot for their fun, sports, hobbies, and entertainment, but they complained about a $2.00-per-car entrance fee at state parks.

When she casually asked the parks director whether it might be possible to attract new visitors by putting in things like a mountain bike mogul racing track or a skate park for in-line skating and skateboarding, he wasn't very responsive. He did, however, ask her to look into some alternatives to bring new life to the park system. Nina knew a big career opportunity when it stared her in the face. If she handled this right, the park system could bring in considerably higher fees and possibly even get involved in selling the equipment needed for these new activities. She was pretty sure that a successful transformation of the department's offerings could put her in line to be the next parks director.

Nina wisely decided that she had to research leisure and entertainment by population segment and would need to be very creative about what a park of the future could be.

Assignment:

You are Nina. Review the strategic planning process and the process for new offering creation. Segment the market in the way that is most appropriate. Consider the behavior of each segment of the target public. Plan the details of each offering for which your projections show revenue exceeding cost. Consider whether it would be possible to attract individual and corporate sponsors to pay for the costs of construction and perhaps subsidize operation in lower-income areas. Prepare a report to the parks director with your detailed recommendations and cost projections. The Minicase assignment at the end of Chapter 6 is part B. There you will be asked to set prices and design promotions for the offerings you pick now.

Bibliography

Álvarez González, L. I., Santos Vijande, M. L., & Vázquez Casielles, R. (2003). The market orientation concept in the private nonprofit organisation domain. *International Journal of Nonprofit and Voluntary Sector Marketing, 7*(1), 55–67.

Andreasen, A., & Kotler, P. (2003). *Strategic marketing for nonprofit organizations* (6th ed.). Upper Saddle River, NJ: Prentice Hall.

Bennett, R., & Savani, S. (2004). New product development practices of urban regeneration units: A comparative international study. *International Journal of Nonprofit and Voluntary Sector Marketing, 9*(4), 291–308.

Burns, L. R., DeGraaff, R. A., Danzon, P. M., Kimberly, J. R., Kissick, W. L., & Pauly, M. V. (2002). *The Wharton School study of the health care value chain.* San Francisco: Jossey-Bass.

Chandra, A., Pettry, C. E., & Paul, D. P. (2005). Telemedicine from a macromarketing viewpoint: A critical evaluation with proposed licensing strategies. *Journal of Nonprofit & Public Sector Marketing, 13*(1–2), 111–135.

Chaves, M., & Tsitsos, W. (2001). Congregations and social services: What they do, how they do it, and with whom. *Nonprofit and Voluntary Sector Quarterly, 30,* 660–683.

Christopher, M. (1998). *Logistics and supply chain management: Strategies for reducing cost and improving service* (2nd ed.). London: Prentice Hall.

Croft, N. (2003). Product quality strategy in charity retail: A case study. *International Journal of Nonprofit and Voluntary Sector Marketing, 8*(1), 89–98.

Donovan, R., & Henley, N. (2004). Social marketing: Principles and practices. *Social Marketing Quarterly, 10*(1), 31–34.

Everard, L. J. (2000). *Blueprint for an efficient health care supply chain.* White paper. Norcross, GA: Medical Distribution Solutions.

Fein, A. J. (2000). *Leaning on the promise: Online exchanges, channel evolution, and health care distribution.* New York: Lehman Brothers.

Feiock, R. C., & Jang, H.-S. (2003, October 9–10). The role of nonprofit in the delivery of local services. Paper presented at the meeting of the National Public Management Research Association, Washington, DC.

Gelders, D., & Walrave, M. (2003). The Flemish Customer Contact Centre for Public Information from a marketing and management perspective. *International Journal of Nonprofit and Voluntary Sector Marketing, 8*(2), 166–180.

Herron, D. B. (1997). *Marketing nonprofit programs and services: Proven and practical strategies to get more customers, members, and donors.* San Francisco: Jossey-Bass.

Knowles, P. A., & Gomes, R. (1997). Use of the Customer Value/Mission (CV/M) matrix in strategic nonprofit marketing analysis. *Journal of Nonprofit & Public Sector Marketing, 5*(2), 43–63.

Lampkin, L., Romeo, S., & Finnin, E. (2001). Introducing the nonprofit program classification system: The taxonomy we've been waiting for. *Nonprofit and Voluntary Sector Quarterly, 30,* 781–793.

Lloyd, J. (2005). Square peg, round hole: Can marketing-based concepts such as the product and the marketing mix have a useful role in the political arena. *Journal of Nonprofit & Public Sector Marketing, 14*(1–2).

Lovelock, C., & Weinberg, C. B. (1988). Planning and implementing marketing programs in nonprofit organizations. In E. Skloot (Ed.), *The nonprofit entrepreneur* (pp. 53–71). New York: Foundation Center.

Lovelock, C., & Weinberg, C. B. (1989). Public and nonprofit marketing (2nd ed.). San Francisco: Jossey-Bass.

Maibach, E. W. (2002). Explicating social marketing: What is it and what isn't it? *Social Marketing Quarterly, 8*(4), 7–13.

McFadden, C. D., & Leahy, T. M. (2000). *US healthcare distribution: Positioning the healthcare supply chain for the 21st century.* New York: Goldman Sachs.

Nitterhouse, D. (2003). Nonprofit and social marketing. *Nonprofit Management and Leadership, 9*(3), 323–328.

Prakash, A. (2002). Green marketing, public policy and managerial strategies. *Business Strategy and the Environment, 11*(5), 285–297.

Quarter, J., & Richmond, B. J. (2003). Accounting for social value in nonprofits and for-profits. *Nonprofit Management and Leadership, 12*(1), 75–85.

Rados, D. L. (1996). *Marketing for nonprofit organizations* (2nd ed.). Westport, CT: Greenwood Publishing Group, Inc.

Ritchie, R., Swami, S., & Weinberg, C. B. (1999). A brand new world for nonprofits. *International Journal of Nonprofit and Voluntary Sector Marketing, 4*(1), 26–42.

Ritchie, R. J. B., & Weinberg, C. B. (2000). A typology of nonprofit competition: Insights for social marketers. *Social Marketing Quarterly, 6*(3), 64–71.

Rodgers, J. H., & Barnett, P. B. (2000). Two separate tracks? A national multivariate analysis of differences between public and private substance abuse treatment programs. *American Journal of Drug and Alcohol Abuse, 26*(3), 429–442.

Schuler, K., & Kurtz, J. M. (2002). An internet opportunity for museums: "Museum." *International Journal of Nonprofit and Voluntary Sector Marketing, 7*(1), 13–18.

Self, D. R. (2001). Promotional products: Adding tangibility to your nonprofit promotions. *Journal of Nonprofit & Public Sector Marketing, 9*(1–2), 205–213.

Te'eni, D., & Young, D. R. (2003). The changing role of nonprofits in the network economy. *Nonprofit and Voluntary Sector Quarterly, 32*(3), 397–414.

Weller, J. (2000). History of successful ballot initiatives. *Cancer, 83*(S12A), 2693–2696.

Wharf Higgins, J., & Lauzon, L. (2003). Finding the funds in fun runs: Exploring physical activity events as fundraising tools in the nonprofit sector. *International Journal of Nonprofit and Voluntary Sector Marketing, 8*(4), 363–377.

6

Offers in Nonprofit Organizations

Promotion and Price

Learning Objectives

On completion of this chapter, the
reader will

- Understand where promotion and price
  fit into the marketing mix

- Understand the role that promotion
  plays in customer-oriented nonprofits

- Explain the various promotion
  objectives

- Identify the different sorts of
  promotional tools

- Understand promotional mix and
  integrated marketing communication as
  they relate to nonprofits

- Understand the complexity of prices in
  nonprofits

Opening Vignette: Megan Dusenberry, Executive Director, XYZ MidWest Charities

Glad to have some time to think, Megan Dusenberry was driving to work by a slightly longer route. It was a bright spring morning, and as usual, Megan was imagining all the possibilities for marketing her latest idea for raising money for charities that make a real difference in people's lives. If her planning went well, this time next year would find her organization hosting a regional charity pro-am golf tournament. She was wondering about how she might attract 50 or 60 golf professionals from the Professional Golfers' Association tour, an equal number of known sports and minor celebrities, and several major stars from Hollywood, television, sports, and politics to top it off. To say that Megan was excited about the opportunity to organize the event would be a huge understatement.

After arriving at her office at XYZ MidWest Charities, Megan decided she needed to do a little marketing research into other pro-am sponsoring organizations. She located some pro-am sites with Google.com and uncovered the names of the organizations involved. A quick stop at GuideStar.com brought her to each organization's Internal Revenue Service (IRS) Form 990, listing the financial aspects of its last pro-am. She found one from a city much like her own in terms of average income and population (around 500,000 including immediate suburbs), and it too had several upscale local golf courses. She searched through the forms for information that might help her make decisions on promotion and prices to charge. She didn't expect that the data would make her decisions easy, but she felt it was definitely better to learn from the successes of others.

Megan's notes after going over the website and Form 990 from the pro-am in the city much like her own were as follows:

72-hole event, three golf courses simultaneously involved, each of 30 charities split $500,000. The 30 charities also sold general admission day tickets at $25 each and kept half of the price of each ticket. "Clubhouse" tickets at $100 each included breakfast, lunch, and parking. VIP tickets at $300 included the same, except the meals were with the pros and celebrities. To actually play in the tournament cost $1,500. In all, 65 local and national businesses provided sponsorship at several levels; television broadcast rights and business sponsorships totaled $1,500,000. Last year's attendance was 50,000, and rain the previous year had reduced it to 35,000. The total purse for professional winners was $600,000; the amateurs and celebrities competed for prize winnings to go to their favorite charity. Some 150 volunteers actually paid $50 each to help out on event days (but received a free T-shirt to wear). Other expenses: gift packages for players, $50,000; lodging, $50,000; meals and entertainment, $50,000; prizes, $300,000; fund-raising, $300,000; misc. program expenses, $200,000; celebrity appearance fees, $200,000; advertising, $75,000; marketing and public relations, $175,000; event planner, $150,000. As intended, the organization broke even after donating what remained after costs to the 30 charities.

From this information, Megan surmised that celebrities were paid a fee to participate and received luxurious gift packages, and all their travel, lodging, and dining were complementary. Some of these expenses were probably also covered for the professional players. Megan knew that quite a few additional expenses would need to be estimated on the basis of her professional judgment, but other income streams were probably available, too. Overall, Megan felt that her pro-am would probably be only 75% to 80% as large as the one she researched, but she could probably save costs by doing the event planning, advertising development, and PR work with her in-house staff.

From all this information, Megan needed to arrive at ticket and participation pricing for her pro-am event. She assigned her deputy executive director the job of designing and estimating an appropriate marketing/advertising/publicity/public relations program. Megan also decided to assign her college interns the job of deciding what promotional items to sell and at what prices. Event golf shirts, hats, and carryall bags all needed to be considered. With 30,000 to 50,000 attendees, any of these promotional items could represent serious income, particularly since they could be "prestige priced" at high margins.

Assignment:

(a) Help Megan decide on preliminary ticket and participation pricing. (b) Help the deputy executive director plan and estimate the cost of an appropriate promotion campaign. (c) Help the interns decide what promotional items to offer and at what prices (hint: Use Google to search on *promotional items*). Much of this work will require planning 10 to 12 months in advance, so you need to get started immediately. Have a preliminary outline for Megan to consider by the beginning of next week and a more formally developed and costed proposal for the following week.

In Chapter 5, two of the four controllable variables that nonprofit marketers have at their disposal when it comes to meeting the needs of their target publics were addressed: product and place. Besides those factors, nonprofit marketers have at their disposal two other controllable variables that should be considered: promotion (marketing communication with target publics) and **price** (monetary charges and nonmonetary costs incurred by target publics). Some nonprofits, perhaps because they tend to equate promotion with manipulative or even unethical behavior, may feel uncomfortable considering promotion of their offers. Other nonprofits may not charge any monetary price for their offers and therefore believe they do not have to worry about price issues. However, understanding how nonprofits may manage both promotion and price issues is important when it comes to making decisions about where to allocate scarce resources. Promotion and price issues are addressed separately in this chapter.

Promotion: Marketing Communication

Before we can discuss promotion, we need to address the validity of several common ideas. The first is that the terms *promotion* and *marketing* refer to the same thing. True or False? The answer is false. Many people, however, including those who work or volunteer for nonprofits, believe that the statement is true. They think that if you market something, you are simply promoting it. Indeed, a quick search on the Internet yielded a definition that began, "Marketing is simply communicating effectively with folks. . . ." Promotion is part of marketing, but it is not, by itself, marketing. Recall the definition in Chapter 5: Marketing consists of the 4 P's, an offer (product), where and when it is available (place), and its price (nonmonetary and monetary), as well as promotion (marketing communication). Nonprofit managers who believe that marketing refers only to promotion may ignore product, place, and price aspects and very likely will fail to develop a marketing mix that is appropriate for a particular target public.

The second and third ideas that need to be addressed are that *promotion* and *advertising* refer to the same thing and that promotion and selling refer to the same thing. Both these statements are false as well. Difficulties arise if nonprofit managers believe that promotion is the same thing as advertising or selling. Those beliefs may result in nonprofit personnel who not only ignore the other aspects of the marketing mix but also ignore the other aspects of promotion. Those personnel may envision marketing as something that necessarily involves hard-sell advertising; is manipulative, calculated, and controlling; and is appropriate only as a tool of big business. With these preconceptions, it is no wonder many nonprofit managers have negative views of promotion.

In actuality, **promotion** refers to any activity of an organization that intends to inform, persuade, or remind its target publics about the organization or its offers, when and where they are or will be available, and other pertinent information the target market may need in order to change its feelings, beliefs, or behavior. More succinctly, promotion is the way that nonprofits communicate with their target publics. It is sometimes referred to as **marketing communication**. Regardless of what a nonprofit proffers, if its target publics are not told about an offer and if they have to guess where and when the offer is available or how much it may cost, it is very likely that the offer will not succeed. If nonprofit managers focus on promotion as simply a way to communicate with their various important publics, then perhaps they will develop a more positive attitude toward using this important element of the 4 P's.

Another difficulty when it comes to nonprofits is the common observation, "Nobody seems to know who we are or what we do." When marketers investigate that complaint, they often find the statement is true, and they quickly find the reason behind it. The answer usually is, "Nobody knows who you are or what you do because you don't tell them." A big reason for this problem can usually be traced to the budget (or lack thereof) for marketing communication. One rule of thumb is that budgets for marketing communications should be rather more than 10% of a nonprofit's total budget. For nonprofits that seek to provide goods, services, or programs to their target publics, such a budget would allow promotion, as well as place and price, to play a role in supporting and facilitating use of their offers. However, for nonprofits that advocate causes to their target publics, such as nonprofits that advocate vaccinating children or wearing helmets when riding bicycles or motorcycles, marketing communication *is* the offer they provide. Indeed, social cause nonprofits often do not make actual contact with their various target publics. For these kinds of nonprofits, the budget for marketing communications would need to be much higher.

Much of what happens in marketing communication in nonprofits needs to be addressed in ways that are very similar to those of for-profit organizations. For example, nonprofit marketers need to be aware of the **communication process**, or establishing commonness or understanding between a sender and a receiver. The process, which involves actual and physiological noise throughout, consists of a source (the nonprofit), which encodes a message that is transmitted via some sort of channel (medium) to an intended receiver, which must in turn decode the message; after the receiver decodes the message, feedback may or may not be given to the nonprofit source.

Decisions also need to be made when it comes to the level of marketing research that should be done to learn about the nonprofit's target publics, the entity that will put together the marketing promotion program for the organization (in-house vs. hired help), the timing for introducing various communications to target publics, and the frequency with which they should appear. Whenever a promotional plan is put in place, it should incorporate measurable goals so that the nonprofit can learn which methods are effective and efficient for the organization. Furthermore, the plan should include the nonprofit's mission statement so that everyone involved in developing marketing communications will remember that the promotional plan is intended to advance that mission.

Promotion Objectives

Promotion objectives should derive from the nonprofit's marketing objectives, which should derive from the nonprofit organization objectives. As indicated in the definition of promotion and as seen in Exhibit 6.1, promotion (marketing communication) is used most basically for one of three reasons: to inform, to persuade, and to remind.

Informing Target Publics

First, promotion may be used to inform target publics about the availability and characteristics of a new benefit or a new offer or about the nonprofit itself. Also, if a nonprofit is trying to approach a new target market, an informational message may be in order. Informative communication is typically used when offers are being brought to the target public for the first time and tends to build **primary demand**, or demand for a program in general rather than for the specific program of a nonprofit organization.

Target publics, including donors, volunteers, users, the media, and so on, need to learn about a nonprofit and its offers before they can make a decision to donate, volunteer, attend a program, engage in an activity, or take other action. Promotional methods used to inform target publics are discussed in the "Promotional Mix" section of this chapter.

❖ **Exhibit 6.1** Three Objectives of Promotion

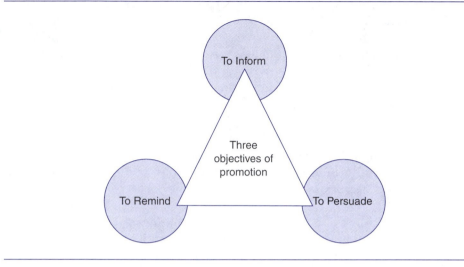

Persuading Target Publics

A second purpose of promotion is to persuade target publics to use the nonprofit's offers rather than offers from another nonprofit or no offers at all. Persuasive marketing is more likely to occur as more and more members of the target public become aware of a nonprofit offer. Persuasion may result in an increase in demand for an existing offer. If a nonprofit's target publics know about it and its offers but similar offers are available from other nonprofits, then persuasion should be the goal of the promotional message. Persuasive communication can be used to build **secondary demand**, or demand for a particular brand of offer rather than demand for an offer class in general. Nonprofit personnel who understand that promotion is simply one of the 4 P's of marketing may, nonetheless, believe that persuasive communication is inappropriate for their nonprofit because they think such communication has to be hard sell or aggressive. And, indeed, there are nonprofits that use aggressive communication. For example, the U.S. Postal Service (USPS), responding to the growing use of e-mail marketing, developed a direct mail piece—a bimonthly custom magazine called *Deliver*—about strategies and trends that are shaping the world of marketing and advertising. The USPS sends *Deliver* to a targeted audience of 350,000 CEOs, corporate marketers (at such companies as Procter & Gamble and Coca-Cola), and their creative agencies (e.g., WPP Group's Ogilvy & Mather). Another nonprofit, the Rainforest Action Network (RAN; www.ran.org), challenges corporate America to change its investment policies, adopt environmental and human rights policies, make fuel-efficient vehicles, and stop clear-cutting virgin forests. Among other actions to get attention, RAN has set up shop outside various corporate headquarters and grilled and handed out tofu dogs while questioning bank workers about their bank's investment practices.

Nonprofits that rely on aggressive communications tend to rely on advertising sales promotions, interactive websites, e-mail, and the like to reach their target publics.

While aggressive communications tend to be more noticeable and, therefore, more unforgettable, it is true that communications at either extreme are subject to faults. Nonprofits that engage in aggressive communication run a risk of committing an **error of commission**. In other words, when nonprofits use aggressive communication, they run a risk of saying or doing something that is wrong or perceived as being inappropriate. Aggressive communication can be ethical, however, and in fact may be the best way to reach a particular target public. The American Legacy Foundation's Truth Campaign (www.americanlegacy.org) reaches teens (ages 12–17) by speaking to them in their own language, without being preachy, via outlets that teens pay attention to: print, radio, the Internet, and television, especially youth-oriented outlets such as MTV, the WB, and UPN. Because teens tend to live in the moment and not consider long-term effects of behavior, a hard-sell message may be the only way to get their attention and make the message meaningful to them.

Nonprofits do not have to engage in aggressive or hard-sell communication. Many that choose minimal marketing or communication assume that demand for an offer will grow simply because the organization offers it or offers it well. They tend to engage only in fund-raising or public relations. For example, GuideStar.org (www.guidestar .org), an organization that offers information about the programs and finances of more than 1 million charitable organizations recognized by the IRS, basically relies on articles, word-of-mouth, and press releases to communicate with its various publics. Another nonprofit that, at least currently, seems to rely on minimal communication is the European Network for Smoking Prevention (www.ensp.org), which sponsors conferences and makes available many reports about the effects of smoking.

Many, many other nonprofits, such as hospitals, universities, and museums, similarly engage in minimal communication with their publics. However, if a nonprofit's target publics do not know about its offers, the nonprofit will, at best, operate well below its potential. Therefore, nonprofits that engage in minimal communication risk committing an **error of omission**. Although minimal marketing may appeal to a nonprofit's sense of professional dignity, it risks not reaching its target publics and, hence, wasting its donations, grants, or tax monies. Minimal communication makes a nonprofit more likely to lose effectiveness and efficiency; furthermore, the nonprofit may in fact become unethical if it makes contact with only some people in its target publics but not others. Therefore, it would behoove any nonprofit engaging in minimal communication to examine the results of its decision from time to time to ensure that it is not ignoring large portions of its target publics.

On the whole, marketers may develop communications that fall anywhere along a continuum from aggressive to minimal. In sum, both aggressive and minimal communication have advantages and disadvantages, and persuasive communication may be the ticket to convincing target publics to attend one of a nonprofit's programs, use one of its services, change a behavior, donate, or volunteer.

Reminding Target Publics. Finally, a third purpose of promotion is to remind target publics that a nonprofit or its offers are available. If a nonprofit has been around for a long time or if one or more of its offers has reached the mature stage of the offer life cycle, the nonprofit might find that much of its target public has forgotten about

❖ **Exhibit 6.2**   Tools Making Up the Promotional Mix

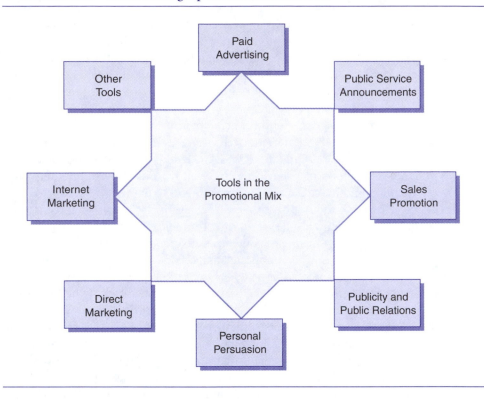

it or has moved on to donate or volunteer at other, newer nonprofits. An example of a nonprofit that is currently using reminder communication is the USPS. The USPS has initiated a "Be Here" advertising campaign that aims to remind business customers about the effectiveness of direct mail. This sort of advertising is used not only to win back target publics but also to keep a brand name in the minds of consumers.

The Promotional Mix

Traditionally, promotion consists of a **promotional mix** (also known as a **communication mix**). As can be seen in Exhibit 6.2, the promotional mix consists of advertising and public service advertising, sales promotions, publicity and public relations, personal persuasion, direct marketing, Internet marketing, and other tools. When it comes to the tools of promotion, some nonprofit boards believe that certain tools (e.g., advertising) are inappropriate for them, even if they grant that promotion is necessary. On the other hand, many other nonprofits seem to overemphasize advertising relative to other promotional tools, probably for several reasons. First, many nonprofits still equate marketing with advertising and believe they have to have ads. Second, nonprofits often solicit or hire advertising agencies to develop promotional materials for them, and the result is very likely to be ads. A nonprofit that wants to hire or ask

❖ **Exhibit 6.3** Factors in the Communication Process

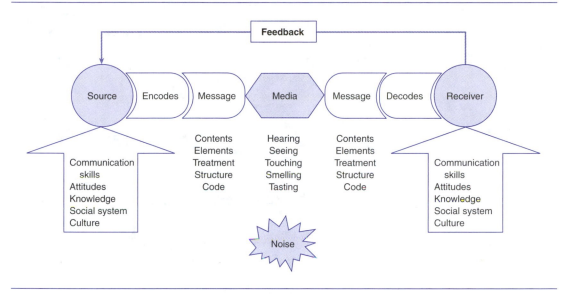

an agency for help might do best to approach a full-service marketing agency. That way, the nonprofit is more likely to end up with a portfolio of promotional tools that can be used with different target publics and at different times to achieve different objectives. Given the assortment of promotional tools available to nonprofits, any nonprofit should be able to put together a good mix to meet its objectives. A discussion of some necessary considerations for any sort of communication tool is followed by a brief description of each of the most popular tools.

The Communication Process. Each of the promotional tools discussed in this section can be used to inform, persuade, or remind target publics about an organization and its offers. Since promotional tools are communication tools, the reader may wish to review the communication process. As seen in Exhibit 6.3, the basic process involves a source (e.g., the nonprofit marketer), who encodes a message. How well a message is encoded depends on the source's communication skills, attitudes, knowledge, social system, and culture. The message is transmitted through some medium and then decoded by the receiver. The terms *encoding* and *decoding* give a hint of the difficulties that may arise, not only when translating one's own thoughts into words and symbols, but also when interpreting the words or symbols of others into terms we can understand. The message that is encoded is characterized by its contents (what it says) as well as by its elements (how the message is presented) and its treatment, structure, and code. The media used may range from print or broadcast modes to a person who seeks individually to persuade target publics; media must be selected such that the sensory cues that make the strongest impression are exploited. Finally, how accurately the message is decoded depends not only on the receiver's skills, attitudes, and knowledge, for example, but also on how well

❖ **Exhibit 6.4**   Steps to Effective Communication for Nonprofits

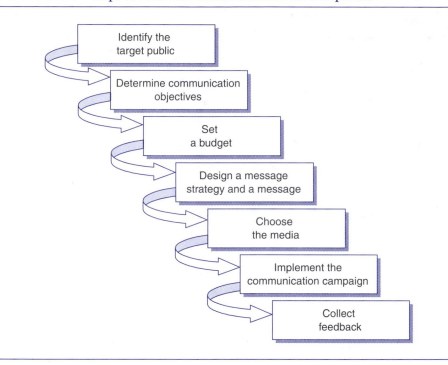

the source understands the nonprofit's target publics. In order to assess the effectiveness of the message, the nonprofit should put into action some sort of feedback loop, formal or informal. Finally, the nonprofit must realize that noise (both auditory and physiological) is present throughout the communication process, as indicated in the Exhibit.

Developing Effective Communication. In addition to considering the communication process, several steps can help a nonprofit develop effective marketing communications. Some researchers and practitioners argue for five steps while others argue for seven. Drawing from a number of published research reports and books, we have synthesized seven steps that are likely to lead to effective communication for nonprofits. They are depicted in Exhibit 6.4 and discussed in more detail below.

1. **Identify the target public.** A nonprofit's target publics may include donors, users, media, and elected officials, among others. For each communication campaign, a nonprofit must clearly specify which publics will be targeted.

2. **Determine the communication objectives.** The three main objectives of promotion— to inform, to persuade, and to remind—were discussed above. At this point, in addition to deciding which of those main objectives the nonprofit wishes to pursue, the marketer must also set objectives for each element of the promotional mix; in

other words, decide specifically what each promotional item is intended to achieve. Objectives should be specific (they should state clearly what, where, when, and how a situation will be changed), measurable (anyone should be able to compute changes in a situation), achievable (they should, given the nonprofit's resources and capabilities, be able to be accomplished), and they should include a time frame (in which the objective can be expected to be achieved). Each promotional item in the nonprofit's promotional mix should target a specific target public and be expected to produce some specific, measurable result. For example, a portfolio for a state park system may include a direct mail piece intended to remind former and current campers that they need to make reservations now for the coming fall, and the objective may be to get at least 75% of those campers to make a reservation. The portfolio could also include a mailing to noncampers in the same area. Its intention might be to persuade them to try camping this year, and its objective might be to induce at least 20% of those families to camp.

3. **Set a budget.** Nonprofits can employ a number of budgeting methods, but the best method by far is the objective and task method. The objective and task method involves setting promotional objectives and then deciding on the tasks the organization will need to accomplish in order to reach those objectives. Next, the organization should estimate how much money will be needed to achieve the tasks it needs to get done. That estimate is the promotional budget. Many nonprofits use budget methods that result in poorly executed promotional efforts because of a lack of money. If a nonprofit has little money, it can do one of three things: It can find the money (via grants or donations or by shifting money from other areas), it can focus on using promotional tools that are free or that do not require much money, or it can rework or drop some of its objectives and focus on achievable outcomes.

4. **Design a message strategy and a message.** Many good sources are available to guide an organization in choosing a message strategy and developing and encoding a message. Among things to consider are the message's content (rational, emotional, or moral appeals), structure, and format. The encoder has a number of decisions to make concerning everything from whether to use humor to whether color or black-and-white would be best. Decisions have to be made about visuals—whether to use drawings or pictures, for example.

5. **Choose the media.** The nonprofit may choose to employ personal (e.g., personal persuaders) or impersonal (e.g., advertising) communication media to transmit its message. It may wish to encourage positive word-of-mouth, which can exert a strong effect. Among media that may be used are television, radio, newspapers, magazines, posters, billboards, direct mail, transit advertising, signs, in-store displays, and point-of-purchase media. Each has advantages and disadvantages that the nonprofit must consider before making a decision about which to use.

6. **Implement the communication campaign.** Once the communication campaign is ready and its media have been selected, the time has come to implement it. On the basis of its decisions about the frequency (the number of times a target public is exposed to a message within a stated time) and reach (how many different people will be exposed to the message at least once within a stated time of the message), the nonprofit will establish a communication campaign schedule.

7. **Collect feedback.** Feedback can be formal or informal. For example, a nonprofit could simply measure the dollar value of goods sold in a museum gift shop as a measure of the effectiveness of a local ad encouraging local shoppers to consider coming there for birthday, Christmas, or other holiday shopping. Or it could add up the value of donations received or count the number of volunteers recruited, letters written to politicians, traffic injuries, or any of a host of other measures. More formally, it could measure awareness of a specific social issue or intention to use a particular offer in the future, both before and after the appearance of a message.

Promotional Tools

Paid Advertising. Marketing managers should understand several important components of the definition of advertising. First, advertising is a paid form of promotion, which means that the nonprofit pays for the development, execution, and placement of the ad. Second, it is a form of mass, impersonal presentation. *Mass* means it will reach a relatively large number of people, including a nonprofit's target publics, who are geographically dispersed. *Impersonal* means the message cannot be changed for each individual who sees or hears the ad. Third, advertising requires an identified sponsor so that viewers of an ad can know who paid for the message they have just seen, heard, or read. Fourth, advertising is presented to its target publics in a formal communications medium so that people can know that the message is sponsored and not a news story. Therefore, **paid advertising** is any paid form of mass, impersonal presentation of an offer by an identified sponsor via a formal communication medium. When it is used, advertising tends to be the most visible form of impersonal promotion.

Advertising can be used regardless of the type of product (good, service, social behavior program, or cause). When it is used to present an offer, it is called **product advertising**, which entails a message to promote a nonprofit offer such as membership. An example would be an ad meant to inspire a nonprofit's target publics to register for one of the nonprofit's programs. A nonprofit can also employ **institutional advertising**, or a message to promote a nonprofit organization as a whole or a concept, idea, or philosophy. Examples of nonprofit institutional ads include those that promote not an offer but an institution, such as the Red Cross or the U.S. Army, and that encourage people to volunteer, vote, or donate money or services. Such advertising may help support a nonprofit's activities but not necessarily its own offers or programs; for example, a Red Cross ad might simply encourage people to give blood but not include its telephone number or Web address.

Advertising has some powerful advantages. It can dramatize a message by combining color, sound, and visuals. It is effective at building awareness, knowledge, and a long-term image for an offer. It reaches the masses, and it can have a fairly low cost per individual reached. Further, because advertising has become increasingly international, nonprofits may be able to reach people around the world with their socially valuable offers and reach donors anywhere. For current examples of advertising from the American Red Cross, go to www.redcross.org/press/psa/psa.html.

But advertising also has disadvantages. It is impersonal and expensive to produce and place, and the message is not adaptable to individuals. Also, there is usually a lot of clutter surrounding advertising, so it is difficult to get the attention of a nonprofit's target publics. Further, it is difficult to measure the effectiveness of advertising campaigns. Last, advertising by nonprofits may lead critics to claim that particular ads are deceptive or a waste of money.

Public Service Advertisements. A public service advertisement (PSA) is any form of advertising (mass, impersonal presentation of an offer by an identified sponsor via a formal communication medium) in which some part of the development, production, or distribution is free. Public service advertisements developed by Erwin-Penland (part of Hill, Holliday, Connors, and Cosmopulos) for a local United Way agency appear in Exhibit 6.5.

Local advertising or promotion agencies may be willing to donate time developing advertising for a nonprofit. Sometimes called public service announcements, these ads are intended to promote an idea or influence behavior, such as encouraging people not to use illegal drugs or smoke cigarettes, or they may encourage people to adopt safer, healthier lifestyles. Because PSAs are advertisements, they share many of the same characteristics as paid advertising, discussed earlier. For example, a PSA is a form of mass, impersonal presentation, so it reaches large numbers of people, and its message cannot be adapted to different individuals. PSAs also list sponsors somewhere in the ad (usually in a bottom corner of a print ad) so that viewers can know who paid for the message they have just seen, heard, or read. Finally, PSAs are presented in a formal communications medium so that people can know the message is sponsored and not a news story.

Although some part of the development, production, or distribution of a PSA is free, a nonprofit usually has to pay any of the out-of-pocket production expenses of the ad agency producing the ad.

Sales Promotion. Sales promotion is defined as any short-term incentive intended to result in target publics' buying more, buying now, buying a nonprofit's offers instead of another organization's offers, or not buying anything at all. The term *buying* should not imply that nonprofits should use sales promotions only for offers that are sold for a monetary price. They may also be used to encourage people to do a better job of changing their behavior, for example (perhaps by exercising more!), to change their behavior now (rather than later), and to use the nonprofit's offers rather than those offered by another nonprofit or no offers at all. Sales promotions usually have a deadline or an expiration date and can target any of a nonprofit's publics, including input, internal, partner, and consuming publics. For example, a nonprofit could run a contest among its volunteers and reward those who managed to sign up the most new members, solicited the most donations, or encouraged the most people to start or stop a behavior. Sales promotions tend to have short-lived effects and can damage a nonprofit's brand-building efforts in the long run if they are misused. For example, if a nonprofit theater group offered target publics a "buy one, get one free" promotion for its performance tickets, there is a risk that those publics may become unwilling to pay regular prices for performance tickets. Thus, successful sales promotions must promote building relationships with a target public, not by giving away or cheapening the core offer, but by giving away something that would enhance the nonprofit's core offer. For example, instead of giving away free or half-price tickets to a play, a local nonprofit

❖ **Exhibit 6.5**

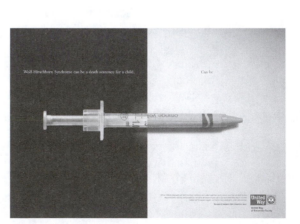

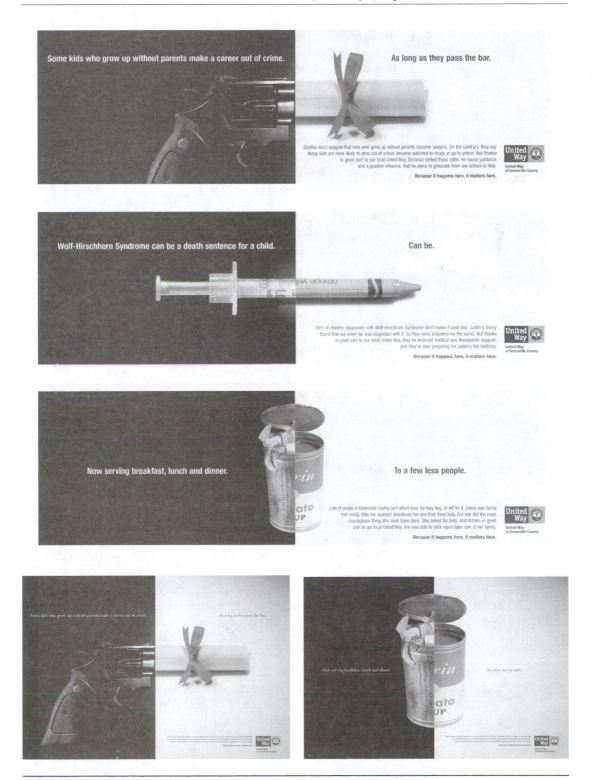

theater group might consider offering free refreshment cards to people who become members at a higher level of giving than most.

Among the various types of sales promotions are samples, coupons, prices off, premiums, prizes, tie-in promotions, demonstrations, and specialty objects, such as pens, cup holders, calendars, and the like (with the nonprofit logo on them, of course). Several steps can help make sales promotions effective in the long run: (a) Make sure the promotion is justified (run it when you need it, not as the standard way to get attention for your nonprofit or its offers), (b) tie the promotion to the offer's brand image, and (c) evaluate every possible sales promotion tool in terms of the sales job it can do as well as the communication it carries.

Publicity and Public Relations. **Publicity** involves news stories about an organization or its offers that are carried by the media but are not paid for by the organization or run under identified sponsorship. Like advertising, publicity is a form of mass communication. Publicity and public relations are **not** synonymous in that **public relations (PR)** involves building good relations with a nonprofit's various publics by attaining favorable publicity, building up a good image, and handling or forestalling unfavorable rumors, stories, and events. The PR person tries to obtain editorial space in all media that might be read, seen, or heard by the nonprofit's target publics. Marketers handling PR should be proactive and plan some press events and releases and schedule interviews in order to support their nonprofit's overall communication objectives. Once press releases or other information is sent out, the PR marketer should follow up with phone calls or e-mails to bring attention to the nonprofit's story. If interviews are scheduled, the PR marketer should be sure to develop different topics that are relevant to each of the nonprofit's publics. Press kits should be on hand, not only at the organization but also on the nonprofit's website, so that reporters can find information easily. In order to ensure that people in your nonprofit can intelligently discuss your organization and its offers, spend some time training them to do so. Develop a crisis-control plan, which means thinking up possible crisis situations and ways to handle them. If a crisis pops up, work actively to end it by acknowledging the problem, showing real concern for people who may be negatively impacted by the problem, limiting any damage, and realizing that the media people who are bugging you this week about the crisis will be back tomorrow to help with one or more of its offers. It is also important for a nonprofit to be flexible and respond to criticism positively. News stories and features reported in neutral media have a great deal of credibility in that target publics are more likely to respond to the story as news and not as sponsored communication. Thus, an advantage of PR is that it has greater credibility than all other forms of promotion that a nonprofit may pay for. It can improve an organization's prestige and image with the public. For many nonprofits, it is an efficient, albeit indirect, promotional alternative, and for some, it is the only form of promotion used. Another advantage of PR is its cost, which is minimal compared with other promotional tools. PR uses a variety of marketing communications, such as press releases, speeches by top management and volunteers, special events, interviews, written and audiovisual materials aimed at target publics, news conferences, article placements and story ideas in other media, nonprofit identity materials such as logos and brochures, websites, and public service activities (e.g., sponsorship of events) meant to generate publicity for an organization. The key to public relations is to have a story that is interesting enough to be told to various publics using a variety of media. A disadvantage of PR is that once a story or news release is sent to the media, the nonprofit loses control of it. Editors can and do edit stories so that they are more interesting, and thus a story can end up conveying information that may not be true. Another disadvantage is that the story will run when the media director decides it will run, so the nonprofit has no control over when the story will appear or if it will appear at all. Given these disadvantages, PR can never be as effective as a promotional tool that remains under the control of the nonprofit.

Personal Persuasion. **Personal persuasion**, or **person-to-person communication**, is defined as a nonprofit "seller" having a conversation with one or more prospective target members in order to encourage them to use the nonprofit's offers, donate, volunteer, or act on an idea. An advantage of personal persuasion is that it is a personal medium in which the message can be tailored to the target public. Two disadvantages are that it can be costly if the persuaders are paid by the nonprofit, and the delivered message will likely vary if different persuaders are involved. Personal persuaders may be called recruiters, donor recruitment departments (at blood banks), change agents, account reps, fund-raisers, canvassers, or lobbyists, depending on what their job entails. Sometimes nonprofits have volunteers available to present their message. Using those volunteers can help the nonprofit provide a warm, human touch to its messages, and volunteers can be very effective at making the "sale"; some examples are Girl Scouts selling Girl Scout Cookies and museum shop volunteers who handle sales.

Direct Marketing. **Direct marketing** refers to those marketing messages a nonprofit sends out to specific individuals from whom it seeks a response such as making a donation or completing a survey. The use of direct marketing tactics by nonprofit organizations is the focus of the next chapter and will be discussed in detail there.

Internet Marketing. E-engagement has become a very important tool in the nonprofit promotional mix. In 2004, Guidestar surveyed 6,434 nonprofit organizations. The study reported that about 97% of nonprofits use the Internet to provide information (e.g., mission, goals, financials, how to take action offline) and that about 55% use it to gather support (e.g., memberships, donations, and volunteer sign-up).

In 2004, Network for Good (NFG) surveyed 2,055 individuals about their use of the Internet. The findings of the survey showed that about 60% of the U.S. population has Internet access. Younger individuals reported higher rates of Internet access. The study found that Internet use is growing and is skewed toward younger individuals. Almost half of the surveyed individuals (49%) said they had visited nonprofit websites and did such things as search for information about a specific cause and look for a place to volunteer. More than 75% who said they visited nonprofit websites said they engaged in some further activity while there. When it comes to what makes up a good nonprofit website, individuals indicated that the top five characteristics were (a) significant content about the nonprofit's cause, (b) information about how donations are spent, (c) ease of use, (d) information about how to get involved, and (e) information about how to become a member. According to the study, nonprofit websites that are engaging are those that give supporters ways to get involved (volunteer, donate, advocate) and good information about the nonprofit's cause and that change their content frequently. Nonprofits can increase the number of website visits by advertising on other organizations' websites via Internet ads, banner ads, and multimedia ads.

Other Tools. Nonprofits might want to use other sorts of promotional tools as well. These include event promotion, joint promotion, and point-of-purchase communications, among others.

Event promotion is publicizing an offer that is tied to a meaningful athletic, entertainment, cultural, social, or other type of high-interest public activity. By publicizing the event and inviting the media to cover it, the nonprofit turns it into a promotional tool. For example, a local nonprofit may sponsor a well-publicized chili cook-off and invite all local religious leaders to cook a pot of chili. Congregations can be encouraged to attend and "vote" for their favorite pot of chili by putting a dollar in a box. The winner could receive some small prize, such as a trophy that spends the year in the winner's parish, and the money raised may go to a local food bank or other nonprofit. Event marketing is a way to break through the myriad communications that people face every day and may be an effective way to contact hard-to-reach publics.

Joint promotion is any promotion activity undertaken by two or more organizations jointly, for example an arrangement whereby people may earn tokens from local blood banks in order to get a free T-shirt from a local clothing store. It is a method of leveraging marketing efforts: The local blood bank would not have to do all the promotion; it would receive some help from the local clothing store. Joint promotions, sometimes called cross promotions, can be beneficial to nonprofits that join forces with other trustworthy organizations with similar values and target publics. Signs, posters, and flyers promoting both organizations can be posted or distributed. Also, both organizations may print joint promotional messages on their receipts or share inexpensive ads in local shopping papers or at either nonprofit's events. Other suggestions can be found at www.sayitbetter.com/articles/sel_attract_custs.html.

Point-of-purchase (POP) promotion is used to attract target publics' attention to particular offers, provide information, affect perceptions, and ultimately influence shopping behavior. POP promotion is one of the marketer's last points of contact with target publics as they make decisions. It can be used by nonprofits that sell goods or services or have joint promotion or sponsorship relationships with other organizations. It includes signs, displays, and various in-store media displays, among other tools.

Integrated Marketing Communication

Although this section has to do with "promotion" of nonprofit organizations, marketing communication, in order to be effective, should be coordinated such that the organization engages in what is called **integrated marketing communication (IMC)**. IMC is defined by George and Michael Belch (2004) as a concept of marketing communications planning that recognizes the added value of a comprehensive plan that evaluates the strategic roles of a variety of communication disciplines and combines these disciplines to provide clarity, consistency, and maximum communications impact. For example, IMC may include advertising, direct response communication, sales promotion, public relations, and even personal persuasion. In other words, instead of independently developing an advertising campaign, a sales promotion activity, or a public relations plan, nonprofits should first set their communication objectives and strategy, decide which tasks they need to accomplish in order to reach their objectives, set a budget, and then choose the promotional tools that will best work together to achieve the nonprofits' objectives.

IMC is more than making sure the same message appears on print and broadcast ads as well as on public relations and sales promotion tools. It should specifically relate what is known about target publics to the promotional tools in such a way that every communication is consistent with one message and one strategy aimed at each target public. A nonprofit effectively implementing IMC might use newsletters, websites, brochures, speeches, broadcast or print advertisements, and sales promotions, each element of which consistently presents the same logo, color, message, visuals, and "feel." The actual words and visuals do not have to be identical, but the rule of thumb is that someone exposed to a marketing communication tool from a nonprofit should be able to tell that the communication came from that nonprofit even if the nonprofit's name were not immediately obvious.

PalmettoPride is a nonprofit, 501(c)(3) organization comprised of South Carolina state agencies, concerned citizens, corporate sponsors, and community and civic organizations. It focuses on four essential areas of concern—education, enforcement, awareness, and pickup—and has a stated goal of encouraging "behavioral change" in the state's citizens when it comes to litter. Its ultimate objective is to stop litter at its source: the people who do it. Public service announcements and news releases, along with educational programs and community outreach, are used to increase awareness of the problems surrounding litter. Furthermore, PalmettoPride engages in community outreach (e.g., Community Pride Grants), trash pickup programs (e.g., Prideways), litter enforcement (e.g., "Litter Busters" Toll-Free Hotline), education (e.g., "Litter Trashes Everyone" puppet show), and other programs, such as targeting commercial waste haulers. It has an interactive website (www.palmettopride.org/default.asp), which begins with a picture of a littered park; online visitors are asked to pick up a piece of litter and see what happens. Once the litter is picked up, the park becomes beautiful, the birds sing, butterflies flutter, and a squirrel happily shakes its tail while "50 Ways You Can Help Clean Up" scrolls over the picture. The website also has a media area, where visitors can see current public service announcements and read news releases. Also, visitors can visit the KidZone, meet Louie the Lion, find more information, and even download brochures, handouts, and other printed materials.

Prices in Nonprofit Organizations

When it comes to nonprofits, price is a more complex subject than it is for most for-profits. The role of pricing in the for-profit sector is typically fairly clear: to recover all or most costs of an offer and enable the firm to make a profit. For nonprofit organizations, however, the idea of charging or increasing a monetary price for one or more offers may seem inappropriate. By definition, nonprofits have nonfinancial objectives rather than financial ones and exist to fulfill a mission that involves a charitable, educational, scientific, or literary purpose recognized by federal law. They are prohibited from redistributing profits from operations or other sources to board members or trustees. Managers earn a salary, of course, an expense to the organization, but they do not receive profit distributions. In addition, nonprofits can gather donations and win grants, and some may be eligible to receive federal or state tax monies.

Given nonprofits' nonfinancial objectives, IRS restrictions, and reliance on the goodness of donors, foundations, and federal and state legislatures, there are many who believe they should neither engage in seeking earned income by imposing monetary prices for offers that have traditionally been free nor increase prices for offers already offered for money. However, under state and federal tax laws, nonprofits may take in more money than they spend and can even earn a surplus revenues as long as they are organized and operated for a recognized purpose and have secured the proper tax exemptions.

Nonprofits' charging money for their offers is not a completely new situation, but monetary prices have traditionally hidden behind terms such as fees, rates, tuition, tolls, fares, and charges. What is new is the number of nonprofits that believe they have no choice but to find sources of earned income by imposing monetary charges for offers they previously offered for free. Others are faced with the need to increase the amounts for offers that have traditionally been offered for a nominal fee. A problem that often arises in these situations is that nonprofit managers often have little or no experience in pricing.

Monetary Prices

When a nonprofit makes a decision to charge some monetary price for one or more of its offers, three issues should be considered. The first, of course, is how much revenue monetary prices will bring in. The nonprofit also needs to consider which target publics will pay the price and which programs will carry a monetary price. When it comes to a question of which programs will carry a monetary price, nonprofits can choose to impose a price for any of their offers—core, supplementary, or resource-attraction. Charging a price for a core offer carries the most risk for a nonprofit and is most likely to cause problems and perhaps negative publicity if the price is considered inappropriate or excessive. This is because of the so-called rationing effect of price: Charging for offers tends to reduce the number of people who can or will buy them. If reducing the number of people who are served by a nonprofit goes against its mission, the nonprofit really must find other ways to fund its offers, perhaps with donations, grants, or tax monies.

In other words, there are situations in which it makes perfect sense for nonprofits to charge a monetary price for an offer, and there are situations in which nonprofits should not charge a monetary price. These situations are summarized in Exhibit 6.6 and are discussed in the next two sections.

❖ **Exhibit 6.6**   Why to Charge and When Not to Charge Monetary Prices

---

Reasons to charge monetary prices:

To encourage awareness of offer value.
To discourage overuse of an offer.
To encourage feelings of ownership or commitment.
To preserve users' dignity.
To motivate a customer orientation by management and staff.
To measure output.

When not to charge monetary prices:

When imposing or raising prices is likely to threaten the mission.
When offers are meant to benefit the general public.
When offers cannot be withheld from individuals who refuse to pay for them.
When prospective customers are unable to pay.
When collection costs are excessive relative to revenue generated.

When to charge monetary prices. Sometimes it makes sense for a nonprofit to charge monetary prices for its offers. The rule of thumb is that imposing or raising fees for offers must be a mission-enhancing step in order to be acceptable to the nonprofit's target publics. Among reasons to charge monetary prices are the following:

• To encourage awareness of offer value. Research has shown that people value offers more if some sort of monetary payment is required. In an example from India, when condoms were offered free at local drugstores, they tended to be ignored. As it turned out, many believed that the free condoms must be substandard in some way, and they did not want to risk using them. When a small price was imposed on the condoms, they were easily sold. In other research, Yoken and Berman (1984) found that patients who expected to receive psychotherapy for free expected to get less out of the experience than did patients who were told there would be a fee for the service. Finally, Kotler, Roberto, and Lee (2002) found that once a hospital in South America decided to charge a fee for patient care, the number of patients increased markedly. When those same patients were offered free health care at the same hospital, they tended to avoid the hospital. Therefore, although in general, imposing prices on offers tends to decrease demand for them (if there is elasticity of demand), in some cases, perhaps counterintuitively, the reverse is true: Higher prices may lead to a general perception of higher quality and an increase in use of an offer.

• To discourage overuse of an offer. In some cases, the supply of free offers may be very quickly exhausted, at least partly by individuals who may not really need them. If that happens, the danger is that people who truly need those offers may not be able to get them. In addition, availability of free offers may result in what is called a "moral hazard," which means that target publics that know that an offer is free may, with time, lose their motivation to take care of themselves. Therefore, given that monetary prices tend to ration an offer among target publics, a nonprofit may feel it needs to impose a monetary price to limit the number of people that use it. For example, most health insurance carries some level of deductible that must be met before the insurance kicks in. Furthermore, even after the initial deductible has been met, clients often have to pay a percentage of the cost of any doctor visits, tests, and procedures. Requiring these payments accomplishes two outcomes. First, insurers are able to keep insurance premiums lower. Second, because doctor visits, tests, and procedures are expensive, imposing (or raising) very low prices may motivate potential users to think about the necessity of that care and reduce the number of unnecessary health care visits. If people make fewer unnecessary visits, patients who are truly ill will have more opportunity to receive needed health care.

- To encourage feelings of ownership or commitment. The Boys and Girls Clubs of America charge a small fee for membership in a child's local club. This fee, though small ($5), seems to help the children feel they have an investment in the club—that they deserve to be there. However, because nonprofits are concerned about not only how many people they serve but also who those people are, if a neighborhood child could not afford the fee, the Boys and Girls Clubs would most likely waive it. Other organizations may choose to impose some type of sliding fee structure. Habitat for Humanity is another organization that charges monetary fees in order to encourage a sense of ownership; it requires a monetary contribution as well as sweat equity from the future owners of the houses it builds. Finally, medical treatment programs may charge fees in order to increase the likelihood that patients will feel more committed to a program and continue with it.

- To preserve users' dignity. A nonprofit may consider imposing prices if doing so will help its target publics to maintain their dignity. According to Oster, Gray, and Weinberg (2004), when it comes to users who are "newly needy," it seems that paying a small fee is preferable to paying no fee at all.

- To motivate a customer orientation by management and staff. Sometimes, if a nonprofit does not charge any monetary price for its offers, management and staff may come over time to act as if zero fees equal zero value. Charging or raising monetary prices for a nonprofit's offers may not only cause target publics to value the offer more but may also cause management and staff to become more attentive to those publics' needs.

To measure output. If prices are charged for services, then when services are purchased, revenues will be generated. Revenues can be measured easily. **When not to charge monetary prices.** Sometimes situations demand that nonprofits not charge monetary prices for their offers. For example, a nonprofit should not charge a monetary price for one of its offers in the following circumstances:

- When imposing or raising prices is likely to threaten the mission. Even in situations in which nonprofits could impose prices and people would pay them, nonprofits should cautiously consider whether doing so involves pricing core offers. It is generally safer to price supplemental or resource-attraction offers. If research shows that imposing prices will send the wrong message to existing and potential target publics or if imposing prices would reduce the number of individuals who would be able to use the organization's core offers, then the nonprofit should consider other options, such as grants or membership programs.

- When offers are meant to benefit the general public. There are situations in which a nonprofit's withholding its offers from individuals who did not wish to pay for them would put the general public at risk. Examples of such offers include police and fire protection. Withholding such protection from individuals who choose not to pay for them would ultimately be detrimental to people living nearby who would choose to pay. For instance, if police opted not to offer protection to citizens who do not want to pay for that protection, then criminals would remain at large to assault or injure other citizens who would pay. Similarly, fires need to be put out wherever they occur in order to protect the property of individuals who are willing to pay for fire service. Because these sorts of services are intended to protect everyone, they tend to be funded via taxation.

- When offers cannot be withheld from individuals who refuse to pay for them. In some situations, offers simply cannot be withheld from some people and not others; examples include national defense and weather information. Sending soldiers to fight for the continuance of a country's way of life cannot be done for some citizens but not others. Nor can tornado sirens be targeted only to weather information "subscribers." Again, funding for these types of offers tends to come from taxes.

- When prospective customers are unable to pay. A country's citizens may believe that certain offers should be available even if the people who will benefit cannot pay for them. Some countries provide free medical care. Some believe that even the poor should have access to legal aid, job counseling, emergency health care, and food.

- When collection costs are excessive relative to revenue generated. In some situations, charging monetary prices for use of an offer makes no practical sense. Theoretically, at least, monetary prices for some offers could be imposed only on people who use an offer; for example, states could charge road or bridge tolls so that only people who use the bridges would have to pay for them. However, if the cost of collecting tolls is high—as it would be if people had to staff monitoring sites on those roads and bridges—and the prices charged were low, then monitoring and collecting would likely cost more than the tolls would bring in. Thus, charging such fees would make no sense at all. Charging monetary prices is also not practicable when it comes to nonprofits that advocate behavior changes such as stopping smoking but offer no particular services or programs that could carry a monetary price.

Pricing Objectives

If a nonprofit decides to set monetary prices on one or more of its offers, it should begin by deciding what it wants to achieve with those prices. **Price objectives** are measurable performance levels that an organization uses prices to accomplish. For example, nonprofits may wish to impose prices in order to raise revenue, to control demand for their services, or to become more consistent with similar nonprofits. Often, one organization will end up with several offers that have very different price objectives. Furthermore, monetary objectives may change over the life of an offer or with different target publics. Each broad pricing objective is discussed next.

Revenue-Oriented Objectives. It sometimes surprises people to find out that nonprofits may want to price in order to increase revenues, but nonprofits can in fact use **revenue-oriented pricing objectives** and set prices in order to increase profits or recover some or all the costs of providing their offers.

- Profit-seeking objectives. Although profit seeking is more common in for-profits, nonprofits may choose to set prices in order to earn a profit. There are two sorts of profit-seeking objectives. One of these is surplus maximization, in which profits earned by setting a high price for an event, program, or service may be used to fund other new or existing offers of the nonprofit. Or a nonprofit may have as a goal to set up or add to an endowment. Nonprofits like universities, hospitals, and churches that have high overhead (e.g., employees and buildings) may even be said to have a moral mandate to establish or increase an endowment in order to ensure continued operation, even in poor economies. Benefit dinners for which the price per person is much higher than the actual cost of the meal are an example of pricing to achieve a healthy surplus. Instead of surplus maximization, nonprofits may choose to simply try to achieve an acceptable profit by setting fairly high but not extreme prices. This is often the case when a nonprofit prices items in a gift or museum shop. The USPS, for example, strives to achieve an acceptable profit when it sells first-day covers to stamp collectors, and the United Nations Children's Fund has the same goal when it prices its annual Christmas cards.

- Cost-recovery objectives. Another type of revenue-oriented pricing objective is cost recovery. A nonprofit may wish to price on offer so that it can just recover overhead costs involved in running the organization. Or it may price so that an offer essentially pays for itself. Finally, it may price so that the cost of providing the offer to one additional user is covered (incremental cost recovery).

Operations-Oriented Objectives. Some nonprofits have offers that are perishable. Perishability refers to services. Because services are produced and consumed simultaneously and cannot be stored for future use, we consider them to be perishable. For example, if a patient fails to keep an appointment for health care services at a nonprofit clinic, that health care service, which could have been provided to the patient, is lost. Some nonprofits have limited space. They may use **operations-oriented pricing objectives** to fix these problems. In addition, some nonprofits have missions that impel them to work to get people to stop doing things they want to do. Many times, those nonprofits must work to decrease the number of people engaging in those behaviors.

- Matching supply and demand objectives. If a nonprofit offers a service or program that is perishable or that traditionally has peak and off-peak periods, it runs the risk of having too few people attending some programs or performances and too many people trying to attend at other times. Having too few or too many people partaking of an offer may cause a nonprofit to appear ineffective or inefficient to its target publics, including potential donors or other supporters. Nonprofits in such situations may wish to price so as to "smooth" demand. Museum restaurants, for example, may offer "value pricing" on Mondays through Wednesdays or in the early evening to encourage patrons to dine when the restaurant is not full. Other examples are nonprofit recreation centers and museums that increase prices during high-peak times and reduce prices during off-peak times in order to better match the supply to the demand.

• Market disincentivization objectives. Alternatively, a nonprofit may wish or need (because of its mission) to discourage individuals from using an offer. In many crowded cities in the United States, people are discouraged from driving their own cars to work by fines for single-occupancy cars traveling in the fast-moving high-occupancy vehicle lanes. Another example is tolls to use bridges or roads that are heavily traveled. The tolls compel drivers to use other routes to or from work if they want to avoid the toll and the inevitable delay at the toll booth. Nonprofits that strive to end smoking or reduce drinking may work to support additional taxes on cigarettes and alcohol because such taxes effectively raise the costs of using those items.

Patronage-Oriented Objectives. Some nonprofits simply do not or cannot have problems with the number of people that can use their services. In fact, they may believe that the more users, the better and that their mission demands increasing the size of their target publics. In this case, they may wish to set prices with **patronage-oriented pricing objectives** in mind.

• Market size maximization objectives. Nonprofit environmental organizations such as the Sierra Club and the World Wildlife Fund (WWF) may feel that their missions can best be accomplished by maximizing their membership rather than their profit. One way to do that is to have low membership fees. Having large memberships will likely allow them to wield more weight in their lobbying activities than having more money would. The Sierra Club, for example, could probably charge more for membership than it currently does, but doing so would likely reduce its 700,000-strong ranks. Of course, maximizing market size is not an option for every nonprofit because there is likely to be a trade-off between membership clout and potential customer-derived revenues. On the other hand, a nonprofit may choose to charge relatively low prices for a program or performance in hopes that people who attend those offers may eventually become more involved or become donors. Other examples of nonprofits that may wish to set prices in order to increase market size are public libraries or museums that are rarely crowded. Sometimes having a full house will result in increased visibility that can bring the nonprofit good publicity. However, nonprofits must keep in mind that their target publics do not necessarily prefer busy or large crowds. When it comes to the best price for maximizing a nonprofit's customers, it is important to understand that the best price may or may not be a zero price. Indeed, this point was made in the subsection "To encourage awareness of offer value" under "When to charge monetary prices."

- Social equity objectives. Some nonprofits wish to price such that they contribute to social equity. In order to do that, they may wish to engage in price discrimination, which is legal as long as the organization has a reason for charging different prices to different individuals and that reason is established before they begin charging different prices. Even in the for-profit arena, some organizations, such as movie theaters and restaurants, charge different prices to senior citizens, middle-aged adults, students, and children. Pricing to support social equity, then, might involve charging higher prices to the wealthy and charging much lower fees to low-income individuals. Another strategy that would help achieve social equity is to let members choose the level of membership they wish. The WWF, for example, allows members to choose the amount they pay for membership, with suggested amounts ranging from $15 to $250 and including an "other" category, which could be any dollar amount.

Setting Prices

Once the nonprofit has decided on its pricing objectives—what it wants pricing to accomplish for the organization—then it has to decide on exactly what the price will be. A mistake made by many nonprofits (as well as for-profits) is to try to institute what is called "cost-plus" pricing. As its name implies, this method begins with the costs of providing an offer and then adds a suitable markup to those costs to arrive at a price. There are several difficulties with such pricing, including the fact that it is often difficult to determine just what should be included in figuring the costs to provide a particular offer direct program costs? shared overhead costs? It may help nonprofit marketing managers to know that, in reality, the cost of an offer may end up having very little to do with its asking price. As shown in Exhibit 6.7, when it comes to arriving at a price for an offer, it may help to consider three important aspects of price, including not only costs to be recovered but market demand and the competition.

In Exhibit 6.7, one can see that costs set what might be called the "**floor price**" of an offer—the lowest price an organization could ask that would allow it to recover the costs of producing an offer. At the top of the figure is the highest price an organization could ask for an offer—the "**ceiling price**," which reflects what the market is willing and able to pay for an offer and is determined through research about a nonprofit's target publics. The third component of this three-step price consideration model is to determine what competitors charge for their offers. Knowing what competitors charge can help a nonprofit determine where, within the range between the floor and ceiling prices, the actual price should be set. Now, if for-profits find that the ceiling price is actually lower than the floor price, they would most likely opt not to continue with that offer. Nonprofits, however, often have missions that result in trying to get target publics to do things they may not really want to do, such as exercise, donate money, or volunteer, or to stop doing things they want to do, including smoking, eating too much, or drinking too much. Therefore, when it comes to nonprofits, it would not be surprising if research found that the ceiling price for their target publics was, in fact, lower than the floor price. If that were the case, but a nonprofit still wanted to pursue an offer, it could do several things, including competing for grants or donations to

❖ **Exhibit 6.7** Relationship of Costs, Competition, and the Market to Actual Price

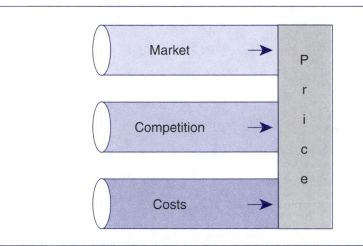

cover or partially cover the costs of providing the offer. The idea is to try to lower the floor price until it becomes lower than the ceiling price. For example, if a nonprofit clinic sought to provide vaccinations to impoverished children, the ceiling price is near zero because the children and their parents cannot afford to pay for this health care. However, the floor price may be relatively high because of the cost of the medicine, health care staff, and facilities. Therefore, in order to provide the service to the target public, the ceiling price must be lower than the floor price. In these cases, funding must be provided by another source, such as government grants or charitable giving.

Oster, Gray, and Weinberg (2004) have suggested some questions for nonprofits to consider when making pricing decisions. Some of those questions (some slightly edited) appear in Exhibit 6.8 and are discussed below.

- What kind of offer is being priced? Target publics are likely to be more forgiving of prices for supplementary or resource-attraction offers than for core offers. (See Chapter 5 for a discussion of the different kinds of offers.) Therefore, it is generally thought that whereas supplementary or resource-attraction offers may be priced not only to cover their own costs but also to contribute to overhead costs of the nonprofit, core offers should either be offered free, with their costs covered by other offers, or be offered for very nominal fees. If a nonprofit chooses to price supplementary offers (e.g., parking or child care), it should carefully consider the effect of doing so on use of its core offers by its target publics. If pricing supplementary offers leads to reduced use of the nonprofit's core offers, then the nonprofit may want to consider funding supplementary offers via grants or donated resources.

- How will the price affect competitive position? Pricing products may result in an altered competitive position in that an offer that was very competitive at a zero price may become more or less competitive once a price is applied.

❖ **Exhibit 6.8** Questions to Guide Nonprofits in Pricing Their Offers

- What kind of offer is being priced?

- How will the price affect competitive position?

- How will the price affect the bottom line?

- How will the price affect the organization's mission?

- How will the price affect other funding alternatives?

- What information will the price convey about the organization and its offers?

- To what offers does a membership fee entitle members?

- How will the price affect the bottom line? Although it may be exciting to contemplate the increase in money that may come into the nonprofit by charging x dollars for some offers, it may be that the nonprofit will actually end up with less money than before. This is especially true when the nonprofit offers have elastic demand, meaning that increasing prices often results in less demand for an offer. Furthermore, if the nonprofit does end up with more money in the till, donors or funding agencies may very well decide that if it is asking prices for its offers, it no longer needs their support.

- How will the price affect the organization's mission? Nonprofits have to carefully consider the effect that pricing their offers will have on achieving their mission. Pricing offers will likely exclude some current or potential target publics. If those publics are closely aligned with a nonprofit's mission or if current funding agencies intended the nonprofit's funds to be used by a particular target public, then pricing should not be considered. Alternatively, a nonprofit may consider engaging in price discrimination (discussed in "Social Equity Objectives, under "Patronage-Oriented Objectives," above) to ensure that important target publics are served.

- How will the price affect other funding alternatives? Foundations providing grants to a particular nonprofit may encourage or discourage charging prices for particular offers aimed at particular target segments. For example, some foundation grants are intended to fund a nonprofit's offers so that they can be offered free, but others may be intended to fund particular offers only partially, with the nonprofit charging monetary prices. Clearly then, if a nonprofit has applied or is applying for grants to fund particular offers, it needs to pay close attention to any grantor expectations.

- What information will the price convey about an organization and its offers? In the for-profit sector, price is often used to reflect the quality of an offer, and there is no reason to think this is not the case for nonprofits as well. However, while pricing offers may bring in needed revenues for nonprofits, it also may send the wrong message about them. Nonprofits need to be judicious when setting prices so that those prices will not send the wrong message about what a nonprofit stands for and who it serves.

- To what offers does a membership fee entitle members? The question here has to do with the appropriateness of setting prices for membership (a resource-attraction offer) and asking additional prices for supplementary or core offers. It is fairly common for nonprofits such as WWF to have membership programs that include a regular newsletter as well as access to the nonprofit's interactive website. Some also offer premiums such as stuffed toys, hats, umbrellas. and the like for particular amounts paid. Often, as in the case of the American Marketing Association, benefits of membership include reduced prices on journals, books, and conferences. The rule of thumb here is that the more similar a nonprofit's target publics, the easier it is to charge fairly large membership fees that include access to many other offers. More diverse target publics are likely to prefer a smaller membership fee with other offers available on an à la carte basis.

Nonmonetary Prices of Nonprofit Offers

In addition to monetary prices, marketers need to be acutely aware of so-called nonmonetary prices. **Nonmonetary prices**, also referred to as **social prices**, are aspects of offers that a nonprofit's target publics may take into consideration when presented with a marketing offer. Some of these nonmonetary prices are obvious, but some are very difficult to ascertain. What's more, it is unlikely that all individuals within a target public will consider the same aspects, and it is likely that, even if they do consider the same aspects, they will be affected by them in different ways. Still, it behooves a nonprofit to consider all possible costs of an offer. Exhibit 6.9 depicts six types of these nonmonetary costs for consideration.

Time Costs. If target publics are asked to drive a long distance to use an offer or to volunteer, or if using an offer or volunteering takes a long time, time costs might be a reason they do not participate. Further, individuals may believe that an offer (say a program) does not last long enough to be worth the investment of their time. When it comes to time, it seems that the majority of people feel they do not have enough of it. Target publics are likely to have family, work, or personal responsibilities that leave them with little discretionary time. To give that "left over" time to any nonprofit takes a real commitment. If a nonprofit's publics are faced with time barriers related to a nonprofit's offer, the nonprofit can take a number of steps. It could try to decrease the time necessary to use an offer or to engage in an advocated behavior. If the problem lies in the length of time spent traveling to a nonprofit, the nonprofit may actually consider changing its location (if many people have this barrier). If target publics routinely have to wait for long periods in order to receive a nonprofit offer, a nonprofit may be able to reduce the waiting period by hiring more staff or attracting more

❖ **Exhibit 6.9** Six Types of Nonmonetary Costs of Nonprofit Offers

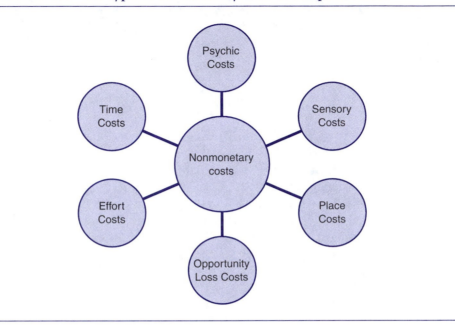

volunteers. When it comes to diet and exercise, many people complain that it takes too long to exercise and that they do not have time to do so during the workweek. A nonprofit could reduce the number of times that someone needs to exercise from daily to three or four times a week. It could reduce the duration of the exercise session from an hour to 30 minutes per day. Indeed, recently, we have seen 30-minute sessions broken up into three 10-minute segments throughout the day. The nonprofit could even encourage people to park farther from their place of work in order to have a 10-minute walk to and from the car and to walk up and down stairs during the day to add another 10-minute exercise segment. Such flexibility and such a needs-centered orientation may be received warmly.

Sensory Costs. Sometimes a nonprofit's offers are unpleasant to one or more of the five senses (seeing, hearing, tasting, touching, and smelling). Nonprofits have to find ways to lesson the negative impact of sensory costs so that these costs will not create a barrier to people's using the offers. For example, a nonprofit dental clinic may be associated with pain for some people in the target market. Therefore, the clinic will have to communicate to its target market that it focuses on gentle care.

Effort Costs. Some nonprofit offers may involve a lot of physical or mental effort to use. If possible, the nonprofit may choose to reduce the effort required, either objectively or subjectively. Exercising with music, for example, may seem far less of an effort than marching up and down stairs at work or using a treadmill in a quiet room. If the effort cannot be eliminated or significantly reduced, then the nonprofit may need to emphasize costs (monetary and nonmonetary) of *not* adopting behavior. For instance, stopping smoking takes quite a lot of mental effort and entails some uncomfortable physical effects. In addition to suggesting products that may help reduce those physical effects, a nonprofit may want to emphasize the risks (costs) of continuing to smoke, including heart problems, asthma, emphysema, lung cancer, and the like.

Psychic Costs. At times, nonprofit offers may carry with them certain psychological costs. These include feelings of discomfort, inferiority, social disapproval from others, or even fear. For example, teens may avoid going to a free clinic advocated by a Council on Teen Pregnancy Prevention to be tested for sexually transmitted infections because they are afraid of what the tests will show. Or they may be concerned that people from their school or church might see them and express social disapproval. Nonprofit marketers may try to emphasize the benefits of being tested and finding an infection early or to stress that people know that going to a free clinic does not necessarily imply sexual behavior at all. Potential volunteers with Local Friends of Guardian ad Litem groups may fear physical harm if they volunteer to follow a child through a legal case involving the child's parents or guardians. In this case, the nonprofit may be able to appeal to volunteers on the basis of morality. Alternatively, for some offers, a nonprofit may be able to work with legislatures to impose some legal mandate or introduce some economic incentive to engage in an advocated behavior.

Place Costs. For any number of reasons, it is possible that a place cost might arise due to the location of a nonprofit or its offers. If Boys and Girls Clubs were located not in the inner city but out in the suburbs, many of the Clubs' target publics would not be able to attend. The organization might consider including supplementary offers (bus rides to the club), or it may choose to locate closer to the children it seeks to serve.

Opportunity Loss Costs. An important nonmonetary cost has to do with target publics' making choices between nonprofit offers and other opportunities in their lives. If someone chooses to donate a sum of money to one nonprofit, then that money cannot be given to another. Someone who decides to attend a symphonic performance could certainly do other things instead. To address this sort of cost, a marketer may consider emphasizing one or more benefits of attending the symphony. For example, an individual may be able to see friends or network with others.

Managerial Issues

The following issues are relevant for nonprofit managers:

   1. **Promotion, price, and the marketing mix.** In Chapter 5, two marketing mix variables were addressed: product and place. Here, the two other controllable variables of the marketing mix were addressed: promotion and price. Although some nonprofit managers may feel uncomfortable about these issues, they are usually just as important to nonprofits as they are to for-profits. In addition, the use of promotion and

price by nonprofits will likely be different enough from their use in for-profits that it behooves a nonprofit's manager, director, and even board to address these topics and set parameters for their use.

2. **What promotion is.** People, sometimes even nonprofit managers, sometimes refer to promotion as marketing, selling, advertising, or even shopping, but promotion is nothing more or less than how the organization communicates with its target publics.

3. **Promotional tools.** Promotional tools range from advertising, public service advertising, sales promotions, publicity and public relations, direct marketing, websites and Internet marketing, and other tools, such as sponsorships and event marketing.

4. **Integrated marketing communication.** In the past 20 years, all sorts of companies and many nonprofit organizations have come to realize the importance of strategically planning the promotional mix so that every type of marketing communication that comes from the organization is clear and consistent and lends itself to maximum communications impact.

5. **Different kinds of prices.** It is likely that any particular nonprofit manager will not have the "luxury" of working only with objective, monetary prices. Instead, most nonprofits must consider both monetary and nonmonetary prices and costs. For instance, even when a nonprofit gives away its offers for free, it still has to address various social prices: time costs, psychic and sensory costs, place costs, costs of opportunity loss, and effort costs.

Summary

The nonprofit marketing issues presented in this chapter are summarized here according to the chapter learning objectives they meet.

Understand where promotion and price fit into the marketing mix. Whereas in Chapter 5 we addressed product and place, in this chapter we looked at the two other controllable variables that should be considered, promotion and price. Some nonprofits have some trepidation about engaging in promotion activities or raising monetary prices, and this attitude often seems to result from a basic misunderstanding of these two marketing mix variables.

Understand the role that promotion plays in customer-oriented nonprofits. Promotion refers to a nonprofit's communications to various publics. Through promotion, a nonprofit communicates the mission and programs of the organization.

Explain the various promotion objectives. Most basically, organizations may use promotional activities to inform, persuade, or remind target publics of their various offers. Informing target publics about offers may include developing primary demand, which is demand for a product class rather than a specific offer. When it come to persuasion, marketers usually find themselves trying to develop selective demand for their particular offers. Reminding is most likely associated with the long-standing offers of a nonprofit.

Identify the different sorts of promotional tools. Promotional tools include advertising, public service advertising, sales promotions, publicity and public relations, direct marketing, websites and Internet marketing, and other tools, such as sponsorships, event marketing, and POP marketing.

Understand promotional mix and IMC as they relate to nonprofits. IMC uses the various tools of the promotional mix to reach target publics with comprehensive plans. The tools begin with evaluation of the strategic roles of a variety of communications disciplines and then combine these disciplines to provide clarity, consistency, and maximum communications impact. The point is that every piece of marketing communication that comes from a nonprofit should be clear and fit with every other piece such that a consistent message reaches a nonprofit's target publics.

Understand the complexity of prices in nonprofits. Price is a significantly more complex subject for nonprofits than it is for most for-profits. Whereas the role of pricing in the for-profit sector is typically fairly clear—to recover all or most costs of an offer and enable the firm to make a profit—the case of nonprofits is different. The idea of charging or increasing a monetary price for one or more offers may seem inappropriate to nonprofits or their publics because, by definition, nonprofits have nonfinancial objectives rather than financial ones and exist to fulfill a mission that involves a charitable, educational, scientific, or literary purpose recognized by law. Legally, they may expand their offers or lower prices, but they must abide by certain constraints. In addition, nonprofits can gather donations, win grants, and some may be eligible to receive federal or state tax monies. Given nonprofits' nonfinancial objectives, IRS restrictions, and reliance on the goodness of donors, foundations, and federal or state legislatures, many people believe that nonprofits should not seek earned income by imposing monetary prices for offers that have traditionally been free and should not increase prices already established. However, under state and federal tax laws, nonprofits may take in more money than they spend and may even earn a profit as long as they are organized and operated for a recognized purpose and have secured the proper tax exemptions.

Understand the role of monetary prices in nonprofits and when and when not to charge them. Sometimes it makes sense for a nonprofit to charge monetary prices for its offers, and sometimes it does not. Generally speaking, imposing or raising fees for offers must be a mission-enhancing exercise in order to be acceptable to the nonprofit's target publics. A nonprofit should charge prices in order to encourage awareness of offer value, discourage overuse of an offer, encourage feelings of ownership or commitment, preserve users' dignity, motivate a customer orientation by management and staff, and measure output. One should not charge or raise prices if doing so is likely to threaten the mission, if offers are meant to benefit the general public, if offers cannot be withheld from individuals who refuse to pay for them, if prospective customers are unable to pay, or if collection costs are excessive relative to revenue generated.

Understand the various pricing objectives. If a nonprofit decides to set monetary prices on one or more of its offers, it should begin by deciding what it wants to achieve with those prices. Price objectives are measurable performance levels that an organization is trying to accomplish with its prices. Often one organization will end up with several offers, each having very different price objectives. Furthermore, monetary objectives may change over the life of an offer or with different target publics. Pricing objectives may pertain to revenue, operations, or patronage.

Understand how nonprofits might consider setting monetary prices. Once a nonprofit has decided on its pricing objectives—what it wants pricing to accomplish for the organization—then it has to decide exactly what the price will be. Rather than focusing too narrowly on costs and which costs should or should not be included when figuring prices, marketing managers should remember that the cost of an offer may end up having very little to do with its asking price. A helpful approach is to think of costs as setting the floor price of an offer and to think of demand as setting the ceiling price. The competition helps a nonprofit decide whether it wants to set prices near the top of the price range, in the middle, or at the bottom. In addition, the nonprofit marketer can use a systematic series of questions to arrive at the best price for an offer.

Identify nonmonetary prices. Not only may nonprofits set monetary prices for offers. They also must consider nonmonetary costs incurred by target publics. One might mistakenly focus on the monetary value given by a donor and not realize that there may be other costs to donating that have little to do with money, including time, effort, place, and opportunity costs and sensory and psychic costs. Often these costs will not be obvious to nonprofit marketers, and so they must engage in research to identify and understand them for each target segment and offer.

Glossary

Ceiling price. Highest price an organization could ask for an offer.

Communication mix. See *promotional mix*.

Communication process. Establishing commonness or understanding between a sender and a receiver.

Direct marketing. Marketing messages a nonprofit sends to specific individuals from whom it seeks a response such as making a donation or completing a survey.

Error of commission. Saying or doing something wrong or that is perceived as being inappropriate.

Error of omission. Minimal marketing; remaining silent or inactive, not reaching one's target publics, and therefore wasting donations, grants, or tax monies.

Event promotion. Publicizing a nonprofit's offer that is tied to a meaningful athletic, entertainment, cultural, social, or other type of high-interest public activity.

Floor price. The lowest price an organization could ask that would allow it to recover the costs of producing an offer.

Institutional advertising. Advertising that presents a message on behalf of a nonprofit organization as a whole or promotes a concept, idea, or philosophy.

Integrated marketing communication (IMC). A concept of marketing communications planning that recognizes the added value of a comprehensive plan that evaluates the strategic roles of a variety of communication disciplines and combines these disciplines to provide clarity, consistency, and maximum communications impact.

Joint promotion. Any promotion activity undertaken by two or more organizations together.

Marketing communication. See *promotion*.

Nonmonetary prices (social prices). Aspects of offers that a nonprofit's target publics may take into consideration when presented with a marketing offer.

Operations-oriented pricing objectives. Pricing used by nonprofits with perishable offers, limited space, or a mission to stop a particular behavior (e.g., smoking) when they price in order to match supply with demand or to encourage target publics not to engage in the behavior.

Paid advertising. Any paid form of mass, impersonal presentation of an offer by an identified sponsor via a formal communication medium.

Patronage-oriented pricing objectives. Pricing so as to encourage as many users as possible.

Personal persuasion, or person-to-person communication. A nonprofit "seller's" conversation with one or more prospective target publics encouraging them to use the nonprofit's offers, donate, volunteer, or act on an idea.

Point-of-purchase (POP) promotion. Tool to attract target publics' attention to particular offers, provide information, affect perceptions, and ultimately influence shopping behavior.

Price. Monetary charges and nonmonetary costs incurred by target publics.

Price objectives. Measurable performance levels that an organization intends to accomplish with its prices.

Primary demand. Demand for an offer class rather than for a particular offer.

Product advertising. A message to promote a nonprofit offer, including the offer of membership.

Promotion. Any activity of an organization that intends to inform, persuade, or remind its target publics about the organization or its offers, when and where they are or will be available, and other pertinent information the target market may need in order to change its feelings, beliefs, or behavior; sometimes referred to as marketing communication.

Promotional mix (also known as communication mix). Advertising and public service announcements, sales promotions, publicity and public relations, personal persuasion, direct marketing, Internet marketing, and other tools.

Publicity. News stories about an organization or its offers that are carried by the media but not paid for by the organization or run under identified sponsorship.

Public relations (PR). Building good relations with a nonprofit's various publics by attaining favorable publicity, building up a good image, and handling or forestalling unfavorable rumors, stories, and events.

Public service advertisements (PSAs). Any form of advertising (any form of mass impersonal presentation of an offer by an identified sponsor via a formal communication medium) in which some part of the development, production, and/or distribution is free.

Revenue-oriented pricing objectives. Pricing offers so as to generate revenue; includes profit-seeking and cost-recovery subcategories.

Sales promotion. Any short-term incentive that is intended to result in target publics' buying more, buying now, or buying one nonprofit's offers instead of another organization's offers.

Secondary demand. Demand for a particular brand of offer rather than demand for an offer class in general.

❖

QUESTIONS FOR REVIEW

1. Define *promotion* and *price*.

2. What role does promotion play in customer-oriented nonprofits?

3. What are the various promotion objectives?

4. What is the promotional mix, and what are all the tools in the mix?

5. What is integrated marketing communication?

6. Why is pricing in nonprofits more complex than pricing in for-profits?

7. When should monetary prices be charged for offers of nonprofits?

8. When should monetary prices not be charged for offers of nonprofits?

9. What are the various pricing objectives?

10. How might nonprofits consider setting monetary prices; that is, what questions should be answered?

11. What are the various nonmonetary prices?

❖

QUESTIONS FOR DISCUSSION

1. What is the problem with someone's defining promotion as simply advertising? Selling? Marketing? Why is it important to know the correct definition of promotion?

2. What are the pros and cons of using promotion in nonprofits?

3. In what situations should nonprofits use each of the main promotion objectives?

4. How might a nonprofit combine promotional tools in order to effectively engage in integrated marketing communication?

5. What are some real-life examples of situations in which a monetary price should be charged for a nonprofit offer?

6. What are some real-life examples of situations in which a monetary price should not be charged for a nonprofit offer?

7. What are some real-life situations in which each of the main pricing objectives should be used?

8. What might be some nonmonetary prices for one or more real-life nonprofit offers?

❖

INTERNET EXERCISES

1. Look up the following Web addresses and develop a presentation illustrating the types of aggressive promotion that the following nonprofits engage in.

A. Progress for America, Inc., an organization that promotes nonpartisan, conservative policies that improve the quality of life for the American people: www.pfavoterfund.com

B. Riverkeeper, Inc., whose mission is to safeguard the ecological integrity of the Hudson River, its tributaries, and the watershed of New York City (protecting the city's drinking water supply) by tracking down and stopping polluters: www.riverkeeper.org/campaign.php/indian_point/we_are_doing/645

C. ArtsMarketing.org, a project of Arts and Business Council of Americans for the Arts. Arts and Business Council is the national headquarters of the Arts and Business Council Inc., Arts and Business Council of New York, and Business Volunteers for the Arts national affiliate network and operates the National Arts Marketing Project.

Next, using an Internet search engine, find at least three other organizations that use aggressive promotion and include these organizations and their tactics in your presentation. Be creative in your search, "aggressive nonprofit ads" or "aggressive nonprofit marketing."

2. Search online for examples of nonprofits that seem to be using revenue-, operations-, and patronage-oriented pricing objectives. Further, be sure to note the exact type of each objective, such as profit seeking or cost recovery, for revenue-oriented objectives.

3. Search online for examples of primary-demand and selective-demand promotions and prepare a short presentation about what you find.

4. Go to the Adopt-A-Minefield website (www.landmines.org.uk), choose one program explained there, and analyze the way it is promoted and priced.

❖

TEAM EXERCISES AND ROLE PLAYING

1. Say that you as a class are creative services personnel in a well-known promotion agency. Say a nonprofit organization asks your firm to develop an IMC program for a new offer it has developed. Form teams. Teams will compete to develop the most creative, cohesive, and consistent IMC program for that nonprofit. The class will vote on the best program.

2. In teams of two, complete a 4-column table that considers the nonmonetary prices that potential target publics of a nonprofit's offer may have to "pay" to use the offer. Select a nonprofit and select one of its offers. Then, for each of the various publics (input, internal, partner, consuming), give at least one example (internal publics = management, staff, board members) and then indicate what nonmonetary prices it may be likely to pay for that offer.

MINICASE: Working for the Director of State Parks—Part B

Students: Please review "Working for the Director of State Parks—Part A" in Chapter 5 before proceeding.

Working for the Director of State Parks was a big change for Nina Black. Right from college she had gone to work for a major aeronautical company. She had enjoyed her assignments, which involved her in several of the company's major government projects. Soon it became clear that she was on the fast track for advancement, but it was a career path that would require frequent transfers to other company locations. She loved her job, but not the moving. The job with the parks department sounded like it would be even more fun than working with airplane contracts, and she would finally be able to settle down in one place.

As soon as she started interacting with other state departments, Nina began to really wonder if anyone in government service understood marketing. They were all wonderful people, but they seemed to have very conservative and traditional perspectives. For example, although the world had changed dramatically, park offerings were pretty much the same as when she was a girl. Nina did have fond memories of her parents taking her to state parks for swimming, hikes, and picnics, but she did not think that would be very attractive to today's kids and their families. The steady decrease in state funding for parks seems to support her worry that perhaps the public viewed parks as old fashioned.

Since Nina had taken marketing classes in college, she knew that tastes change and that service providers had to constantly differentiate themselves and keep up with the times. She thought about what was different about peoples lives today compared to 20 years ago. She was particularly interested in what activities attract groups. Where did groups of kids go to play today, and what do they play. She asked herself the same question about tweens, teenagers, young adults, families and senior citizens. She thought about today's amusement parks, attractions, and the activities scheduled for visitors of popular resorts.

She wondered if state parks should rethink their offerings and become involved in more of today's leisure activities. She knew that people today did not hesitate to spend a lot for their fun, sports, hobbies, and entertainment, but strangely they complained about a two-dollar per car entrance fee at state parks.

When she casually asked the Parks Director if it might be possible to attract new visitors by putting in things like a mountain bike mogul racing track, or an area like a skate park for in-line and skateboarding, he wasn't very responsive. He did, however, ask her to look into some alternatives to bring new life to the park system. Nina knew a big career opportunity when it stared her in the face. If she handled this right, the park system could bring in considerably higher fees, and possibly even get involved in selling the equipment needed for these new activities. She was pretty sure that a successful transformation of the department's offerings could put her in line to be the next Parks Director.

Nina wisely decided that she had to research leisure and entertainment by population segment, and based on that would need to be really creative about what a park of the future could be.

Assignment for Part B:

As in Part A of this two-part case, you are Nina. For Part A, you went through the initial steps in both the strategic planning and the new offer creation processes. You segmented the market and analyzed buyer behavior and the consumer decision process for each segment. You probably realized that you would have to do this at least twice: once for the market of park service users and a second time for the separate market of potential charitable donors and grantors (governments or corporate and nonprofit foundations). By taking a rough first pass at considering the possible offering alternatives in Part A, you should now have the information necessary to confirm the target market segments, finalize the prices you will be charging, set donor dollar contribution targets, and actually create specific ads and other promotional elements consistent with an IMC program. The ads and other promotional elements should be clearly derived from the segment's behavior and decision process and should be doable considering your projected budget. You will probably need a separate campaign for each target segment (although some elements may be shared). Similarly, you need to show how dollar prices and donor targets are consistent with segment characteristics and will produce the desired results.

In the assignment for Part A, you were reminded to make sure that you could reasonably forecast that each of the offerings you design will "attract more revenue than it costs." A similar reminder is in order for Part B. You need to formally project specific park usage increases and donor dollar amount increases that each campaign will produce and show that the campaign costs are justified.

Be sure you understand that this assignment is *not* asking you to make up numbers based on some hypothetical promotional elements and campaigns. It is asking you to create actual ads, story boards, and so on, and then find their costs as a real-world marketer would. That will require some online research, media choices, and probably discussions with some ad agency and possibly PR people. You instructor will advise you if there are local alumni or other resources available. Although all these people can advise you in general terms, do not expect them to make strategic choices and estimates for you. That is your job.

This may seem like a difficult and involved assignment, but keep in mind that it is what nonprofit marketers do for a living. Most professionals would say that this type of applied assignment is very consistent with the whole point of studying nonprofit marketing. Through it, you will acquire the skill and confidence to properly apply business theory and the strategic planning process to reach organizational objectives and provide client-sector services that make a positive difference in people's lives.

Always remember that your organization's management and board will hold you personally accountable for achieving the results you forecast. There will be no "pointing fingers" at others if the campaign does not work. A marketer creating a strategic campaign takes responsibility for design and implementation. If the campaign is successful, the marketer can expect to receive credit for business wisdom, creative insight, and coordination skills in implementation and monitoring (i.e., adjusting the plan effectively as market realities shift). If the campaign fails to meet expectations, it reflects directly and negatively on the ability of the marketer. That is why it is so important that you clearly understand how the chapter topics you have studied thus far are applied in the real world.

The objective of this case is to create a campaign worthy of inclusion in your professional portfolio and one that clearly demonstrates your marketing knowledge and professional capability.

References and Bibliography

Andreasen, A. R. (1996). Profits for nonprofits: Find a corporate partner. *Harvard Business Review, 74*(6), 47–50, 55–59.

Ansari, A., Siddarth, S., & Weinberg, C. B. (1996). Pricing a bundle of products or services: The case of nonprofits. *Journal of Marketing Research, 33,* 86–93.

Arnold, M. J., & Tapp, S. R. (2003). Direct marketing in non-profit services: Investigating the case of the arts industry. *Journal of Services Marketing, 17*(February), 141–160.

Barberis, M., & Harvey, P. D. (1997). Costs of family planning programmes in fourteen developing countries by method of service delivery. *Journal of Biosocial Science, 29,* 219–233.

Belch, G. E., & Belch, M. A. (2004). *Advertising and promotion: An integrated marketing communications perspective* (6th ed.). New York: McGraw-Hill/Irwin.

Black, D. R., Blue, C. L., Coster, D. C., & Chrysler, L. M. (2002). Corporate social marketing: Message design to recruit program participants. *American Journal of Health Behavior, 26*(3), 188–199.

Bonk, K., Griggs, H., & Tynes, E. (1999). *The Jossey-Bass guide to strategic communications for nonprofits: A step-by-step guide to working with the media to generate publicity, enhance fundraising, build membership, change public policy, handle crises, and more.* San Francisco: Jossey-Bass.

Brinckerhoff, P. C. (2005). Charitable Australians sick of hard sell. *The Age.* Retrieved October 22, 2005, from www.theage.com.au/news/National/Charitable-Australians-sick-of-hard-sell/2005/02/25/1109180086031.html

Brown, K. G., & Geddes, R. (2006). Image repair: Research, consensus and strategies (A study of the University College of Cape Breton). *Journal of Nonprofit & Public Sector Marketing, 15*(1–2), 69–85.

Cain, L., & Meritt, D., Jr. (1998). Zoos and aquariums. In B. A. Weisbrod (Ed.), *To profit or not to profit: The commercial transformation of the nonprofit sector* (pp. 217–232). Cambridge, UK: Cambridge University Press.

Callow, M. (2004). Identifying promotional appeals for targeting potential volunteers: An exploratory study on volunteering motives among retirees. *International Journal of Nonprofit and Voluntary Sector Marketing, 9*(3), 261–274.

Carrick, B. (2002). Appealing to the unchurched: What attracts new members? *Journal of Nonprofit & Public Sector Marketing, 10*(1), 77–91.

Caywood, C. L. (1997). *The handbook of strategic public relations and integrated communications.* New York: McGraw-Hill.

Colby, S. J., & Rubin, A. (2005). The strategic value of a shared understanding of costs. *Strategy and Leadership, 33*(February), 27–32.

Dees, J. G. (1998). Enterprising nonprofits. *Harvard Business Review, 76*(1), 54–67.

Dermody, J., & Scullion, R. (2005). Young people's attitudes towards British political advertising: Nurturing or impeding voter engagement. *Journal of Nonprofit & Public Sector Marketing, 14*(1–2).

EU farm commissioner visits China to promote tasty Europe. (2004, March 19). *Europaworld.* Retrieved October 16, 2005, from www.europaworld.org/week169/eufarm19304.htm

Ford, J. B., & Mottner, S. (2003). Retailing in the nonprofit sector: An exploratory analysis of church-connected retailing ventures. *International Journal of Nonprofit and Voluntary Sector Marketing, 8*(4), 337–348.

Foster, W., & Bradach, J. (2005). Should nonprofits seek profits? *Harvard Business Review, 83*(2), 92–100, 148.

Fousekis, P., & Revell, B. (2002). Primary demand for red meats in the United Kingdom. *Cahiers d'économie et sociologie rarales, 63,* 32–50.

Gomes, R., & Knowles, P. A. (2001). Strategic Internet and e-commerce applications for local nonprofit. *Journal of Nonprofit & Public Sector Marketing, 9*(1–2), 215–245.

Granik, S. (2005). Membership benefits, membership action: Why incentives or activism are what members want. *Journal of Nonprofit & Public Sector Marketing, 14*(1–2).

Gray, C. M. (2001, April 15). Pricing issues for the nonprofit manager. *The NonProfit Times,* 22.

Gregory, J. (2006). Using message strategy to capture audience attention: Readers' reactions to health education publications. *Journal of Nonprofit & Public Sector Marketing, 15*(1–2), 1–23.

Griffin, D., & O'Cass, A. (2004). Social marketing: Who really gets the message? *Journal of Nonprofit & Public Sector Marketing, 12*(2), 129–147.

GuideStar. (2004). *Improve your web strategy: What new research says about donor needs and nonprofit programs.* Presented at Nonprofit Technology Conference, March 26, 2004. Retrieved October 20, 2005, from www.networkforgood.org/npo/download/NTCResearch2004.pdf

Harvey, P. D. (1994). The impact of condom prices on sales in social marketing programs. *Studies in Family Planning, 25*(1), 52–58.

Helmig, B., Jegers, M., & Lapsley, I. (2004). Challenges in managing nonprofit organizations: A research overview. *Voluntas: International Journal of Voluntary and Nonprofit Sector Marketing, 15*(June), 101–116.

Janowitz, B., & Bratt, J. H. (1996). What do we really know about the impact of price changes on contraceptive use? *International Family Planning Perspectives, 22,* 38–40.

Kline Henley, T. (2001). Integrated marketing communications for local nonprofit organizations: Communications tools and methods. *Journal of Nonprofit & Public Sector Marketing, 9*(1–2), 157–168.

Kline Henley, T. (2001). Integrated marketing communications for local nonprofit organizations: Developing an integrated marketing communications strategy. *Journal of Nonprofit & Public Sector Marketing, 9*(1–2), 141–155.

Kline Henley, T. (2001). Integrated marketing communications for local nonprofit organizations: Messages in nonprofit communications. *Journal of Nonprofit & Public Sector Marketing, 9*(1–2), 179–184.

Kotler, P., Roberto, N., & Lee, N. (2002). *Social marketing: Improving the quality of life.* Thousand Oaks, CA: Sage.

LaMay, C. L., & Weisbrod, B. A. (1998). The funding perils of the Corporation for Public Broadcasting. In B. A. Weisbrod (Ed.), *To profit or not to profit: The commercial transformation of the nonprofit sector* (pp. 249–267). Cambridge, UK: Cambridge University Press.

Lavack, A. M. (2004). Ads that attack the tobacco industry: A review and recommendations. *Journal of Nonprofit & Public Sector Marketing, 12*(2), 51–71.

Lesly, P. (1998). *Lesly's handbook of public relations and communications* (5th ed.). Lincolnwood, IL: Contemporary Books.

Maibach, E., & Holtgrave, D. R. (1995). Advances in public health communication. *Annual Review of Public Health, 16*, 219–238.

McClure, N. R., Kiecker, P., & Wood, V. R. (1997). Is price a signal of service quality? Challenging conventional wisdom in the health care industry. *Journal of Nonprofit & Public Sector Marketing, 5*(4), 27–46.

Mizerski, D., Mizerski, K., & Sadler, O. (2001). A field experiment comparing the effectiveness of ambush and cause related ad appeals for social marketing causes. *Journal of Nonprofit & Public Sector Marketing, 9*(4), 25–45.

Morton, C. R., & Villegas, J. (2005). Political issue promotion in the age of 9–11. *Journal of Nonprofit & Public Sector Marketing, 14*(1–2).

Moscato, S., Black, D. R., Blue, C. L., Mattson, M., & Galer-Unti, R.A. (2001). Evaluating a fear appeal message to reduce alcohol use among "Greeks." *American Journal of Health Behavior, 25*(5), 481–491.

Network For Good. (2004). Improve your Web strategy: What new research says about donor needs and nonprofit programs. Presented at Nonprofit Technology Conference, March 26, 2004. Retrieved October 20, 2005, from www.networkforgood.org/npo/download/NTCResearch2004.pdf

O'Cass, A. (2005). Political campaign advertising: Believe it or not. *Journal of Nonprofit & Public Sector Marketing, 14*(1–2).

O'Cass, A., & Griffin, D. (2006). Antecedents and consequences of social issue advertising. *Journal of Nonprofit & Public Sector Marketing, 15*(1–2), 87–104.

O'Neil, J. (2003). The challenge of promoting a cohesive institutional identity: An investigation of the impact of external audiences, task specialization, and the overall organization. *Journal of Nonprofit & Public Sector Marketing, 11*(2), 21–42.

Oster, S., Gray, C. M., & Weinberg, C. B. (2004). Pricing in the nonprofit sector. In D. R. Young (Ed.), *Effective economic decision-making by nonprofit organizations*. New York: The Foundation Center.

Peattie, S. (2003). Applying sales promotion competitions to nonprofit contexts. *International Journal of Nonprofit and Voluntary Sector Marketing, 8*(4), 349–362.

Philippi, C. (2002). *Understanding buyer behavior: Primary demand vs. selective demand*. Retrieved October 16, 2005, from www.zeromillion.com/marketing/buyer-behavior.html

Rose, J. (2003). Government advertising and the creation of national myths: The Canadian case. *International Journal of Nonprofit and Voluntary Sector Marketing, 8*(2), 153–165.

Tuckman, H. P., Chatterjee, P., & Muha, D. (2003). Nonprofit websites: Prevalence, usage and commercial activity. *Journal of Nonprofit & Public Sector Marketing, 12*(1), 49–68.

Vakratsas, D., & Ambler, T. (1999). How advertising works: What do we really know? *Journal of Marketing, 63*(1), 26–43.

Van den Bulte, C., & Lilien, G. L. (2001). Medical innovation revisited: Social contagion versus marketing effort. *American Journal of Sociology, 106*(5), 1409–1435.

Weisbrod, B. A. (1998). *To profit or not to profit: The commercial transformation of the nonprofit sector*. New York: Cambridge University Press.

Yoken, C., & Berman, J. S. (1984). Does paying a fee for psychotherapy alter the effectiveness of a treatment? *Journal of Consulting Clinical Psychology, 52*(2), 254–260.

Part II

Marketing to Donors and Volunteers

7

Direct Marketing Tactics

❖

Content

Learning Objectives

On completion of this chapter, the reader will

- Understand the advantages and different types of direct marketing

- Understand how to develop a direct marketing program

- Identify opportunities for the use of direct marketing in the marketing mix

- Understand some of the ethical issues involved in fund-raising

- Learn a base of concepts and skills that will facilitate further learning and thinking in the direct marketing area

Opening Vignette: Alliance of Confessing Evangelicals, Inc.

According to Independent Sector (www.independentsector.org), religious organizations are the largest category of nonprofit organizations in the United States. Like most nonprofits, religious organizations must attract donations and membership support to fulfill their missions. Direct marketing tactics are frequently used to communicate the organization's needs to interested supporters.

The Alliance of Confessing Evangelicals (www.alliancenet.org) is a religious organization that seeks to strengthen evangelical churches by advocating and teaching doctrine consistent with the Reformation. The organization accomplishes its purpose by producing radio programs and by publishing a magazine and a variety of books, videos, music tapes, and compact disks. The online catalog of the Alliance of Confessing Evangelicals, www.ReformationalResources.org, offers 3,800 products. The Alliance also conducts workshops, seminars, and conventions across the United States. Because the Alliance's mission is fulfilled by widely disseminating doctrinal messages, its products and services are priced low. Most of the Alliance's revenues are the result of soliciting individual contributions through direct marketing activities, which are responsible for 80% of the organization's annual revenues.

Of a supporter base of 65,000 individuals, about 8,000–10,000 support the Alliance only by purchasing its products. The remainder of the supporter base is made up of contributors who make periodic donations of varying amounts.

A first-time product purchase is viewed by the Alliance's CEO, Robert Brady, as an entry point or introduction to the organization. Through direct marketing efforts, the Alliance builds on this initial event to introduce the organization and inform the customer about the programs and important work of the Alliance. Customers are nurtured into becoming contributing supporters.

The database of contributors categorizes donors as small, medium, and large, depending on a statistical evaluation of several factors. For example, a supporter may be classified as a large donor through a large contribution (>$10,000 U.S.), a history of donations that accumulate to a substantial sum, or a capacity for substantial giving, such as a large net worth. Small donors comprise about 50%, medium donors about 30%, and big donors about 20% of the Alliance's supporter base. Mr. Brady says that donor classification directs how the Alliance interacts with donors. Large donors typically receive personal contact from an Alliance representative. Mr. Brady personally communicates with about 200 of the Alliance's biggest donors. Medium donors receive a combination of direct mail and invitations to Alliance events. Small donors receive regular direct mail and the least personal interaction from the Alliance.

About 2,000 of the Alliance's 65,000 supporters give monthly through automated credit card payments or checking account withdrawals agreed to in advance. For the remainder of the supporter base, direct marketing activities from the Alliance prompt contributions. E-mail addresses are available for 12,000 supporters, who received biweekly e-mail messages. Small and medium donors receive periodic direct mail.

The Alliance manages about 14 direct mail campaigns each year. Direct mail is usually directed at attracting support for a specific Alliance program, of which there are several. Therefore, the number of direct mail solicitations a supporter would receive is determined in part by the programs that donor has supported previously. Some donors give without linking their contribution to a specific program, allowing the Alliance to use these funds to support the organization's operations.

The information in this opening case was obtained in a personal interview with Mr. Robert Brady, the Alliance's CEO, on May 21, 2004.

Importance of Direct Marketing

As the opening case demonstrates, many nonprofits rely on direct marketing tactics to attract contributions. Nonprofit managers use direct marketing for fund-raising, membership recruitment, product sales, and so forth. The purpose of this chapter is to introduce readers to direct marketing. After reading this chapter, you will have a better understanding of what direct marketing is and how it can be used to further your objectives and goals. Numerous books are available to assist you further, and this chapter will provide a foundation for subsequent in-depth, self-directed learning.

Status of Direct Marketing Among Nonprofits

Direct marketing refers to those marketing messages a nonprofit sends to specific individuals, seeking a response such as making a donation, completing a survey, or some other action. Examples are telemarketing, direct mail, and Internet direct marketing using e-mail messages.

According to the American Association of Fundraising Counsel, in 2002, individuals in the United States contributed about $184 billion to nonprofit organizations. According to the Association of Direct Response Fundraising Counsel (2004), Americans give nonprofits more than $100 billion annually as a result of direct marketing solicitations. As in the example provided in the Opening Vignette, donors differ markedly in the amount they contribute. However, a common feature among many donors is that most made their first contribution in response to a letter they received asking for help.

Nonprofit managers use direct marketing for many purposes. They use direct marketing to establish their reputations. Direct marketing, properly used, can help build relationships with supporters. It can help the organization grow, communicate the organization's programs, and attract operating funds. Direct marketing can be a useful tool in identifying supporters willing and able to donate large sums and make bequests in their estate plans.

Unfortunately, some managers have unrealistic expectations for direct marketing or plan and implement campaigns ineffectively, and sometimes they become skeptical of direct marketing as a result. It is important, then, that nonprofit managers properly understand the practical and effective use of direct marketing in achieving their goals.

CHAPTER INSIGHT   **Direct Marketing Response Rates**

According to the Direct Marketing Association (DMA), in October 2003, nonprofit organizations generated higher response rates from their direct marketing activities than did other types of organizations.

For example, as reported in the *DMA 2003 Response Rate Study,* for all industries, the average response rate from a direct marketing campaign was 2.61%. However, for nonprofit fund-raisers, it was 5.35%. The overall response rate using telemarketing was 7.44%. For nonprofit fund-raisers, telemarketing resulted in a 19.42% response rate.

More results from this study are available on the DMA's website (www.the-dma .org/).

❖ **Figure 7.1**   Characteristics of Direct Marketing

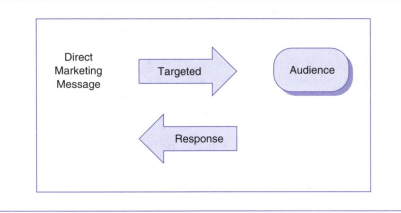

Characteristics of Direct Marketing

Direct marketing is distinguished from other types of marketing in that it seeks to obtain a measurable response from its target audience. Effective direct marketing relies heavily on use of a database. Nonprofit organizations, like the one in the opening case, develop and maintain supporter databases. These are useful in helping managers make more effective decisions.

Our definition of direct marketing does not include face-to-face solicitations made between individuals. (We consider this activity to be personal selling.) Nor does our definition of direct marketing include communications that are not targeted to individuals, such as mass advertising and public speaking engagements. We view direct marketing as a type of communication directed to a selected group of individuals. The targeted group members receive the message through a medium such as the postal system (direct mail), the Internet as e-mail (Internet direct mail), or the telephone system (telemarketing). Therefore, as depicted in Figure 7.1, direct marketing is targeted, and it seeks a **response** from the message recipient.

The nature of the response a nonprofit manager may seek in a direct marketing campaign can vary. The action or response a campaign seeks may be a financial contribution, membership, or some other type of assistance or information. For example, advocacy groups involved in issues marketing (discussed in a later chapter) may ask their supporters to petition policy makers on behalf of their cause. Obviously, not everyone in your targeted audience who receives your message will respond. The **response rate** refers to the percentage of the group receiving the direct marketing message that responds favorably.

Advantages of Direct Marketing

Direct marketing has several advantages: flexibility, targetability, measurability, accountability, and privacy. **Flexibility** refers to your ability to send the message you want when you want, and in the format of your choosing. **Targetability** refers to your ability to send your message to the individual(s) of your selection rather than broadcasting it to a mass audience. **Measurability** refers to your ability to test, track, and analyze the various dimensions of your campaigns to improve effectiveness. **Accountability** is linked to measurability. Because you are able to measure and analyze the various components of a specific campaign, you can know which campaigns and tactical elements are effective and which are not. **Privacy** refers to (a) your ability to send your message to individuals without its being easily received by unintended audiences and (b) your supporters' improved likelihood of receiving your message without typical distractions inherent in broadcast communication clutter.

CHAPTER INSIGHT	National Do Not Call Registry

The federal government recently established a National Do Not Call Registry (www.donotcall.gov). U.S. residents can visit the website and register their telephone numbers. This registration, good for 5 years, is intended to shield consumers from unwanted telemarketing calls.

Not all organizations are required to purge registered telephone numbers from their lists, however. Registered consumers may still receive calls from political organizations, charities, telephone surveyors, or companies with which they have an existing business relationship.

Although viewed by the direct marketing industry as an infringement on free speech, these new restrictions may actually benefit nonprofit organizations. The exemption for nonprofit organizations may give them greater credibility to consumers. Also, because consumers will be receiving far fewer telemarketing calls than in the past, there will be less competition for consumers' attention and fewer distasteful telemarketing experiences in consumers' recent memories.

Types of Direct Marketing

There are various types of direct marketing. Each has its strengths and weaknesses. No type is best in all situations. Rather, managers should understand each type and decide which communication medium or combination of media is the most appropriate for a given situation. The types of direct marketing used most commonly by nonprofit organizations are direct mail, Internet direct e-mail, and telemarketing. Table 7.1 shows how these direct marketing media compare across several dimensions.

Speed. Among the three, direct mail takes the longest to deliver a direct marketing appeal. This is generally due to postal delivery time, especially for direct mail using the less expensive bulk mail postage rates. Sending direct mail to individuals outside your country's postal system can add substantial delays. Conversely, marketing messages are sent rapidly over the telephone network and the Internet.

Cost. Telemarketing is typically the most costly because of the labor expense. Organizations often use telemarketing firms to perform this function. Organizations having sufficient resources

❖ **Table 7.1** Comparison of Major Direct Marketing Media

	Direct Mail	Telemarketing	E-Mail
Speed	slowest	medium	fastest
Cost	medium	most	least
Multimedia	limited	none	greatest
List availability	best	limited	good
Back-end integration	worst	good	best
Personalization	good	very good	very good
Flexibility	limited	moderate	very good

(e.g., computers, telephone lines) are able to recruit volunteers for periodic campaigns. Direct mail is moderately expensive because of the substantial printing and ever increasing postage rates. Effective implementation and planning of direct mail campaigns, however, can make its use quite cost effective. Internet direct e-mail marketing is least expensive. E-mail appeals can be sent to a large number of individuals inexpensively.

Multimedia. **Multimedia** refers to the ability of a communication medium to allow different formats, such as print, sound, or animation. Telemarketing, of course, has the least multimedia capability because it is limited to a telephone call. Because the components of a direct mail packet (outer envelope, inner envelope, cover letter, brochure, inserts, gifts, and so forth) can be modified considerably, direct mail is a bit more flexible. Direct mail is limited to the capability of print media, however. The technology available on websites and in e-mail messages allows for a high level of flexibility. Internet technology accommodates digital pictures, searchable databases, video animation, video streaming, and audio streaming. Managers continue to learn creative approaches to using Internet technology.

Scalability. **Scalability** refers to the capability of a system to increase its operating capacity without substantial modifications. This quality pertains to direct marketing tactics using Internet technology, such as e-mail and e-newsletters. The quality of scalability refers to the quality of using Internet technology in which, once an investment in equipment and software is made, the expense to send 100,000 mail messages is not much greater then the expense to send 100 e-mail messages (the fixed cost in equipment is the primary expense, so the total expense is not greatly effected by volume). In contrast, the cost of using traditional direct mail rises in proportion to the volume because the main expense, postage, is not a fixed expense but varies with volume.

List availability. As mentioned earlier, direct marketing targets specific individuals. Therefore, lists of individuals and their contact information must be acquired. Lists can be either internal or external to the nonprofit organization. A nonprofit's internal database of supporters or members, also known as its **house list**, can be analyzed to retrieve the subgroup of individuals most likely to respond to a specific campaign. External lists can be rented by a nonprofit for one use in a campaign (see Chapter Insight, page 199). Individuals from a rented list who respond to a campaign are added to the nonprofit's house list.

Mailing lists are readily available from a variety of sources. List brokers can find a mailing list for almost any group of individuals a nonprofit manager might care to target. Telephone lists are generally available, too. (Some states in the United States prohibit mobile phone solicitations.) Fortunately, nonprofit organizations generally face fewer telemarketing restrictions than commercial organizations do.

Lists of e-mail addresses are becoming more available. However, their availability still lags behind the more established media. Although virtually everyone has a postal address and a telephone, a sizable portion of the population still does not have Internet access. Also, people tend to change e-mail addresses more frequently than they change telephone numbers or postal addresses, reducing an e-mail list's accuracy.

Nonprofit managers are now adding supporters' e-mail addresses to their supporter databases. You may recall from the opening vignette that the Alliance of Confessing Evangelicals had e-mail addresses for approximately 12,000 of its 65,000 supporters. E-mail and e-newsletters are increasingly popular vehicles for nonprofits to use to communicate with their supporters because of the scalability and multimedia capability discussed earlier.

CHAPTER INSIGHT — **External Lists**

Thousands of lists can be rented for one-time use. A small number of lists may be traded on a one-to-one basis for your organization's donor list. You can select from three different types of lists:

Donor lists. Donor lists, containing contact information of persons who have donated to a charity, usually generate the highest response rates. You can find donor lists among

- Nonprofits that have a mission similar to your organization's (these usually generate best response rate)
- Nonprofits that do not have a mission similar to your organization's

Compiled lists. Compiled lists are developed by combining donor or membership lists from more than one nonprofit organization and creating new compiled lists from similar subgroups of the input lists. These lists would be representative, not of a single organization, but of groupings of individuals, such as individuals who are members of environmental groups and individuals who are members of opera house guilds.

Commercial lists. Commercial lists are developed by aggregating individuals from other sources, then creating subgroups having similarities. The most responsive lists will include only individuals who have responded to some type of direct marketing offer previously. Individuals who are aggregated into commercial lists are identified from an array of sources, such as magazine or newspaper subscriptions, hobbies, catalog buyers, directories, public records, voting lists, and so forth.

Back-End Integration. Back-end integration refers to the relative ease with which the response generated from a direct marketing message can be handled in an automated fashion by the organization's computer network. Supporter responses generated using Internet technology often have the highest level of back-end integration. For example, it is possible to have a prospect make a contribution online by credit card and have the donation accepted using only software, no human intervention. Supporters can complete surveys online, and the data can be compiled and summarized by software. Advocacy groups can have supporters send e-mail letters and petitions to their policy makers very quickly, in large numbers, electronically.

Responses generated through telemarketing activities require the employee to manually enter supporter responses into the employee's computer. Once entered, the information can be processed by software.

Direct mail typically provides supporters a response form and an envelope or a response card to return to the nonprofit through the postal system. This requires transportation of the response form, then personal handling when received by the nonprofit. Direct mail may also provide supporters with a toll-free telephone number to call. This alternative avoids mail delays and may be preferred by some supporters (because it involves speaking to a person and providing credit card information more securely), but it is somewhat costly because of labor and telecommunication expenses.

Personalization. Personalization refers to the ability to tailor a message to an individual. The level of personalization can range from addressing the individual by name to analyzing donor data in your database and custom-tailoring an offer for each individual.

All three media afford the basic personalization tactic of including the supporter's name in the message. Direct mail typically offers the least personalization because marketers usually keep these communications brief, anticipating that few people will take the time to read a lengthy letter. Also, the more materials included in a direct mail packet, the more it weighs, increasing the postage expense.

Telemarketing offers more personalization opportunities than direct mail does. Employees making calls are typically guided in what to say by a script on their computer monitors. Because employees are using computers, they can quite simply access records of people they call who are already supporters.

Internet technology offers the potential for a substantial level of supporter personalization. It is possible for regular supporters to receive a personalized experience when visiting the nonprofit's website. Software can collect a history of supporter website viewing and record this information on the supporter's computer so that supporters see only information of interest to them, along with their name and possibly news or recommendations of personal interest.

Flexibility. Direct mail is flexible in the sense that nonprofit managers have many alternatives for developing the direct mail packet. However, the elements of the packet are typically standardized for mass production and reduced-rate postage. Telemarketing is more flexible than direct mail because the employee can interact with the supporter and react to various supporter questions or responses. Internet technology allows for considerable flexibility because supporters can have a high level of control over the information they retrieve.

❖ **Figure 7.2**   Developing Your Direct Marketing Plan

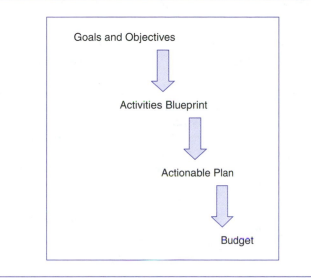

Developing a Direct Marketing Program

We will now discuss how a nonprofit manager would develop a direct marketing program. Because nonprofit organizations rely on direct mail the most, we will demonstrate how to develop a program using this medium.

A direct mail program typically consists of the following steps:

1. Develop plan.

2. Research and purchase mailing list.

3. Develop creative materials for direct mail campaign.

4. Produce, test, and mail direct mail packets.

5. Measure results and refine program.

Step 1: Develop Your Plan

In this step of your direct mail program, you need to carefully consider what you want to achieve and how you will go about implementing your program. Figure 7.2 shows the tasks involved in this step.

Identify goals and objectives. Your first task in developing a direct marketing program is to decide what you want to accomplish. What is your objective? Do you want to attract donations? Increase membership? Sell season tickets for your symphony? It is better to develop objectives you can measure, such as selling all 5,000 available season symphony tickets. Measurable goals allow the managers to assess how effective the implementation of marketing activities has been in a given time.

CHAPTER INSIGHT   **Economics of Direct Mail**

In commercial direct marketing, managers are very interested in comparing the resulting orders with the campaign cost, for obvious reasons.

In the nonprofit sector, the economics are not as clear. It may be shortsighted to simply compare the donations or membership fees received with the cost of a direct mail campaign. Direct mail expenses have increased. In the past 10 years, nonprofit postage in the United States has increased from $18 to $125 for every 1,000 pieces mailed. If nonprofit managers gauge the success of a program by its ability to produce an immediate return (revenues in excess of costs), then fewer direct mail programs will be approved.

When products are sold to obtain operating revenue, such as season tickets to a symphony, obviously sales should exceed campaign cost by a large margin. However, when the goal is to attract new members or new donors, a loss on the direct mail campaign that acquired them may be considered a donor-acquisition expense.

If the goal is to increase bequests, legacy giving, first-time contributors, or new members, it may be wise to consider the direct marketing expense as an investment that will produce future returns.

Develop activities blueprint. Developing an **activities blueprint** will help you to better manage a complex program by dividing it into its various components. The blueprint will also help you develop a time frame for implementing your program. To develop your activities blueprint, you will need to begin at the completion date and work backwards. For example, you must first decide when your direct mail pieces must be sent to your target audience.

Figure 7.3 shows an example of an activities blueprint. It is usually wise to send out a test mailing to a smaller subset of your list prior to sending out the main mailing (called *rollout*). The results of the test mailing will help you detect problems and determine what components of your packet need revising. For simplicity, however, Figure 7.3 does not show the test phase.

Draft actionable plan. An **actionable** plan is a plan that provides sufficient detail to enable implemented. A completed blueprint can guide the development of a detailed plan that can be implementation. Building on the blueprint, we now need to add (a) a description of activities that must be done to meet milestones; (b) persons responsible for ensuring activities are completed; and (c) an estimated cost of the creative work (if done outside the nonprofit), printing, insertion, and postage. This task requires considerable thought, but the benefits are worthwhile.

This step will enable you to determine the level of outsourcing required. It will also enable you to determine the budget constraints, plan the relative size of the mailing (the number of people on your lists), and develop alternatives. For example, you might discover that the expense will not be as great as expected and that you can add more names to your list. Or you may find the expense is too great, and you will have

❖ **Figure 7.3** Activities Blueprint for Direct Mail Campaign to Sell Season Tickets to a Symphony

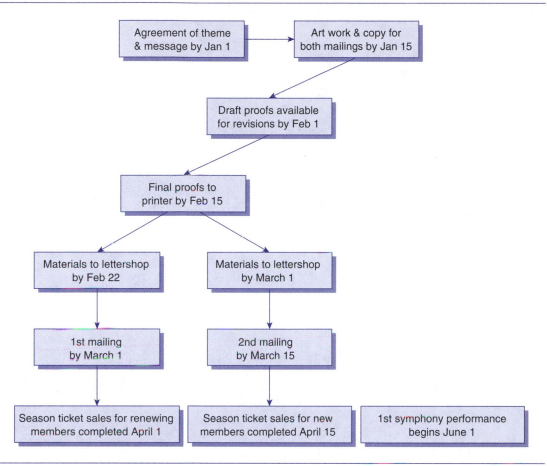

to reduce costs. In this case, you may choose to reduce the number of names in your lists, reduce the complexity of your brochure, or reduce the number of pages to bring weight and postage expense down.

Develop budget. Managers should develop a tentative budget. Table 7.2 provides an example of a budget.

In examining a tentative budget such as the one in Table 7.2, managers may make alternative decisions depending on organizational resources and priorities. A nonprofit may feel the cost of the campaign is lower than expected and decide to increase the target audience. Or the nonprofit may seek to improve the campaign results by finding ways to reduce costs or increase the response rate.

❖ **Table 7.2** Proposed Direct Mail Campaign Budget

Expected costs:	
List rental	$150 per thousand
Artwork/agency fees	$5,000
Production and postage	$750 per thousand
Premiums	$1,000
Campaign revenues:	
Mailing quantity	10,000 mail packets
Response (7%)	700 new donors
Total new donations	$24,500
Campaign effectiveness:	
List rental	$1,500
Art work/agency fees	$5,000
Production and postage	$7,500
Premiums	$1,000
Total costs	$15,000
Net campaign results:	**$9,500**

Step 2: Research and Purchase Your Mailing List

Now that you know your goals and objectives and you have a plan to guide your implementation, you can more closely define your target audience. You can use part or all of your internal list (house list), you can purchase an external list, or you can do both. For the symphony example, let us assume that you will send a direct mail piece to last year's season ticket holders, followed by a mailing to a list purchased from an external source, such as a list broker. List brokers can be a valuable resource. They have many contacts, and they have experience working with clients to find the most productive list. Getting a good list from a reputable list broker can be an important component in the success of your direct mail program.

List Brokers. List brokers are intermediaries who match mailers with list owners. Lists are usually rented. (For examples, perform an Internet search using *list broker* as keywords.) The price of a list is not more expensive if you use a broker. The broker's commission comes from the list's owner. List brokers can recommend lists that should be the most responsive for your specific mailing. List brokers will also seek the list owner's approval of your direct mail packet and your desired date.

Prior to meeting with your list broker, assemble as much detail about your direct mail plans as possible so that you can give the list broker the most accurate perception of your organization, your direct mail goals, and your desired audience.

CHAPTER INSIGHT **Finding a Successful List**

How do you find the best external list? Usually, the best prospects are those individuals who are similar to your current members or donors. The following may guide you in locating the best list.

1. Look for your best donors. Who are they? What makes them best: amount of donation, frequency of donation, length of time they have been a donor?

2. Model your best donors. Now that you have identified your best donors, try to understand what they have in common. What characteristics do they share?

3. Locate your potential donors. Armed with a description of the characteristics you are seeking in individuals, you can enable a list broker to locate a productive list.

Step 3: Develop Creative Materials for Your Direct Mail Campaign

Now that you know your goals and objectives and to whom you will send your direct mail, it is time to develop the materials that will comprise your packet. There are many choices.

Copy refers to the words that will be used to state your message. Art work refers to all other visual elements of the direct mail packet. You can chose a traditional mail packet, which includes an outer envelope, letter, brochure, response device, and inner reply envelope, or a **self-mailer**, which is a direct mail package that does not use an outer envelope.

Cover Letter. If you are seeking contributions, how much money should you ask of an individual? When soliciting donations from current supporters, your records should show the amount of their previous donation. You can usually ask for an amount slightly greater. If you are seeking first-time donations using an external list, you have to decide what an entry amount should be. Most solicitations show several amounts, from lowest to highest, but you can also recommend an amount that would really help.

The length of your letter is also a consideration. Generally, for nonprofit causes, the longer the better *as long as you have something significant to say*. If your cause is important, it will probably take more than one page to describe your needs. Also, a longer letter is more similar to the personal visit a potential large donor would receive. Organizations with well-known names, however, are able to use briefer letters.

Craft your letter according to the following guidelines.

1. Begin with a compelling opening to obtain interest.

2. State your problem, the enemy (useful for advocacy or political nonprofits), or both.

3. Describe your cause in terms of the people you serve, the needs to address, or your successes.

4. Tell a story such as an evocative case history.

5. Use familiar words, short sentences, and plenty of white space around text. Write with emotion (if you do not feel strongly about your mission, will your reader?).

6. Ask directly for a donation near the beginning and at the end of the letter. Include something significant in a postscript; ask for money again and mention a premium donors can receive by responding by a specific date.

Response Device. You must include a card or form for donors to return to you. If you are using a windowed return envelope, you need to ensure that the response form fits in the envelope properly and that the address on the form can be seen by postal system workers. The form should have a box or statement the donors can mark to indicate their gift amount. Make sure the response device has clear instructions for writing a check, calling, or going online to make a contribution. More nonprofits are encouraging online responses because they are faster and less expensive to process; however, they take more effort, and many people may not have Internet access. Be sure to include information about the tax deductibility of the gift, if applicable.

The response device will provide you with another opportunity to suggest a more generous donation. Suggested amounts are usually placed lowest to highest, with an "other" blank the donor can fill in if desired. You can gently direct the donor's attention to a suggested amount by putting it in bold type, circling the amount, or putting it in a different color.

Outer Envelope. Typically, business (No. 10) envelopes are used. They are widely available and inexpensive. However, because business envelopes are so common, a larger or smaller or oddly shaped envelope may gain greater attention. Many organizations used windowed envelopes because they don't require personalized letters to be matched with an envelope with the correct address label. Rather, the addressed letter can be folded and inserted in the windowed envelope so that the address on the letter is displayed.

You may decide to print words (copy) or illustrations (art work) on the outer envelope. This is called a **teaser**. If a teaser is linked to the package theme and is interesting or curious, it may help get the envelope opened.

Reply Envelope. A reply envelope is usually included in the direct mail packet for the donor's convenience. Many reply envelopes are **business reply envelopes** (BREs). The postal service charges the nonprofit a postage expense for each BRE returned by a donor. Nonprofits would like to avoid this expense if possible. In general, **house mailings** (mailings to a house list) will not require a BRE. A BRE is usually necessary for mailing to external lists. A nonprofit may print copy on the stamp location that says the donor's paying the postage will also help the organization.

Other Materials. Other items can be included in the direct mail packet. They may include brochures, decals, testimonials, endorsements, questionnaires, gifts, newsletters, magazines, and so forth. Many articles and books have been written about ways to develop superior creative materials, so help and advice are readily available.

The Complete Package. The various elements that comprise your direct mail package are part of a whole and should work together to communicate a consistent, focused message. Keep in mind that your central message should permeate your entire package, from a central theme to the various subparts that support that core message. Ensure that there is a focused, central message that is clearly communicated by the package. Include enough information to make a compelling appeal, but avoid information that adds little to the impact of the message. As always, your organization's reputation is its most important asset. Before mailing the package, be sure that all information in it reinforces the integrity of your organization.

CHAPTER INSIGHT   **Unified Registration Statement**

Forty-three states in the United States require nonprofit organizations that solicit funds to register and report to them. The National Association of State Charities Officials and the National Association of Attorneys General have developed a Unified Registration Statement (URS), which allows nonprofits to complete a single form to use in most states.

Of the 43 states that require registration, Alaska, Arizona, Colorado, and Florida do not accept the URS and have their own registration forms. Six of the participating states that will accept the URS require supplemental forms to also be completed.

The Multi-State Filer Project has developed a useful website to help nonprofit managers comply with these requirements. It is located at www.multistatefiling.org.

Step 4: Produce, Test, and Mail Direct Mail Packets

Now that you have developed your creative materials, it is time to have them printed and assembled into your direct mail packages, then placed in the postal system for delivery. Most large organizations, however, perform testing prior to the final mailing. For example, a large organization such as the National Geographic Society may send out 1 million to 3 million direct mail packets internationally in one mailing. These large campaigns are generally targeted toward increasing subscriptions to the nonprofit's magazine, *National Geographic.* However, prior to sending out the large mailing, *National Geographic* will send out a test mailing of approximately 50,000 packets. This provides an adequate estimate of the response rate the primary mailing would generate. If a test mailing generates an unsatisfactorily low response rate, a nonprofit will try to make the necessary correction to the materials included in the packet before sending out the main mailing.

There are several reasons for testing before your primary mailing. To test, you send out a mailing to a small portion of your target audience before you send your direct mail to the entire list. This may help you locate weaknesses and detect problems so as to improve the effectiveness of your program and avoid costly mistakes. (Testing should be incorporated in your Activities Blueprint.) Therefore, you typically have a **testing phase** first and then a **rollout phase** (the primary mailing).

An in-depth discussion of testing is beyond the scope of this chapter. However, for organizations that use direct mail regularly, testing all the various components of a direct mail program, from the list to the response device, should be an ongoing activity. Many books and articles are available on testing, including Mal Warwick's *Testing, Testing, 1, 2, 3: Raise More Money With Direct Mail Tests* (2003).

Production. There are many businesses that can help with various components of your direct mail program. We have already discussed list brokers. There are marketing research firms, direct mail consultants, businesses to help improve your art work, printers, and **lettershops,** which personalize, label, sort, and stuff envelopes in preparation for mailing.

Step 5: Measure Results and Refine Your Program

One of the primary advantages of direct marketing over alternative marketing tactics, such as mass advertising, is that you can measure the effectiveness of your activities. You can learn from each direct marketing campaign and apply that learning to the next campaign, improving your effectiveness with experience.

Many organizations have a **house piece,** which is the most successful direct mail packet to date and the standard by which future programs will be evaluated. Each time a new campaign is planned, managers develop new creative elements to test. If the new package generates a better response than the house piece, it becomes the new house piece. If the new package generates a lower response than the house piece in a test, then the house piece is used in the rollout.

You will find it useful to measure various aspects of your direct marketing activities. This will provide you with information for improved decision making. Also, it will provide you with accountability data you can use to report to your board of directors or other constituencies. Table 7.3 illustrates an example of calculating the cost of acquiring a new donor. The campaign depicted in Table 7.3 shows that 20,000 packets were mailed to individuals who had not previously contributed to the

❖ **Table 7.3** Donor Acquisition Campaign Outcomes

Total mailings	20,000	
Total number of contributions	1,400	(New donors)
Response rate	7%	(1,400/20,000)
Total contributions	$32,200	
Average donation	$23	($32,200/1,400)
Total campaign cost	$35,000	
Average cost/donation	$25	($35,000/1,400)
Campaign net revenue (loss)	($2,800)	($32,200 - $35,000)
Donor acquisition cost	$2/donor	($2,800/1,400)

nonprofit. The cost for the list of names and addresses, printing, and postage was $35,000. Of the 20,000 individuals receiving the mail packet, 7% responded with a contribution. The total contributions generated by the campaign were less than the cost of the campaign. This outcome may, at first, appear to indicate a failed campaign because it resulted in a loss of $2,800. If the mailing had been sent to existing contributors, it would be correct to interpret the campaign as a failure. However, since the mailing was sent to people who had not previously contributed to the nonprofit, the proper interpretation is that the nonprofit spent $2 to acquire each new donor. This is actually a favorable response rate because the expense is an investment in new donors, some of whom may become regular contributors to the nonprofit.

Ethical Issue

The two largest professional organizations for direct marketers are the Direct Marketing Association and the Association of Fundraising Professionals. The Association of Fundraising Professionals has a thoughtfully developed code of professional ethics and standards. The Direct Marketing Association's Nonprofit Federation also has a set of ethical guidelines for its members. For a comprehensive treatment of ethical issues in fund-raising, the reader is encouraged to visit each organization's website.

Readers having an interest in the professional standards of different countries are encouraged to visit websites of those organizations. There are international direct marketing associations around the world. The Direct Marketing Association's website contains a comprehensive listing of related international organizations.

Online Fund-Raising

Although traditional direct mail has received emphasis in this chapter because it is the most popular type of direct marketing among fund-raising professionals, online fund-raising is growing rapidly in importance. Nonprofits typically send individuals e-mail messages, encouraging them to click on a link that will take them to the nonprofit's website, where a donation can easily be made with a credit card. Nonprofits also include the organization's website address in their direct mail materials because some supporters may find donating online more convenient than returning the direct mail response card.

The basic framework described above for traditional direct mail is also appropriate for Internet direct mail. Because the Internet is a different medium, however, the development of creative materials will be different. Most e-mail applications allow for multimedia text and visual elements. This combination creates opportunities for much greater creativity in fund-raising offers. Furthermore, because links can be embedded into the message, much more information can be made available to receivers who desire it.

There are several reasons online fund-raising is growing. The proportion of the population that has an Internet connection continues to grow. The proportion of the Internet-connected population that has a high-speed Internet connection also continues to grow. The availability of e-mail lists is greatly improving. Compared with traditional direct marketing methods, Internet direct mail is much faster and much less expensive. The response rates of Internet direct mail are comparable to, if not better than, traditional direct marketing methods.

CHAPTER INSIGHT   **Spam or Fund-Raising?**

The European Federation of Direct Marketing (http://www.fedma.org) is emphasizing the importance of permission in direct marketing. The Marketing Federation of Southern Africa (http://www.mfsa.co.za/) has an antispam campaign. See each organization's website for more information.

When is sending an e-mail fund-raising message spam (i.e., unsolicited e-mail)? This is an important issue because spam annoys the people who receive it and, in some locations, may be illegal. A nonprofit's good reputation is vitally important to maintain.

The way for the nonprofit manager to avoid spamming is to obtain permission from an individual prior to sending a fund-raising request. This is known as permission e-mail marketing, or "opt-in" e-mails. The most preferred process is known as a double opt-in procedure, in which interested individuals give you permission to send newsletters, alerts, and other messages (fund-raising e-mails) by registering on your e-mail list. People register by typing their e-mail addresses into a simple form on your website. This is the first opt-in. As you receive the e-mail addresses, you then send those people an e-mail verifying their registration. To verify, they reply to your message (the second opt-in). This second opt-in prevents people from registering others by typing their e-mail address into your website form.

Managerial Issues

The following issues are relevant for nonprofit managers.

1. **Blended approach.** Successful direct marketing campaigns rely on building multiple paths to current and future supporters. Nonprofit managers should do this using both online and offline tactics. When more than one path (method) to supporters is used, the different methods reinforce each other. Opening up additional avenues for giving cannot but help. The low costs of e-mail campaigns and the growing number of individuals using e-mail suggest that complementing direct marketing programs with e-mail campaigns will enhance results (increase response rates and lower costs). As postage rates continue to rise, the reliance on e-mail as a complement to direct mail will continue to grow.

2. **Program, not organization, focus.** People want to contribute to a cause, not an organization. All components of the direct marketing program must support a central theme—the need, the cause, or the program for which you are asking their help.

3. Targeted campaigns. Members of your house list should not receive every mailing, only mailings for campaigns related to a program they are likely to have an interest in. If your organization has 20 different programs supporting its mission, not everyone is interested in supporting all 20 programs. Send your direct marketing campaign to those most likely to respond. Those most likely to respond will probably be those supporters who have contributed to the target program in the past.

4. Supporter database. Nonprofits should have a database of their supporters. A database should include supporters' names, postal addresses, e-mail addresses, telephone numbers, and contribution histories. Contribution histories should show the dates and amounts of each contribution, identify programs that were supported, and show the communication medium through which they responded.

Summary

In this chapter you learned the following nonprofit marketing concepts as they related to our learning objectives:

Importance of direct marketing. Some nonprofit organizations communicate to mass audiences through mass media, but they use direct marketing tactics to communicate to selective audiences or when they seek a desired response, like a contribution or some other action. Using mass media is appropriate when building awareness or reputation, such as in branding activities. When specific messages are needed for specific groups of individuals, then direct marketing tactics allow for higher selectivity, increased personalization, and greater effectiveness.

Advantages of direct marketing. Direct marketing is flexible. You can send the message you want, in the format of your choosing. Direct marketing is targetable and more private than mass marketing. You can select whom to send your message to. Because direct marketing is measurable, you can analyze, assess, and refine various dimensions of your program. Therefore, each dimension of your program becomes accountable. The effectiveness of each dimension is testable and can be modified for improvement.

Direct marketing media. The major types of direct marketing used by nonprofits are direct mail, e-mail, and telemarketing. Direct mail is most common. E-mail is the fastest growing. No direct marketing medium is best for all situations. The best choice is dependent on your time and cost constraints, the availability of a suitable list, the level of personalization desired, and the complexity of your message. A blended approach that uses a variety of communication vehicles to bring your message to your target audience is often preferred.

Program planning. A direct mail program can be developed by a series of steps. Managers need to determine their goals and objectives first, then carefully lay out the necessary activities, time lines, and responsible individuals. Allowing for testing is also necessary. The house list should be analyzed to identify those most likely to respond to your request. Managers may consult a list broker to locate and rent the most productive list of potential supporters. Creative materials need to be developed and compared with the standard house piece. Testing allows managers to refine the package's various elements prior to the rollout. The materials need to be printed and delivered to a lettershop for collation, insertion, and delivery to the postal system. Managers can then measure the subsequent response rates and program effectiveness, learning from successes and disappointments to develop more effective programs in the future.

Glossary

Accountability. Accountability is linked to measurability. Because you are able to measure and analyze the various components of a specific campaign, you can know which campaigns and tactical elements are effective and which are not.

Actionable plan. A plan of your direct marketing campaign that provides sufficient detail to enable the campaign to be implemented. It would include the various tasks that need to be completed, who is responsible for task completion, and target completion dates.

Activities blueprint. A detailed chart of your direct marketing program that portrays event milestones that must be completed as subparts of your overall plan. It guides the development of your actionable plan.

Art work. All visual elements of the direct mail packet other than words (see *copy*).

Back-end integration. The relative ease with which the responses generated from a direct marketing offer can be taken or fulfilled in an automated fashion.

Business reply envelope (BRE). A return envelope a direct mail respondent can use to return a donation or other response device to an organization without paying postage. BREs are usually printed with the nonprofit's postal address and other coding required by the postal system so that it can charge the nonprofit for each BRE returned.

Commercial lists. Contact lists of individuals that have been compiled from commercial sources like magazine subscription lists, business client lists, and so forth. These are used to send direct marketing communications to individuals not currently identified by the nonprofit as supporters.

Compiled lists. Direct marketing lists that are developed by combining donor or membership lists from multiple nonprofit organizations and creating new, compiled lists from similar subgroups of the input lists. These lists would be representative, not of a single organization, but of groupings of individuals, such as "individuals who are members of environmental groups," "individuals who are members of opera guilds," and so forth.

Copy. The words that are used in formal marketing communications such as brochures, Web pages, or direct mail cover letters (see *art work*).

Direct marketing. Marketing communications a nonprofit, seeking a donation, information, or some other response, sends to specific individuals. Examples are telemarketing, direct mail, and Internet direct marketing using e-mail messages.

Donor lists. Contact lists of supporters of other nonprofit organizations. Donor lists are typically derived from nonprofits similar to your own or from nonprofits whose supporters are similar to your supporters.

Flexibility. A characteristic that distinguishes direct mail from advertising. Direct marketing is flexible in the sense that the nonprofit manager has many alternatives for developing the direct mail packet. However, the elements of the packet are typically standardized for mass production and reduced-rate postage. Telemarketing is more flexible than direct mail because the employee can interact with the supporter in reaction to various supporter questions or responses. Internet technology allows for considerable flexibility because supporters can have great control over the information they process.

House list. An organization's database of supporters.

House mailings. Direct mail sent to your organization's house list (see *house list*).

House piece. The direct mail package that has been the most successful so far. It is the package by which future direct mail packages are gauged. When a more effective direct mail piece is developed, it becomes the new standard or house piece.

Lettershops. Companies that label, sort, and stuff direct mail envelopes before they are submitted to the postal system for delivery.

List broker. An intermediary with access to numerous list owners. A list broker is used to help locate a desired list.

Mail packet. The compiled direct mail piece, which typically includes an outer and inner envelope, a cover letter, a response card, and possibly a brochure.

Measurability. Your ability to test, track, and analyze the various dimensions of your campaigns to improve effectiveness.

Multimedia. The quality of a communication medium that allows the use of various formats, such as print, sound, or animation.

Personalization. The ability of a message to be directed at a specific person, possibly even taking a person's donation history and program support into account.

Privacy. When used to refer to a characteristic of direct marketing, the ability to restrict marketing communications to specific individuals.

Response. When used in a direct marketing context, a requested action from a targeted individual. For example, in direct mail, you may be interested in attracting contributions. A response would be a donation that is generated by your direct marketing solicitation.

Response device. Any means of receiving a desired action from an individual who receives a direct marketing communication.

Response rate. The percentage of people receiving a direct marketing message who respond favorably.

Rollout or rollout phase. The delivery of direct marketing communications to the main lists following a period of test mailing(s) to sample groups in order to refine campaign elements.

Scalability. The capability of a system to increase its operating capacity without substantial modifications. For example, once an investment is made in technology to develop an interactive website, the cost of handling 100,000 transactions is little more than that of handling 10 transactions. Such a system is scalable.

Self-mailer. A direct mail package that does not use an outer envelope.

Targetability. A characteristic of direct marketing that refers to the ability to send a message to specific individuals.

Teaser. The printed words (copy) or illustrations (art work) on the outer envelope of a direct mail piece that is part of neither the address information nor the postage information. Teasers are used to stimulate interest of the mail recipient and increase the nimber of direct mail pieces that are opened.

Testing phase. Stage in a direct marketing program in which the various components of the program are tested on list samples. This phase is used to detect problems and revise materials prior to the rollout (defined above).

❖

QUESTIONS FOR REVIEW

1. Define *direct marketing*.

2. List and describe the advantages of direct marketing.

3. What are the most common types of direct marketing that nonprofit organizations use?

4. If getting your message to your target audience as rapidly as possible was your greatest concern, which type(s) of direct marketing would you use?

5. Define *scalability*.

6. List the five steps in planning a direct mail program.

❖

QUESTIONS FOR DISCUSSION

1. In the Chapter Insight on page 195, we learned that direct marketing response rates tend to be greater for nonprofit organizations than for other types of organizations. Why do you think this is so?

2. How does direct marketing differ from traditional marketing?

3. In the Chapter Insight on page 197, we learned that charities or political organizations are exempt from Do Not Call rules. Why do you think they were exempted?

4. From the Chapter Insight on page 199, which list type would generally produce the highest response rate? The lowest? Why?

5. What is an activities blueprint, and what is its use?

6. Can a direct mail campaign that produces a net loss (costs of program exceed donations) ever be considered a success?

7. Figure 7.3 is conspicuously missing a step. Can you identify this step?

8. Is it important for a return envelope to have prepaid return postage?

❖

INTERNET EXERCISES

1.   Visit the Direct Marketing Association Nonprofit Federation website at www.the-dma .org/nonprofitfederation/index.shtml. What is the purpose of this organization? Who are its members? What are current issues of interest?

2.   Visit the CharityChannel website at charitychannel.com. What resources are available there to nonprofit managers? What are the differences among the various international versions of CharityChannel? Visit the Career Search Online portion of the site. What are the available positions?

3.   Visit the *Chronicle of Philanthropy's* direct marketing Web page at philanthropy .com/directmarketing/. What direct marketing services are available? Describe the types and variety of services related to lists.

4.   Visit the website www.wilbers.com/fund-raising.htm. It discusses a 10-step process for writing a direct mail cover letter. How does this information compare to this chapter's recommendations?

5.   Internet direct e-mail is a relatively new direct marketing medium. Visit www.nonprofits .org/if/idealist/en/FAQ/CategoryViewer/default?category-id=106&sid=36611365-117-RznnF. What issues concern nonprofit managers regarding Internet direct e-mail?

❖

TEAM EXERCISES AND ROLE PLAYING

1.   In teams, interview a nonprofit's manager to learn how that organization uses direct marketing. In class, report findings and discuss the importance of direct marketing in meeting organizational objectives. How is direct marketing used? What types of direct marketing are most used? For what purpose? What types of lists are typically used? What variables are included in the house list?

2.   In teams, develop telemarketing scripts for a suicide hotline volunteer recruitment drive. Role-play in class using your scripts.

3.   Acquire a direct mail packet from home (one that a team member has received) or from a nonprofit organization. Identify the components of the packet, using direct mail jargon. Evaluate the quality of each component.

4.   Investigate the effectiveness of using premiums as a direct marketing response incentive for nonprofit organizations (a controversial topic). Teams can use the Internet to make the information search more efficient (one site worth checking is www.cdmdirect.com/ dmpremiums.htm). You should discover the prevailing arguments for and against the use of premiums for nonprofit organizations in such direct marketing activities as fund-raising. Draft a brief team report describing the arguments pro and con and present your own conclusions and the evidence and arguments you based them on.

MINICASE: Volunteer Metro

Volunteer Metro is an urban umbrella organization that recruits volunteers from the community and matches them to an agency with a need for their preferred volunteer role. Area nonprofits send their requests to Volunteer Metro, which posts the volunteer positions on its website. The metropolitan area is home to more than 1,600 nonprofit organizations. However, not counting churches or membership organizations like the Rotary Club, the number of organizations relying on volunteers is about 200. These organizations include a wide array of social welfare organizations, as well as youth development organizations, educational organizations, and health organizations.

Susan Maxell, Volunteer Metro's marketing manager, is worried. She has just attended a board meeting, chaired by Volunteer Metro's executive director, Marita Shipley, in which the financial troubles of the organization were made abundantly clear. Susan, now at her desk, realizes for the first time that unless something changes within the next year, Volunteer Metro may have to close, and with it will go her job.

In its 10-year history, Volunteer Metro has been funded by the city government. Over the past decade, however, as the federal government has reduced taxes, it has also reduced its funding of state programs. States, although receiving less federal funding, have also reduced taxes, which in turn lowered state funding to cities. Revenues from the state, which used to make up 60% of cities' funding, have fallen to 35% of city revenues. Fortunately, during this period, real estate values increased. Because considerable city revenues are derived from real estate taxes, the revenue shortfall created by the reduction in state funding is not as serious as it might be. However, cities are having to reduce services and grant funding to compensate for lower revenues. (Politically, raising taxes is not considered an option.) Local museums, historical sites, arts and culture organizations, and other nonprofits have received sharply reduced city funding. In some instances, city funding has been eliminated.

Susan learned in the board meeting that the city will reduce its funding to Volunteer Metro by 50% next year and 75% the following year. As marketing manager, Susan has been responsible for recruiting volunteers, primarily through publicizing the organization's website in local public service announcements. She also spends a large amount of her time communicating with the city's nonprofit organizations to assess their recruitment needs. Marita asked Susan to develop a marketing plan to attract new funding sources for Volunteer Metro to compensate for the city's cuts. Susan has to develop her marketing plan and present it at next month's board meeting.

Susan works most often with 50 of the city's 200 volunteer organizations. On average, Volunteer Metro places about 2,500 volunteers in local nonprofits annually. In a marketing study Volunteer Metro conducted last year, Susan learned that about 50% of the city's population has heard of the nonprofit and understands its mission. Volunteer Metro has a favorable public image in the community. In the past, Susan has focused on Volunteer Metro's relationship with the nonprofit organizations it serves. Communication with the public has been aimed at encouraging local volunteerism. Susan's database contains contact information for the area nonprofit organizations and the volunteers she has placed over the past 5 years.

Susan is considering her options. Who can she solicit for funding? Can she rely on local nonprofits, many of which may be experiencing funding shortfalls similar to hers? Can she attract contributions from volunteers she has placed? City residents?

Questions for the Case

1. If you were Susan, who would you target for fund-raising? Rank your list of targets in terms of potential for producing the greatest levels of funding.

2. What lists would you use or acquire for a direct mail program?

3. Develop a direct mail program that includes goals and objectives, list descriptions, an activities blueprint, draft copies of creative materials, and a budget.

Bibliography

American Association of Fundraising Counsel. (2004). *Charity holds its own in tough times.* Retrieved May 22, 2004, 209.224.198.45/press_releases/trustreleases/charityholds.html

Association of Direct Response Fundraising Counsel. (2004). *What your organization needs to know about direct mail fundraising.* Retrieved May 22, 2004, from www.malwarwick.com/direct4.html

Bass, G., & Berry, J. (2004). Lobbying and advocacy by nonprofit organizations: Rethinking the legal constraints on nonprofit voices. *Snapshots, 34*(May), all pages.

Berry, T., & Wilson, D. (2000). *On target: The book on marketing plans.* Eugene, OR: Palo Alto Software.

Bly, R. W. (1998). *Business to business direct marketing: Proven direct response methods to generate leads and sales* (2nd ed.). Chicago: Contemporary Books.

Geller, L. K. (2002). *Response: The complete guide to profitable direct marketing.* New York: Oxford University Press.

Hitchcock, S. (1999). Is it OK to take a loss on a direct mail campaign? Retrieved October 20, 2005, from www.malwarwick.com/direct7.html

Lautman, K. P. (2001). *Direct marketing for nonprofits: Essential techniques for the new era.* Gaithersburg, MD: Aspen Publishers.

Lister, G. J. (2001). *Building your direct mail program.* San Francisco: Jossey-Bass.

Miller, T. W. (2005). *Data and text mining: A business applications approach.* Upper Saddle River, NJ: Pearson Education.

Nash, E. (2000). *Direct marketing: Strategy, planning, execution* (4th ed.). New York: McGraw-Hill.

Self, D. R., Wymer, W. W., Jr., & Henley, T. K. (2002). *Marketing communications for local nonprofit organizations.* Binghamton, NY: Best Business Books.

Spiller, L., & Baier, M. (2005). *Contemporary direct marketing.* Upper Saddle River, NJ: Prentice Hall.

Stone, B., & Jacobs, R. (2001). *Successful direct marketing methods* (7th ed.). New York: McGraw-Hill.

Thomas, B., & Housden, M. (2002). *Direct marketing in practice.* Oxford, UK: Butterworth-Heinemann.

Warwick, M. (2003). *Testing, testing, 1, 2, 3: Raise more money with direct mail tests.* San Francisco: Jossey-Bass.

8

Strategic Approaches to Attracting Major Gifts

Learning Objectives

On completion of this chapter, the reader will

- Understand that individuals give more money to nonprofits than do corporations, foundations, or government sources

- Understand three approaches to identifying a nonprofit's largest donors

- Understand the importance of looking at a nonprofit's offer from the point of view of potential donors

- Understand the importance of the potential major gift information file

- Understand the various traditional tactics for major gift fund-raising

- Understand the individual major gift donor profile

> ## Learning Objectives (Continued)
>
> - Describe and understand the tasks related to effective major gift fund-raising
>
> - Understand when and how to make the "close," or ask for the major gift
>
> - Understand some alternative major gift formats

Opening Vignette: First-to-College

It was a bright spring morning outside, but it was a bit dreary in the tiny offices of the First-to-College organization. Kaitlyn Bowen, the organization's newly hired director of development, was pondering her next move. Kaitlyn's background included a degree in marketing and several internships in large but decentralized nonprofits, such as the American Red Cross and the United Way. In those organizations, a great many small donations were solicited across many segments of society and commercial organizations because people from all walks of life are likely to understand the needs of the Red Cross when it comes to helping disaster victims or collecting blood for victims of car or other accidents. However, because of its focus on students who would be the first in their families to go to college, Kaitlyn thought that First-to-College needed a different approach. Although she planned to continue a traditional, small-donation program, she was fairly sure that relying only on small donations would result in the organization's falling far short of what was needed to cover client services; First-to-College seemed to be a type of organization that would not interest large numbers of individual donors. Kaitlyn believed that, with creative methods, she would be able to attract a major sponsor or maybe even several major sponsors.

Background

First-to-College is a 5-year-old organization that addresses the reality that preparing for and taking SATs, selecting a college, completing application paperwork, applying for financial aid, choosing among various housing options, and registering for classes can be very daunting to someone who is the first in a family to attend college. First-to-College provides services and social marketing programs to help students and their families through the complicated processes involved in getting into college. Among offers of the organization are seminars for the families of these students, SAT training and review, talks and meetings with interested students in local high schools, and mentoring for individual students from the junior year in high school through their first year in college. Among the area's social outreach programs, First-to-College is well regarded and is perceived to be successful in providing a valuable service that positively impacts many young lives. The organization's initial funding came from a multiyear start-up grant, but it will run out in just over 2 years and is nonrenewable. At first, the clients were all minority students, but the program quickly grew to include students from low-income rural areas. If Kaitlyn does not find major new funding support, many of the programs will have to be drastically reduced and perhaps discontinued altogether. Although close to a major city, Kaitlyn has little in the way of a travel and expense budget. She knows that she needs to find some major gifts and quickly.

When it comes to strategic approaches to attracting major gifts, it is important to note a few important points. First, a "major gift opportunity" is a type of resource-attraction offer for a nonprofit organization (see Chapter 5). On the one hand, resource-attraction offers are intended to develop additional funds and volunteers. On the other hand, like any offer of a nonprofit organization, resource-attraction opportunities should be developed after marketing research, market segmentation, and target market selection. In addition, benefits and costs of the major gift need to be identified (see Chapter 6 for a discussion of "price" issues), and 4P marketing mixes need to be developed around the unique characteristics of the nonprofit's target market(s).

Furthermore, because a major gift is a marketing offer, it makes sense that a marketer should be involved in developing and promoting it. Therefore, although many nonprofits employ so-called fund-raisers to develop major gifts, those fund-raising individuals are actually a special type of marketer. Like all marketers, they need to think carefully about the offer (opportunity to give) and what benefits major gift givers might seek. For example, San Diego Hospice and Palliative Care offers three benefits to giving: an exclusive new member welcome reception in the spring, a private evening with San Diego Hospice and Palliative Care Fellows in the fall, and special recognition displayed prominently in the Donor Library and included in the annual report (see www.sdhospice.org/helpmakeadif.htm). Universities, many of which are well versed in developing major gifts, often have a hierarchy of membership levels commensurate with giving amounts; for example, the University of Kentucky has five levels, ranging from University Fellows, who give at least $10,000 in cash or who bequeath at least $50,000, to Presidential Fellows, who give at least $1,000,000 or who bequeath at least $5,000,000 (www.uky.edu/Development/supporters.htm). Clemson University has five Major Gift Clubs for gifts from $1,000 to $25,000 and above, two Legacy Societies for those who wish to remember Clemson in their will, and seven Cumulative Societies, where lifetime cumulative gifts of $50,000–$10,000,000 or more are honored (www.clemson.edu/giving/societies/index.htm).

Major Gifts From Individual Donors

In the United States, gifts from individuals represent nearly 88% of all charitable giving. Although many donations are modest, there is an important category of donor prospect that nonprofit marketers should be willing to spend a great deal of time and effort to cultivate. That category is the small set of prospects who have the capability and the inclination to make major gifts. How large a gift must be in order to be considered major depends on the size of the nonprofit's operating budget. For some non-profits, major gift categories may begin at $5,000, and for others, six- or seven-figure donations are appropriate. The French American International School, for example, designates a major gift as a donation of $5,000 or more (www.faispdx.org/supportingfais/majorgift.asp), whereas the Los Angeles Philharmonic Association asks for a minimum of $10,000 (www.laphil.com/support/major_gifts.cfm) and major gifts

❖ **Exhibit 8.1**   !!News Releases!!

- May 2005—Children's Hospital announced a major gift from Ashley Turner, who contributed about $270,000, including a challenge to triple others' donations, during a radiothon by Oldies 107.9 for Children's Miracle Network, benefiting Children's Hospital of Greenville, North Carolina.
- April 2004—The University of South Carolina announced a $45 million gift from Darla Moore; this was in addition to her $25 million gift in 1988.
- February 2003—The San Diego Symphony announced a $120 million gift from Irwin and Joan Jacobs.
- July 2002—The University of Michigan announced a $25 million gift from Ann Lurie; this was in addition to her previous gifts totaling $12 million.
- April 2002—University of California Santa Cruz alumnus Gordon Ringold and his wife Tanya Zarucki provided a gift of $500,000, the largest outright gift the campus has ever received from an alumnus.
- July 2000—A $9.7 million construction plan for Royalton's K–12 school received a breathtaking boost this week with the announcement of a $350,000 donation from long-time residents Dick and Polly Ellis.

to the National Constitution Center begin at that amount also (www.constitution center.org/support/MajorGifts/index.shtml). World Vision UK's website (www.world vision.org.uk) suggests that major gifts begin at £5,000. Exhibit 8.1 presents news releases for six gifts that were considered major by the organizations that received them. **Major gifts** are defined as donations that are significantly beyond the typical donor's gift to a nonprofit; they often represent 10%, 20%, 30%, or more of the nonprofit's total yearly budget. The importance of such a gift to the success of a capital campaign or to reaching an organization's goals is so great that the nonprofit's director and major fund-raising officer are willing to spend considerable time planning, developing, and nurturing a relationship with a potential major gift donor. How these potential major gift donors are found, nurtured, and turned into repeat major gift donors is the subject of this chapter.

A Nonprofit's Largest Donors

There are several views when it comes to identifying a nonprofit's donor segments. Three of these are the rule of thirds, the 80/20 axiom, and the 90/10 axiom.

The Rule of Thirds. The **rule of thirds** crops up in several fields, but in the context of nonprofit fund raising, it suggests that one third of annual donations (in dollars) will come from the top 10 to 20 donors, one third from the next 80 to 100 donors, and one third from all the remaining nonprofit supporters. One caveat, however, is that it seems that, more and more, the top 10–20 patrons must actually be asked for more than one third of the fund-raising goal, perhaps even as much as one half.

❖ **Exhibit 8.2**   An Example of the Rule of Thirds as Applied to a Nonprofit Wishing to Raise $100,000

No. of Gifts	Amount of Gifts	Total at This Level	Cumulative Total	Percentage of Goal
1	$10,000	$10,000	$10,000	10.00
1	$8,000	$8,000	$18,000	18.00
1	$5,000	$5,000	$23,000	23.00
2	$2,500	$5,000	$28,000	28.00
5	$1,000	$5,000	$33,000	33.00
One third of the $100,000 goal will come from the top 10 donors.				
15	$750	$11,250	$44,250	44.25
20	$500	$10,000	$54,250	54.25
25	$250	$6,250	$60,500	60.50
25	$150	$3,750	$64,250	64.25
30	$75	$2,250	$66,500	66.50
One third of the goal will come from the next 115 donors.				
50	$70	$3,500	$70,000	70.00
75	$65	$4,875	$74,875	74.88
100	$55	$5,500	$80,375	80.38
150	$50	$7,500	$87,875	87.88
...	...	...	...	...
n			$100,000	100.00
The campaign goal of $100,000 will be met with many gifts of less than $50.00.				

SOURCE: Goettler Associates (2000).

To use the rule of thirds heuristic to raise $100,000, nonprofits may consider putting together a table such as that shown in Exhibit 8.2.

The 80/20 and 90/10 Axioms. Another common view that can be applied in many situations is the 80/20 axiom, which says 20% of donors will provide 80% of the funding (often with 10% from one gift). A more aggressive view suggests that 10% of donors provide 90% of the funding. In either case, the ability to attract, involve, and motivate the top major gift donors by and large determines a campaign's success or failure.

The rule of thirds, the 80/20, and the 90/10 views of fund-raising are very different from the naïve approach that inexperienced marketers might express as, "If you need to raise $600,000, then all you need to do is find 1,000 people willing to give $600 each. Rather than building a marketing campaign to attract $600 donors, an experienced marketer using the rule of thirds would design a campaign to attract several donors in the $50,000 range, a larger group in the $2,000 range, and an even larger group in the $100–$500 range. Because each donor group likely differs from the others not only in terms of gift potential but also in terms of donor behavior and decision making, strategists need to consider the cost-benefit trade-off of creating a customized marketing approach for each group. For example, a nonprofit would, of course, change its monetary request for each group, but the benefits offered and the initial approaches to each should be different as well. Unless a nonprofit's budget is extremely limited, not only will it benefit the nonprofit to approach each segment separately; it may also be cost effective to create subsegments within each group because there may be differences within each donor group. Much of the groundwork for a custom approach to different donor segments and subsegments will come from the situation analysis of the strategic planning process, which was covered in detail in Chapter 4.

As with all organizational strategy, there are many factors, including the nature of the nonprofit's offer(s), the environment, organizational resources and structure, and leadership, that may impact the way each potential donor group should be approached. Nonetheless, some general approaches to each of the two or three donor groups identified by the rule of thirds and the 80/20 and 90/10 axioms seem to be effective for most nonprofits. Generally, the large number of small givers may be approached with mass marketing techniques, including broadcast advertising or public service announcements, direct mail solicitation, public relations events, publicity, and the like. The middle third, who give medium-size gifts, may be approached with traditional fund-raising campaigns that will be described in Chapter 9. Finally, the top third or the 20% or 10% who give the most should typically receive personal attention from the nonprofit's top fund-raising and operational executives, who will likely rely on individualized marketing approaches and very personal communication and solicitation. For example, the nonprofit may practice **supporter relationship management,** which refers to those aspects of a nonprofit's strategy that relate to techniques and methods for attracting and retaining supporters.

The top donors represent relatively few individuals, but finding them and gaining their support are critical to the success of most capital campaigns.

Seeing Through the Eyes of the Potential Donor

As with large-scale strategic planning, it would be best for a nonprofit to start with an objective analysis of itself and its offer(s) through the eyes of the potential donor. In this chapter, we are concerned with seeing through the eyes of donors capable of making five-, six-, seven-, and even eight-figure major gift donations. It is very important to segment within this group because major gifts can come from several sources, such as individuals, corporations, charitable foundations, and the government. Each will have its own giving objectives and its own way of considering how well a particular nonprofit fits with its interests.

❖ **Exhibit 8.3**   Example of an Objective Offer Analysis

Program Name: _____

In order to put oneself in the position of a potential donor, one must evaluate each of the following:

1. **Cause, mission, and vision:** *How well does the offer address what donors see as social priorities?*

2. **Differential advantage:** *Compared to others addressing these social priorities, what is this offer's differential advantage, special capability, or unique approach?*

3. **Value proposition:** *How realistic is the nonprofit's set of statements that describe the real benefits its target publics will receive from this offer?*

4. **Impact:** *How many people will benefit from the program? How will they benefit?*

5. **Measurable results:** *What objective, measurable approach will be used to assess the offer's performance in providing target public benefits, meeting program objectives, and conforming to budget?*

6. **Timeliness:** *Why is this the time to address this need?*

7. **Realistic time frame:** *What is a reasonable time frame for identifying potential donors, identifying personal values, building relationships, and closing funding agreements? (This often takes more time and effort than many nonprofits realize—months and years.)*

8. **Non-financial support from referent public figures:** *What other important public figures are willing to have their name associated with this offer?*

9. **Media attention:** *How much interest will the media have? How might this ability (or lack of it) to attract media be used in our capital campaign's strategic and tactical design?*

10. **Offer enhancement:** *What is the nonprofit not doing that would really capture the interest of potential major gift donors?*

A useful first step when it comes to seeing offers from the point of view of a donor is an objective review of each of the nonprofit's offers (whether goods, services, or social behavior programs) as the potential donor is likely to see it. A checklist of items from the donor's point of view appears in Exhibit 8.3. The checklist can help managers prepare the offers they use to solicit major donations. Several of the items in the checklist help managers view the situation from the prospect's perspective. Not only should a nonprofit examine each of its offers with such a checklist; it should also complete the checklist for each current and potential public, including different groups of current or potential donors. Different groups of publics may respond to many offers similarly; however, offers that different segments or individuals may see differently should be clearly noted in the donors' reference file.

The Potential Major Gift Information File

As a reference for those internally involved in a nonprofit's fund-raising efforts, it is important that the organization set up a computer file folder for each individual or organization with major gift potential. The file information will be important in designing a custom strategy to interest, involve, and maintain the donor-organization relationship. The files will also be helpful in finding and understanding other potential donors with similar profiles.

Exhibit 8.4 shows typical information that would be collected and maintained for an individual donor. The file for a corporate, foundation, or government donor would be similar, but with detailed information on the group, its history, its giving objectives, and its key executives. As in the business world, fund-raising executives must make a

❖ **Exhibit 8.4**   Content of Potential Major Gift Information File—Individual Donor

Name

Date of birth

Family members and relationship

Address and contact information (including their administrative assistants)

Detailed personal and professional history

Income, net worth, giving record

Financial and legal advisors

Professional organization membership and leadership positions

Civic and charitable organization membership and leadership positions

Hobbies

Hot buttons (Issues this individual feels strongly about, either positively or negatively)

Chronological record of contacts (date, mode, summary of interaction, planned follow-up or next step)

Our relationship-building plan and current stage

Target major gift amount (a reasonable starting point might be in the range of a traditional 10% of annual income over a period of time to reach a total amount or a one-time gift equal to 2% to 5% of net worth)

special effort to keep these files up to date. Notes on all supporter contacts should be included, as should special issues to mention and those too sensitive to bring up.

Traditional Tactics for Major Gift Fund-Raising

Analyzing needs, taking advantage of market opportunities, and creating valued offer mixes have always been fundamental responsibilities for marketers. Through a strategic planning situation analysis (see Chapter 4) and an objective offer analysis (see Exhibit 8.3), strategists try to make sure that all their approaches and tactical elements are solidly based on the needs of particular clients and the funding interests of particular donors. Although it is wise to be skeptical of any list of general observations, there are a few traditional fund-raising ideas and philosophical approaches that have stood the test of time and deserve consideration. Because an individual major donor's needs and motivations could be quite different from those of average donors, strategists need to use their own professional judgment about the appropriateness of the following guidelines in a particular situation.

Focus on individuals. Because individuals provide the majority of all philanthropic support for nonprofits, nonprofit marketers must identify individuals with major gift potential, plan a powerful and creative individual-specific campaign, and implement it with passion and persistence. There are likely to be thousands of millionaires in any particular nonprofit's state, hundreds in its closest city, and several in its town. The nonprofit marketer will never know how many of these individuals might support the nonprofit's cause unless the marketer is committed to finding them, uncovering the issues that are important to them, designing and presenting a compelling offer (including benefits to the giver), and personally asking for their financial support. The nonprofit marketer tasked with major gift development must passionately believe in the "dream" that the nonprofit is trying to recruit others to support.

Focus on donor benefits. The donor's decision usually does not revolve around the nonprofit's need. Individuals give for emotional reasons. Tax benefits for giving may make the decision easier, but it is rarely the number one motivator. Major donors almost always need to develop a great deal of affection and respect for the nonprofit and involvement with it before significant support will begin. Major gift donations usually bring donors personal satisfaction in areas such as the following:

- Doing their share to help others
- Gaining recognition and influence
- Feeling pride of association
- Experiencing the joy of giving
- Feeling they make a difference

There is seldom a single dominant reason for a donation. It is up to the marketer to build the relationship with a donor and gain insight into the donor's unique personal mix of motivations. A future major donor is almost always one who has a history of supporting a cause in a smaller way, so it is very likely that nonprofits already have some donor knowledge that will be helpful. The marketer should not expect to uncover prospects who will quickly write checks with a high dollar value, however. Major gifts almost always require time, relationship building, and nurturing.

Ask for the gift. A business-world marketer would recognize this as the imperative "need to close" (ask for the objective of the interaction with the client). Experience suggests that the larger the gift request, the better it is that the close be made by the nonprofit's most senior executive and, if possible, a social peer at the board level. In any case, the closer needs to be someone the potential donor holds in high regard and someone capable of selling the excitement of the program. If a program the nonprofit is trying to fund does not create excitement, the nonprofit really should rethink the offer.

Remember board members. Involved board members are important sources for a nonprofit's funding. Research has shown that major donors give their biggest gifts to organizations they serve in board or volunteer officer positions. Board members know they are expected to make and recruit major gifts, and it is a great honor to be asked to serve on a nonprofit board. However, with the honor comes the responsibility of financially supporting the organization in a significant way and helping find others to do the same. Board members who believe in a cause are excellent recruiters of others from their social and professional strata.

Express appreciation. Donors usually welcome sincere and tasteful recognition. Expressing gratitude for a major gift should involve more than one kind of thank-you and usually should recognize the donor's spouse as co-donor. What will be most appreciated by any specific donor should be uncovered via the fund-raiser's interpersonal skills prior to receipt of any major gift, but a letter of appreciation from the nonprofit director and board would be a good start, perhaps followed by letters of appreciation from public figures who are relevant to the donor and who are willing to have their names associated with the cause (e.g., a personal thank-you from the state's governor or a nationally recognized business person). A nonprofit may follow up its thank-you letters with a donor recognition dinner or ball, when the nonprofit can introduce individual major gift donors and donor couples and present them with a plaque. The nonprofit may later arrange an event at which donor names are added to a permanent bronze plaque in the organization's headquarters lobby. Still later, the nonprofit could organize an event at which donors (individuals and couples) are inducted into an appropriate donor level, such as the Founders Club, President's Club, or Sponsors Club.

The Individual Major Gift Donor Profile

Once a nonprofit marketer understands the importance of seeing through the eyes of the potential donor and has read about some of the traditional approaches to major gift fund-raising, it is important to consider the nature of individual major donors in more detail. This section begins with individuals because they are the source of the

❖ **Exhibit 8.5**   Typical Major Donor Profile

- Age 50–70
- Conservative
- Educated
- Cares and shares
- Is a successful entrepreneur or professional or a member of a wealthy family
- Has an involvement in the cause
- Has a long history of donations (probably progressively larger donations even if not approaching major gift level)
- Has grown and financially secure children
- Is financially knowledgeable
- Has total personal assets 20 to 50 times the amount you are seeking as a major gift
- Is planning for a lifestyle change such as retirement or planning for some significant rearrangement of finances.

majority of nonprofit donations. Yes, that number includes giving to churches and other religious institutions, but if one were to look around a college campus, one would almost certainly find many plaques, monuments, and buildings that testify to the importance of individual gift donors. In fact, many universities carry the name of the original major gift donor who made their creation possible. Some of you who are reading this textbook may be studying in a college of business that carries a donor's name, and perhaps faculty who hold donor-named chaired professorships have taught you in a class. The amount of donation required for this type of recognition varies, but good ballpark figures would be $1 million to $5 million for the professorship and $50 million to $100 million to have a college in a university (e.g., a college of business) named after the donor or a donor's loved one in perpetuity.

A typical major donor profile is presented in Exhibit 8.5. The nonprofit marketer should consider each piece of information about the typical major donor and use it to put together an approach to specific potential donors. That is not to say that all major donors will neatly fit the profile presented in Exhibit 8.5, but most do, and it can be a good starting point for identifying candidates worthy of more detailed research.

Tasks Related to Effective Nonprofit Major Gift Fund-Raising

Effective major gift fund-raising requires several tasks: engaging in marketing research to identify potential donors of major gifts; rating good prospects, which helps in deciding where to spend time and resources; developing strategies for building relationships and moving a potential donor to an involved major gift donor; determining how many major gift donor prospects to assign to each marketer or fund-raiser; and anticipating and handling a prospect's concerns about and objections and barriers to a request for a major gift.

Marketing Research: Identifying Potential Donors of Major Gifts

Although the reader may have studied the marketing research chapter in this textbook (Chapter 3) or even taken a marketing research course, the type of marketing research appropriate for identifying potential major donors is typically much different from the statistical research approaches taught in undergraduate marketing classes and used to understand specific problems. For example, when it comes to identifying potential major donors, it would be logical to start with the nonprofit's own board members and have them list the people they know who would make good prospects. Other important people in the community as well are often willing to add individuals they know to the list. Membership contact lists of the local chamber of commerce, country club, and private business clubs could be reviewed (of course, that may require the cooperation of a member who has access to the information). Prospective major gift donors are likely to live in a very prestigious housing development or have a house that stands out because of its size. If you know the address of a house, you can search county real estate records and uncover its exact valuation, price paid, and loan amount at the time of purchase. To find out who own other multimillion-dollar homes in the area, collect addresses and use a city directory to get the names of the people who live there. In addition, use Internet directories such as www.switchboard.com to find telephone numbers. There are national and regional directories for doctors and lawyers by specialty (and your own doctor and lawyer can help identify the best directories for the area). Local yellow pages may be a starting point, but a good professional directory will help separate the interns, HMO physicians, and strip mall lawyers from the truly wealthy, successful professionals. Other nonprofits in a nonprofit's area may list their major donors, and these names can be added to at least the first draft of a list of possible donors. At some time or other, the business and society sections of your local newspaper have probably covered most of the high-potential donors in your area. Accessing the paper's archives for particular types of stories can provide a wealth of background information about potential donors. The section of a publication (e.g., business announcements, cotillions, fraternal organizations) that covered one potential donor may be a source of more names.

Local university or city reference librarians can be a big help in uncovering public information. Imagine a person who has one or more degrees and years of experience in finding just the kind of information you need. Fund-raisers would be wise to make use of their expertise. Often the library will allow you free access to databases that normally require a subscription. LexisNexis is an online database that will usually turn up past news and magazine coverage of successful people. The Thomson Gale Biography Resource Center (www.galegroup.com/BiographyRC) is another online resource for information on public figures. Who's who books in various professional areas can be found in libraries and online (for example *Marquis Who's Who On-Line*, www.marquiswhoswho.com/index.asp). The Thomson General Business File (infotrac.thomsonlearning.com) is a good online source of information to connect a donor to a company. The online *D&B's Million Dollar Databases* (www.dnbmdd.com/mddi) shows the companies in a nonprofit's state and the names of their top management. See philanthropy.com/stats/donors/ for information on the type of people who make the very largest donations. In hard cover, Standard and Poor's *Register of Corporations, Directors and Executives* and *D&B's Reference Book of Corporate Managements* are good sources of information.

When uncovering information on individuals, surrogate indicators are often useful. A **surrogate indicator** is some factor that is related to another variable of interest. For example, nonprofit marketers often do not have direct access to an individual's income, but they do have access to surrogate indicators such as job title and size and type of employer (surveys of income by title and company type are available at employment websites such as www.dowjones.com/Careers/Careers.htm). If prospects are officers in public companies, their income, bonus, stock plan, and retirement plan are likely to be available in U.S. Securities and Exchange Commission filings (www.sec .gov); a nonprofit employee can search for a public company's filings and look in proxy filings if available. The company's 10K filings usually include a professional biography for each corporate officer, including age and time with the company.

It is important to note that nonprofit managers can also use service providers to help with prospect research. These are businesses that specialize in research to identify potential large donors. Big Online (www.bigdatabase.com) and PRO Online, also known as iWave (www.iwave.com), are two examples.

Rating Good Prospects: Where to Spend Precious Time and Resources

If a nonprofit has a great many prospects and a staff of marketers working as fund-raisers, marketers will probably want to devise a formal approach to rating prospects according to their dollar ability to give (based on their net worth or assets), adjusted by the rater's judgment (expressed as a percentage) of how likely each is to provide the gift. Then, prospects would be assigned to specific marketers in such a way as to balance their load and give everyone an approximately equal chance of being successful. The CEO and high-level marketers at the nonprofit would handle the very-high-dollar major gift prospects.

In small organizations, it is likely that only one or two marketers will have to make most of the fund-raising efforts. Therefore, they need to allocate their limited time and resources to prospects that are most likely to donate. Building donor involvement and a good relationship takes considerable time and effort. It will be difficult, but the seeds for future donations have to be planted and nurtured at the same time that a marketer is harvesting ripe opportunities. So for each prospect (and the list should be long), a nonprofit marketer should assess the following key factors:

- How much each prospect is capable of giving
- How likely it is that each prospect will give
- How long it will take to bring each prospect to the point of giving (closing)

For those prospects capable of being "closed" for a current campaign, the nonprofit marketer needs to determine how best to approach each and should assign a specific marketer the responsibility of making face-to-face contact. The marketers for each prospect should listen to and interact with them to uncover motivations and needs. They have the responsibility of building a custom approach to their assigned prospects, seeing the approach is implemented, and providing regular updates to the main office. Even smaller nonprofits can use one of a number of supporter relationship management and sales-contact software packages to organize this effort. It is important that a nonprofit store all prospect assessments and information in some sort of master contact reference files that will be available to top management and to others who may also be assigned to deal with a particular prospect.

Strategies for Building Relationships

Prospects need to be identified and evaluated and an involvement program designed, implemented, and monitored—and revised as appropriate. Involvement program elements should each facilitate prospects' movement from one step of their decision process to the next. Individuals support organizations that they feel involved in and believe in, whose leadership team they respect, and whose dream they share of making something special happen, making a difference, or having an impact. A nonprofit's next major gift donor will most likely be a donor who has progressed well along the pattern of progressively larger donations represented by the AIDTIM model, shown in Exhibit 8.6. The model represents the various steps (Awareness, Interest, Desire, Trial, Information, and Major Gift Action) through which a nonprofit should move a prospect so that the prospect progresses from unawareness to close involvement with the nonprofit's offers and its mission. The marketer would use the framework illustrated in Exhibit 8.6 to outline a plan for building a relationship with a potential donor. Then, specific details about how to develop awareness, interest, and so forth would be added so that the plan could be implemented.

Awareness—The Mission, People, and Vision. To begin developing prospects into major gift donors, a nonprofit needs to build awareness of its mission, its people (both the people in the organization and the people whom the nonprofit seeks to help), and its vision. Furthermore, the nonprofit needs to develop excitement about its mission. It is important to determine levels of awareness about the nonprofit's mission, people, and vision at the beginning and at the end of the process of moving a prospect through AIDTIM.

Interest—Building Involvement. During interest building, the model's second step, the nonprofit's goal is to begin encouraging involvement on the part of its potential major gift donors. Research has consistently shown that people are more likely to give to an organization once they have become involved with it. Major involvement tends to follow moderate involvement, which tends to follow minor involvement. In the case of raising funds for a university, for example, fostering minor involvement by a prospect might involve inviting the prospect to speak to a class or student club on an appropriate topic.

Desire—Status Building. To move potential major gift donors from interest to desire, the nonprofit should "up the ante" a little. Meeting and having lunch with the dean of a prospect's college degree program might be a next step as the nonprofit attempts to move the potential major gift donor from interest and minor involvement to desire via

❖ **Exhibit 8.6**   High-Involvement Donor Decision-Making Model and Donor Relationship Management Program Elements to Facilitate Donor Movement Toward Major Gift Action (AIDTIM)*

Awareness

   Mission, People, and Vision Excitement (Planned program steps 1, 2, 3, . . .)

Interest

   Involvement Building (Planned program steps 1, 2, 3, . . .)

Desire

   Status Building (Planned program steps 1, 2, 3, . . .)

Trial (small commitment or donation)

   Expression of Appreciation (Planned program steps 1, 2, 3, . . .)

Information

   Formal Proposal, Estate and Tax Planning (Planned program steps 1, 2, 3, . . .)

Major Gift Action

   Follow-Up (Planned program steps 1, 2, 3, . . .)
   Expression of Appreciation (Planned program steps 1, 2, 3, . . .)
   Relationship Maintenance (Planned program steps 1, 2, 3, . . .)
   Planning for Next-Stage Gift (Planned program steps 1, 2, 3, . . .)

SOURCE: Gomes and Knowles (2005).

Note: In a real application, detailed, planned program steps would be listed. Here they are represented by "Planned program steps 1, 2, 3, . . ."

status building. At or following the luncheon engagement, the dean might be asked to solicit the prospect's advice on some important matter facing the college. Perhaps the prospect would be willing to lend business or other expertise to a new college project or student initiative. At some point, there may be an invitation to interact with board members or major donors in a formal or informal way (perhaps to attend a meeting or a luncheon with spouses or to play golf). If a board member has a yacht, a day trip or fishing expedition might be attractive to many prospects and may cause them to feel that it would be enjoyable to join the "club" of major donors and make a "real" difference. Generally, prospects are more likely to become major gift donors if they feel valued, involved, and important. That means keeping them involved in events and the communications loop for current efforts and activities. Tours, coffees, luncheons, tailgating and seats in the president's box at sporting events, invitations to speak at campus conferences, and nomination to be responsible for some part of recruiting or fund-raising all can play a part in building the prospect's relationship and involvement with the nonprofit. But none of this just happens. Nonprofits need to plan for moving prospects to levels of more and more involvement.

Trial—Expression of Appreciation. As in business-to-business (B2B) marketing, a nonprofit marketer should not be building up to just one donation from each prospective donor (or, in the B2B case, one sale) but should actually be building a long-term relationship that will lead to a whole progression of donations (sales). But before donors will become major gift donors, it is likely they will make a smaller donation. Depending on the nonprofit's response to the first donation, donors will either give more when asked or may feel they have done enough for one nonprofit and move on (and away from the nonprofit). Earlier in this chapter, we discussed the importance of expressing appreciation for donations. Even though a potential major gift donor has given only one small gift so far, a thank-you is very important when it comes to moving that donor to the next level of involvement.

Information—Formal Proposal, Estate and Tax Planning. At the appropriate point in the relationship, potential donors who are being groomed for a major gift actually expect a request for financial support. They expect that such a request will be made in a professional manner with a well-conceived and compelling verbal presentation (compelling because it has been designed around their passion, motivation, and personal interest), delivered by someone they have come to trust and substantiated by a brief written proposal they can share with their spouse or financial advisers.

Major Gift Action—Follow-Up, Expression of Appreciation, Relationship Maintenance, and Planning for the Next-Stage Gift. Of course, once donors have become major gift donors, it is important that the nonprofit and the marketer remember them, continue their contacts, and otherwise be sure that the major donor continues to feel appreciated. Perhaps the most critical and challenging recognition for the fund-raiser to arrange is having the board and other major gift donors include new major gift donors in their social functions (e.g., golf, a night at the opera with spouses, dinners at members-only clubs). It is usually important to show donors that they have become a part of something special in which they can meet people similar to themselves who also support the cause. It also shows such donors that they are liked for themselves and not just for their money. This show of appreciation, followed by social acceptance and involvement, will encourage major donors to continue their support of the nonprofit.

Number of Accounts Per Marketer

How many prospects individual marketers can manage at the same time depends on many factors, including the donor development activity of the total organization, their energy, their ability to prioritize and organize work, their ability to understand and bond with diverse individuals, how much they learn from experience and their mistakes, how much they learn from other fund-raising team members, and, of course, the nature of the prospects they are assigned. Donors with the most promise, those with significant assets, will probably be contacted one or two times per month. If individual marketers are each assigned 10 to 20 of these sorts of prospects, they will likely have their hands full. In situations where their social and professional position can be an advantage, nonprofessional marketers, such as board members, may be assigned a few prospects to develop and manage. It helps if those board members have already given a significant gift (and it is certainly expected of board members that they either give a significant amount or personally raise a significant amount for their nonprofit). If board members have already given or raised a major gift, they can express how personally important the cause is to them and prove it by showing the prospect how much time and resources they have committed to its success.

With a limited staff and many prospects, it is easy to see why nonprofit major gift fund-raising efforts need to be organized and prioritized. One approach would be to give the set of highest-priority prospects to the nonprofit's staff with the strongest track record and a larger group, perhaps 20–40, of lower-priority prospects to each of the other marketers, with an expected average contact frequency of once every 4–6 weeks. Another approach would be to give each marketer a mix of large, medium, and smaller prospects. This would allow more contact continuity as donors progress from small gifts to major gifts.

Anticipating Prospect Objections, Concerns, and Barriers to the Major Gift

In making a major sale, B2B marketers expect objections along the way. Similarly, marketers working with potential major gift donors should also expect donor objections, concerns, and other barriers. Handling objections is where good marketers use their training and "closing" skills. This does not mean they should use manipulation or pressure, like a stereotypical used-car salesperson. That misuse of closing skills would be inappropriate because we are talking about supporter-value-driven marketers who truly care about the best interests of the donor and seek to create a win-win outcome. The process for handling sincere objections is a valuable skill set for any professional because, when used correctly, it creates the habit of seeing situations through the eyes of the donors, it avoids confrontation, and it assures that the donors have access to all the information relevant to the decision they are facing.

Handling Prospect Objections, Concerns, and Barriers to the Major Gift

Clarify your understanding. The first objective when dealing with an objection, concern, or barrier is to be sure to know exactly what the prospect is saying and what those words mean. That means fund-raisers need to ask questions and listen carefully to a donor's answers in order to clarify their understanding. A commonly heard prospect objection is, "I don't have that kind of money." That may sound like a pretty clear communication, but it isn't necessarily. The marketer has to determine whether the prospect feels too poor to consider such a large gift or whether the donor's money is tied up in assets that would be impossible to turn into cash. Or it might be an indication that the marketer has not brought the prospect to the point of being ready to make that kind of commitment. The point is that such a statement could mean many things, and it would be a mistake to guess at the meaning. When a prospect makes such a statement, it is important for the marketer to be caring enough to tactfully ask questions and listen carefully to the prospect's reasoning. A clear understanding of the prospect's thinking will be the basis for the fund-raiser's approach to removing the objection, concern, or barrier.

Acknowledge and validate the donor's reasoning. The marketer should begin by empathizing with the prospect, saying something like, "I understand why you may feel that way." Saying this does not mean the marketer necessarily agrees with the prospect. It just means that the marketer understands. Prospects are typically highly successful professionals, and if pushed, they will probably win in a clash of wills. Because objection handling is a routine part of moving toward a major gift, there is no need for marketers to inject an adversarial tone into the relationship they have been working so hard to build.

Offset the objection, relieve the concern, remove the barrier. The approach the marketer takes in this step will depend on the reason for the objection and the marketer's insight into the prospect's personality, values, and motivation. A marketer may be able to offset an objection with a greater benefit that the prospect was not considering. The fund-raiser may be able to provide a creative, alternative way of approaching the timing or nature of the gift that will better fit the prospect's situation. It may be possible to turn an objection into a lead-in to providing more information. For example, the marketer may say, "I should have gone over some of the latest ways of structuring planned gifts that make excellent use of nonliquid assets while retaining a lifetime steady income for you and your spouse."

Fund-raising is an art form based on understanding and caring about people. Being able to effectively handle an objection is an important interpersonal skill. Marketers who are nervous about handling objections may do well to practice objection-handling skills on an objection made by a friend on a particular issue.

The Close—Asking for the Major Gift

We hope it is very clear that marketers should not and generally do not just ask for a major gift. First, the prospect is carefully identified and evaluated, and then a donor-specific progressive relationship-building plan is designed and implemented. Asking for a gift comes as a natural progression and is done by the right person at the right time. It should not be a surprise to the donor, but it has to be handled with finesse. Similar to business-to-business salespeople, good marketers learn how to read the mental state or attitude of important prospective donors. They have taken the time to really get to know their prospective donors, and they can read the body language and signals the prospects are sending. Effective marketers use their knowledge to decide if, when, and how they should ask for the donation. There are a number of important points to keep in mind:

- Remember the motivations and values you have uncovered for this prospect that will help you decide on an approach and timing.
- Remember to stress the impact the gift will have.
- Remember to go over the aspects of the program that generate excitement and passion for this particular prospect (the prospect's hot buttons).

- Remember to mention that you will work with the prospect's financial adviser and attorney to make the whole giving process smooth, painless, and professional.
- Remember to mention the planned recognition (e.g., the events and process of naming the business school after the prospect's father—a name the college will carry in perpetuity).
- Have a written proposal the prospect can discuss with spouse and advisers.
- Although you have calculated a gift amount based on a percentage of the prospect's net worth, offer alternative levels. It is better to have a prospect considering what level to give than whether to give.
- Listen carefully, uncover barriers, and handle sincere objections, questions, and concerns.
- Even if the prospect does not respond positively in your first "asking for the donation" attempt, you will have learned a great deal from the interaction and can better plan your next approach.

If you are sincere and truly believe in the worthiness of your cause, then you should not feel any hesitation about using your people skills and marketing ability to find ever better ways to approach the prospect. When appropriate, invest more in building the relationship, and be sure to enlist the aid of your supporters among the prospect's social circle.

Alternative Major Gift Formats for Prospect Consideration

Although nonprofits love to receive unrestricted, immediate, cash gifts, there are many other common approaches that may be more suited to a donor's financial situation. The fund-raiser's detailed knowledge of these options often makes the difference in turning a major gift prospect into a major gift donor. Although we will list some of these options here, their actual tax consequences to a particular donor would need to be determined by the donor's financial and tax advisers. Internal Revenue Service rules can change, and state and local tax procedures are not uniform across the country. Fund-raisers must be familiar with the tax rules in their locality in order to present viable giving options. Gifts can be available immediately, they may take effect at a later time, or they may be given as a bequest (available on the death of the donor and spouse). Some examples of gifts appear in the following list.

1. Immediate gifts: Can be held, used, or turned into cash. The gift may be unrestricted or given with specific limitations on use.
   - Cash
   - Stock
   - Land, buildings
   - Gifts of equipment, art, boats, or anything of value that the nonprofit would be willing to receive

2. Gifts that provide the donor with income
   - Charitable gift annuity: In return for a gift, the nonprofit may agree to provide the donor with regular income payments for life (or for a set period).
   - Trust: A donor's gift is placed in trust (usually with a financial institution), typically with the donor receiving regular income payments for life (or for a set period).
     a. Charitable remainder annuity trust: At the donor's and spouse's death, the "remainder" (principal amount) in the trust goes to the nonprofit. The donor's income is set at regular periodic payments of a fixed amount.

    b. Charitable remainder unitrust: Same as annuity trust except regular income payments vary based on the performance of the trust's investments.

    c. Charitable remainder pooled income fund trust: Same as unitrust except a number of donors' individual gifts are pooled for investment, and the returns (income) are distributed according to investment performance and how much of the pool the donor contributed.

3. Gifts that provide the nonprofit with income
   - Charitable lead trust: The regular investment income from the trust goes to the nonprofit, either for the donor's or spouse's life or for a specified period of years. Then the trust is ended, and the remaining principal returns to the donor, estate, or beneficiary.

       a. Charitable lead annuity trust: Because this is an annuity, the income from the trust is set at a fixed periodic amount.

       b. Charitable lead unitrust: The income from the trust varies based on the performance of the investments.

4. Gifts to the nonprofit that allow the donor to retain use
   - Life estate agreement: The gift gives the nonprofit ownership of something of value such as a house or yacht, but the donor retains the right to occupy and use the property for life or for a set period of time.

5. Bequest: The donor makes the gift in his or her last will and testament.

6. Life insurance: The donor typically makes regular premium payments to the insurance company, and the insurance company pays beneficiaries a set amount when the donor dies.
   - The donor may own the policy and name the nonprofit as beneficiary.
   - Alternatively, the nonprofit may own the policy. In this case, the donor still makes the premium payments, and the nonprofit is still the beneficiary.

As you can tell from this partial list of typical ways donors can provide a major gift to a nonprofit, there are many alternatives and issues for the donors and their financial advisers to consider. Marketers who are knowledgeable in major gifts and estate planning can provide real value to the donor. A marketer who knows the donor's values and objectives will customize and fine-tune the terms of the agreement to make the offer more attractive and more likely to be accepted by the donor. The specifics of all the alternatives are set out in legal documents written with the involvement of lawyers representing the donor and lawyers representing the nonprofit.

The number of possible ways a donor can provide value to a nonprofit is limited only by the fund-raiser's and donor's ability to think creatively. Southern Wesleyan University's Alumni Association Web page (www.swu.edu/alumni/101ways.php) lists 101 ways alumni can support their university. Although many of them could not be added to the financial results of a capital campaign, they all could represent additional ways to involve a prospect in the success of the university. Each involvement could bring the potential donor one step closer to feeling personally motivated to make a major gift.

Managerial Issues

The following issues are relevant for nonprofit managers:

1. **Importance of individual donors.** Individuals give more money to nonprofits than corporations, foundations, or government sources. Although it might be tempting or seem easier to write grants for funding from corporations, foundations, or the government (because grant writing is probably an existing skill set in many nonprofits), a nonprofit may do better to look to individuals for major gifts.

2. **Identifying large donors.** There are several ways for a nonprofit to go about identifying potential large donors. Three rules, the rule of thirds, the 80/20 axiom, and the 90/10 axiom, may be used to shape the thinking of the nonprofit when it comes to developing donor sources. Many nonprofits have important information already available concerning their most consistent donors. The next major gift donor is most likely to come from the most consistent 1/3, 20%, or 10% of a nonprofit's current donors.

3. **Your nonprofit's offer(s) from the point of view of potential donors.** Rather than taking a cause or a funding point of view, nonprofits would do best to look at their offers from the point of view of their donors. Because donors often are not clients of the nonprofits to which they donate, nonprofits need to look at the benefits that donors may receive from donating and emphasize those benefits in communications with current and potential donors.

4. **The potential major gift information file.** In order to ensure that marketers in a nonprofit have all the information they need before approaching potential major gift donors, it is important for a nonprofit to develop a potential major gift information file and keep it current.

5. **Traditional tactics for major gift fund-raising.** It is important to learn and apply the traditional tactics (ones that have stood the test of time): Focus on individual donors (each donor is unique and should be treated as such), focus on benefits to the donor (e.g., a sense of pride, a feeling of involvement), ask for the gift (the equivalent to "closing a sale"), remember board members (they may be major gift donors themselves or know people who could be), and express appreciation (a simple thank-you expressed in terms that are appropriate to the donor).

6. **The major gift donor profile.** Nonprofits should develop a major gift donor profile that is relevant to them. What is true for nonprofits in general may not be true for a specific nonprofit.

7. **Nonprofit major gift fund-raising tasks.** It is important to understand and train marketers in the tasks related to effective major gift fund-raising. These tasks include identifying potential donors of major gifts via marketing research; rating good prospects so that the marketer knows where to spend precious time and

resources; and implementing strategies for building relationships, which include tactics for moving a prospect from unawareness of a nonprofit or its offers to to engaging in major gift actions through the intermediate steps of awareness, interest, desire, trial, and closing.

8. Making the "close," or asking for the major gift. If the nonprofit marketer has paid careful attention to moving a potential major gift donor though the stages of the AIDTIM model, then after the donor has made a first donation, it may be appropriate to close, or ask for a major gift. As noted in the AIDTIM model, this step is referred to as "providing information" because the marketer now needs to present a formal request with suggestions for a major gift that will be appropriate to that donor.

9. Alternative major gift formats. A good marketer will be able to offer a potential major gift donor a number of different giving formats and should be knowledgeable about each.

Summary

The nonprofit marketing issues presented in this chapter are summarized here according to the chapter learning objectives they meet.

Understand that individuals give more money to nonprofits than do corporations, foundations, or government sources. Gifts from individuals represent nearly 88% of all charitable giving. Although many of those donations are modest, there is an important category of donor prospect that nonprofit fund-raisers should be willing to spend a great deal of time and effort to cultivate: the major gift donor prospect.

Understand three approaches to identifying a nonprofit's largest donors. There are several views when it comes to identifying a nonprofit's donor segments. The rule of thirds says that about one third of annual donations (in dollars) will come from the top 10–20 patrons. The 80/20 axiom says that 20% of a nonprofit's donors will give 80% of the money. Finally, the 90/10 axiom says that 10% of a nonprofit's donors will give 90% of the money. If a nonprofit set a goal of raising $600,000, a wise marketer would likely design a campaign to attract several donors in the $50,000 range, a larger group in the $2,000 range, and an even larger group in the $100–$500 range.

Understand the importance of looking at a nonprofit's offer from the point of view of potential donors. To avoid what is called marketing myopia, a useful first step in understanding potential major gift donors is to prepare an objective review of each of the nonprofit's offers (goods, services, social behavior programs) as the potential donor is likely to see it. Not only should a nonprofit examine each of its offers with a checklist such as the one presented; it should also complete the checklist for each current and potential public, including various groups of current or potential donors.

Understand the importance of the potential major gift information file. As a reference for those internally involved in a nonprofit's fund-raising efforts, it is important that the organization set up a computer file folder for each individual or organization with major gift potential. The file information will be important in custom designing a strategy to interest, involve, and maintain the donor-organization relationship. The files will also be helpful in finding and understanding more potential donors.

Understand the various traditional tactics for major gift fund-raising. Among the time-tested tactics for major gift fund-raising are the following: (a) focus on individual donors (each donor is unique and should be treated as such), (b) focus on benefits to the donor (e.g., a sense of pride, a feeling of involvement), (c) ask for the gift (the equivalent to "closing a sale"), (d) remember board members (they may be major gift donors themselves or know people who could be), and (e) express appreciation (say a thank-you in terms appropriate to the donor).

Understand the major gift donor profile. The nonprofit marketer might begin by considering a typical major gift donor profile (one is presented in Exhibit 8.4). Each piece of information from the nonprofit's typical major donors should be considered and plugged into the nonprofit's major gift information file for use by marketers who must put together an approach for specific potential donors. That is not to say that all major gift donors will neatly fit the profile presented in Exhibit 8.4, but most do, and it can be a good starting point for identifying candidates worthy of more detailed research.

Describe and understand the tasks related to effective major gift fund-raising. It is important to understand and train marketers in the tasks that are related to effective major gift fund-raising. The tasks discussed in the chapter include (a) identifying potential donors of major gifts via marketing research, (b) rating good prospects so that marketers knows where to spend their precious time and resources, and (c) implementing strategies for building relationships, which include moving a prospect from unawareness of a nonprofit or its offers to a major gift action through the intermediate stages of awareness, interest, desire, trial, and closing. After the major gift action, follow-up involves showing appreciation, maintaining the relationship, and preparing for the next stage.

Understand when and how to make the "close," or ask for the major gift. Marketers should not and generally do not simply ask a donor for a major gift. The prospect must first be carefully identified and evaluated, and then a donor-specific, progressive relationship-building plan is designed and implemented. Asking for a gift should come as a natural progression and should be made when the time is right and by the right person. If the process is handled correctly, the donor will not be surprised by the request; however, the request has to be handled with finesse. Good marketers learn how to read the mental state or attitude of important prospective donors and take the time to really get to know and read their body language and the signals they send. The effective marketer uses this knowledge to decide whether, when, and how to ask for the donation, bearing in mind a number of important points.

Understand some alternative major gift formats. A good marketer should offer many types of major gift formats to a potential major gift donor. Some formats will be more suited to a donor's financial situation than others, and it is the fund-raiser's detailed knowledge of these options that can make the difference in turning a major gift prospect into a major gift donor. Donors will no doubt want to review the various tax consequences with their financial and tax advisers because Internal Revenue Service rules change and state and local tax procedures are not uniform across the country. Gifts may be available immediately, they may take effect at a later time, or they may be given as a bequest (effective on the death of the donor and spouse).

Glossary

80/20 and 90/10 axioms. Situations in which 80–90% of something (say donations) is given by 20% or 10% of a nonprofit's target publics.

Major gifts. Donations that are significantly beyond the typical donor's gift to a nonprofit; often represent 10%, 20%, 30%, or more of the nonprofit's total yearly budget.

Rule of thirds. One third of annual donations (in dollars) will come from the top 10–20 patrons, one third from the next 80–100, and one third from all the remaining nonprofit supporters.

Supporter relationship management. Those aspects of a nonprofit's strategy that relate to techniques and methods for attracting and retaining supporters.

Surrogate indicator. Some factor that is related to another variable of interest.

QUESTIONS FOR REVIEW

1. Define the term *major gift*.

2. Explain the difference between the three methods one could use to identify a nonprofit's largest donors: the rule of thirds, the 80/20 axiom, and the 90/10 axiom.

3. Define *supporter relationship management*.

4. Be able to list the traditional tactics that have been used successfully in reaching nonprofit donors.

5. Explain the areas where a major gift donor may feel personal satisfaction.

6. Know the steps in the AIDTIM model presented in this chapter as well as the overriding purpose of the model.

QUESTIONS FOR DISCUSSION

1. Given the rules one can use to find a nonprofit's largest donors, how might a nonprofit go about raising $1,000,000?

2. What kinds of questions should be part of an objective offer analysis and why?

3. What kinds of information should a nonprofit gather about its individual donors?

4. What does it mean to say that a nonprofit should "focus on individuals" and "focus on donor benefits" when it comes to major gift fund-raising?

5. How might a nonprofit go about engaging in marketing research to identify potential donors of major gifts?

6. What is involved in moving a potential major gift donor from unawareness to full involvement with the nonprofit?

7. What kinds of objections, concerns, and barriers to a request for a major gift should a nonprofit marketer anticipate? How could each be handled?

8. What are alternative formats for major giving?

INTERNET EXERCISES

1. Enter http://philanthropy.com/stats/donors/works and develop a list of the 10 most generous charitable donors.

2. Enter philanthropy.com/ and from the list on the left, click on "Jobs." Then, in the center, under "Browse Jobs by Position," click on "Fund-raising," then click on "Major Gifts," then on "Sort by State." Then pick out some jobs in your state that interest you and become familiar with how nonprofits describe the positions and responsibilities.

3. Enter fdncenter.org/pnd/, which is the website for *Philanthropy News Digest*. Read up on the latest issues and events in nonprofit major gift fund-raising.

4. Enter www.givingandvolunteering.ca/, look through the "Fact Sheets" and "Reports and Manuals," and investigate how Canadian gift and major gift donors may differ from U.S. donors.

TEAM EXERCISES AND ROLE PLAYING

1. At the website of the Association of Fundraising Professionals, http://www.afpnet. org/, in the left column click on "Ethics," then review the material under "Guidelines, Codes, Standards" and "The Donor Bill of Rights." In teams, propose something you have noted around the university that would be worthy of multimillion-dollar funding. Then list the terms your team would require if it were a wealthy major gift prospect considering funding that project. What would a wise prospect require in assurances? In the eyes of the prospect, where could the university go wrong after the funds were given?

2. Bob Smith was a successful business person who pledged $50 million to his alma mater, MidState U. The donation was to be $10 million per year for 5 years. Bob was inducted into the university's elite President's Club for top donors. In June of the second year, Bob passed away. Bob's will left his entire estate to his son, Bob Jr. Bob Jr. has notified the university that he feels the university used improper influence on a senior citizen with reduced mental capability. Bob Jr. has no intention of completing the pledge payments. How many students in the class believe the university should sue Bob Jr.? Those who do should form a group (at the next class meeting) to debate those who believe that the university has a lot to lose in initiating court action.

MINICASE: Departmental Major Gifts

The department of marketing at your university has hired you to uncover potential major gift donor information for them. If approved by your instructor and your university's senior funding officer, you will make contact and deliver a funding proposal. Based on your knowledge of this chapter, you will be asked to apply what you have learned to real-world situations. Be sure to be professional in all your research, contacts, and interactions. The quality of your enthusiasm, initiative, preparation, and work will reflect directly on the prospect's perception of your university.

The parts of this exercise are independent, so your instructor may assign one, two, or all three parts. It is also likely that your instructor will want to adapt this assignment with special instructions. Each part deals with the same case.

Part 1

Step 1. Go to philanthropy.com/stats/donors/ and search the listing for the donors who are the 60 largest individual charitable contributors in the United States. The listing has a "search by state option," so begin by seeing if any of these donors come from your state. If any are from your state, they will probably know your college or university, and that is a good start. The recipients of some of their past donations will be listed, so enter each into Google (or another search engine) and see what those nonprofits are involved in and what the donor has funded in the past. At this point, you are simply trying to gain a bit of insight into what issues seem to be important to the donor. You will use this and other insights you can uncover to creatively design an initiative that will interest the donor in considering a donation to your university. Note: If the above website does not work (and web addresses change frequently!), use a search engine to search on "philanthropy.com" or on something like "biggest gift," followed by your state. If there are no donors on the list from your state, choose prospects from the closest state to your location.

Step 2. Pick three prospects that seem to have good potential and put their names in a search engine; for example, enter "John A. Smith" (be sure to include the quotation marks and, of course, use the name of a prospect you found). See if you can uncover information that can give you some insight into wealth, employment, interests, and professional history. Check with your business reference librarian for online resources and databases. If you have access through your school's library subscription, check to see if your prospects are listed in www.marquiswhoswho.com/index.asp and www.galegroup.com/BiographyRC (as described in the section above titled "Marketing Research: Identifying Potential Donors of Major Gifts"). In many schools, you will need to access the database from the library itself. Also, search on the prospects' names in LexisNexis. Your objective is to prepare a report about what you have been able to uncover about these prospects. Use whatever additional marketing research approaches you can come up with. Think creatively as well as ethically.

Part 2

Step 1. In this part of the case, you will be assigned to find major gift prospects by looking for top corporate managers. Senior managers have high incomes, and some of them may make good candidates. Check the online *D&B's Million Dollar Databases* (www.dnbmdd.com/mddi) for corporations in your state and their top management (check with your school's business research librarian for instructions on accessing this database). Pick some CEOs or executives at the board chairman level from public companies that seem large enough to have highly paid senior managers. If you cannot access the D&B database, pick some large public companies in your region and go on to Step 2.

Step 2. Once you have found names of companies that may have highly paid leaders, go the Securities and Exchange Commission website (www.sec.gov) and click on company filings. Enter the company name and look in filings named *proxy* and *10K*. Each filing is split into several parts, so you will want to scan them to find sections that deal with the company's officers and board of directors. See what you can learn about any of these prospects' professional history, income, and stock holdings. Your objective is to prepare a report containing what you have been able to uncover about several of the best of these prospects. Use Exhibit 8.4 as a checklist and try to fill it out as completely as you can. Use whatever additional marketing research approaches you can come up with. Again, think creatively as well as ethically.

Part 3

Step 1. This part is more advanced and should be completed only under the direction of your instructor. Your instructor should first seek the approval of your university's senior fund-raising officer because we would not want your actions for this assignment to interfere with an active relationship development effort with a prospect. It is likely that at least some of the prospects you identified will not already be active targets of your university's fund-raising efforts. Your activity may be seen as a good icebreaker. Your university's senior fund-raising officer will definitely want to review your plans, make suggestions, and possibly even veto a particular action or strategy before you implement it.

Step 2. As you have probably already guessed, in this assignment you will attempt to uncover one prospect's contact information and invite the prospect to become involved with the marketing department in some way. This will be the first step in creating involvement and starting to build a relationship. Even a simple request will be a good start. However, do *not* use e-mail for the contact.

Some examples for beginning to involve a major gift donor prospect might be the following:

- Invite the prospect to speak to your class on a topic of interest to him or her.
- Invite the prospect to speak to your American Marketing Association student chapter.
- Invite the prospect to join in a roundtable discussion with other senior business executives from the area.
- With your dean's permission, invite the prospect to have lunch or dinner in the formal faculty dining area.
- Request a meeting at the prospect's location.

Step 3. Once you have met the prospect and learned about his or her interests through personal interaction, careful listening, and observation, think about something small that the prospect may be willing to fund or to brainstorm outside funding sources for. Search the Internet for examples of well-crafted proposal documents and cover letters. Create a proposal document and decide how to present it to the prospect. Again, do *not* use e-mail. Present the proposal, and follow up. Your objective is to prepare a report containing what you have done, what the results were, and what next steps you recommend to close on the small request for funding. Also detail your recommendations for the next steps the department should implement to advance the prospect's involvement and interest in your department. One more time, think creatively as well as ethically.

References and Bibliography

Bennett, R. (2006). Predicting the lifetime durations of donors of charities. *Journal of Nonprofit and Public Sector Marketing, 15*(1–2), 45–67.

Cermak, D. S. P., File, K. M., & Prince, R. A. (1994). A benefit segmentation of the major donor market. *Journal of Business Research, 28*, 121–130.

Chang, C. F., Okunade, A. A., & Kumar, N. (1999). Motives behind charitable bequests. *Journal of Nonprofit and Public Sector Marketing, 6*(4), 69–85.

Dove, K. E., Spears, A. M., & Herbert, T. W. (2001). *Conducting a successful major gifts and planned giving program: A comprehensive guide and resource.* San Francisco: Jossey-Bass.

Eveland, V. B., & Crutchfield, T. N. (2004). Understanding why people give: Help for struggling AIDS-related non-profits. *Journal of Nonprofit and Public Sector Marketing, 12*(1), 23–36.

Fredricks, L. (2001). *Developing major gifts: Turning small donors into big contributors.* New York: Aspen Publications.

Goettler, R. H. (1996). Announcing the "four Ws" of major gift solicitation. *Fund Raising Management,* (April), 40.

Goettler Associates. (2000). What is a major gift? *Fund Raising Matters, 5*(3), 1–4. Retrieved October 23, 2005, from www.goettler.com/goettlerweb.nsf/$LookUpFilesType/FRM%2018%20Final.pdf/$file/FRM%2018%20Final.pdf

Gomes, R., & Knowles, P. (2005). *AIDTIM prospect decision-making model* (Working Paper).

Greenfield, J. M. (2001/2). *The nonprofit handbook: Fund raising.* Hoboken, NJ: John Wiley & Sons Inc.

Heiser, R. S. (2006). Normative influences in donation decisions. *Journal of Nonprofit and Public Sector Marketing, 15*(1–2), 127–149.

Hurd, H., & Latimer, M. (Eds.). (1994). *The millionaire givers: Wealth and philanthropy in Britain.* London, UK: Directory of Social Change.

Lawson, M. (1995). Major gift development in your organization. *Fund Raising Management,* (May), 18–21.

Luck, M. F., & Evans, G. A. (1992). Making major gifts happen. *Fund Raising Management,* (September), 28.

Marland, J. (1999, June). *Developing major gift and membership programmes for the British Museum.* Presentation at Fundraising for Museums, the Arts and Heritage, Henry Stewart Conferences, London, UK.

Pitt, L. F., Keating, S., Bruwer, L., Murgolo-Poore, M., & de Bussy, N. (2001). Charitable donations as social exchange or agapic action on the Internet: The case of Hungersite.com. *Journal of Nonprofit and Public Sector Marketing, 9*(4), 47–61.

Prince, R. A. (2001). *The seven faces of philanthropy: A new approach to cultivating major donors.* San Francisco: Jossey-Bass.

Reuther, V. (1998). Debunking the myth of Bill Gates: Finding major donors. *Nonprofit World,* (March/April), 46.

Sargeant, A. (1999). Charitable giving: Towards a model of donor behaviour. *Journal of Marketing Management, 15*, 215–238.

Sargeant, A. (2001). Fundraising direct: A communications planning guide for charity marketing. *Journal of Nonprofit and Public Sector Marketing, 9*(1–2), 185–204.

Sargeant, A., Jay, E., & Lee, S. (2006). Benchmarking charity performance: Returns from direct marketing in fundraising. *Journal of Nonprofit and Public Sector Marketing, 16*(1–2), forthcoming.

Sargeant, A., Lee, S., & Jay, E. (2002). *Major gift philanthropy: Individual giving to the arts.* Centre for Voluntary Sector Management, Henley Management. Retrieved October 23, 2005, from 195.167.181.209/Asp/uploadedFiles/file/Philanthropy.pdf

Schervish, P. G. (1999). Major donors, major motives: The people and purposes behind major gifts. *New Directions for Philanthropic Fundraising, 17*, 59–87.

Smith, P. (1997). Managing a successful major gifts program. *New Directions for Philanthropic Fundraising, 16*(5), 67–81.

Steckel, R., Simons, R., & Lengsfelder, P. (1989) *Filthy rich and other nonprofit fantasies: Changing the way nonprofits do business in the 90's.* Berkeley, CA: Ten Speed Press.

Taylor, M. A., & Shaw, S. C. (1997). Women as philanthropists: Leading the transformation in major gift fundraising. *New Directions for Philanthropic Fundraising, 16*(5), 43–48.

Walton, R. C. (1999). The psychology of major gifts. *Fund Raising Management, 29*(12), 16–19.

Weiss, M. J. (2003). Great expectations. *American Demographics, 25*(4), 26–35.

Williams, M. J. (2001). Overview of major giving. In J. M. Greenfield (Ed.), *The nonprofit handbook: Fund raising* (pp. 604–614). Hoboken, NJ: John Wiley & Sons Inc.

Wood, E. W. (1997). The four Rs of major gift fundraising. *Developing Major Gifts, 16*(5), 12–18.

Special Events in the Nonprofit Sector

Barry O'Mahony

Michael Polonsky

Content

Learning Objectives

On completion of this chapter, the
reader will

- Define special events and understand
  the role of special events in the
  nonprofit sector

- Describe the different types of nonprofit
  events

- Describe the factors that influence the
  objectives of special events

- Understand the issues involved in
  producing special events

- Understand the risks associated with
  hosting special events

Learning Objectives (Continued)

- Describe the procedures involved in managing special events
- Understand the importance of marketing and public relations for special events in the nonprofit sector

Opening Vignette: The Great Victorian Bike Ride

Bicycle Victoria is an independent, nonprofit, community-based organization. It was established in 1975 with the sole purpose of increasing the profile of cycling in Victoria, Australia. Since that time, its mission has been to get "more people cycling more often." Its main promotional program has been an annual event called the Great Victorian Bike Ride, and it operates a range of other cycling events. The Great Victorian Bike Ride tries to include celebrities in the ride to gain additional publicity and also links with various charities. In 2004, Tara Moss, the writer and "ex-super model," worked with the organization to raise money for the Bone Marrow Institute.

The Great Victorian Bike Ride started in 1984 and is staged annually. Participation has been growing since it started, and in 2003, it attracted more than 20,000 participants, as well as several thousand volunteers supporting the riders. The event lasts nine days and involves a long-distance social cycling "tour." The route changes each year and is designed to cover the most scenic areas of the state of Victoria. The organization closely controls and monitors the route and provides meals, entertainment, social activities at the end of each day, and camping facilities for participants, all included in the cost of participation. The event is complex, requiring coordination of organizational activities as well as coordination with a range of state and local bodies, businesses, sponsors, and other nonprofit organizations.

The targeted participants comprise a range of groups, including families, couples, and singles of all ages. The event has broad appeal because of the perceived leisure, health, and social and personal development opportunities that it provides. The extensive volunteering program and fund-raising link have been used to allow nonriders to participate.

One of the aspirations of Bicycle Victoria is for the Great Victorian Bike Ride to be the best bike ride in the world. It also aims to provide a lasting memory rich in friendship and fun, which will create a positive experience and encourage bicycle riding more generally. It also promotes teamwork and regional involvement and evokes community spirit (Bicycle Victoria, 2005).

Special Events: Definition, Rationale, Planning, and Design

Everybody loves to celebrate. Indeed, according to Goldblatt (1990, p. 1), the need to celebrate is "perhaps even more vital to the sustenance of the human spirit" than are the basic physical needs of food, clothing, and shelter. The importance of celebrations to the welfare of communities is recognized in most cultures with public displays marking significant occasions such as harvest time, the beginning of a New Year, and various cultural and religious festivals. In some cases, these activities have developed well beyond their traditional focus. For example, in the United States, Saint Patrick's Day is celebrated by more people and often with more activities and parades than occur in Ireland, where it originated. In fact, events frequently expand beyond their original focus and become part of the broader community.

Events can be organized by a range of international and local nonprofit organizations and include global activities such as the Olympics or Clean Up the World day; national events such as the 40 Hour Famine or celebrations of national identity; and local activities, such as a local nonprofit organization's annual fund-raising ball.

Events can be fun and can add something to the lives of those involved in hosting them as well as those attending. This entertainment and emotional value represents an opportunity that many organizations seek to leverage in planning events. It is also a feature that sponsoring organizations value highly because it allows them to cut through the marketing clutter.

Globally, nonprofit and for-profit events have grown so substantially as to have become a major area for investment. Indeed, events have been described as "one of the most exciting and fastest growing forms of leisure, business, and tourism related phenomena" (Getz, 1997, p. 1). According to Getz, "their special appeal stems in part from the limited duration and innate uniqueness of each event" (p. 1). Thus events are similar to most service experiences in that they are perishable and distinctive in some way. Since most successful events are presented as leisure activities, fun and enjoyment are among the core values sought by event participants as part of the overall experience. As a result, the planning, preparation, production, and evaluation of events are even more challenging (see Exhibit 9.1 for the planning process involved).

From a nonprofit perspective, hosting events is attractive because of their limited duration and immediate source of revenue. Another appeal is that participants are in a heightened state of emotion during the event and likely to be more susceptible to an organization's message. However, planning an event requires considerable investment from the organization if the event is to be successful and reach its full potential.

The global growth in events has created a level of competition equal to the competition for products or services. Individuals and organizations have limited leisure time, which means that events compete for public support as well as government or business patronage. For nonprofit organizations, the situation is even more complex because they often seek support from for-profit organizations as well. Consequently, for-profits face increasing requests for assistance from an ever-growing number of nonprofits. In this way, nonprofit events face both supply-side and demand-side competition. A further complexity is that scheduling competition exists in both the timing of events and the type of events. It is unlikely, for example, that members of a local community would support two different jazz festivals on consecutive weekends. The organizations involved might also have difficulty attracting appropriate musicians to participate. Thus timing becomes a core planning issue that needs to be considered.

❖ **Exhibit 9.1**   Stages in Event Management

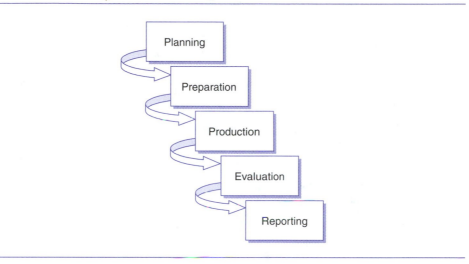

It should be clear from this introduction and the opening vignette that staging events can be an extremely complex process requiring extensive planning and coordination. This chapter is designed to introduce readers to the core elements of the events industry and to provide insights into the structured and strategic processes required to successfully manage nonprofit events. As the chapter proceeds, we will draw on a range of examples from around the world to highlight the scope of events in the nonprofit sector (Exhibit 9.2 provides one such example in more detail).

Defining Special Events

A diverse range of activities can be classified as **special events**: civic events, often linked with culture and national pride (e.g., 4th of July parades); fairs and festivals (e.g., World Fairs); sporting events (e.g., Olympics or World Masters games); musical events (e.g., New York's Concerts in Central Park); and many others. For nonprofits, events can be equally diverse. For example, nonprofits may organize annual balls, golf tournaments, fun runs, telethons, walkathons, or charity art auctions. Nonprofit organizations may also get involved in events that focus on communication, such as awareness campaigns or program launches. For example, the Cancer Council might promote skin cancer prevention at beaches nationally in summer or focus its activities on specific regions. Exhibit 9.3 shows how one organization may have a diverse range of events.

As noted above, the taxonomy of special events is so broad that Getz (1997) advises that "it will never be possible to come up with a universal, standardized definition, nor a classification of which types of events are exceptional or special. It is clearly a matter of perspective or preference" (p. 4). However, in terms of defining events, the perspectives

❖ **Exhibit 9.2**   Live 8: A Complex Global Event

One of the largest global special events ever seen was held in 2005: Live Aid 8. This was a massive event integrating 10 separate concerts around the world—London, Paris, Berlin, Rome, Philadelphia, Barrie, Tokyo, Johannesburg, Moscow, Eden Project. Most of the concerts were free and were funded from a range of sources (see table below). The musical artists donated their performances.

Main Sources of Income (Millions of Euros)

Sponsorships	8.948
Text income	1.366
Hospitality income	0.648
International TV sales	1.540
Sky texting	0.023
Advance merchandise sales	0.575
Advance DVD sales	0.215
Wrist band income (potential)	16.191
Other (photo, downloads, etc.)	not announced
TOTAL	**29.506**

The goal of the series of concerts was to raise awareness of the problem of poverty in Africa. The concerts were also designed to put political pressure on leaders of the G8 nations (Canada, France, Germany, Italy, Japan, Russia, the United Kingdom, and the United States) to assist the poorer nations of Africa by granting debt relief to these countries. Large sums of money were also donated to charities participating in the event, however.

While the number of people attending the concerts was limited, it was suggested that 2 billion people around the world watched part of the concerts. In addition, many ways to participate were offered, such as sending e-mails of support or sending messages to political leaders.

The international coordination for the event was massive, and the financial exposure (i.e., risk of losses) by the organizing body, Band Aid Trust, was several million dollars. This does not include the financial exposure of local organizing groups for some locations of the concert. The event reached a very wide audience, and the G8 did make some concessions on debt relief. Thus it could be argued that this was one of the most successful nonprofit events of all time.

SOURCE: Adapted from information at www.live8live.com/, retrieved August 8, 2005.

of two **stakeholders** should be considered: (a) the organizers or producers of events, including their associates (i.e., sponsors and other business partners), employees, or **volunteers** (people who elect to assist, without financial reward, with the staging of an event) working at the event; and (b) the customers of events, also referred to as guests,

❖ **Exhibit 9.3**   **Having a Stable of Events: The Asthma Society of Canada**

In many cases, organizations will have a diverse set of activities. These may be designed to cater to different segments or interests or donors. Each event needs to be managed separately, the events must also be coordinated. It is possible that individuals and sponsors will want to participate in multiple activities and thus build integrated links with the non-profit. On the other hand, multiple events like these may lead to event fatigue on the part of donors and the nonprofit's employees involved. The Asthma Society of Canada held the following five events between August and October 2004:

The Great Urban Adventure: a team of between 50 and 200 in a team-building "Urban Scavenger Hunt"

Alexander's Challenge: a day of cycling, walking, or jogging (3 different days in various communities)

Crystal's Walk in the Clouds: a day of walking in memory of a person who passed away from an asthma attack

Asthma Celebrity Open: celebrities and guests playing on a prestigious golf course

Infusion: A Wine Experience: a wine tasting, with food prepared by award-winning chefs

These events were generally coordinated in different areas by different people. In some cases, the events were local in scale, such as Crystal's Walk in the Clouds. Others, such as the Asthma Celebrity Open 2004, were nationally coordinated activities with much broader objectives and appeals.

SOURCE: Adapted from Asthma Society of Canada. (2004). *Special events*. Retrieved December 2004 from www.asthma.ca/corp/events/

visitors, participants, or the audience. It is important to consider the goals and expectations of both parties when developing special events. With this in mind, Getz (p. 4) has suggested two definitions, one applying to each stakeholder group:

> To the organizers, a special event is a one-time or infrequently occurring event outside the normal program of activities of the sponsoring or organizing body.

> To the customer or guest, a special event is an opportunity for a leisure, social, or cultural experience outside the normal range of choices or beyond everyday experience.

A further defining feature is that "If events are held frequently they will become routine for their organizers. If they do not offer the customer something out of the ordinary, they become mundane" (Getz, 1997, p. 4). Because events are unique from each party's perspective, nonprofit organizations need to continually reinvent their event to maintain internal and external interest.

❖ **Exhibit 9.4**   Special Olympics European Basketball Week

The Federated International Basketball Association (FIBA) worked with the Special Olympics in Europe to organize a range of activities associated with enhancing and promoting basketball in the disabled community. This multinational collaboration involved 21 countries and more than 7,000 Special Olympics athletes. Each individual "event" is unique and needs to be planned separately; however, overall coordination among the events is also necessary.

The scope of the activity is enormous: It will potentially "bring opportunities to 15,000 new players by 2006." The benefits of the FIBA are also extensive. It will promote basketball more widely, building grassroots support. In this way, the event is about creating opportunities for those with disabilities while at the same time enhancing the profile of basketball in Europe: the elusive win-win solution.

SOURCES: Adapted from the following:

Special Olympics. (2004, May 15). Press Release: FIBA Europe and Special Olympics Europe/Eurasia sign agreement to bring new opportunities to players with intellectual disabilities. Retrieved November 11, 2005, from http://www.specialolympics.org/Special+Olympics+Public+Website/English/Press_Room/Global_News_Archive/2004+Global+News+Archive/FIBA+Signing.htm

Special Olympics. (2004, November 16). Press Release: FIBA Europe to support inaugural Special Olympics European Basketball Week. Retrieved November 11, 2005, from www.specialolympics.org/Special+Olympics+Public+Website/English/Press_Room/Global_News_Archive/2004+Global+News+Archive/European+Basketball+Week.htm

Scope of Events in the Nonprofit Sector

According to Montgomery and Strick (1995), there are two criteria for holding an event: cost and convenience. For nonprofit events, however, these criteria may be broadened to include publicity, which covers issues related to creating awareness and knowledge about the cause and the event.

Nonprofit events may be held by for-profit organizations or nonprofit organizations. The critical issue in defining nonprofit events is whether the object is to generate revenue for a for-profit organization. A charity event might be held by a for-profit organization, and other activities, such as cause-related marketing, discussed previously, frequently have both for-profit and nonprofit objectives. In general, however, nonprofit events are designed to attract revenue to support charities and community activities or to educate the public about broader issues of social concern.

Nonprofit events frequently involve multiple groups, including community-based non-profits, governmental bodies, for-profit organizations, and private groups. They can be designed for leisure, educational, or social purposes. They also have a range of aims and objectives, which may in fact vary among those involved in the event. Improving sport, health, and social integration within a community is one example of the objectives a nonprofit might have for an event (see Exhibit 9.4). Nonprofits might

❖ **Exhibit 9.5**   Stakeholders in Nonprofit Events

sponsor arts and cultural festivals to foster appreciation for and participation in the arts as well as to garner political support for increased funding. In fact, each event can have multiple community benefits. Several features of event management are distinctive of nonprofit events. These include the goals of the event organizer, the concepts for special events, and the criteria by which the success (or failure) of an event is measured.

As noted in Chapter 3, most nonprofits have at least two important publics, their clients and their donors. Similarly, the planning of a nonprofit event needs to take account of a number of internal and external stakeholders so that these stakeholders can identify the benefits they can bring to the event as well as the rewards they seek. Exhibit 9.5 shows the internal stakeholders (middle ring) that are essential for staging events, as well as the external stakeholders (outer ring) that support events.

As stated earlier, events are temporary in nature and of fixed duration, thus making them highly perishable. Like most service experiences, when an event is over, you cannot experience it again, and this fact has major implications for marketing activities. Getting it right, which is often measured in terms of the number of participants attracted or the amount of revenue raised, is crucial.

Planning an event involves a number of strategically oriented processes that must be coordinated to ensure that objectives are achieved. Therefore, detailed and specific guidelines need to be created for every event. As Goldblatt (1990) suggests, events may appear spontaneous, a feature that enhances the ability of the event to produce unexpected pleasure within the audience, but detailed planning and fastidious management are the hallmarks of any successful event. Because many for-profit and nonprofit events are conducted infrequently, and because event management personnel are often employed on a casual basis, detailed planning is especially critical to ensure that an event will be well managed.

Many special events occur outdoors, and they are therefore seasonal in nature and usually have a leisure component associated with them. For example, a music festival in the park is a day out for the whole family. More leisure time provides an opportunity for having more events; however, there is a danger that too many events can lead to audience fatigue as well as aggressive competition for corporate support. Given that each nonprofit organization can control only its own events, and that providing a unique, fun experience is crucial to an event's success, it is vital that scheduling take other organizations' events into account. Doing so may result in coordinated planning of the events calendar by nonprofits or even joint staging of events.

Objectives of Special Events

Why Nonprofit Events?

As previously mentioned, events are not always about profit. Indeed, in Chapter 1, it was noted that the growth in the number of nonprofit organizations in the United States has been phenomenal, with 1.8 million new organizations appearing in the year 2002 (Lee, 2004). This increase in nonprofit organizations, coupled with the decline in the traditional nonprofit funding base, has prompted nonprofit managers to explore different ways to increase their resource base as well as get their message to targeted communities. Events provide an attractive alternative for furthering the cause of the nonprofit sector.

However, producing special events is a complex process, especially when nonprofit events are required to attain multiple goals, such as creating awareness, fund-raising, and educating the community, and at the same time the nonprofit must carry on its regular programs, i.e. helping those in need and working with volunteers and community members. Moreover, different stakeholders often have different perspectives on the value of an event (see Exhibit 9.6). Thus, the nonprofit organization may be concerned with generating interest in an issue, but its for-profit cosponsor might be more concerned with polishing its public image and has decided to link itself with a worthy cause to achieve this goal.

The operation of nonprofit events can also have political ramifications that involve social, environmental, and cultural costs in addition to the financial costs of producing an event. For example, many seaside communities (e.g., Sea Isle, New Jersey) host a range of events to attract tourists. However, overly successful events can result in unforeseen pressures. Visitors may, for instance, complain of crowded

❖ **Exhibit 9.6** Governmental Bodies Also Stage Special Events

---

While we traditionally consider special events to be associated with "charities," the scope of nonprofits is quite broad and includes governmental activities. These relate to specific events in local communities or broad-based regional events. For example, within the European Union, there is a "Committee of Regions," which runs a youth program designed to "promote voluntary activities, intercultural dialogue and active participation of young people in society." The objectives are broadly to integrate youth and at the same time to stimulate discussion among people of different countries and backgrounds. Such activities require both coordination among the various member countries and centralized programs where the debate takes place and the various presentations occur.

The Council of Europe also has a broad-based event entitled "European Heritage Days." This program, while broadly coordinated across Europe, is designed to "bring European citizens closer to their cultural heritage" while recognizing differences among cultures. The objectives also include protection of local cultural sites. The program also emphasizes education, and thus events are designed to be integrated into school curricula as well.

Compiled from: 10th Anniversary of Committee of Regions. (2004, November 17). Retrieved December 2004 from http://europa.eu.int/comm/youth/index_en.html accessed December 2004.

European Heritage Days 2004. (October 15, 2004). Retrieved December 2004 from www.di-ve.com/dive/portal/portal.jhtml?id=152655&pid=91

---

conditions, and local support may decline because of overcrowding or other problems caused by a large influx.

Notwithstanding these challenges, events can provide significant financial benefits for nonprofit organizations and their constituencies. Many of these benefits can be measured quantitatively by a range of survey or modeling approaches. There are also a number of long-term benefits for communities that host events, including marketing the destination to attract tourists and creating and projecting an image of the destination as an ongoing tourist attraction. For example, it has been suggested that one of the major benefits of hosting the Olympic Games is the ability to showcase a nation and a city in a way that could not be done otherwise. In addition, the event fosters event tourism, or people traveling to attend national or international events. In addition, major events can provide the impetus for redevelopment of rundown areas (urban transformation) and for development of infrastructure.

Setting Objectives

Setting objectives refers to developing a set of aims for an event that specifically states exactly what the event is designed to achieve. It has already been mentioned that managing events is complex, mainly because it involves planning and controlling multifarious activities that have critical deadlines and that may require input from a range of stakeholders. Moreover, because many events in the nonprofit sector are conducted infrequently or only once, a nonprofit's managerial competency in hosting events or learning from past experience is severely limited. Furthermore, nonprofit organizations traditionally have not possessed the same range of managerial skills required in for-profit settings, which is understandable because the objectives of nonprofit and for-profit organizations have differed. Therefore, undertaking events within the nonprofit sector has sometimes been quite difficult and has caused nonprofit managers considerable uncertainty over how events should be produced.

To boost managers' confidence, not to mention an event's chances of success, it is crucial to establish objectives that state exactly what the event is supposed to achieve. Objectives also need to be measurable because they will become the criteria by which the event will be evaluated after it has been staged. The next step is to identify the stakeholders who should be included. Objectives need to be formulated by, and agreeable to, all stakeholders. They need to be realistic in terms of being achievable, and timelines must be set for individual objectives, even though, as was mentioned previously, each stakeholder may have different objectives.

Allen, O'Tooel, McDonnell, and Harris (2001) use the acronym SMART (specific, measurable, agreeable, realistic, and time specific) as a reminder of the issues involved in developing event objectives. Setting and recording objectives also serve as a form of organizational memory and thus allow the nonprofit to improve performance in the future, even if the next event will be planned and carried out by someone else in the organization.

A nonprofit organization might establish a range of objectives for an event. Some of these are presented in Table 9.1, and in many cases they are interrelated. For example, informing the community about the need to assist in reforestation might result in increased awareness of the importance of the issue (i.e., knowledge) as well as participation in replanting programs (i.e., direct action). The two objectives will be evaluated differently, and the evaluation measures must be established when planning the initial event.

Objectives should be established during the initial planning of the event and need to be realistic in respect to the activities and investments associated with the event. Once the objectives have been defined, strategies for achieving the objectives must be developed.

Feasibility

Determining the **feasibility** of special events requires an assessment of the internal and external business environment, an analysis of requirements for hosting the event, and an assessment of the broader event concept or idea. To assess the external environment, the organization will need to have an extensive amount of information. The main concern for the nonprofit event organizer is to assess the competition in relation to the geographic area, the targeted population, the type of event, and the type of organization that is seeking support. By identifying the number of events held annually in the region, the nonprofit organization can design the most appropriate type of event as well as the most suitable time to host or produce it.

From this initial analysis of what others do, the organization should be able to define a concept suitable for the target market. The market's preferences and size will also

❖ **Table 9.1**   Objectives for Special Events

Objective	Examples	Measurement
Fund-raising	• An organization holds a charity art auction • An organization holds charity concert	Increases in donations or more people attending the event
Raising profile through direct nonprofit involvement in a community event	• Appeal for volunteers to assist with event, such as Clean Up the World day • Campaign to solicit contributions of gifts for toy drive for Christmas	Increases in numbers of people who participate in the event Less binge drinking Fewer drunk driving deaths
Awareness campaign through Indirect nonprofit action Information	• Motivate target audience to behave more responsibly in terms of drinking • Program to explain global warming	More recycling taking place People more concerned with the issue (revealed in a survey of attitudes and knowledge)

need to be considered; as with all "products," one does not want to develop a product for thousands if the market is only hundreds. Generally, one will develop events with a number of market segments in mind, such as local communities, couples, and families.

Other external factors include the political environment, that is, permits, licenses, and traffic management; likely levels of sponsorship; the need for special equipment, catering, and insurance; the availability of accommodations (in terms of facilities to host event and hotel accommodations for participants and guests); and the lead time required to plan and organize the event.

From an internal perspective, the organization has to undertake a needs analysis for any event. This means answering a series of questions about the rationale for hosting the event. The first question should be, Is this the best way to achieve our objectives? Other matters that need to be addressed include who the event is being held for (the target market), why the target market would want to attend, and who will benefit from the event. The feasibility analysis should include an audit of the organization's financial and human resources in order to identify shortfalls and devise strategies to meet them. This can be done using a traditional strengths, weaknesses, opportunities, and threats (SWOT) analysis.

The SWOT Analysis

The major reason to make a SWOT analysis is to determine the core focus of the event based on internal **organizational factors** (strengths and weaknesses) and external **environmental factors** (opportunities and threats). Used effectively, a SWOT analysis ensures that the firm knows where it is today and so can focus on ways its positives (strengths and opportunities) can be maximized while negatives (weaknesses and threats) are minimized.

Strengths relate to the organization's competencies and abilities—what it has the ability to do. Weaknesses, on the other hand, identify internal issues that would inhibit the organization's ability to achieve its objectives for an event. While a weakness such as a declining support base might be used to focus an event, it would also make hosting a major event less feasible. Thus, negatives and positives need to be considered together to provide a holistic picture of the dimensions of the proposed event.

Issues outside the organization also need to be analyzed. In some cases, changing business environments create an opportunity; for example, an increased interest in social responsibility might make potential sponsors more likely to support a given event than they would have been previously. External environments can represent threats as well. For example, liability issues might raise insurance premiums high enough to render some events infeasible.

Once the external and internal environments have been assessed, a business plan should be developed, and it may be critical in attracting sponsors and other funding bodies. The plan should include a description of the event and concept; the objectives of the event; economic, social, and environmental considerations; a market analysis and marketing strategy; and the management structure.

Organizations will then need to select a site or venue for the event. **Venue selection** refers to choosing an event location that is in line with the needs of the identified target audience. The old real estate adage "Location, location, location" is also of paramount importance when staging events because people need to be able to access the venue easily. Having a for-profit rock concert in an isolated area might make sense, but having a jazz festival to raise money for charity in the same location could be inappropriate. Once a location has been chosen, then venue-specific resource needs may arise. These include the availability of transportation, amenities, and utilities, all of which will be directly linked to the needs of the identified target audience. Exhibit 9.7 provides some of the core issues that need to be considered.

Strategic Issues in Producing Special Events

Organizational Structure for Events

The manner in which special events are produced and staged is critical to the success of an event as well as to the health and safety of participants and stakeholders. To ensure that all critical issues are considered, nonprofit organizations need to set up a structure to administer and support their event. When nonprofits have little or limited relevant past experience, they need to decide whether to hire an experienced event management company to run the event.

The specific approach adopted will vary with the type of event and the organization(s) involved. Small events may be managed by a nonprofit organization's existing staff members, especially those in the communications or publicity department. However, larger events might require focused committees with expertise drawn from across the organization. In other cases, these committees may be even larger, drawing

❖ **Exhibit 9.7**   Ten Secrets From Fundraising Experts

In 2002, Lisa Hurley, a professional event planner, interviewed five fund-raising experts, who identified the following secrets of successful fundraising:

1. Choose a venue that has attractive features as well as potential for innovative decorations.

2. Don't have too many decorations; rather, be innovative with more impact, which might include lighting and unique centerpieces. Less may be better.

3. Catering needs a good working relationship with the chef and the catering manager to ensure you stay within your budget.

4. Make sure that fund-raising time is spent effectively. If you could raise more money than you could receive in "in-kind" goods, you would be better off raising the money.

5. Volunteers need to feel important because they are the number-one ambassadors for events.

6. Managing sponsors is critical and should be done by appropriate staff.

7. While events should be unique, radical changes in events might not be warranted. As long as those attending had a great time last year, they will most likely attend again.

8. Events should not be simply about having a social event; they should make a real contribution to the issue.

9. "Create impulse buying opportunities throughout the event" to increase giving.

10. Involve sponsors from this year to assist in planning next year's event and thus maintain a solid base to allow an increase in targets.

SOURCE: Hurley, L. (2002, June 1). Secrets of successful fund-raisers. *Special Events Magazine.* Retrieved November 2005 from specialevents.com/fundraisers/meetings_secrets_successful_fundraisers/

---

on expertise of various stakeholders, such as partner organizations, sponsors, and the local community.

The larger the event, the more complex the management activities involved in producing it and the more formal the **organizational structure** needed to administer it (see Exhibit 9.8). According to Getz (1997), the organizational framework for an event can be classified under one of five headings: a simple structure, a functional structure, a network structure, a task force, or a committee.

For small events, a simple management structure is sufficient. It involves an event manager and a few core employees working closely with the manager. By virtue of the many tasks that need to be accomplished, these employees need to be flexible and multiskilled. A simple structure allows for centralized control and defined levels of accountability generally, with everybody reporting to the event manager.

❖ **Exhibit 9.8** Example of a Functional Structure

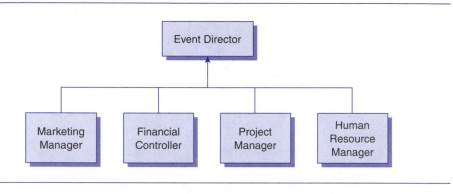

A functional structure applies to slightly larger events. It involves an event manager or director, who may be employed elsewhere in the organization. A number of employees with specialized skills are then engaged to oversee various management tasks. Each employee is responsible for a specific function or activity of the event. These activities are usually aligned with an organizational department, hence the term *functional structure*. The functional structure is good for large-scale events produced by nonprofit organizations because it allows those who have some skills or involvement in a specific area of the larger organization to take responsibility for similar activities or functions of an event. This arrangement ensures little or no duplication of roles. However, functional structures place a heavy emphasis on the event director's ability to coordinate a variety of functional activities, and thus frequent formal meetings and ongoing departmental reporting are required.

A network structure is a flexible approach to managing an event. It involves either an event director or a directorate consisting of several people. In this situation, key activities are outsourced to specialists (possibly through short-term contracts) rather than completed in-house. This structure allows the organization to utilize the expertise of individuals who have specific knowledge in given areas. A major benefit of the network structure is the ability to precisely control costs; it can do this because, in most cases, each contracted individual or organization has a specified budget to work within. On the other hand, the network structure means that the organization is reliant on skilled and reliable contract personnel to produce the event. In addition, the nonprofit may not develop an effective working relationship with its stakeholders if external contractors manage the stakeholder relationships. There is also limited **organizational learning**, which may be a significant disadvantage if the organization plans to host other similar events in the future.

A task force is a temporary structure created by an organization to produce a one-off event. It relies on the employment of staff with appropriate skills who can cross various functional lines, and it generally uses both internal and external resources to achieve organizational goals. Thus there are similarities between the task force and both the functional and the network structures. This structure may also include representatives from various partner organizations as well as external stakeholders and experts from specific bodies such as the police and emergency services.

An event management committee is sometimes used in large, volunteer-based nonprofit organizations. It is similar to a task force in that it is engaged specifically to produce an event, but it is designed to draw on a variety of individuals from within the organization. In practice, the management committee relies on a number of subcommittees set up along departmental or functional lines, for example, finance, marketing, and human resource management. This structure may become rather slow and burdensome but allows the organization to minimize costs by relying on a cross section of internal resources. A major weakness, however, is that the structure assumes that the organization's staff people have the relevant expertise to manage events, which may not be the case. If resources allow, the various subcommittees might be able to engage external assistance. However, these kinds of contractual arrangements are often beyond the means of smaller nonprofit organizations and relatively small-scale events.

Human Resources

As noted earlier, an organization needs to identify the human resources necessary to produce the event. This means not only that the organization has the expertise but that the expertise can be allocated to this specific task. A factor that further complicates this process for nonprofit organizations is extensive reliance on volunteers, who in some cases take on core managerial roles as well as the roles required to successfully produce an event. Managing volunteers is in itself a difficult task and requires the development of clear guidelines for their recruitment, induction, training, and supervision, all of which must be commensurate with the level of responsibility the volunteers are given.

Fiscal Control

Fiscal control refers to the management of incoming and outgoing funds as well as to ensuring that the financial objectives of an event are met. As noted earlier, a business plan needs to be developed for each event. Budget projections are a main feature of the event business plan and the main control factors for the event. The budget must identify all possible sources of income as well as all the expenses associated with producing the event. Income or revenue will include ticket sales (or gate fees), merchandising, competitions, raffles, program advertising, grants received, concession and booth rental fees, and television rights (if applicable). Expenses (i.e., costs) would include things like insurance, fees for contractors or organizing staff (i.e., administrative costs), venue and equipment rent, license fees, entertainment fees, catering, promotional costs, and merchandising expenses.

Careful financial planning is critical, and although the objective of the event may not be to make money, the potential for shortfalls is high; furthermore, any shortfalls would need to be covered by the nonprofit organization, which may not have sufficient reserves. It is, therefore, critical that the budgeting process be based on the financial objectives of the event, which might be to break even (i.e., not lose money). To this end, it is strongly recommended that the organization undertake some scenario analysis, which simply means playing with the budget numbers to see what would happen if costs in given areas were to increase or revenues were to decline. For example, an outdoor concert might break even on a warm, sunny day but lose substantial sums on a day that is rainy, cold, and windy. These eventualities can then be planned for by allowing a variance in the budget to cover any predicted increased costs or a potential reduction in revenue. In some cases, allowing a variance might require the removal of a programmed activity; in others, it may simply involve a marginal increase in ticket prices.

When developing the budget for an event, an organization must consider the importance of each of the activities associated with the event. In some cases, skimping on costs could have a substantial impact on the viability of the whole event. In others, aspects of the event program can be reduced or removed with little or no impact on the overall quality of the event.

Financial Management

Another aspect of fiscal management that nonprofits need to control is the people who will have access to incoming funds. At many nonprofit events, attendees use cash to pay for entry or to purchase merchandise at stalls or booths. Consequently, the host organization will need to implement security, monitoring, and coordinating activities to eliminate the risk of robbery or fraud. One way of doing this is to sell tickets at a central point only, thus controlling the flow of monies. This central point can also sell vouchers that can be exchanged for goods at booths or stalls. It is also vital to determine who is allowed to access bank accounts and who can make purchases, incur debts, or sign checks on behalf of the event.

If an organization is using its members or volunteers to raise funds, for example by selling raffle tickets, raising sponsorships for walkathons, or selling products (e.g., chocolates or cookies), the nonprofit will need a monitoring mechanism to supervise the distribution inventory. A critical aspect of these monitoring procedures is to identify both the receipts and the unsold products returned by individuals. If a nonprofit is running an officially sanctioned lottery, competition, or raffle, then in order to meet legal requirements, the organization will need to ensure that all tickets sold are entered into the draw. Furthermore, unsold tickets must be collected and retained for future auditing purposes.

Finally, if the organization is to reimburse individuals for expenses, it is essential that clear procedures be put in place specifying eligible expenses as well as the procedures for reimbursement. Exhibit 9.9 provides examples of ways technology can assist in the planning (financial and otherwise) and management of special events.

Attracting Government Grants

Governments frequently see nonprofit organizations as fulfilling valuable societal roles and thereby supporting governmental activities. For example, charities that support homeless youth will reduce a range of social problems. A nonprofit organization involved in this area might hold events to generate funds for promoting its goals, educating youth about the plight of those less well off, and intervening to help those at risk. In some cases, government funding and corporate support such as sponsorships or collaborative

❖ **Exhibit 9.9** Technology Can Assist With Planning and Managing Special Events

An increasing number of online software solutions exist to help nonprofit organizations manage events. They can assist in various areas.

Managing guests:
- Sending invitations and tracking responses
- Purchasing tickets and merchandise online or making a donation
- Sending thank-you letters
- Sending reminder notices to guests and potential guests
- Recording information on special dietary needs or special seating requirements

Managing volunteers:
- Recruiting volunteers
- Tracking activities undertaken
- Scheduling work activities
- Sending thank-you letters for participation

Helping with broader management activities:
- Tracking expenses
- Setting out work plans and schedules online
- Displaying receipts
- Tracking solicitations to organizations

SOURCE: Compiled from Events.org. (2003–2005). *Event management*. Retrieved August 8, 2005, from www.events.org/services.aspx#EventManagement

programs are a critical part of a nonprofit's overall activities. However, governmental support may bring with it additional program requirements for the nonprofit. Frequently, these requirements are designed to allow governments to show that their activities have made a difference. The implication for nonprofits is that they need to develop mechanisms that can measure the success of events in terms of the stated goals. This ability to justify how governmental funds were spent may place nonprofits in a better position to integrate evaluation mechanisms and thus attract funding in the future.

Sponsorship

Event **sponsorship** involves an external individual's or organization's providing an event with financial resources or various in-kind contributions. Sponsorship often fills key roles in organizing events, and in most cases, it entails a partnership or collaboration with governmental organizations, for-profit organizations, or even other nonprofit organizations. More often than not, however, sponsorship involves a partnership between a nonprofit organization and the business sector.

As will be highlighted in Chapter 12, the "primary motivation for nonprofits to develop a relationship with a company is financial." The nonprofit organization is seeking financial or in-kind support to assist with the costs of hosting an event. The sponsoring organization sees sponsorship as an opportunity to invest in the commercial potential of the event and will have specific objectives. These will of course vary but may include increased sales, brand differentiation, new and deeper community connections, improved public reputation, enhanced brand image, a demonstration of shared values with a target market, and enhanced community relations. For example, a local council might sponsor a local fun run to be seen to be contributing to the local community as well as assisting with promoting healthy lifestyles.

Sponsors can also bring a diverse range of nonfinancial benefits to the nonprofit event. These can include managerial expertise, volunteers, increased promotional coverage, and increased credibility. For example, a newspaper might promote an event in return for being named as a sponsor. If the nonprofit organization and its sponsoring partner each have different objectives for the event, that difference has implications for the measures used to evaluate the event, and the nonprofit and its partner should therefore coordinate their activities and objectives.

Nonprofits also need to be aware that while they gain from the support of a partner, there are also potential risks. For example, would having a major oil company sponsor an environmental cleanup day send the right message? Inappropriate sponsorships can place at risk a nonprofit's most valuable asset: its brand. In other words, there needs to be a clear link between the event and the sponsors. In evaluating event sponsors, the nonprofit could follow a process similar to that suggested in Chapter 12 for recruiting corporate partners. (See Table 9.2 for a list of potential sponsors.)

The Legal Environment

When staging events, nonprofit organizations need to consider many legal issues. Some of these will even affect whether an event can be classified as nonprofit (i.e., having charity status). The specific legal issues faced when organizing a nonprofit event, as well as the agencies involved, will vary depending on the locale. As a result, it is impossible to survey all the possible legal issues; however, we will briefly survey some of the more important bodies to consider.

Government Bodies

Government bodies frequently have to approve an organization's and an event's having nonprofit status. Governments may also have various regulations regarding nonprofit organizations and events. These include things such as licenses, permits, and regulations for various activities associated with events, such as competitions and raffles, firework displays, walkathons, bikeathons, or other events conducted in public spaces.

Governmental bodies will also deal with basic event issues such as food safety and public liability requirements. It is essential that a nonprofit learn what governmental and statutory requirements must be met for an event to proceed and how long the approval process takes. In many cases, the planning and approval process can involve several months.

❖ **Table 9.2**   Examples of Potential Sponsors for a Fun Run

Newspapers	Tourism bodies
Magazines	Transport services
Local radio	Hotels
Health funds	Restaurants
Health clinics	Sports clothing retailer
Health clubs/gymnasiums	Sports shoe companies
Multivitamin companies	General retail stores
Bottled water companies	Cell phone companies
Energy drink companies	Financial institutions
Snack food companies	Government agencies

Who Owns the Event?

One crucial legal issue that needs to be addressed well in advance of its staging is the event's exact legal ownership. This will often be based on the structure of the organizing body, but it may need to be determined with the assistance of a legal expert. Ownership is especially important when multiple parties are involved. For example, who is the owner of a charity ball for the Red Cross: the local organizing committee or the national body or both? Legal discussions should address the legal status and levels of responsibility of the management or organizing committee, as well as who can enter into contracts on behalf of the organization.

Venue Agreements

To protect both contracting parties, venue agreements, like all business contracts, should be in writing. While these contracts can be quite simple, large sums of money may be at stake. For example, a charity organization hiring a large outdoor stadium for a concert may incur substantial costs. Even if the facility is "donated" at a reduced fee, it is critical to identify the rights and responsibilities of both parties. For instance, clauses designed to indemnify the venue owner or operator against damages are often included in venue contracts. These contracts will also involve some form of consideration, usually in the form of a security deposit, to cover cleaning, repairs, security, and cancellation. Access times for equipment to be brought into and removed from the venue (known as bumping in and bumping out) also need to be negotiated and documented. In many cases, penalties are imposed for not finishing on time. The nonprofit also needs to consider the cost and implications of providing free house seats for venue management, as well as additions or alterations to internal structures and approvals for signage.

Sponsor Contracts

Sponsor contracts also need to be negotiated, and rights and responsibilities need to be documented and agreed to. As Chapter 12 will show, these contracts may involve agreement between the contracting parties to use the other's trademarks or logos. For this reason, sponsors often insist on the right to monitor and control the quality of the program and on hospitality rights for their staff and guests. In simple cases, this may merely be the provision of a number of complimentary tickets. In other cases, however, the costs can be substantial.

Entertainment Contracts

Entertainment contracts are often extremely complex. The major focus of the contract is usually clear; however, additional aspects, known as riders, or special attachments, can be extensive and can sometimes threaten the viability of the event. These usually consist of requirements for the provision of food, drink, accommodations, and transport in addition to the artist's fees. The idiosyncratic whims of some artists can require a substantial financial commitment, and thus all special attachments need to be specific, documented, and agreed to.

Another important aspect of booking artists is exclusivity clauses. These are provisions designed to protect the unique aspects and value of the event so that the artist coming to town does not take advantage of the free airfare and accommodations to make additional appearances unrelated to the event. Exclusivity becomes more complicated, however, when artists are performing free or at reduced fees, as is the case at many nonprofit events. Negotiations are also difficult when the nonprofit organization is dealing with an agent. As a precaution, the nonprofit should seek written proof that the agent represents the act and has the authority to sign on its behalf.

Media Broadcast Contracts

In large national or international events, media broadcast contracts may be fundamental to the financial success of an event. The television rights to broadcast the Olympic Games, for example, represent a major source of revenue that is so essential for the survival of the Olympics that media issues influence the scheduling of activities.

In some cases, attracting media sponsorship is a major goal of an event, simply because of the opportunities to publicize the event or the issue being promoted. The 2003 AIDS concert organized in conjunction with Nelson Mandela in South Africa is a good example (see Exhibit 9.10).

Risk Management

Many legal issues relate to risks associated with events. Unfortunately, risk is inevitable; however, it is possible for organizations to identify potential hazards and undertake activities that minimize any associated risks. **Risk management** is a core part of any event. For an event organizer, risk management involves anticipating what could go wrong and developing strategies and action plans to manage and control incidents that might occur. Some of these incidents are outlined in Table 9.3.

❖ **Exhibit 9.10**   Give a Minute of Your Life for AIDS Campaign

In 2003, former South African president Nelson Mandela and a number of high-profile music icons (including Bob Geldof, Bono, Brian May, Annie Lennox, Beyoncé, and Anastacia) supported the Give a Minute of Your Life for AIDS campaign, which was staged in Cape Town.

In the lead-up to the event, many of the musicians repeatedly promoted the concert, providing an unprecedented level of publicity. The concert promoted awareness of the HIV issue globally, and the media rights also contributed to the financial success of the event. Media broadcast contracts will generally identify specifically the territory or area to which the event will be broadcast, which may be increasingly important in a global environment. In this case, the concert was broadcast free on the Internet to more than 15 countries. It was also shown on BBC1 and MTV online and later released on CD and DVD.

Some types of events may have added complexities, such as concerts in which performers' copyright (normally controlled by a publishing company) may also be an issue. Negotiations will need to address such things as repeat broadcasting (after the event); extracts; sublicensing arrangements; merchandising via CD-ROMs, cable television, and the Internet; and access to stage and celebrity areas; as well as listed titles and credits.

SOURCE: Compiled from information on *46664.com*, retrieved December 30, 2005, from 46664.com

❖ **Table 9.3**   Types of Risk Associated With Events

Types of Risk	Examples
Crowds	Security, health, and comfort issues
Visibility	Crime, prostitution, terrorism
Celebration	May lead to revelry and lawlessness
Activities	Competitions, sports, thrill rides
Alcohol	Overindulgence, underage drinking, glass vessels
Target markets	Clash of cultures
Setting	Site-related risks
Weather	Dehydration, sunstroke
Quality control	Variability with occasional or one-time events
Financial areas	Mega events (i.e., high up-front costs)
Volunteers	Quality assurance and sourcing

The first step in the risk management process is to identify all likely risks and assess their potential for occurrence. Risks are identified either by risk assessment specialists or by organizational committees at risk assessment meetings. These meetings need to involve members from all functional areas or departments so that employees responsible for all aspects of the event are represented. For most events, it is also useful and prudent to include external individuals or agencies, such as police, ambulances, and fire departments. As a result of increasing litigation, it is also crucial that all risk-related discussions be documented. Documentation provides evidence a nonprofit can use to demonstrate that it has done all that is possible to minimize potential risks (i.e., exercised due diligence).

Insurance

Insurance is a core part of events, and in some countries, such as Australia, the cost of insurance is a key reason many proposed events are abandoned. Rising insurance rates have had particularly harsh repercussions on the event planning of smaller nonprofits.

Nonprofits can invest in various categories of insurance. Some policies may insure for specific types of risks or liabilities. For example, an organization may be able to insure a venue for damages. Other insurance policies might also be needed, such as personal accident (including volunteers), public liability, directors' liability, professional indemnity, and workers' compensation, to name a few.

Health and Safety Issues

Many health and safety issues are associated with events, and each carries its own particular requirements. The provision of food, for example, adds a dimension to the management of an event because a range of food safety issues must be considered. These issues are particularly complex if volunteers are engaged to provide food, and even when contractors are appointed to operate food concessions, any bad publicity from food-related incidents still reflects poorly on the event.

If alcoholic beverages are to be served at the event, another range of issues needs to be dealt with. Not only must appropriate licenses be obtained, but a raft of other requirements must be met, such as ensuring that alcohol is not sold to minors and that intoxicated people are not served. Serving alcohol may also involve security issues if patrons become unruly. Moreover, in recent international cases, those serving alcohol to individuals who are already drunk have been found to bear partial responsibility for any drunken behavior.

Sanitation is another basic requirement that is sometimes not fully considered. Local laws often dictate the number of toilets considered sufficient for an event as well as requirements concerning refuse collection and disposal. All these matters can be managed if adequate lead-time is allowed for planning and obtaining advice and permits. Estimating the costs involved and planning effectively may be complicated because they depend on the number of people attending.

Managing Special Events

We have previously identified various organizational structures that can be used to manage events. Generally, however, one person will be responsible for all the activities associated with the coordination of the event. This person, the event manager, needs

❖ **Table 9.4**   A Systematic Approach to Decision Making

1. Collect all the information (most problems have many points of view).
2. Consider the pros and cons of your decision in terms of those who will be affected.
3. Consider the financial implications of your decision.
4. Consider the moral and ethical implications of your decision.
5. Make the decision and do not look back.

SOURCE: Goldblatt, 1997, p. 56.

to possess certain core skills and attributes, including leadership skills, organizational skills, communication skills, vision, and creativity, in order to manage and control the macroenvironment and the finer details of the **planning process**. One of the major management issues is the ability to make decisions in a competent and timely manner. Goldblatt (1997) provides a useful and systematic approach to decision making (Table 9.4). These are the basic types of decision processes that are needed in any managerial role in an organization. At the same time, as discussed in the preceding sections, event planning entails some very unique issues.

Marketing and Promoting Special Events

Marketing is that function of events management that can keep in touch with an event's participants and visitors (consumers), read their needs and motives, develop products that meet those needs, and build a communication program that expresses the event's purpose and objectives (Hall, 1997, p. 136).

Events are products (i.e., service experiences) that both nonprofit and for-profit organizations need to develop and manage so that they fit within the organization's broader philosophy. And like all service experiences, these events need to be marketed if they are to achieve organizational objectives.

One of the major challenges in marketing events is that many events are one-off occurrences, and thus an organization does not have internal information or experience on which to make effective decisions. Even if an event has been held previously, nonprofits seek to ensure the event is perceived to be new and exciting each time it occurs. Furthermore, radical changes in the event's focus or schedule are almost as complicated as developing a totally new event. Thus in many cases, nonprofit organizations do not have extensive internal information on which to base decisions. In addition, given that nonprofits may have restricted budgets, they may have very little ability to undertake extensive research about the type of focus they should be using. All the while, any activities to be undertaken need to be consistent with the nonprofit's broader mission, and this mission will be manifested in the objectives that are established during the event planning stage. Moreover, the SWOT analysis will have identified some key issues that may need to be considered in both the strategic direction of the event and the specific **marketing mix** of the event. For example, broad objectives might be to increase membership in the nonprofit organization, raise awareness of the event in the community, increase the profile of the organization, and generate resources to be used to further the nonprofit's cause.

Segmenting and Positioning

Segmenting and positioning is a marketing process designed to identify a market segment (or segments) not satisfied by other events. As with all marketing activities, the nonprofit needs to carefully consider which potential groups to target. As has been said before, several market segments must often be considered at once. Generally speaking, an event should be based on a market segment that is large enough to make the event viable and expandable in the future and that may be attractive to business organizations. The most successful events reach across several market segments or deal with a demand that has not been satisfied by other events.

The Marketing Mix

To address special event marketing by nonprofits appropriately, it is necessary to expand the 4P marketing mix discussed earlier in this book to include some additional considerations. The result is an 8P list, which includes product, price, promotion, place, people, packaging, programming, and partnership. The discussion in this section is designed to briefly cover the core issues associated with events and not to replace the detailed discussion of marketing more generally. Remember that the marketing mix consists of several elements that combine to make one offering. Consequently, activities need to support one another if the overall offering is to meet the specific objectives of the nonprofit organization.

Product

Product "encompasses all of the elements that make up the event" (Allen et al., 2001, p. 164). Thus product involves more than just the tangible elements of the event; it includes all aspects associated with the event experience. In this way, the event, like all product offerings, has a personality that is supported across the marketing mix. Marketers frequently discuss five levels of a product, the core benefit, basic offer, expected offer, augmented offer, and potential offer. Events have similar levels. The core product might relate to the issue involved or the type of event. Tangible aspects of the event might include the venue rented. However, many of the support activities contribute extensively to the product. For example, the decorations selected will assist in developing a theme that in turn will influence the overall experience. The augmented features might include specific unique features, such as unique performers at the event. While the event is a product, it is more like a service, in that the tangible aspects frequently have relatively little importance (as occurs for all services) and those participating evaluate the overall experience.

Pricing

Price is "the value consumers place on the event experience and are prepared to pay" (Allen, 2001, p. 164). Calculating the value of an event is frequently difficult. For example, why will some people pay hundreds of dollars to attend one charity event but only $20 to attend another? Is the value derived by consumers based solely on the quality of the food and entertainment? In many cases, the value might be associated with simply being "seen" at a specific event and thus is similar to the consumption of other prestige "goods."

When considering pricing, the nonprofit organization needs to recognize that there is a downward-sloping demand curve. This means that nonprofit organizations need to consider how various prices, in cash or in terms of effort, are required to achieve the objectives, financial or nonfinancial. The organization also needs to consider how changes in price and perceived value will affect participation. There is some optimal price for a black-tie dinner. The level of effort people are asked to contribute will also affect their participation.

From a traditional economic perspective, however, an event will need to cover all fixed and variable costs to break even. Given the variability in circumstances, such as weather conditions, an organization may want to set prices such that it breaks even, that is, does not lose money, even if demand is somewhat lower than anticipated.

In summary, pricing is complex. Indeed, in some cases, pricing of events might not in any way relate to the ticket price charged. For example, in the United Nations' Clean Up the World event, individuals contribute their time and effort rather than money, although there are corporate sponsors as well. How does one design an event that will encourage participants' support and be commensurate with the "value" participants expect to receive?

Promotion

In terms of events, promotion "includes all of the marketing communications techniques of advertising, personal selling, sales promotions, merchandising and public relations" (Allen et al., 2001, p. 164). This is sometimes made more complex because promotion may not only be part of the activities to inform potential audiences of the event; it may also be part of the product. For example, an event designed to raise awareness of skin cancer would be deemed successful if it generated extensive publicity.

We traditionally think of promotion as advertising, which is a core part of an event. People do not attend an event if they are unaware of it. Advertising takes the form of paid impersonal communication (television, radio, outdoor media). In some cases, media companies (television stations, radio stations, and newspapers) provide free advertising spots as in-kind sponsorship.

Other forms of promotion include publicity and public relations. This is unpaid promotion that usually appears in the form of a media story. While it is not paying for this advertising, an organization needs to do something to generate media interest. For example, one organization publicizing breast cancer held a 10-kilometer race in Washington, DC, in which the vice president of the United States handed out medals to those finishing. This sort of celebrity participation generated extensive media coverage that could not have been purchased.

The negative side of publicity is that the organization does not control what is said about the event. Moreover, on busy media days, activities designed to attract publicity may fail. It is also possible that publicity could be negative; for example, a campaign against drunk driving could be harmed irreparably if the celebrity spokesperson were arrested for drunk driving. Thus, while publicity and public relations can cut through the advertising clutter, they are often difficult to manage and control.

Sales promotion is sometimes used to promote an event as well. It usually takes the form of an invitation to purchase a ticket or attend the event. In many cases, it would be part of a cause-related marketing program in which a for-profit sponsor might subsidize entry to the event for patrons who bring one or more of its labels or proof-of-purchase tokens. In this way, the event entices people to participate with discounted tickets. Other forms of promotions, such as free gifts, may be used infrequently in connection with events.

Personal selling is another form of event promotion. While we may think it is seldom used for nonprofit events, this is not the case. Indeed, personal selling is frequently undertaken by volunteers or members of the sponsoring nonprofit organization. These individuals try to "sell" tickets or seek contributions from friends, acquaintances, and colleagues. In many cases, this practice is very successful because individuals are motivated more by their sense of obligation to the seller than by a commitment to the event or issue it supports. This may not be problematic if the sole focus of the event is to raise money. If other objectives are sought, however, such as increased awareness of an issue, personal selling may be less important.

Place

Place is often discussed as "the geographical location of the event, as well as the purchase point for tickets" (Allen et al., 2002, p. 164). It is relevant to ask how a location might be found that will appeal to the target audience as well as be consistent with the desired image of the event and its overall objectives. In many cases, the type of event will determine the appropriate venue. For example, an outdoor concert needs to be in a venue both capable of holding the appropriate number of people and accessible to the target audience. Location may be critical in attracting the right group. For example, many local government bodies in Australia support open-air movies in parks in the summer months because they not only provide a service to residents but also allow residents to increase usage of resources that are usually untapped. The distribution of tickets for events as well as transportation to events may be critical to their success. For example, at the 2000 Sydney Olympics, a ticket to an event also entitled patrons to free public transportation for the day, making access to event locations easier.

People

In the services area of marketing, it is recognized that people are critical to the success of operations. The same is true in the case of events. However, managing people may be more difficult at events because nonprofits frequently rely on volunteers. Nonprofit organizations need to ensure that the experience is as enjoyable as possible for patrons and that the service provided is of an appropriate level. This can be a major challenge because many events are short-term in nature, and thus there is little time for training regular employees or volunteers. As a result, dealing with the service delivery problems that are often experienced at events becomes more difficult.

Programming

Programming generally refers to **event scheduling** but also includes the processes associated with the implementation of the event such as running sheets and other event checklists. Activities need to flow smoothly yet appear spontaneous. This requires extensive levels of coordinated effort across all the activities associated with the planning and staging of the event. Thus, some of the activities discussed previously under marketing mix, for example training volunteer staff, would be part of the process of delivering a coordinated event.

Partnerships

The concept of partnerships has been discussed in several areas in this chapter and elsewhere in the book. A nonprofit needs to collaborate with others—other nonprofits, governmental bodies, and firms—to draw on the resources necessary to develop an event that achieves its objectives. Of course, the objectives of all parties must be congruent, and identifying appropriate partners may or may not be easy, depending on the event. It is essential that the nonprofit be able to clearly explain how the partnership will benefit all parties. This can be a difficult marketing task. Nevertheless, partnerships are becoming increasingly important in events, especially as the issues being tackled grow in complexity. In many cases, nonprofits seek to draw together large groups interested in a common issue, which has the benefit of amassing larger resource bases. It may also lead to a coordinated effort focused on issues of common concern, which reduces competition for the same audience pool.

Packaging

Packaging is the total integrated nature of the event, that is, the way it is presented. In many ways, all the previous marketing mix activities determine how the event finally appears. In essence, this is the integrated result of all activities. Having a $500-per-head charity dinner will need to be supported throughout with "top class" actions, from the initial promotion through the event and any follow-up activities, ensuring a consistent image across activities.

Evaluating Special Events

As with all activities, it is essential to evaluate the success or lack of success of a nonprofit event. This is a critical part of the overall event process, but unfortunately, some nonprofit organizations may not see it as an essential formal task, or they may realize its importance but not want to allocate valuable resources to evaluation. The evaluation process should in fact start well before the event has even begun. For example, a nonprofit organization that wants to hold an event to increase awareness of an issue needs to measure the awareness level in the community both before and after the event. Without such activities, it would be impossible to verify the success of the event. The evaluation process is essential to overall learning within an organization and also contributes to the organization's ability to host successful events in the future.

When **evaluating events**, nonprofits will frequently require a range of qualitative and quantitative techniques. These need to focus on all the event's objectives and should also identify opportunities for improvement in the future. The organization needs to use formal processes to collect information from internal and external sources.

Ideally, the objectives for an event will have been defined before the event takes place, and this will require a range of pre-event information. In some cases, this information is readily accessible. For example, an organization can identify a short-term increase in the number of new members or the funds raised from a given event. On the other hand, identifying changes in attitudes toward an issue of social concern will most likely require pre-event research. For instance, if an objective of the event is an increase in awareness of the dangers of sunburn, some measure of pre-event awareness on the part of the target audience must be available.

The objectives need to consider all stakeholders and partners in the event. The local government, for example, might be more concerned with increased spending in the region and less about satisfaction with the event itself, but sponsors may be interested in consumers' levels of recall of the sponsor Thus, multiple measures of success may need to be developed to satisfy the needs of all the partners. Consequently, measuring the overall success of an event will be extremely complex because it may be difficult, if not impossible, to aggregate objectives and outcomes in a manner acceptable to all the parties involved. Moreover, what one party perceives to be a highly successfully event could be viewed by another as a failure.

Summary

The nonprofit marketing issues presented in this chapter are summarized here according to the chapter learning objectives they meet.

Define special events and understand the role of special events in the nonprofit sector. Nonprofit organizations produce occasions or special events that are diverse and include civic events, fairs, and festivals; sporting events; musical events; and many others. A range of international and local nonprofit organizations can produce events. Events are organized for a variety of reasons and, therefore, may have multiple objectives and multiple benefits to several different entities, including governments, the community, and corporations.

Describe the different types of nonprofit events. A diverse range of activities can be classified as nonprofit special events. Nonprofit organizations may also get involved in events for many reasons, including communication and awareness campaigns and program launches at both regional and national levels. Two major stakeholders need to be considered: the organizers or producers of events and the customers of events.

Describe the factors that influence the objectives of special events. Objectives are developed by answering a series of questions: Why is the event being held, what is the event to achieve, and who are the event stakeholders? Objectives also need to be measurable because they will become the criteria by which the event will be evaluated after it has been staged. Setting and recording objectives is furthermore a form of organizational memory that can assist the nonprofit in improving performance in the future.

Understand the issues involved in producing special events. Several administrative structures can be employed to successfully manage an event. These range from in-house personnel to a network of partners. Human resources and the management and motivation of employees are very important, as is the induction of volunteers. Fiscal control and the importance of budgeting were also highlighted, and issues relating to attracting external revenue from both government and corporate sponsors were discussed. Legal issues and the role and responsibilities of event managers were also explained.

Understand the risks associated with hosting special events. Risk management is a process that begins with the identification of all likely risks as well as the likelihood of their occurrence. Risks are identified either by risk assessment specialists or by organizational committees at risk assessment meetings. All stakeholders need to be represented at risk assessment meetings, and it is important to document the meetings so that a nonprofit can demonstrate due diligence.

Describe the procedures involved in managing special events. Although various organizational structures can be used to manage events, ultimately the event manager will be responsible for all the activities associated with the coordination of the event. The skills required to manage an event include the following: leadership skills, organizational skills, communication skills, vision, creativity, and decision-making skills. Managing events includes the following procedures: planning, preparation, production, evaluation, and reporting.

Understand the importance of marketing and public relations for special events in the nonprofit sector. Many events in the nonprofit sector represent a major marketing challenge because they are one-off occurrences and some organizations do not have the necessary internal information or experience on which to base effective decisions. Regardless of the event concept, the activities to be undertaken need to be consistent with the nonprofit's broader mission. This mission needs to be reflected in the objectives that are established during the event planning stage and which will subsequently inform the SWOT analysis. In terms of defining the market for an event, the event concept needs to be broad-based in order to attract a large enough market to make the event viable. The 8 P's of the marketing mix (product, price, promotion, place, people, packaging, programming and partnership were also discussed.

Glossary

Environmental factors. Factors that are external to the organization but need to be analyzed (in a SWOT analysis) to ensure an event will achieve broader strategic objectives.

Evaluating events. A process of collecting and analyzing data in order to assess whether an event has been successful or not.

Event scheduling. Choosing a date and time to stage an event.

Feasibility. A process of analysis used to determine whether an event is viable.

Fiscal control. Managing incoming and outgoing funds as well as ensuring that the financial objectives of an event are met.

Marketing mix. The elements that combine to make one event offering. Also known as the 8 Ps of event marketing (product, price, promotion, place, people, packaging, programming and partnership).

Organizational factors. Internal competencies and abilities that reinforce an organization's ability to stage an event, as well as inherent weaknesses that may inhibit the organization's ability to achieve its objectives for an event.

Organizational learning. The experience gained as a result of holding an event; important if the organization plans to host similar events in the future.

Organizational structure. The management hierarchy and levels of responsibility required to produce an event.

Planning process. The design and documentation of a number of strategically oriented processes developed to ensure that event objectives are achieved.

Programming. Event scheduling and the processes associated with the implementation of an event.

Risk management. The formal process of anticipating what could go wrong and developing strategies and action plans to manage and control incidents that might occur.

Segmenting and positioning. A marketing process designed to identify a market segment (or segments) not satisfied by other events.

Setting objectives. Developing a set of aims for an event that states exactly what the event is designed to achieve.

Special events. A diverse range of activities ranging from civic events to product launches that are unique and temporary and staged for a specific purpose.

Sponsorship. An external individual's or organization's provision of financial resources or various in-kind contributions to an event.

Stakeholders. A range of individuals and bodies, such as partner organizations, sponsors, and the local community, that have a specific interest in an event.

Venue selection. Choosing an event location that is in line with the needs of the identified target audience.

Volunteers. People who elect to assist, without financial reward, with the staging of an event.

❖

QUESTIONS FOR REVIEW

1. Define *special event* from a sponsor's perspective.

2. Define *special event* from a customer's perspective.

3. Explain feasibility in terms of a special event.

4. Describe a network structure.

5. Explain the primary motivation for nonprofits to develop a relationship with a company.

6. List the eight elements of the marketing mix for special events.

❖

QUESTIONS FOR DISCUSSION

1. What happens if events do not offer a customer something out of the ordinary?

2. What is the critical issue in defining nonprofit events?

3. What are the purposes for which nonprofit events are designed?

4. Why is detailed planning critical when conducting events?

5. What are the benefits of producing special events?

6. Why should objectives be measurable?

INTERNET EXERCISES

Visit the website of Trick-or-Treat for UNICEF (www.unicefusa.org/trickortreat/). Based on the information provided:

- Define the segments being targeted.
- Discuss how this event positions itself differently from other types of charity appeals.
- Discuss how the Web page describes the 8 Ps.
- Provide a method to evaluate the various objectives of the event.

TEAM EXERCISES AND ROLE PLAYING

1. This assignment is designed to highlight the roles of different stakeholders when planning a large outdoor concert organized to promote a social issue of your group's choosing. Divide your group into representatives of government, a corporate sponsor, a community leader, and a nonprofit executive. Convene a meeting to formulate the objectives of the event and discuss how the event should be marketed to achieve your objectives. Document the meeting and present items for follow-up.

2. Go to the office of your local government and identify the permits you would need to host a charity concert with an expected attendance of 10,000 people. The concert will include the supply of both food and alcoholic beverages at the venue.

MINICASE (suitable for term project assignment)

In this chapter, you have been exposed to a number of issues that are important in the production of special events. Major planning activities include a feasibility analysis, which is a process that can be used by nonprofit organizations to determine whether an event is viable, and a SWOT analysis, which is used to determine how internal strengths can be capitalized on and external weaknesses can be downplayed.

In groups of no more than four, brainstorm a concept for a nonprofit event. Develop objectives and conduct a feasibility and a SWOT analysis. The results should be presented as a business plan with the following headings:

- Executive summary
- Description of the event and concept
- Feasibility analysis

- SWOT analysis (including planning considerations)
- Proposed organizational structure
- Market analysis and marketing strategy
- Potential government support and corporate sponsorship
- Risk assessment and management strategies
- Financial considerations (including budget and cash flow information)

- Logistics and staging issues (such as permits, crowd and traffic control, and safety concerns)

The business report should be approximately 5,000 words in length (1,250 words per person), and the event is to be presented as a new concept rather than an analysis of an existing event.

References and Bibliography

Allen, J., O'Tooel, W., McDonnell, I., & Harris, R. (2001). *Festivals and special event management* (2nd ed.). Queensland, Australia: Wiley.

Appenzeller, H. (1998). *Risk management in sport: Issues and strategies* (2nd ed.). Durham, NC: Carolina Academic Press.

Armstrong, J. (2001). Planning special events. San Francisco: Jossey-Bass.

Astroff, M. T., & Abbey, J. R. (1995). *Convention sales and services* (4th ed.). Cranbury, NJ: Waterbury Press.

Berlonghi, A. (1900). *The special event risk management manual.* Dana Point, CA: Alexander Berlonghi.

Betteridge, D. (1997). *Event management in leisure and tourism.* London, UK: Hodder & Stoughton.

Bicycle Victoria. (2005). Retrieved November 2005 from www.bv.com.au/

Catherwood, D. W., & Van Kirk, R. L. (1992). *The complete guide to special event management : Business insights, financial advice, and successful strategies from Ernst & Young, advisors to the Olympics, the Emmy Awards, and the PGA Tour.* New York: Wiley.

Damster, G., & Tassiopoulos, D. (2000). *Event management: A professional and developmental approach.* Lansdowne, South Africa: Juta Education.

Getz, D. (1997). *Event management and event tourism.* New York: Cognizant Communication.

Goldblatt, J. (1990). *Special Events: The art and science of celebration.* New York: Van Nostrand Reinhold.

Goldblatt, J. (1997). *Special events: Best practices in modern event management.* New York: Wiley.

Goldblatt, J. (1999). *Dollars and events: How to succeed in the special events business.* New York: Wiley.

Goldblatt, J., & Nelson, K. (2001). *The international dictionary of event management.* New York: Wiley.

Goldblatt, J., & Schiptsova, J. (2004). *Special events : Twenty-first century global event management.* Amsterdam, the Netherlands: Elsevier Butterworth-Heinemann.

Hall, C. M. (1997). *Hallmark tourist events: Impacts, management and planning.* Chichester, UK: Wiley.

Hoyle, L. H. (2002). *Event marketing: How to successfully promote events, festivals, conventions, and expositions.* New York: Wiley.

Ickis, M. (1970). *The book of festivals and holidays the world over.* New York: Dodd, Mead.

Lee, M. (2004). The coming nonprofit crash. *PA Times, 27*(9), 5, 9.

Masterman, G. (2002). *Strategic sports event management* (3rd ed.). New York: Wiley.

Montgomery, R., & Strick, S. (1995). *Meetings, conventions and expositions: An introduction to the industry.* New York: Van Nostrand Reinhold.

Shone, A., & Bryn, P. (2004). *Successful event management: A practical handbook* (2nd ed.). London, UK: Thomson Learning.

Skinner, B. E., & Rukavina, V. (2003). *Event sponsorship.* New York: Wiley.

Sonder, M. (2004). *Event entertainment and production.* Hoboken, NJ: Wiley.

Stedman, G., Goldblatt, J., & Delpy, L. (1995). *The ultimate guide to sport event management and marketing.* Chicago: Irwin Professional.

Tarlow, P. E. (2002). *Event risk management and safety.* New York: Wiley.

Marketing to Volunteers

Learning Objectives

On completion of this chapter, the reader will

- Understand the importance of volunteers to nonprofit organizations

- Understand the various reasons people volunteer

- Describe ways to recruit volunteers effectively

- Describe virtual volunteering and its growing importance

Opening Vignette: Girl Scouts

Founded in 1912, Girl Scouts started with a membership of 18 girls. By 1929, the membership had grown to more than 200,000. In 2003, the membership has grown to more than 2.8 million girl members and almost 942,000 adult members. More than 50 million American women experienced Girl Scouting while growing up. Young women and girls continue to be attracted to Girl Scouting's mission of helping young women between the ages of 5 and 17 develop their potential (Girl Scouts of America, 2005).

Unfortunately, some young women are unable to join Girl Scouts. Many prospective Scouts are being placed on waiting lists because of a shortage of adult women volunteers. The shortage is greatest in rural, urban, and other areas with sizable transient populations. Because so many adult women were once Girl Scouts, it might seem surprising that recruiting and retaining sufficient numbers of volunteers is a challenge. Not so. With historically high divorce rates, a sizable number of women are fully employed and managing single-parent households (CNN, 2003).

To cope with the shortage of volunteers, Girl Scouts has asked volunteers to be responsible for more girl members. In some cases, Girl Scouts has adapted to women's time constraints, asking some mothers to serve on weekends or to meet with their troops monthly instead of weekly. One of the greatest challenges Girl Scouting faces in the future is recruiting and retaining enough volunteers (Maldonado, 2003).

Importance of Volunteers

As the Girl Scouting vignette illustrates, many nonprofit organizations rely heavily on volunteers to accomplish their missions. Volunteers are defined as persons who willingly perform a service, without pay, through a group or organization. Volunteers allow nonprofit organizations to direct a greater proportion of their resources toward program objectives because the organizations do not have to pay for their labor. Volunteers also attract resources to the organization because (1) volunteers usually make financial donations to their organizations, and (2) they often recruit other volunteers and solicit donations.

Status of Volunteering in the United States

The U.S. Bureau of Labor Statistics (BLS, 2003) reported that about 59 million people performed some type of volunteer service in a recent year. This figure represents just over one in four Americans older than 16. BLS also reported that women tend to volunteer at higher rates than men do. Fully employed people volunteer more than underemployed people do. The majority of volunteers served in religious or educational and youth-service organizations. Volunteers served, on average, 52 hours during the year of the BLS study (BLS, 2003).

Independent Sector, a nonprofit organization that commissions biennial surveys of American giving and volunteering, estimated the economic value of volunteering in the United States to be $239.2 billion in 2001 (Independent Sector, 2003). Clearly, many Americans give of their time to further the work of nonprofit organizations. Volunteering has a great economic value to the economy as well as a great cultural value to citizens.

However, pressures on nonprofits and their volunteers are bringing about changes. First, Americans volunteer for nonprofit organizations, but they work in businesses that have been profoundly affected by the information economy. Competition is intense and global. Americans are working harder and longer in the new economy than in the former, mass production, industrial economy (Reich, 2002). Second, the number of nonprofit organizations has been steadily growing. For example, from 1995 to 2002, the number of nonprofit organizations in the United States increased by 200,000 (Lee, 2004). Third, the U.S. federal government has been steadily decreasing funding to the nonprofit sector yet at the same time promotes the nonprofit sector as a more appropriate provider of social services than the government (Adams, 1987; Bush, 2002; Carnegie Corporation of New York, 2003; Etherington, 2001).

However the nonprofit sector responds and adapts to these pressures, volunteers will continue to be a vital resource. **Volunteer program managers** (VPMs) are individuals with the authority and responsibility for organizing and directing the activities of an organization's volunteers. In small nonprofit organizations, VPMs may be volunteers. In larger nonprofits, they are usually paid staff. These individuals will continue to find ways to recruit and retain valuable volunteers in a climate of increasing competition both from other nonprofit organizations and from the many other ways volunteers could spend their time.

Status of Volunteering in Other Countries

Volunteers in many different nations donate their time to charities and other nonprofit organizations. For example, according to the Australian Bureau of Statistics, volunteerism in Australia is strong and growing. Approximately 32% of civilian adult Australians volunteer for at least one volunteer organization (Wesley Mission Sydney, 2001). Some other examples follow:

- More than one in four Canadians (27%) volunteer for a charity or nonprofit organization, according to Statistics Canada (2000). This represents more than 1 billion hours of donated labor annually.
- The Institute for Volunteering Research (1997) reports that about half (48%) of the adult population in the United Kingdom volunteers for a nonprofit organization or charity.
- Volunteer Development Scotland (2004) reports that 43% of adults in Scotland volunteer.
- About 16% of adult Brazilians report volunteering for a nonprofit organization (Salamon et al., 1999).

Classifying Volunteers

Before we describe the various types of volunteers, it is appropriate to be more precise about how we define a volunteer. The term **volunteer** is used to refer to an individual who serves in a nonprofit organization without being paid. Freely giving one's personal services to a charity, for example, implies that there is no coercion (such as a company's expecting its managers to serve on local nonprofit boards) or monetary payment for services (such as in military service). We will now discuss different ways to classify volunteers. As depicted in Figure 10.1, we will classify volunteers by type (based on regularity of service) and by the roles in which they serve.

Episodic Versus Ongoing Volunteering

Episodic volunteers are volunteers who serve on an as-needed basis or who serve during special events or on projects of limited duration. An example is a Girl Scout's mother who participates in a yearly bake sale to raise money for her daughter's troop.

❖ **Figure 10.1**   Classification of Volunteers

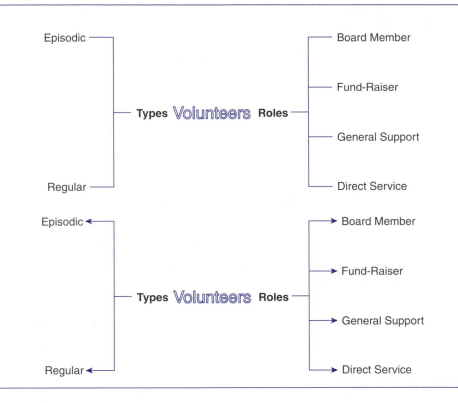

In contrast to episodic volunteers, **ongoing volunteers** work regularly. An example would be a Girl Scout troop leader who conducts weekly troop meetings.

Many nonprofit organizations rely on their regular, ongoing volunteers to maintain their programs and regular activities. Big Brothers and Big Sisters of America, for example, was established with the idea of matching adult ongoing volunteers with at-risk children.

Volunteer Roles

Nonprofit organizations have a variety of volunteer positions to staff. It is useful to think of volunteer roles as falling into one of the following categories: (a) board member or managerial, (b) fund-raising, (c) general support, and (d) direct service (Heidrich, 1988). Understanding the various roles is important because each attracts different types of people. Each role will be discussed in turn.

Board members or **managerial volunteers** are those volunteers who serve on the nonprofit's board of directors or who otherwise play a leadership or unpaid administrative role. These volunteers are responsible for overseeing the various functions of the organization in fulfillment of its mission. Board members are more likely than other types of volunteers to have higher levels of education, higher levels of income, and higher-status employment.

Fund-raising volunteers' primary tasks involve raising money by soliciting contributions. These volunteers may also be responsible for writing proposals for grants. For many organizations, fund-raisers may be the most difficult volunteers to recruit. Fund-raising volunteers are more likely to be outgoing and socially oriented. Fund-raising involves setting challenging goals, working in a team, and feeling energized by a challenge. Fund-raisers also serve a public relations role because they represent the nonprofit to the community and influential persons.

General support volunteers get the necessary, behind-the-scenes work done. They staff telephones, do filing, work on mailings, help write newsletters, work on maintenance projects, do cleaning, do driving, run errands, and so forth. General support volunteers do not seek positions of authority, but they feel a duty to help where they are needed.

Direct service volunteers provide the organization's services directly to its clients or members. They may be a scout troop leader, a Sunday school teacher, a Little League coach, a counselor, a companion, and so forth. Direct service volunteers want to make a meaningful contribution to the nonprofit. They want to feel that what they are doing is significant and improves the condition of the organization's clients.

Understanding Volunteer Motivations

In order to recruit volunteers through marketing activities, managers need to understand what influences individuals to volunteer. In this section, we will present a model of such influences.

A consistent finding in national surveys is that, when asked why they volunteer, people say they volunteer so that they can help others (Pearce, 1993). Unfortunately, for the person responsible for marketing to volunteers, this finding is not very helpful. There are many ways in which people can offer help to others. Nor does this finding help us understand why some people decide to help others by volunteering for the library and other people decide to help others by volunteering for a hospice.

Volunteering is generally considered to be an other-oriented activity. Although volunteers are giving up scarce free time, and thereby incur a cost (i.e., the opportunity to do something else with the time given to volunteering), they are also receiving benefits. For example, the parent who volunteers to be a troop leader enjoys spending time with her daughter and other young people. The troop leader feels good about being part of Girl Scouting, which was part of her own childhood experience. The troop leader feels that her service is validation of being a good parent, which is how she wants to define herself. The troop leader sees herself as a nice, kind, helpful, fun-loving person who is liked by children. Being a troop leader allows her to express these values.

Determinants of Volunteering

The motivations of volunteers are complex and involve various factors. In Figure 10.2, the motivational determinants of volunteering are depicted.

❖ **Figure 10.2**   Determinants of Volunteering

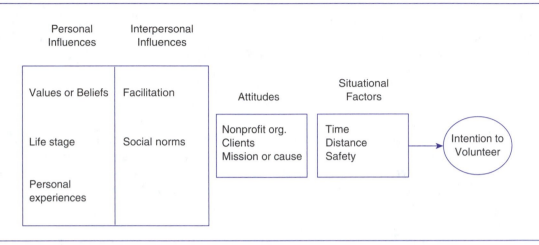

A person's decision whether to volunteer, the decision to volunteer for a particular organization, and the decision to volunteer for a specific role are dependent on multiple factors.

The model depicted in Figure 10.2 takes into account personal influences on behavior, interpersonal influences, attitudes, and situational factors. **Personal and interpersonal influences** stimulate a general disposition regarding volunteering as well as preferences for volunteering in specific areas, such as youth development, arts and culture, religion, or health care. Nonprofits that meet preference criteria are screened by a person's **attitudes**, which may be directed toward the nonprofit itself, the nonprofit's cause or mission, or the clients served by the nonprofit. **Situational factors** also influence volunteer behavior. A person may decline to volunteer for a nonprofit if there is insufficient time for volunteering, if the volunteering takes place too far away, or if personal safety may be at risk. All these types of influences affect a person's intention to volunteer for a nonprofit (Wymer, 1996).

Values and Beliefs. A **value system** consists of those issues people care about. We care about some issues more than others. Those issues we care most about, and that most influence our attitudes, beliefs, and choices, are our **core values**. Our core values are ranked in importance. People are defined by their values, especially their core values. People act in ways that appear to be consistent with whom they perceive themselves to be. People avoid acting in ways inconsistent with their core values.

Life stage. On our journey through our lives, we pass through different stages. Figure 10.3 provides a simplified depiction of a traditional person's **life stages**. The basic determinants of the traditional view of life stage are marital status, the presence or absence of children, and the age of the youngest child (Watson, 1999).

❖ **Figure 10.3** Life Stage Determinants

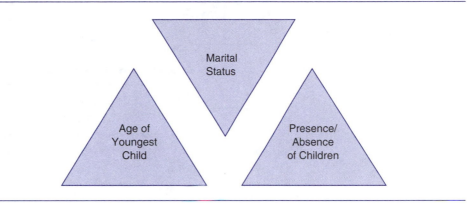

Our life stage influences our values and priorities. The City of Wellington, New Zealand, commissioned a study on volunteering in its city. The following findings were reported:

> Volunteering with different organizations at different times of their lives depending on their interests and family commitments was seen to be a general pattern. People often started volunteering by becoming involved with their children's activities then moving to more formal roles within those organizations. Volunteers might work for several organizations at the same time but usually with varying levels of commitment. (Feeney, 2001, p. 3)

Perhaps one of the most significant life stage transitions that influences volunteering is retirement (see Figure 10.4). Our jobs are important to us. They provide our livelihood. They provide us with a means of feeling useful and productive, of making accomplishments. Our jobs partially define who we are. When people retire, they may search for new ways to meet needs that were formerly met through their occupations. Studies of senior volunteers consistently find that seniors volunteer in order to feel useful and productive and to be around other people (Fischer & Schaffer, 1993).

Managers should take life stage into account when identifying prospects for marketing. Parents are good prospects for nonprofits offering services for children. Older adults whose children have left home (i.e., empty nesters) have more freedom and fewer responsibilities and may be good prospects. Middle-aged adults approaching retirement often desire to give back to their communities and are planning for a good quality of life after retirement. They would also be productive prospects.

Personal Experiences. Personal experiences play a role in helping people develop and reform their value systems. Many nonprofit organizations have been started by individuals who found themselves confronted with human privations of which they previously were unaware. Wymer and Starns (1999) examined the motives of 63 hospice volunteers. Many hospice volunteers reported that they learned about the hospice when their terminally ill loved one received hospice services. The experience of a dying

❖ **Figure 10.4** Traditional View of Life Stages

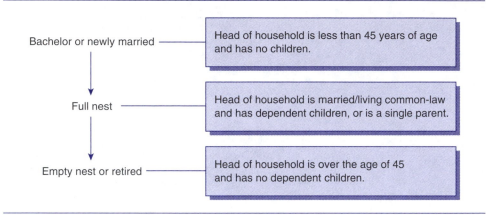

loved one's receiving compassionate care from a hospice volunteer had a major impact. After their loved one's death, many survivors responded to their experience by becoming hospice volunteers.

Another type of personal experience that influences a person's propensity to volunteer is early exposure to volunteering. Young people who are given volunteer experiences can assimilate the experiences into their value systems. If the experience was positive, children and adolescents are likely to view volunteering as a positive behavioral choice when they become adults.

In addition to the personal influences that affect volunteering (see Figure 10.2), interpersonal influences play a role. Two **interpersonal influences on volunteering** will be discussed here: facilitation and social norms.

Facilitation. Facilitation refers to assisting the potential volunteer in becoming a new volunteer and assisting the new volunteer in assimilating into the organization by providing information and social or emotional support. Facilitation helps reduce the stress that people may experience in anticipating a new role or the stress new volunteers may experience in joining a new group of people. A facilitator, then, is a person who serves a boundary role between a potential or new volunteer and the nonprofit. A facilitator provides the potential or new volunteer with information and social support, reducing ambiguity and enhancing assimilation into the organization. A facilitator is usually the friend, family member, or associate of the person being asked to volunteer. When the person who is recruiting is known by the person being recruited, the recruitment effectiveness increases four- or fivefold (Independent Sector, 2000b).

Social Norms. Social norms are those customary patterns of attitudes and behaviors that social groups accept, maintain, and enforce. Some social groups share strong political beliefs, strong feelings about the environment, strong feelings about social welfare, and so forth. These social groups may expect their members to participate in the political process, environmentalism, or social welfare reform, for example, as volunteers. Social groups exert varying degrees of influence on their members. Some social groups encourage volunteering for causes they support (Clary, Snyder, Copeland, & French, 1994; Wymer, Riecken, & Yavas, 1996).

Application Case 10.1

Ethnic Volunteering in the United Kingdom

The ethnic population in the United Kingdom is growing about 3% each year. As the proportion of ethnic citizens increases, so does the importance of better understanding these groups' social norms for volunteering. In one U.K. study, the Asian and Black communities were sampled to learn more about this topic.

The authors of the study found that Black respondents reported a duty to volunteer to help serve their ethnic community. Asians respondents, however, reported that the idea of volunteering to help their community was embarrassing and that they worried about the reactions of their families (Sharma and Bell, 2002).

Attitudes. In addition to personal and interpersonal influences on volunteering, people's own attitudes will affect their desire and motivation to volunteer. A person's motivation to volunteer can be satisfied in many ways. Individuals' personal and interpersonal circumstances help determine the type of volunteering that would interest them. However, a person's attitudes will help select the specific organizations to be considered.

Once a person is inclined to serve, the individual's attitude regarding the organization, its cause, or its clients can enhance or impede that person's willingness to volunteer. Attitudes are derived from values. A person will have negative attitudes toward things that conflict or oppose core values. A staunch conservative or libertarian will be unlikely to have a favorable attitude toward a social welfare organization. A person with strong views against violence will be unlikely to volunteer for a conservative group supporting unregulated freedom to own weapons.

Attitudes are directed toward multiple attitude objects, all of which combine to form an overall favorable or unfavorable attitude (with varying levels of intensity) related to volunteering for a particular organization. A person's overall attitude toward the organization's cause is a primary indicator because it serves as a gatekeeper of further attitude exploration. For example, if an individual's values include staunch opposition to environmental organizations, then that person will likely generalize that attitude to other facets of the organization. However, even if an individual is supportive of an organization's cause, that individual may develop negative attitudes toward the organization's management, staff, clients, volunteers, or other elements.

Situational Factors. Even though individuals may have the motivation to serve, situational factors may impede volunteer service. Many people are experiencing time poverty: They feel they lack sufficient time to devote to volunteering. According to Ellis (1994), lack of time is the number-one reason people state for not volunteering.

When prospects feel they do not have the spare time, there may be several reasons; some may be dealt with effectively during recruitment appeals, and some may be insurmountable barriers.

Numerous other situational factors may serve as barriers to volunteering. A person may live in a rural area or in a suburb remote from a nonprofit the person would like to serve. A person may feel unsafe, either because of the reputation of the nonprofit's location or because of the nature of the nonprofit's clients. Some of these barriers can be overcome by effective recruitment tactics, but others cannot be (Ellis, 1994; Wymer, 1996).

Marketing to Potential Volunteers

Recall the marketing problem described in the vignette that began this chapter: Girl Scouts are having a difficult time recruiting volunteer troop leaders. Some girls wanting to join are being placed on waiting lists. In practice, the organization probably recruits volunteers by asking mothers of Girl Scouts to serve. However, as we learned from the case, things are changing, making recruitment more difficult. For many organizations that must concern themselves with identifying and appealing to prospects, a more systematic strategy is required. The following elements help make marketing to potential volunteers more effective.

Build Your Case

Fund-raising professionals understand that the organization has to make a compelling case before people are willing to give their money. Likewise, the nonprofit has to make its compelling case known before people will be willing to give their time. Building your case means that your organization is making its name and cause widely known; doing things that build its name, reputation, and image; and communicating to outside groups the importance of the cause it supports and the ways its support is making a difference.

Nonprofit managers obtain recognition and build public support for their causes over time by consistently communicating to the outside world. Press releases are regularly sent to the media. Presentations are made to community groups. Advertisements inform the public of the organization's good work. The nonprofit creates events to raise money and to disseminate information. It obtains government grants to build its program. It attracts corporate support. Staff and volunteers alike tell others about the organization and the great things it is doing. The board of directors understands the importance of garnering public support and provides adequate funding for marketing activities. Newsletters are sent to people on the organization's mailing lists regularly. They are told about the great things the volunteers are doing and the difference they are making.

Prepare Your Organization

Before you can sell your organization to the world, you have to promote it to your internal groups. Have staff, current volunteers, and board members been hearing about the importance of volunteers to the cause? Has the organization's leadership been talking about the importance of volunteers?

At first, it may seem obvious that an organization would value volunteers. However, different parts of the organization may not value volunteers enough. Do staff and current volunteers view new volunteers with energy and helpful friendliness? Are staff and current volunteers reluctant to go out of their way to make new volunteers feel welcome and appreciated until the new volunteer has been around for awhile? Does the board support allocating funds to help volunteer recruitment? Do board members actively recruit volunteers?

All persons involved with the organization must feel valued. They have a right to see how their work is connected to the organization's mission. Nonprofit leaders must establish an organizational culture that values and supports volunteers. When regular volunteers feel appreciated and are given meaningful work, they are more accepting of new volunteers. When volunteers are treated with respect and with friendliness, they are more inclined to treat others (e.g., other volunteers, clients, staff) similarly.

Organization leaders must stress the importance of volunteers. If the leadership values volunteers and gives the recruitment and management of volunteers priority, then volunteers will come to have an important value in the organization.

Determine Your Needs

Identify areas where volunteers are needed. Once you have identified tasks that need to be performed, look for ways to create meaningful assignments for volunteers. An advisory team of staff persons or current volunteers could help identify volunteer assignments.

Whether developing a new program, preparing for an event, or helping with current operations, nonprofit managers need to develop assignments that are specific and sufficient for the need. Volunteers dislike having their time wasted by a disorganized leader. They dislike being given a task that is too challenging and therefore frustrating. They dislike being given a task that is insignificant, that does not meet their expectations, and that does not allow them to make a difference. Volunteers like being given assignments that meets their needs and allow them to feel useful and appreciated.

Volunteer Job Descriptions

Volunteer job descriptions achieve many important goals. They help the organization focus on its needs and expectations for volunteers. They help managers plan human resource needs, and they provide a means for the marketer to describe the volunteer's role. Job descriptions help volunteers anticipate their likely volunteer experience and develop expectations. Having realistic expectations helps reduce volunteer turnover from dissatisfaction.

The Texas Commission on Volunteerism and Community Service (www.one starfoundation.org/onestar/download/AmeriCorps_RFP/CallforPeerReviewers.doc) suggests using the following components in developing volunteer job descriptions.

Position Title. A properly selected title helps distinguish volunteer assignments and communicates something about the position. A specific, descriptive title gives the volunteer a sense of identity and helps the salaried staff and other volunteers understand the assigned role. A title should reflect the function of the position.

Work Location. The volunteer needs to know where the work will take place.

Volunteer Impact. To help volunteers understand the importance of their roles, explain how the volunteer job relates to the mission and operation of the organization.

Responsibilities and Duties. As precisely as possible, list the tasks the volunteer is expected to accomplish and the level of performance required.

Qualifications. What skills or other attributes are you looking for in the volunteer in this position? Be clear and concise. List qualifications required for the position. Include education, personal characteristics, skills, abilities, and experience required.

Commitment. How often are you expecting this person to work? How long will a typical shift last? How long do expect this person to remain in this position (weeks, months, years)? People who prefer episodic volunteer roles to ongoing volunteering will want to know the beginning date, the time commitment, and the ending date.

Training. Indicate nature and length of all general and position-specific training required for the assignment.

Date. Indicate the date the description was written and last updated.

Volunteer Supervisor. Identify the person the volunteer will report to and provide contact information.

Another advantage of developing volunteer job descriptions is that they aid recruitment by providing specific information to communicate to volunteers. Rather than announcing a general call for volunteers, an organization can inform prospects precisely what volunteer opportunities are available, what they can expect from the volunteer experience, what qualities the nonprofit is expecting, and how to apply. Written volunteer job descriptions can be given to people you are recruiting or posted on your nonprofit's website.

How to Find Good Volunteers

In looking for volunteer prospects, you are limited only by your imagination. Susan Ellis (see the Energize Inc. website, www.energizeinc.com/) has developed a proximity chart technique that recommends that you walk or drive in concentric circles around your organization's site, writing down everything you see, and then determine how you can approach these neighbors with a recruitment message. Ellis also recommends that your organization hold an open house at least once a year or more often when something special deserves celebration. The point is to do something especially for your neighbors. Send invitations that are different from any general, public announcements. Either make it clear that the event is only for those within a two-block radius or explain that neighbors will be welcome an hour earlier than the general public for special attention.

Many schools and universities are involved in **service learning,** an educational program that provides students with community volunteer experiences. Service learning assumes that youth volunteer experiences will lead to greater adult civic participation. VPMs should contact area high schools and universities to determine if a suitable match exists.

Another approach to finding potential volunteers is to think of them as part of a community. The first community of potential volunteers is those individuals who are part of the social circles of your current volunteers and staff. You can also think of this community as existing in concentric circles. The persons closest to current volunteers and staff are in the innermost circle (our loved ones and family members). The middle concentric circle includes friends and individuals your current volunteers and staff communicate with often. The outermost circle consists of those acquaintances your volunteers and staff associate with periodically. This community is usually the most receptive to recruitment appeals, especially when they are recruited by their social contacts in your organization.

Another community consists of individuals who are not socially connected with people in your organization. Since people in this community are not part of your organization's social networks, the interpersonal influences that help recruitment (see Figure 10.2) are relatively weak. The nonprofit organization may have to communicate with these people through flyers, the newspaper, or other impersonal forms of communication. Since social influences are weak, the best prospects in this community are those with the greatest affinity for your cause.

Some nonprofit organizations have found helpful corporate partners. As discussed in Chapter 12, corporations are supporting the nonprofit sector more and more. Progressive corporations encourage **corporate volunteering,** that is, they allow employees to take time off from work to volunteer. These programs differ greatly, however. Walker (2001) provides VPMs with tips on how to approach corporations.

The Marketing Appeal

There are two general methods for inviting someone to volunteer for your organization: personal and nonpersonal marketing appeals. **Personal recruitment** involves direct interaction between two people, or a dialogue between a recruiter and a prospect. **Nonpersonal recruitment** is a one-to-many type of communication. It is not a dialogue, meaning that individuals receiving the recruitment appeal are not interacting with the recruiter.

Personal recruitment appeals are generally the more effective of the two. Social pressures are such that many people find it more difficult to say no to a person requesting help for a good cause than to a general call for help. Personal recruitment is most effective when done face to face rather than via telephone or e-mail. Personal recruitment is most effective between two people who are familiar with each other.

Obviously, when asking people to volunteer for your organization, you should attempt to learn what concerns or questions they have. People outside your organization may have little knowledge on which to base expectations about serving it.

Personal recruitment appeals allow for questions and reduced uncertainties. Prospects can be helped to anticipate the volunteer experience and to better understand the potential rewards and disappointments. Prospects can also be asked to help the recruiter understand where the individual is likely to make the greatest contribution to the nonprofit. While nonpersonal recruitment appeals are generally not as effective as personal appeals, they should also be used. Sending recruitment appeals to individuals outside the social networks of your current volunteers and staff will increase the number of people you are able to ask, and it will lead to higher levels of diversity in your organization. Nonpersonal recruitment appeals can be made by public speaking engagements, listing volunteer opportunities in the newspaper, advertising in the media, listing volunteer openings on your organization's website, posting flyers in public locations, and so forth.

Application Case 10.2

Volunteer Hampton Roads

Volunteer Hampton Roads (VHR), a nonprofit resource center for southeastern Virginia, works with more than 500 nonprofits to identify and address critical community needs. It has been serving this community since 1957. Its mission is to work with area nonprofit organizations to garner public support for their causes. VHR's website provides the public with information on both episodic and ongoing volunteer opportunities at area nonprofits. VHR also provides information on family volunteer opportunities, youth volunteer opportunities, and court-referred volunteers (people found guilty of an offense and sentenced to community service).

Volunteer Hampton Roads is typical of many areas with sizable populations. It is a referral, or umbrella, organization that serves other nonprofit organizations. Just as the United Way is an umbrella organization that raises funds and distributes them to area nonprofits, area volunteer referral organizations increase awareness of volunteerism and help direct volunteers to area nonprofits.

Virtual Volunteering

Virtual volunteering refers to volunteer tasks that are completed, in whole or in part, via the Internet and a home or work computer. It is also known as online volunteering, cyber service, online mentoring, or teletutoring, among other names. Virtual volunteering allows agencies to expand the benefits of their volunteer programs by allowing more volunteers to participate and by utilizing volunteers who possess unique skills or who live in distant locations.

Online volunteering is aimed at building the capacity of the nonprofit organization by providing volunteer opportunities for people who would not otherwise be able to participate. People with time constraints may find virtual volunteering more convenient since they can serve from their homes. Since volunteers do not have to travel in order to volunteer online, a much wider selection of nonprofit organizations is available for them to choose from. People with disabilities may have physical limitations that reduce their volunteer opportunities. Virtual volunteering may provide a suitable accommodation that allows them to participate more fully.

There are two types of virtual volunteering. One type is **technical assistance**, in which virtual volunteers share their expertise on projects and provide support to staff and other volunteers at the nonprofit. Examples include conducting online research, consulting, translating documents from one language into another, designing and maintaining websites, and managing online databases. Another type of virtual volunteering is providing **direct contact** between a virtual volunteer and a client, such as by electronically visiting someone confined to home, hospital, or nursing home; tutoring; moderating an online chat room; and publishing and distributing electronic newsletters.

Virtual volunteering is in the early stages of development. Over time, increasing numbers of VPMs will learn about virtual volunteering successes in volunteer organizations and will incorporate virtual volunteering in their own organizations. The best resource for the VPM to learn more about virtual volunteering is the Virtual Volunteering Project (visit its website, www.volunteermatch.org/orgs/org6606.html).

Managerial Issues

The following issues are relevant for nonprofit managers.

1. **Professionalism in managing volunteers.** Competition for the discretionary time of individuals is increasing. Work and family demands take priority. People feel as though they have little free time, making leisure and recreational activities very valuable. A large number of worthy causes compete for volunteers. All these factors require that nonprofit organizations place great importance on the recruitment and management of volunteers.

2. **Perception of number of available volunteers.** Locating potential volunteers is limited only by your imagination. Managers can look for new volunteers within the social networks of existing volunteers and in the vicinity of the nonprofit's local operations. Many corporations seek to improve employee morale and the corporation's reputation by participating in corporate volunteering. Virtual volunteers are only a click away in cyberspace.

3. **Retention versus recruitment.** Because it is much more difficult to recruit a new volunteer than to keep a current one, nonprofit managers need to place a high priority on volunteer retention. Volunteer retention begins with proper selection, placement, orientation, and training. Social assimilation of volunteers into the community of individuals in the nonprofit organization is important. Finally, excellent volunteer supervision is vital. The board of directors and the leaders of the nonprofit organization need to place a priority on effective volunteer management. Volunteer recruitment, retention, turnover, satisfaction, and performance can be measured and included in assessment activities.

Summary

The nonprofit marketing issues presented in this chapter are summarized here according to the chapter learning objectives they meet.

Understand the importance of volunteers to nonprofit organizations. About one in four Americans volunteer some time in the American nonprofit sector. This represents an important resource for nonprofit organizations in particular and for society in general. Powerful social forces are contributing to the reduced availability of volunteers. Individuals are under pressure to spend more time at work. The federal government is continuing to reduce financial support for nonprofit organizations and simultaneously emphasizing the nonprofit sector as a more appropriate provider of social services than government. Furthermore, a large and growing number of nonprofit organizations are competing for volunteers. Nonprofit organizations need episodic volunteers to serve on periodic projects or events, and they need regular, ongoing volunteers to help with the continuing operations of the organization. Volunteers can serve in various roles. They can volunteer as a board member, helping to lead the organization. They can serve as fund-raisers, helping to bring in additional resources to support the nonprofit. General support volunteers are needed to handle telephone calls and perform clerical work and other behind-the-scenes activities. Finally, direct service volunteers work directly with the organization's clients.

Understand the various reasons people volunteer. People volunteer for a variety of reasons. Their choices are guided by their values, beliefs, and attitudes. A person's stage in life can also play a role in a decision about volunteering. Experiences that bring people into contact with a nonprofit organization and its volunteers can also impact a decision to volunteer. People who have friends or other social contacts who volunteer are much more likely to volunteer than people whose social circle does not include active volunteers. Being raised in a family with parents who volunteer influences children, who may themselves become volunteers as adults.

Describe ways to recruit volunteers effectively. The more effective organizations have cultures that support the value of volunteers. Volunteers are viewed as a crucial and important resource. The effective VPM spends considerable time developing a compelling case, a message for prospective volunteers that shows why their service is important and helps the organization fulfill its mission. The organization must determine its need for volunteers and develop volunteer job descriptions. Interpersonal recruitment appeals tend to produce better results than nonpersonal, mass appeals made through media. Retaining volunteers is also very important. The foundation for retaining volunteers rests on excellent organizational leadership and superior volunteer supervision. Without these two essential elements, other efforts will prove futile. Effective retention begins with effective volunteer selection, screening, placement, orientation, training, and social assimilation. Volunteer jobs must be carefully designed. Volunteers must be given regular feedback that demonstrates appreciation and notes the way their work makes a difference for the organization. Volunteer performance needs to be monitored and periodically assessed.

Describe virtual volunteering and its growing importance. One recent trend is the increasing use of online volunteers. Nonprofit organizations are finding creative ways to use virtual volunteers. Online volunteers play a support role in some nonprofits. In others, they communicate directly with clients via e-mail or chat rooms.

Glossary

Attitudes. Our thoughts and feelings about something. An attitude is an assessment of what we think and how we feel about a person, place, thing, idea, and so forth.

Board member. One of the four volunteer roles. Board members and managerial volunteers are those volunteers who serve on the nonprofit's board of directors or who otherwise provide unpaid leadership or administrative services. These volunteers are responsible for overseeing the various functions of the organization to fulfill its mission.

Core values. Those principles that are the fundamental tenets that guide the way we work and live. These are the most important, or most closely held, values in our value systems.

Corporate volunteering. Companies' allowing employees time off from regular work to volunteer for a cause or nonprofit organization. Some companies give employees paid time off; others do not. Some companies target a special cause; others allow employees to choose their own volunteer activities.

Direct contact. A type of virtual volunteering in which the volunteer is providing direct services to the nonprofit's clients.

Direct service volunteer. One of the four volunteer roles. These volunteers provide services directly to clients.

Episodic volunteering. Volunteering on an as-needed basis or serving on special events or on individual projects.

Facilitation. Assisting the potential volunteer in becoming a new volunteer, and assisting the new volunteer in assimilating into the organization by providing information and social or emotional support.

Fund-raising volunteer. One of the four volunteer roles. Fund-raising volunteers' primary tasks involve raising money by soliciting contributions. These volunteers may also be responsible for writing proposals for grants.

General support volunteer. One of the four volunteer roles. General support volunteers do work that is very necessary but often invisible. They staff telephones, do filing, work on mailings, help write newsletters, work on maintenance projects, clean, drive, run errands, and so forth.

Interpersonal influences on volunteering. These are social forces that affect our attitudes and choices about volunteering. Two interpersonal influences on volunteering are facilitation and social norms.

Life stage. Distinct periods in a person's life that are marked by different priorities, experience, and responsibilities. The basic determinants of life stage in a traditional view are marital status, the presence or absence of children, and the age of the youngest child

Managerial volunteer. See *board member.*

Nonpersonal recruitment. Recruiting volunteers using a one-to-many form of communication. It is not a dialogue, meaning that individuals receiving the recruitment appeal are not interacting face to face with a recruiter.

Ongoing volunteering. Volunteering on a continual, regular basis, in contrast to episodic volunteers, who work periodically when needed.

Personal influences. Those individual, nonsocial factors that affect a person's volunteering choices; they include personality, values and beliefs, life stage, and personal experiences.

Personal recruitment. Face-to-face solicitations to volunteer for a nonprofit organization or a cause or event.

Service learning. An educational program that provides students with community volunteer experiences. Service learning assumes that youth volunteer experiences will lead to greater adult civic participation.

Situational factors. External, nonpersonal variables that affect an individual's volunteer choices. Some situational factors are an individual's available time for volunteering, the distance that must be traveled to volunteer, and the perceived safety of the volunteer activity.

Social norms. Customary patterns of attitudes and behaviors that social groups accept, maintain, and enforce.

Technical assistance. A type of virtual volunteering in which volunteers share their expertise on projects and provide support to staff and other volunteers.

Value system. An individual's enduring organization of beliefs concerning preferable styles of conduct or end-states of existence. Values are organized in a value system by relative importance.

Virtual volunteering. Volunteer tasks completed, in whole or in part, via the Internet and a home or work computer; also known as online volunteering, cyber service, online mentoring, and teletutoring.

Volunteer. An individual who freely provides labor to a nonprofit organization without an expectation of monetary compensation.

Volunteer job descriptions. Formal, written statements that describe the volunteer position and its duties and responsibilities.

Volunteer program managers (VPMs). Individuals with the authority and responsibility for organizing and directing the activities of an organization's volunteers.

❖

QUESTIONS FOR REVIEW

1. Define *volunteer.*
2. Define *volunteer program manager.*
3. Define *episodic volunteering.*
4. Define *ongoing volunteering.*
5. List the four volunteer roles.
6. Define *facilitation.*
7. Define *virtual volunteering.*
8. Define *corporate volunteering.*

❖

QUESTIONS FOR DISCUSSION

1. What factors are contributing to increased competition for volunteers?

2. Describe the four volunteer roles.

3. Describe the personal influences on volunteering.

4. Describe the interpersonal influences on volunteering.

5. What elements should be included in a volunteer job description?

6. How can individuals' life stages influence their volunteer choices?

7. What is the difference between personal and nonpersonal recruitment appeals? Which is more effective and why?

8. When looking for new volunteers, which group of people includes the most promising prospects?

9. In respect to volunteers, what are some of the qualities of excellent nonprofit leaders?

10. What are some of the qualities of excellent volunteer supervisors?

❖

INTERNET EXERCISES

1. Visit the website www.netaid.org. What is NetAid? Describe its purpose. What are some online volunteering opportunities that appeal to you?

2. Visit the iMentor website at www.imentor.org/. What is the mission of this organization, and who are its clients? Do you think this program will be successful (why or why not)? This program matches adults with children; describe the screening process for potential volunteers.

3. Visit the website www.serviceleader.org/new/virtual/index.php. Select articles on a virtual volunteering topic that interests you and write a one-page summary of what you learn from them.

4. Visit the website www.volunteering.org.uk/missions.php?id=635. Summarize the information on volunteer recruitment, screening, and selection, as well as training, supervising, and disciplining volunteers. Also describe volunteer liability and types of coverage available.

5. Effective managers must have good people skills. Managing staff-volunteer relations is an area in which superior people skills are essential. Visit the website www.vskn.ca/hrm/vrelate.htm and study the section on interpersonal skills. How can nonprofit managers encourage positive relations between staff and volunteers?

6. Visit Sidelines National Support Network at www.sidelines.org. Describe the purpose of the organization. Is this cause suitable for virtual volunteering? What type of virtual volunteer would be appropriate?

❖

TEAM EXERCISES AND ROLE PLAYING

1. A checklist for effective volunteer management is available online at www.mapnp .org/library/org_eval/uw_hr.htm (scroll down to the section that deals with volunteers). In teams, use the checklist to evaluate a local nonprofit organization's management of its volunteers.

2. An online manual was prepared by the Best Practices Subcommittee of the Maryland Advisory Committee on Volunteerism, which is a standing committee of the Governor's Commission on Service and Volunteerism. It is available at www.gosv.state.md.us/ volunteerism/publications.asp. There are 10 sections. Each team should study one or two sections and summarize them for the class.

3. Want to combine your desire to volunteer for a worthy cause with your desire to travel? Go to the website www.idealist.org and click on Volunteer opportunities. Find an international volunteer assignment that appeals to you and present your findings and thoughts to the class.

4. E-activism is becoming very popular among nonprofit advocacy organizations. Form teams of students with similar social concerns (or do this as an individual exercise) and find e-activism opportunities that correspond to your values and interests. Present your findings to the class.

5. Visit the website www.healthassistancepartnership.org/ship-pilot-project/pilot-project-retaining-volunteers.html. Compare and contrast these tips with the concepts presented in this chapter. What surprised you most? What insights did you gain from this site?

MINICASE: Pearisburg Volunteer Fire Department

Eugene (Gene) Kelly is the fire chief of the Pearisburg Volunteer Fire Department. Pearisburg is a small town in Giles County, Virginia, in the heart of the Appalachian Mountains of southwest Virginia. About 925 families make their home in Pearisburg. The population is approximately 2,064. Chief Kelly operates the volunteer fire department with four fire trucks and some 30 trained volunteer fire personnel.

While urban areas have the tax base to support professional, full-time firefighters, smaller communities throughout America do not. There are about 800,000 volunteer firefighters in America. Volunteer firefighters make up almost 80% of America's fire service. There are nearly 28,000 rural fire departments that, like Pearisburg's, serve communities with populations

under 10,000. It would cost taxpayers more than $40 billion to staff these volunteer fire departments with paid firefighters.

Unfortunately, there has been a decline in volunteer firefighting. Young adults are simply not volunteering for their local volunteer fire departments the way their town's older citizens once did. This has become a national problem. For example, small-town fire departments in Connecticut have been experiencing a decline in volunteerism for years. The situation is now at the point that the Connecticut State Firefighters Association has formed a task force on recruitment and retention.

Rural volunteer fire departments report many causes for this volunteer shortage. For one, the federal government has been reducing its funding for rural fire departments. The federal government has been providing some funding through its Volunteer Fire Assistance Program, which is administered by the U.S. Forest Service, but the federal government has been reducing the funding for this program, and only about one in four grant requests from rural volunteer fire departments is receiving funds.

There are many other reasons volunteer firefighting is declining. Potential recruits face growing demands from their employers. Since the number of families with both spouses working full-time to pay the bills is at an all-time high, many potential volunteers have greater family obligations. Younger adults are not assimilating well into the patterns of the traditional, older, male-dominated social communities that most rural fire departments serve.

Compounding these problems is the fact that rural fire departments are being asked to do more with less. In addition to being responsible for putting out house fires, volunteer firefighters are responsible for responding to forest fires and emergency medical response needs. The federal Department of Homeland Security expects these volunteers to help if terrorism emergencies arise. All these expectations necessitate increased training (a disincentive for volunteering) and increased funding (unlikely in a period of political conservatism with an emphasis on smaller government, greater reliance on the private sector, and tax cuts).

Chief Kelly finds himself in a situation similar to that of many rural fire chiefs. Although he claims to have 30 volunteer firefighters, only about 10 or 12 volunteer firefighters respond regularly to emergency calls. Volunteer training consists of providing the bare essentials. The emphasis is on volunteer safety. More training is greatly needed, especially given the growing state and federal requirements regarding terrorism. However, volunteers dislike the time required for training, and frankly, there is no money available to fund training.

During the past 30 years, Chief Kelly has witnessed his team of volunteers getting older. The core group of volunteers has formed a tight social community, but this cohesive team of older, white men, is not attractive to younger men, women, or ethnic groups with little in common with the core group. Consequently, volunteers who quit are not being replaced, and a shortage exists. Chief Kelly has communicated with many other volunteer fire chiefs to find solutions to his problems. He has discovered that his volunteer problems are common and that no simple solution seems to exist. He is considering the following alternative solutions:

1. Consolidate the multiple town volunteer fire departments into one county-wide fire department with five or six paid firefighters.

2. Offer housing and tuition to some local community college students in exchange for working shifts as firefighters.

3. Supplement the volunteers with a core group of paid volunteers. Taxes will have to be raised.

4. Offer volunteers retention incentives such as subsidized mortgage rates, lower insurance rates, or lower local taxes.

Questions for the Case

1. Consider the advantages and disadvantages of each alternative Chief Kelly is considering. Discuss each one's potential for success in terms of recruiting and retaining volunteers, as well as the public's reaction to reduced services or possible tax increases.

2. Which alternative(s) should Chief Kelly implement and why?

3. Identify and discuss other possible alternatives.

4. Chief Kelly is experiencing a situation common to leaders in many small nonprofit organizations. His focus is on the organization's mission and on providing services. He does not have a marketing orientation and has little training in marketing and little time to dedicate to marketing activities. If a government grant could fund you as a marketing professional for the fire department for 2 years, what would you do to improve the situation Chief Kelly faces?

References and Bibliography

Adams, C. H., & Shepherd, G. L. (1996). Managing volunteer performance: Face support and situational features as predictors of volunteers' evaluations of regulative messages. *Management Communication Quarterly, 9*(4), 363+.

Adams, D. (1987). Ronald Reagan's "revival": Volunteerism as a theme in Reagan's civil religion. *Sociological Analysis, 48,* 17–29.

Berger, G. (1991). Factors explaining volunteering for organizations in general and for social welfare organizations in particular. Doctoral dissertation, Heller School of Social Welfare, Brandeis University, Waltham, MA.

Betancourt, H., Hardin, C., & Manzi, J. (1992). Beliefs, value orientation, and culture in attribution processes and helping behavior. *Journal of Cross-Cultural Psychology, 23*(2), 179–196.

Blascovich, J., & Tomaka, J. (1991). Measures of self-esteem. In J. P. Robinson, P. R. Shaver, and L. S. Wrightsman (Eds.), *Measures of personality and social psychological attitudes: Vol. 1* (pp. 115–160). New York: Academic Press.

Bonk, K., Griggs, H., & Tynes, E. (1999). *The Jossey-Bass guide to strategic communications for nonprofits: A step-by-step guide to working with the media to generate publicity, enhance fun.* San Francisco: Jossey-Bass.

Bureau of Labor Statistics. (2003). *Volunteering in the United States.* Retrieved November 10, 2005, from www.bls.gov/news.release/volun.toc.htm

Bush, G. W. (2002). President Bush Implements Key Elements of his Faith-Based Initiative. Speech made at Downtown Marriott Hotel in Philadelphia, Pennsylvania, on December 12, 2002. Retrieved March 4, 2003, from www.whitehouse.gov/news/releases/2002/12/20021212-3.html

Bussell, H., & Forbes, D. (2002). Understanding the volunteer market: The what, where, who and why of volunteering. *International Journal of Nonprofit & Voluntary Sector Marketing, 7*(3), 244–257.

Carnegie Corporation of New York. (2003). *Strengthening the nonprofit and philanthropic sector—Subprogram guidelines.* Retrieved November 10, 2005, from www.carnegie.org/sub/program/spguide.html

Clary, E. G., & Snyder, M. (1991). A functional analysis of altruism and prosocial behavior: The case of volunteerism. In M. S. Clark (Ed.), *Review of Personality and Social Psychology: Vol. 12* (pp. 119–148). Newbury Park, CA: Sage.

Clary, E. G., Snyder, M., Copeland, J. T., & French, S. A. (1994). Promoting volunteerism: An empirical examination of the appeal of persuasive messages. *Nonprofit and Voluntary Sector Quarterly, 18*(2), 167–177.

Cnaan, R. A., & Goldberg-Glen, R. S. (1991). Measuring motivation to volunteer in human services. *Journal of Applied Behavioral Sciences, 27*(3), 269–284.

CNN.com. (2003, January 13). Girl Scout hopefuls short on leaders. Retrieved November 10, 2005, from www.cnn.com/2003/EDUCATION/01/13/girl.scouts.waiting.ap/

Dodson, D. (1993). *How to recruit great board members.* Santa Fe, NM: Adolfo Street Publications.

Dovidio, J. F., Piliavin, J. A., Gaertner, S. L., Schroeder, D. A., & Clark, R. D., III. (1991). The arousal: Cost-reward model and the process of intervention. In M. S. Clark (Ed.), *Review of Personality and Social Psychology: Vol. 12* (pp. 86–118). Newbury Park, CA: Sage.

Ellis, S. J. (1993). Building a circle of resources. *The Nonprofit Times, 7*(Sept.), 14.

Ellis, S. J. (1994). *The volunteer recruitment book.* Philadelphia: Energize.

Ellis, S. J., Weisbord, A., & Noyes, K. H. (1991). *Children as volunteers: Preparing for community service.* Philadelphia: Energize.

Etherington, F. (2001). Volunteers struggle to cope: Study. *The Record,* B 1.

Feeney, B. (2001). *Volunteering in Wellington: Issues and trends.* Retrieved November 10, 2005, from www.volunteerwellington.org.nz/iyvwccrep.htm

Fischer, L. R., & Schaffer, K. B. (1993). *Older volunteers: A guide to research and practice.* Newbury Park, CA: Sage.

Fisher, J. C., & Cole, K. M. (1993). *Leadership and management of volunteer programs: A guide for volunteer administrators.* San Francisco: Jossey-Bass.

Girl Scouts of America. (2005). *Who we are.* Retrieved November 10, 2005, from www.girlscouts.org/who_we_are/

Gora, J. A., & Nemerowicz, G. (1991). Volunteers: Initial and sustaining motivations in service to the community. *Research in the Sociology of Health Care, 9,* 233–246.

Green, S. (2002). Making a difference. *British Journal of Administrative Management,* May/June, 29–38.

Heartbeat Trends. (2001). *Research report: 2001 premier's forum on ageing. Older people and volunteering.* Retrieved March 7, 2003, from www.communitybuilders.nsw.gov.au/download/DADHC.pdf

Heidrich, K. W. (1988). *Lifestyles of volunteers: A marketing segmentation study.* Doctoral dissertation, University of Illinois at Urbana-Champaign.

Himmelstein, J. L. (1997). *Looking good and doing good: Corporate philanthropy and corporate power.* Indianapolis: Indiana University Press.

Hobson, C. J., Rominger, A., Malec, K., Hobson, C. L., & Evans, K. (1996). Volunteer-friendliness of nonprofit agencies: Definition, conceptual model, and application. *Journal of Nonprofit & Public Sector Marketing, 4*(4), 27–42.

Hodgkinson, V. A. (1990). *Motivations for giving and volunteering,* New York: Foundation Center.

Horvath, T. (1995). *Spread the word : How to promote nonprofit groups with a network of speakers.* Indianapolis, IN: Publishing Resources.

Independent Sector. (1992). *Volunteering and giving in the United States: Findings from a national survey.* Washington, DC: Author.

Independent Sector. (1994). *Volunteering and giving in the United States: Findings from a national survey.* Washington, DC: Author.

Independent Sector. (2000a). *Nonprofit size and scope.* Retrieved November 12, 2005, from www.independent-sector.org/PDFs/NA01factsheet.pdf

Independent Sector. (2000b). *Volunteering: Volunteering levels and number of hours recorded.* Retrieved November 12, 2005, from www.independentsector.org/media/grandvsummary_1999.html

Independent Sector. (2000c). The relationship between giving and volunteering. Retrieved November 12, 2005, from www.independentsector.org/GandV/s_rela.htm

Independent Sector. (2001). *The new nonprofit almanac: In brief.* Retrieved November 12, 2005, from www.independentsector.org/PDFs/inbrief.pdf

Independent Sector. (2003). *Giving and volunteering in the United States 2001.* Washington, DC: Author.

Institute for Volunteering Research. (1997). "1997 National Survey of Volunteering in the UK," accessed on November 12, 2005, online at http://www.ivr.org.uk/nationalsurvey.htm

Jackson, E. F., Bachmeier, M. D., Wood, J. R., & Craft, E. A. (1995). Volunteering and charitable giving: Do religious and associational ties promote helping behavior? *Nonprofit and Voluntary Sector Quarterly, 24*(1), 59–78.

Lammers, J. C. (1991). Attitudes, motives, and demographic predictors of volunteer commitment and service duration. *Journal of Social Service Research, 14,* 125–140.

Lee, M. (2004). The coming nonprofit crash. *PA Times 27*(9) 5, 9.

Little, H. (1999). *Volunteers: How to get them, how to keep them.* Naperville, IL: Panacea Press.

Logue, A. C. (2001). Training volunteers: The Junior League wants you!. *Training & Development, 55*(6), 62–69.

Macduff, N. (1991). *Episodic volunteering: Building the short-term volunteer program.* Walla Walla, WA: MBA Publishing.

Maldonado, M. (2003, January 15). Cookie couriers: Girl Scouts are set to begin sales Thursday, but troops say they need volunteers. *South Florida Sun-Sentinel,* 3 B.

Marks, R. B. (1996). *Personal selling: A relationship approach* (6th ed.). Pearson Education.

Marriott Senior Living Services. (1991). *Marriott's seniors volunteerism study.* Washington, DC: Author.

Marshall, K. P. (1999). Volunteerism among non-clients as marketing exchange. *Journal of Nonprofit & Public Sector Marketing, 6*(2/3), 95–106.

McKee, E. M. (1991). *The relationship between self-esteem, mood states, and helping behavior in children.* Doctoral dissertation, United States International University, Nairobi, Kenya.

Miller, L. E., Powell, G. N., & Seltzer, J. (1990). Determinants of turnover among volunteers. *Human Relations, 43*(9), 901–917.

Mitchell, M. A., & Taylor, S. L. (1997). Adapting internal marketing to a volunteer system. *Journal of Nonprofit & Public Sector Marketing, 5*(5), 29–42.

Murk, P. J., & Stephan, J. F. (1991). Volunteers: How to get them, train them, and keep them. *Economic Development Review, 9*(1), 73–75.

Okun, M. A. (1994). The relation between motives for organizational volunteering and the frequency of volunteering by elders. *Journal of Applied Gerontology, 13*(2), 115–126.

Omoto, A. M., & Snyder, M. (1990). Basic research in action: Volunteerism and society's response to AIDS. *Personality and Social Psychology Bulletin, 16*(1), 152–165.

Pearce, J. L. (1993). *Volunteers: The organizational behavior of unpaid workers.* New York: Routledge.

Petrick, A. E. (2000). Energizing and recognizing volunteers. *Association Management, 52*(1), 127–135.

Reich, R. B. (2002). *The future of success: Working and living in the new economy.* New York: Knopf.

Ross, D. (1992). Managing volunteers—When the carrot is not a paycheque. *CMA, 66*(9), 30+.

Rusin, J. B. (1999). *Volunteers wanted.* Mobile, AL: Magnolia Mansions Press.

Salamon, L. M., Anheier, H. K., List, R., Toepler, S., Sokolowski, S. W., et al. (1999). *Global civil society: Dimensions of the nonprofit sector.* Baltimore: Johns Hopkins Center for Civil Society Studies.

Salzman, J., & Salzman, J. (1998). *Making the news: A guide for nonprofits and activists.* Boulder, CO: Westview.

Scheier, I. H. (1993). *Building staff-volunteer relations.* Philadelphia: Energize.

"Seat-of-the-pants" volunteer management deplored. (1998). *Nonprofit World, 16*(1), 55.

Sharma, A., & Bell, M. (2002). Beating the drum of international volunteering? Exploring motivations to volunteer amongst Black and Asian communities. MRS Research 2002: Insight to Action, Paper 5.

Sinisi, C. A. (1993). *The origin of volunteering: Socialization antecedents and personal variables.* Doctoral dissertation, Kansas State University.

Smith, J. (1995). *The new publicity kit.* New York: Wiley.

Statistics Canada. (2000). "Volunteering in Canada," from National Survey of Giving and Volunteering and Participating. Accessed November 12, 2005, online at http://www.givingandvolunteering.ca/pdf/factsheets/2000_CA_volunteering_in_canada.pdf

Sundeen, R. A., & Raskoff, S. A. (1994). Volunteering among teenagers in the United States. *Nonprofit and Voluntary Sector Quarterly, 23*(4), 383–403.

Sutton, C. D. (1992). *Pass it on: Outreach to minority communities.* Philadelphia: Big Brothers/Big Sisters of America.

Taylor, L. (1995). Disability as a part of diversity. *Journal of Volunteer Administration, 13*(2).

Thelen, L. (2001). Volunteer magic: Finding and keeping library volunteers. *School Library Media Activities Monthly, 18*(3), 22–30.

Thurmond, D. P., & Cassell, J. (1996). *Family volunteering: Putting the pieces together.* Washington, DC: Points of Light Foundation.

Tremper, C., & Kostin, G. (1993). *No surprises: Controlling risks in volunteer programs.* Washington, DC: Nonprofit Risk Management Center.

Unger, S. L. (1991). Altruism as a motivation to volunteer. *Journal of Economic Psychology, 12,* 71–100.

Vineyard, S., & McCurley, S. (1992). *Managing volunteer diversity: A rainbow of opportunities.* Downers Grove, IL: Heritage Arts Publishing.

Virtual Volunteering Project. (2000). *Marketing volunteer opportunities online.* Retrieved November 18, 2005, from www.serviceleader.org/new/managers/2003/04/000065.php

Volunteer Development Scotland. (2004). *Volunteering facts and figures.* Retrieved November 12, 2005, from www.vds.org.uk/information/factsNFigures.htm

Walker, F. (2001). Volunteerism under the magnifying glass. *Fund Raising Management, 32*(4), 46–53.

Watson, J. J. (1999). A cross-cultural comparison of the explanatory power of materialism and life cycle stage for important possessions. Proceedings of the Seventh Cross-Cultural Consumer and Business Studies Research Conference, Cancun, Mexico, December 12–15. Retrieved November 12, 2005, from marketing.byu.edu/htmlpages/ccrs/proceedings99/watson.htm

Wesley Mission Sidney. (2001). *Faces of volunteering: Facts about volunteering.* Retrieved November 12, 2005, from www.wesleymission.org.au/publications/volunteers/facts.asp

Wineburg, R. J. (1994). A longitudinal case study of religious congregations in local human services. *Nonprofit and Voluntary Sector Quarterly, 23*(2), 159–169.

Wood, J. R., & Hougland, J. G., Jr. (1990). The role of religion in philanthropy. In J. Van Til et al. (Eds.), *Critical issues in American philanthropy* (pp. 29–33). San Francisco: Jossey Bass.

Wymer, W. W., Jr. (1996). *Formal volunteering as a function of values, self-esteem, empathy, and facilitation.* DBA dissertation, Indiana University.

Wymer, W. W., Jr. (1997a). Church volunteers: Classification, recruitment, and retention. *Journal of Ministry & Marketing Management, 3*(2), 61–70.

Wymer, W. W., Jr. (1997b). Segmenting volunteers using values, self-esteem, empathy, and facilitation as determinant variables. *Journal of Nonprofit & Public Sector Marketing, 5*(2), 3–28.

Wymer, W. W., Jr. (1997c). A religious motivation to volunteer? Exploring the linkage between volunteering and religious values. *Journal of Nonprofit & Public Sector Marketing, 5*(3), 3–17.

Wymer, W. W., Jr. (1998). Strategic marketing of church volunteers. *Journal of Ministry & Marketing Management, 4*(1), 1–11.

Wymer, W. W., Jr. (1999a). Youth development volunteers: Their motives, how they differ from other volunteers, and correlates of involvement intensity. *International Journal of Nonprofit and Voluntary Sector Marketing, 3*(4), 321–336.

Wymer, W. W., Jr. (1999b). Hospital volunteers as customers: Understanding their motives, how they differ from other volunteers, and correlates of volunteer intensity. *Journal of Nonprofit & Public Sector Marketing, 6*(2/3), 51–76.

Wymer, W. W., Jr. (1999c). Understanding volunteer markets: The case of senior volunteers. *Journal of Nonprofit & Public Sector Marketing, 6*(2/3), 1–24.

Wymer, W. W., Jr. (2003). Differentiating literacy volunteers: A segmentation analysis for target marketing. *International Journal of Nonprofit & Voluntary Sector Marketing, 8*(1), 267–285.

Wymer, W. W., Jr., & Brudney, J. (2000). Marketing management in arts and cultural organizations: A customer analysis of arts and culture volunteers. *International Journal of Arts Management, 2*(3), 40–51.

Wymer, W. W., Jr., Riecken, G., & Yavas, U. (1996). Determinants of volunteerism: A cross-disciplinary review and research agenda. *Journal of Nonprofit & Public Sector Marketing, 4*(4), 3–26.

Wymer, W. W., Jr., & Self, D. R. (1999). Major research studies: An annotated bibliography of marketing to volunteers. *Journal of Nonprofit & Public Sector Marketing, 6*(2/3), 107–164.

Wymer, W. W., Jr., & Starns, B. J. (1999). Segmenting sub-groups of volunteers for target marketing: Differentiating traditional hospice volunteers from other volunteers. *Journal of Nonprofit & Public Sector Marketing, 6*(2/3), 25–50.

Wymer, W. W., Jr., & Starns, B. J. (2001). Conceptual foundations and practical guidelines for recruiting volunteers to serve in local nonprofit organizations. *Journal of Nonprofit & Public Sector Marketing 9*(1/2), 63–96.

Part III

Special Topics

11

Social Marketing ❖

<table>
<tr><td>

Content

</td><td>

Learning Objectives

On completion of this chapter, the
reader will

- Define social marketing and issue
  marketing
- Describe the relationship between social
  marketing and changing individual
  behavior
- Describe the AOM model of changing
  individual behavior
- Describe the social marketing plan
- Describe effective tactics that can be
  utilized in an issue marketing campaign
- Describe the inherent conflict between
  corporate self-interest and social
  marketing

</td></tr>
</table>

Opening Vignette: The Mass Media and Health Practices Program

The Mass Media and Health Practices Program was the first major test of social marketing applied
to reducing infant mortality in developing countries. The objective was to reduce infant mortality by providing mothers with the means and the training to rehydrate their infants afflicted with
diarrheal dehydration, which accounted for 24% of all infant deaths in the test country, Honduras.
Before this program, the treatment for diarrheal dehydration was intravenous therapy, which

requires trained medical personnel and a sterile environment, accessible to only a fraction of the population.

The social marketing program focused on applying a treatment mothers could administer by themselves at home: oral rehydration therapy. Using print materials and radio advertisements (30- to 60-second ads), workers instructed the target audience, mothers with children under the age of 5 years, in the benefits of oral rehydration therapy and how to administer it to their children. Mothers were instructed in how to mix a branded salt solution with water and encouraged to continue breast-feeding their infants during diarrheal illnesses.

Surveys indicated that the program was communicating its message effectively. Within little more than a year of the project's start, 93% of the mothers sampled from rural Honduras knew that the program's radio campaign was promoting Litrosol, the brand name of the locally packaged oral rehydration salts used to treat diarrhea, and 71% could recite the radio jingle used to promote the administration of liquids during diarrhea affliction.

The social marketing program was also successful in changing behavior. Mortality rates for children under 5 years of age decreased from 47.5% to 25%. The program was later extended to 12 countries in Latin America and Africa. (The interested reader is referred to www.social-marketing.org/success/cs-massmedia.html.)

Social marketing refers to using marketing tactics in the creation, execution, and control of programs designed to influence social change. The opening vignette illustrates using radio ads, print communication, and branding to change the manner in which mothers in rural Honduras treated their sick children.

Influencing social change usually involves changing public attitudes, behaviors, or both. Social marketers face challenges in influencing human attitudes and behaviors, which are often culturally reinforced (attitudes) and habituated (behaviors). How can a program be designed that will encourage people to quit smoking, to eat healthy foods, to exercise more often, to practice safe sex, or to reduce their reliance on fossil fuels?

Issue marketing refers to a type of social marketing that focuses on increasing public awareness of an important issue and ultimately changing public policy. Although *issue marketing* is a relatively new term, groups within various societies have been pressing for reform, or changing social policy, for a very long time.

In this chapter, we will discuss the challenges social marketers face when attempting to change human behavior. We will also describe the social marketing process, an organized, sequential approach to implementing social change. This will be followed with a discussion of issue marketing, which will include a model for reforming social policy.

Changing Public Behavior

It is important to recognize that ultimately, social marketing and issue marketing are concerned with changing human behavior. It is helpful to distinguish the various areas that social marketers focus on to achieve their goals. Table 11.1 illustrates how social marketers often have to achieve their long-term goals by advocating incremental

❖ **Table 11.1**   Social Marketing Foci

	Individuals	Policy Makers
Short-term change	Focus is educating individuals about consequences of an unhealthy behavior and encouraging reduction of the unhealthy behavior.	Focus is changing ancillary causes of the unhealthy behavior in ways that are politically acceptable.
Long-term change	Focus is cessation of the unhealthy behavior.	Focus is elimination of root causes of the unhealthy behavior.

changes that are more acceptable to their culture at a given time. For example, social marketers may desire to end the production of tobacco products (ultimate goal). However, since this goal may conflict with various cultural values (such as unregulated corporate activities and rights, freedom of consumer choice, and so forth), short-term objectives may be more practical (e.g., a ban on advertising tobacco to children).

Table 11.1 also illustrates the multiple targets to whom social marketers may direct their communications. Generally, social marketers direct their appeals to both individuals engaging in unhealthy behaviors and policy makers having the authority to make changes. Table 11.2 provides an example of these concepts using the growing obesity rate in countries with fast-food companies heavily marketing their products to consumers.

Changing public behavior is a challenge and often a frustration. People tend to resist change, even when it is in their own best interest. Human behavior is complex. Often behavior is influenced by an elaborate array of factors, such as personality, social forces, habit, and so forth. The model we will use in this chapter is the **Ability, Opportunity, and Motivation Model** (AOM). The premises of the model are the following:

1. $X = \alpha + b_1 A + b_2 O + b_3 M$, where A is ability, O is opportunity, and M is motivation.

2. The probability of behavioral change or lack thereof is proportional to the magnitude of X.

3. The greater the positive value of X, the higher the likelihood of change.

4. The greater the negative value of X, the higher the likelihood of no change.

5. A value of X equal to zero (neutral) implies an indifference to change.

In the opening vignette, you read about mothers who were taught how to treat their sick children. This training gave the mothers the ability to change their behavior. The mothers were also given access to inexpensive medicine. This access gave them the

❖ **Table 11.2** Social Marketing Foci for Lowering Obesity Rate

	Individuals	Policy Makers
Short-term change	Teach individuals about health consequences of obesity. Encourage consumers to reduce frequency of eating at fast-food restaurants.	Community level: Provide fruit and vegetable options to school children. Societal level: Restrict the marketing of fast food to children.
Long-term change	Individuals stop consuming processed foods high in sugars, fat, and sodium. Daily caloric intake is limited to maintain healthy weight, and diet is complemented by daily exercise.	Community level: Fast food is banned from schools. Societal level: Advertising of unhealthy food and beverages is banned. Companies that produce unhealthy food products are taxed at rates sufficient to make continued production of these products unprofitable.

opportunity to change. We can assume that mothers were already motivated to help their ill children. As a result of all three factors, behavioral change occurred, and the social marketing program was successful.

In instances in which the barrier to change is lack of ability (which can often be remedied by training) or lack of opportunity (which can often be corrected by access to resources), changes often occur rather quickly because the people affected are already motivated to change. If villagers have unsafe drinking water, they are probably motivated to act once they have training and resources to purify their water. Likewise, people living in disease-prone areas are motivated to get vaccinations when given health education and access to medicine. In these cases, social marketing efforts can be very successful. Social marketers have a more difficult task when individuals are not motivated to change.

Why would people not want to make a change if the change would benefit them? Examples of people doing detriment to themselves are plentiful. Most people are aware that they would be better off if they stopped smoking, avoided being overweight, exercised regularly, ate a more healthy diet, lowered the level of stress in their lives, and practiced safe sex. Yet we know many people who choose not to change their detrimental behaviors. Many people, although they have the ability and the opportunity to make healthy changes, fail to change. They prefer to maintain their unhealthful behaviors. This is very puzzling and irrational—if one assumes that people are rational.

❖ **Figure 11.1**   Influences on Motivation

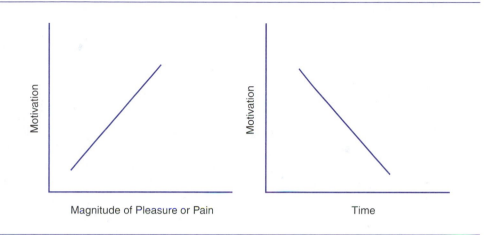

Obviously, we are not. Understanding the factors influencing motivation may help us deal with this conundrum.

Motivation

At the most basic level, we humans are motivated to maximize our pleasure and minimize our pain. The strength of our motivation to acquire pleasure or avoid pain is directly related to (a) the magnitude of each, and (b) the immediacy of the experience. This relationship is depicted in Figure 11.1.

An economic view of behavioral change would frame motivation in a cost-versus-benefit context. People seek to maintain the highest benefit-to-cost ratio (B/C) for any behavioral alternative. Motivation for change is a function of the difference between B/C for the desired (new) behavior and B/C for the undesirable (existing) behavior.

$$\text{Motivation for change} = \text{B/C}_{(\text{new behavior})} - \text{B/C}_{(\text{existing behavior})}$$

Benefits and costs are determined by the individual. Therefore, it is an individual's perception of benefits and costs associated with behavioral change that is important. Also, we must account for the effect of time on perceptions of benefits and costs. Benefits we can experience today have greater value to us than do the same benefits available to us in the future. Costs that we must endure today are felt more strongly than costs we can postpone until the future. Thus, it is the present value of B/C that is important. A more accurate equation for motivation would be the following:

$$\text{Motivation for change} = \text{PVB/C}_{(\text{new behavior})} - \text{PVB/C}_{(\text{existing behavior})}$$

where PVB/C represents the present value of B/C. Seen in this light, it is more apparent why people stubbornly maintain unhealthy behaviors. They perceive their current behaviors to be more desirable than the alternative behavior.

Consumer Recycling

One of us used to live in Bloomington, Indiana. During that time, the city government was attempting to increase residents' participation in curbside recycling. Residents had a recycling container they could place by their trash bins for the trash collectors' weekly visit. This arrangement gave residents both the ability and the opportunity to recycle. Many residents, however, chose not to change their behavior and recycle—they were not motivated. These residents felt the benefits of recycling were not worth the cost, which was the inconvenience of separating their recyclable items before putting out the trash. Because the benefits of recycling are generally realized in the future and accrue to society as a whole, some residents felt taking the time to separate their recyclable items was too great a cost. The city government elected to stimulate residential recycling by increasing the cost of not recycling (keeping existing behavior): it standardized bag size and charged for each bag of trash removed so that residents who didn't recycle used more trash bags. Subsequently, residential participation increased.

Strategies for Changing Behavior

The economic model of behavior change presented above provides strategy choices for the social marketer. We shall use tobacco smoking as our example in this discussion. Table 11.3 lists the four basic strategies for changing behavior, and it presents illustrative examples of ways social marketers (working on behalf of a government agency or a nonprofit organization) would implement these strategies in a social marketing campaign to discourage smoking.

It is worth noting again that social marketers must have an understanding of the perceptions of benefits and costs of the group they wish to help. Without an understanding of the target group's perceptions of the benefits and costs of associated with behavioral change, influencing change is more difficult. Social marketers should also be aware of barriers hampering the target group's ability and opportunity to change its behavior.

The Social Marketing Plan

Social marketers armed with the model of behavior change and strategy options presented above still need to plan their social marketing programs and understand them in relation to the marketing mix. Figure 11.2 illustrates the steps in developing a **social marketing plan**, discussed below.

Step 1: Develop Purpose Statement

The people leading the social marketing effort need to establish a consensus among all interested parties regarding the primary objectives of the effort. Planners need to think in terms of outcomes, not programs, at this stage. Does the group want to decrease the rate of new HIV infections of a target population? Decrease obesity

❖ **Table 11.3** Strategies for Behavioral Change

Strategies	Examples
Increase costs of current behavior	a. Stress high likelihood of getting cancer. b. Stress that smokers subject loved ones to second-hand smoke. c. Impose high taxes on tobacco immediately.
Decrease costs of desired behavior	Provide immediate assistance in quitting smoking.
Decrease benefits of current behavior	Reduce or remove nicotine in tobacco immediately.
Increase benefits of desired behavior	a. Reduce insurance rates for nonsmokers immediately. b. Stress nonsmokers' longer and healthier lives. c. Stress social desirability of quitting smoking (whiter smile, fresher breath, more vitality).

❖ **Figure 11.2** Steps in Developing a Social Marketing Plan

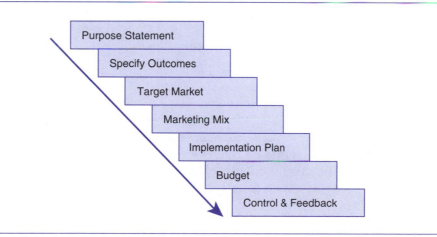

Purpose Statement
Specify Outcomes
Target Market
Marketing Mix
Implementation Plan
Budget
Control & Feedback

rates among an adolescent population? Decrease the infant mortality rate in a Third World country?

The statement of purpose must meet two criteria. First, it must be the result of a consensus among the interested groups. The group must have a common and consistent understanding of its reason for being. Second, the purpose must have focus. The group will remain supportive if its purpose is precisely defined and limited to a specific issue. It is difficult to maintain the support of the group driving the change if the purpose is vaguely defined and too general to focus the group's energy.

Step 2: Specify Outcomes

The purpose statement defines the issue. The next step specifies measurable outcomes tied to a specified time. Measurable outcomes provide a means for the social marketer to assess the group's progress. Outcome measures also focus the social marketing team on its purpose rather than its programs. Also, outcome measures provide the social marketing team with feedback to assess program effectiveness and improve continuously.

For example, if the purpose is to reduce cigarette smoking in the young adult population, a desirable outcome might be to reduce the percentage of this population that uses tobacco from 25% to 20% over 5 years.

Step 3: Identify and Understand Target Market

Define the group that you wish to target. For example, your target group may be 16- to 35-year-old males in Nigeria. The more precisely the target group is defined, the better the social marketer can design a marketing mix to appeal specifically to that group.

Once the target group is defined, the social marketer should try to understand the group as well as possible. By understanding its values, activities, interests, and social influences, the social marketer is prepared to develop an effective social marketing campaign. The message will be more effective and can be communicated through media channels used by the target market.

Step 4: Develop the Marketing Mix

It is now appropriate to develop a marketing mix for the target market. In cases in which there is more than one target market, a marketing plan should be developed for each. We will discuss the marketing mix using the 4P model introduced earlier in this text. The reader will recall that, in Chapter 9, additions to the 4P model were made to address concepts specific to special event planning. In this chapter, we will amend the 4P model to address concepts specific to social marketing planning. For describing social marketing planning, we will add another P, policy, which is important in social marketing, as we will discuss below.

Product. The product is the behavior or idea you want your target market to adopt. It is also the benefits the target market receives by adopting the desired change.

Price. The price represents the costs the target market would experience if it were to adopt the desired change. We discussed cost in the previous section on motivation. Costs represent the target market's perception of the positively perceived benefits that will be sacrificed and the negatively perceived experiences that must be endured to adopt the desired change.

Place. Place is the location where the target market receives the social marketing message. Place also refers to the location of any program services delivered to the target market, such as education or training.

Promotion. Promotion refers to the communications program used to deliver the social marketing messages to the target market. The communications program specifies the message that will be delivered. It also includes the communication vehicles to be used. Communication vehicles may include print material (brochures, direct mail, newspapers, magazines), broadcast media (radio, television), online media (websites, e-mail, e-newsletters, e-zines), publicity and public relations, and person-to-person communication (dialogue, telephone calls).

Policy. According to Social Marketing Down Under (2005), people are more likely to change their behavior if the environment around them is supportive. For example, when children are not bombarded with fast-food advertisements during children's television programming, they are less influenced to make poor meal choices. Social marketing often attempts to influence policy makers and others who are in a position to change the environment. Our concept of policy is not limited to government officials responsible for legislation and regulations. Policy changes can be made inside organizations. For example, a university may set a policy to make condoms available without charge to its students as a tactic to promote safer sexual behavior.

Step 5: Develop Implementation Plan

Specific activities to be performed during a specified time (usually a year or less, depending on the duration of the social marketing campaign) need to be assigned to specific people and times on the campaign timeline. These details allow for the implementation of the marketing mix.

Step 6: Develop Budget

Now that the social marketing planning team has developed a series of activities to achieve desired outcomes, meet its objectives, and fulfill its purpose, the team is prepared to estimate the costs associated with the campaign. Then, if the planning team does not believe it can acquire the necessary funding to carry out the entire plan, it can examine the various activities for cost-saving alternatives. For example, it may be necessary to rely on volunteers more and commercial services less. The team may also have to adjust objectives for the planning period to better match its resources.

Step 7: Control and Feedback

Outcomes can be measured periodically to allow for adjustments during the program period. Feedback can be provided to the social marketing organization for continuous improvement and future planning refinement.

Issue Marketing: Changing Public Policy

The goal of issue marketing is to influence government or corporate policy indirectly by changing public attitudes, beliefs, or opinions about a cause. For example, an advocacy group may want a corporation to change its practices or a government to pass a law or regulation. The advocacy group may feel the best or only way to attain this goal is to influence public opinion, which will pressure the corporation or government to act.

Issue marketers can face several hurdles in accomplishing their aims:

1. The public may not know about the issue.
2. The public may have forgotten about the issue.
3. Public opinion on the issue may have been influenced by the opponent's propaganda.
4. The public may believe the issue is unimportant.
5. The public may not know enough about the issue to have formed an opinion.
6. The public may disagree with the social marketer about the need to act on the issue.

The public level of knowledge and attitude about the issue will determine the appropriate marketing tactic.

For example, most of the world knew for many years that apartheid existed in South Africa. However, in the 1980s, human rights groups became more focused on bringing apartheid to the world's attention. Human rights organizations appealed to governments to oppose the apartheid government but were generally unsuccessful until the news media began to inform the public on a regular basis about what was happening in South Africa. Over time, public opinion began to turn against the white minority South African government. This development led to various advocacy groups' pressuring corporations to stop doing business with South Africa. Later, the governments of some nations issued trade sanctions against South Africa.

Because of South Africa's poor image in the world and the poor economic environment caused by the sanctions, social conditions in South Africa actually worsened for a time. In 1989, sanctions hurt the economy further, the national currency (the rand) collapsed, and reformist F. W. de Klerk came to power. Afterward, virtually all apartheid regulations were repealed, political prisoners were released, and negotiations about forming a new government began. Free elections in 1994 resulted in a victory for the African National Congress, and Nelson Mandela became president.

What would have happened if activists had not been successful in attracting media attention to the problems of South Africa? What would have happened if the public had shown little interest in the early news reports? This example of successful issue marketing was effective because conditions favored the development of a virtuous cycle, in which public concern was aroused about the issue, which in turn stimulated business and government to act. Our discussion will now focus on how the virtuous cycle was germinated. Figure 11.3 represents issue marketing communication patterns in an issue marketing campaign.

Issue marketers present their case to government officials (policy makers). In some instances, one or more officials champion the issue by encouraging a change in

❖ **Figure 11.3**   Issue Marketing Communication Patterns

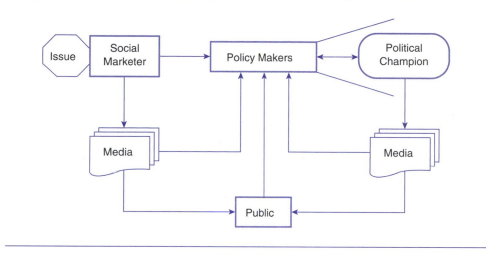

policy (legislative or administrative) and by communicating their support for the issue to the public through the media.

Issue marketers also try to build public awareness and support for the issue by presenting their case to the public through the media. This implies that the media find the issue marketers' case newsworthy. If the public supports the issue, that support can influence government officials to reform policy.

Although issue marketing could be effected by an appeal to a government official who immediately supports the issue and implements policy reform, it is generally the case that policy makers are influenced by public opinion. The success of issue marketers' efforts, therefore, depends on their ability to influence public opinion. For issue marketers to influence public opinion, a virtuous cycle must be created. As depicted in Figure 11.4, if issue marketers can gain the attention of the media and if the media report the issue to the public and if the public shows interest in the issue, a virtuous cycle can begin.

In Step 1 in Figure 11.4, the media report on the issue. Assuming the media's audience shows interest in more reporting on the issue, a positive feedback loop (virtuous cycle) can develop in which the media's reporting increases the public's interest, which increases the media's reporting on the issue, and so on and on. If Step 1 is successful, the media will add a new story to their reporting: the public's growing interest in the issue. As the media's reporting on the issue continues and their reporting on public interest in the issue grows, policy makers begin to focus on the issue as a growing concern (Step 2). Policy makers also perceive an increasing level of constituent support for the issue. If public support continues to grow, policy makers will eventually experience sufficient influence to support the issue.

Issue marketers are challenged to present an important and credible case to the media. If the issue experiences growing support, a faction of policy makers will

❖ **Figure 11.4**   Interrelationship Between Media, Public, and Policy Makers

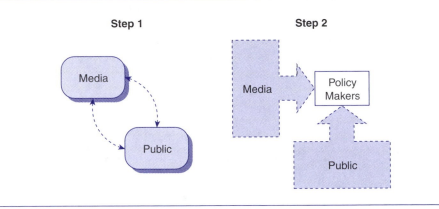

probably oppose it. The opposition will develop a strategy to present its case to the public through the media, which may create a public debate about the merits of the issue.

Interest in issue marketing is growing among social marketers. In the following section, we will discuss more emerging issues in social marketing.

Involvement of the Business Sector

Perhaps the greatest hurdle for social marketers to overcome in future years will be the confounding effect of the business sector on public health. The influence of the corporate sector in society is so pervasive that, at some point, social marketers will have to redefine society's understanding of business's role in modern societies. The following specific instances illustrate this idea.

Corporations: Negligence (Commission of Social Harm)?

Tobacco. Tobacco use is perhaps the most prolific cause of preventable disease in recent times. Millions of lives have been lost to cancer. Billions from public treasuries have been expended to provide health care for victims of tobacco use. Nevertheless, tobacco companies have lobbied to prevent government regulation of the advertising and sale of tobacco products. Government officials have supported tobacco companies at the cost of citizens' health (Kessler, 2001). When countries gradually restrict the activities of tobacco companies, as the United States is doing, tobacco companies have redoubled their marketing efforts in foreign markets, fostering new consumers and heavy users of their products. Social marketers' and public health officials' efforts have been paltry in comparison with the economic might of multinational corporations (Jarvis, 1994; Lantz, Warner, Wasserman, Pollack, & Ahlstrom, 2001).

Obesity. In countries that the fast-food and chain-restaurant industries have penetrated, obesity rates are soaring. Children are evoking public sympathy because they are viewed as having limited volition over poor dietary choices, and it is clear that the effects of obesity on public health are of concern. Unhealthy eating is a precursor of obesity, which is a precursor of a myriad of diseases (Nestle, 2003). Public health social marketing campaigns aimed at encouraging healthier eating have largely been ineffective because the occasional public health message cannot overcome the thousands of marketing messages sent by the food industry each day. The food industry is actively encouraging poor food choices and overconsumption (Brownell & Horgen, 2003). The food industry is also active in schools, gaining the support of educational administrators, who enjoy financial support from the industry (Schlosser, 2002).

The preceding two examples (and there are many others) illustrate how corporations can try to achieve higher sales by encouraging people to engage in unhealthy behaviors. This encouragement is normally communicated through advertising. Social marketers, with comparatively trivial resources, find themselves trying to compete against giant multinational corporations.

Making the social marketers' task even more difficult is the relationship between the corporate sector and the political system. With their enormous wealth, corporations influence some in the political system to protect them. These companies, however, cannot vote. The only way to reform the system is to inform voters and encourage them to demand change from their legislators (Angell, 2004).

Corporations: Benign Neglect (Omission of Improvements to Social Welfare)?

In addition to harming people intentionally, corporations also fail to help people when it is in their power to do so.

Let us briefly examine the example of pharmaceutical companies. They are very profitable. The 10 largest pharmaceutical companies in the world are located in the United States and in Europe. The pharmaceutical companies deploy most of their financial resources in marketing and administration rather than in developing new drugs. In addition, very little innovation in drug development occurs in the industry. Instead, drug companies focus on developing versions of their own and their competitors' drugs, which provides little or no additional benefit. Most innovation occurs in government-funded programs in research universities and small biotech companies. Furthermore, pharmaceutical companies focus on developing drugs for chronic conditions that treat symptoms rather than on developing cures for diseases (Angell, 2004).

The pharmaceutical example illustrates that companies overlook opportunities to provide major benefits to society because their focus is not on benefiting society but on building profits, market dominance, and so forth. The social marketer's task is difficult because it must attempt to obtain a cultural change, which is a very difficult endeavor.

The Main Problem. The purpose of this section is not to persuade the reader that the corporate sector is all bad. There are many examples of good corporate citizenship (see Chapter 12). Rather, we want the reader to better understand that at some time in the future, social marketers and other advocates will realize the futility of trying to change people's unhealthy behavior when the corporate sector will spend tremendous sums to work against those efforts. At some point in the future, social marketers will tire of dealing with symptoms of social problems (smoking, obesity) and will effect change by targeting the root cause (corporate practices and government complicity). Although some groups are already mounting these challenges, they have been portrayed as extremists on the fringe (and, indeed, some are). Until a critical mass of determined public support develops, companies will continue to encourage more cigarette smoking, more alcohol consumption, and more gluttonous eating of processed foods devoid of nutrition.

Until sufficient numbers of voters demand reform, companies will continue to spend fortunes on advertising to convince physicians to prescribe and patients to demand one company's brand of aspirin rather than another's. Until then, pharmaceutical companies will continue to invest in treatments for baldness and erectile dysfunction rather than cures for malaria, tuberculosis, and cancer.

Summary

The nonprofit marketing issues presented in this chapter are summarized here according to the chapter learning objectives they meet.

Define social marketing and issue marketing. Social marketing refers to using marketing tactics in the creation, execution, and control of programs designed to influence social change. Issue marketing refers to a type of social marketing that focuses on increasing public awareness of an important issue and ultimately on changing public policy.

Describe the relationship between social marketing and changing individual behavior. Social marketing's effectiveness is largely determined by its ability to change individual behavior. Human behavior is complex, and behavioral changes that involve people's giving up current behaviors they enjoy in exchange for long-term benefits (e.g., better health in old age) are very challenging.

Describe the AOM model of changing individual behavior. Understanding the target market's ability to change, opportunity to change, and motivation to change inform the strategy decisions of social marketers. Essentially, social marketers should inform their target markets why they should change their behavior, make it as convenient as possible for people to adopt a new behavior, and influence their target markets' motivation by enhancing the benefits and minimizing the costs of change.

Describe the social marketing plan. The social marketing plan consists of seven steps: stating the purpose, specifying outcomes, identifying and understanding the target market, developing the marketing mix, developing the implementation plan, developing a budget, and last, monitoring implementation and incorporating feedback.

Describe effective tactics that can be utilized in an issue marketing campaign. Issue marketing involves influencing local, provincial, national, or international policy makers. Issue marketers may advocate for change by appealing to policy makers directly. However, it is often more effective to also garner public support by getting the news media to develop an interest in the issue and carry a stream of news reports on it.

Describe the inherent conflict between corporate self-interest and social marketing. In some instances, the desired behavioral or policy changes may oppose the self-interest of a portion of the business sector. When an industry has economic and political power, social marketers' goals become much more difficult to achieve.

Glossary

Ability, Opportunity, and Motivation Model (AOM). A model for understanding the forces influencing behavioral change. Social marketers can use the model to develop their social marketing plans.

Issue marketing. A type of social marketing that is focused on increasing public awareness of an important issue and ultimately changing public policy.

Social marketing. Use of marketing tactics in the creation, execution, and control of programs designed to influence social change.

Social marketing planning. A seven-step, organized approach to developing an effective social marketing program that can be implemented.

QUESTIONS FOR REVIEW

1. Define *social marketing.*
2. Define *issue marketing.*
3. Describe the AOM model.
4. What social marketing tactics are used to improve the adoption of new behaviors?
5. Describe issue marketing tactics.

QUESTIONS FOR DISCUSSION

1. Why is social marketing challenging?
2. What are some examples of behavior changes that are easy to adopt and changes that are difficult to adopt? What are the differences in easily changed behaviors compared to difficult-to-change behaviors?
3. Can you think of an issue that could be used in an issue marketing campaign?
4. What are characteristics of an issue that reduce its chances of obtaining policy reform?
5. Describe the relationships between the business sector, the public, and the government that affect policy reforms.
6. How can issue marketers deal with a well-funded advertising campaign by an industry opposed to reform?
7. What tactics should issue marketers use when communicating directly to policy makers? The news media?

INTERNET EXERCISES

1. This assignment is designed to give you the opportunity to better appreciate the breadth of social marketing campaigns and to explore some real examples in areas of your personal interest. Please visit the website www.psaresearch.com/bibsocial.html. Notice the range of

social marketing examples on this site. Explore a couple of examples in an area in which you have an interest.

2. This assignment is designed to give you an opportunity to explore a particular issue marketing example: use of renewable, wind-generated electricity. Go to the website www.awea .org. Describe the strategy this organization uses to achieve its objectives.

TEAM EXERCISES AND ROLE PLAYING

1. As the U.S. market for tobacco products declines, U.S. tobacco companies are refocusing their marketing efforts abroad, and tobacco use in international markets is growing. One team of students should represent a social marketing organization whose task is to convince the public not to use tobacco. Another team should represent an advocacy organization whose task is to convince government policy makers in various countries to pass laws preventing the marketing of tobacco in their country. Another team should represent a major tobacco company whose task is to increase foreign markets of tobacco consumers. Each team should develop an action plan for achieving its goals and then discuss its strategy with the class. Also discuss barriers each team will encounter and how each will likely respond to the actions of the other teams.

MINICASE: Consumer Rights of America

Adrian Love, the executive director of Consumer Rights of America (CRA), is in a dilemma. His board of directors has instructed him to explore ways to influence the U.S. government to change its policy toward its pharmaceutical industry. Adrian is very concerned about his ability to influence reform.

The current U.S. policy protects the industry. For example, the U.S. government does not regulate prices of prescription drugs. A law enacted in 2004 provides some prescription drug coverage for the elderly. The law prevents the government from negotiating with the drug industry for lower prices, which would save U.S. taxpayers many millions of dollars. The U.S. government funds much of the pharmaceutical industry's research and development. More than $25 billion in public funds is distributed through the National Institutes of Health (NIH) to research universities and biotechnology companies to develop new drugs. When a new drug is developed, a pharmaceutical company buys the rights

to the drug, then applies for U.S. monopoly patent protection, which shields the company from competition for 20 years. The U.S. patent protection system allows for high prices, which cost the global market about $400 billion in 2003. Consequently, U.S. consumers pay the highest drug prices in the world. This burden falls disproportionately on consumers who cannot afford health insurance. Insurance companies negotiate lower prices and cover much of the cost for their policy holders. However, since individuals with no insurance coverage have no power to negotiate with drug companies, they pay the highest possible price for a drug—or they go without (Angell, 2004; Consumer Project on Technology, 2004; U.S. Department of Health and Human Services, 2004).

Mr. Love and his board members believe only government regulation of the pharmaceutical industry and price controls can bring drug prices down to levels similar to those in other parts of the world. They also believe that patents for drugs that are (a) not innovations but merely imitations of existing drugs, (b) not more effective than available alternatives, and (c) developed under government research grants should not receive monopoly patent protection.

Mr. Love, after considering the economic and political power of the pharmaceutical industry, believes that any publicity he could obtain for his issue would quickly be dwarfed by a reaction from pharmaceutical companies, their trade association, and supportive politicians and physicians. Since he lacks the financial resources to communicate to the public through paid advertising, Mr. Love must get his message out through the news media. He must also find sympathetic policy makers who will speak out in favor of reform. Mr. Love must develop a plan of action that will help him create a message that will resonate with society. He must develop an effective plan that can be implemented and that can anticipate the strategy of his opponents.

Questions for the Case

1. Mr. Love will have to convince the public that reform is needed. He realizes he does not have the resources to communicate the complexity of the problem to the public. What will his message be?

2. How will Mr. Love get the news media interested in his issue?

3. Drug companies spend millions advertising in the media. Will this discourage the media's news departments from covering his story? What can he do?

4. What will the drug industry's message be in response to Mr. Love's advocacy for reform? What will politicians who support the industry use as their argument against reform?

5. What can Mr. Love do to best improve his chances for success?

References and Bibliography

Akinci, F., & Healey, B. (2004). The role of social marketing in understanding access to primary health care services. *Health Marketing Quarterly, 21*(4), 3–30.

Andreasen, A. (1997). Challenges for the science and practice of social marketing. In M. E. Goldberg, M. Fishbein, & S. E. Middlestadt (Eds.), *Social marketing: Theoretical and practical perspectives* (Chapter 1). Mahwah, NJ: Erlbaum.

Andreasen A. R. (1995). *Marketing social change: Changing behaviour to promote health, social, development, and the environment.* San Francisco: Jossey-Bass.

Andreasen. A. R. (2004). A social marketing approach to changing mental health practices directed at youth and adolescents. *Health Marketing Quarterly, 21*(4), 51–76.

Angell, M. (2004). *The truth about the drug companies: How they deceive us and what to do about it.* New York: Random House.

Bloom, P. N., & Novelli, W. D. (1981). Problems and challenges in social marketing. *Journal of Marketing, 45*, 79–88.

Brownell, K., & Horgen, K. B. (2003). *Food fight: The inside story of the food industry, America's obesity crisis, and what we can do about it.* New York: McGraw-Hill.

Consumer Project on Technology. (2004). *Open letter to U.S. Department of Commerce on drug pricing, July 1, 2004.* Retrieved November 12, 2005, from www.cptech.org/ip/health/rndtf/ drugpricestudy.html

Dalmeny, K. (2003). Food marketing: The role of advertising in children's health. *Consumer Policy Review, 13*(1), 1–7.

Fox, K. F. A., & Kotler, P. (1980). The marketing of social causes: The first ten years. *Journal of Marketing, 44*, 24–33.

Hastings, G. B., & Haywood, A. J. (1991). Social marketing and communication in health promotion. *Health Promotion International, 6*(2), 135–145.

Hastings, G. B., & Haywood, A. J. (1994). Social marketing: A critical response. *Health Promotion International, 9*(1), 59–63.

Hastings, G. B., Hughes, K., Lawther, S., & Lowry, R. J. (1998). The role of the public in water fluoridation: Public health champions or anti-fluoridation freedom fighters? *British Dental Journal, 184,* 39–41.

Hastings, G. B., Stead, M., Whitehead, M., Lowry, R., MacFadyen, L., McVey, D., et al. (1998). Using the media to tackle the health divide: Future directions. *Social Marketing Quarterly, IV*(3), 42–67.

Jarvis, M. J. (1994). A profile of tobacco smoking. *Addiction, 89,* 1371–1376.

Kessler, D. (2001). *A question of intent: A great American battle with a deadly industry.* New York: Public Affairs Books.

Kotler, P. (1994). Reconceptualizing marketing: An interview with Philip Kotler. *European Management Journal, 12*(4), 353–361.

Kotler, P., Armstrong, G., Saunders, J., & Wong, V. (1996). *Principles of marketing, the European edition.* London, UK: Prentice Hall.

Lantz, P. M., Warner, K. E., Wasserman, J., Pollack, H. A., & Ahlstrom, A. K. (2001). *Combating teen smoking: Research and policy strategies.* Lansing: University of Michigan Press.

Lawther, S., Hastings, G. B., & Lowry, R. (1997). De-marketing: Putting Kotler and Levy's ideas into practice. *Journal of Marketing Management, 13*(4): 315–325.

Lawther, S., & Lowry, R. (1995). Social marketing and behaviour change among professionals. *Social Marketing Quarterly, II*(1), 10–11.

Lefebvre, R. C. (1996). 25 years of social marketing: Looking back to the future. *Social Marketing Quarterly* (special issue), 51–58.

Ling, J. C., Franklin, B. A. K., Lindsteadt, J. F., & Gearion, S. A. N. (1992). Social marketing: Its place in public health. *Annual Review of Public Health, 13,* 341–362.

Manoff, R. K. (1985). *Social marketing: New imperative for public health.* Westport, CT: Praeger.

Murray, G. G., & Douglas, R. R. (1988). Social marketing in the alcohol policy arena. *British Journal of Addiction, 83,* 505–511.

Nestle, M. (2003). *Food politics: How the food industry influences nutrition and health (California Studies in Food and Culture).* Berkeley: University of California Press.

Peto, D. (1994). Smoking and death: The past 40 years and the next 40. *British Medical Journal, 309,* 937–938.

Rangun, V. K., Karim, S., & Sandberg, S. K. (1996). Do better at doing good. *Harvard Business Review,* May–June, 4–11.

Schlosser, E. (2002). *Fast food nation: The dark side of the all-American meal.* New York: Perennial.

Social Marketing Down Under. (2005). *Key features of social marketing.* Retrieved November 12, 2005, from social-marketing.co.nz

U.S. Department of Health and Human Services. (2004). *Report on drug importation.* Retrieved November 21, 2005, from www.hhs.gov/importtaskforce/Report1220.pdf

Walsh, D. C., Rudd, R. E., Moeykens, B. A., & Moloney, T. W. (1993). Social marketing for public health. *Health Affairs,* Summer, 104–119.

Wymer, W. W. (2004). Using social marketing strategies to reform social policy: A lesson from British history. *Journal of Nonprofit & Public Sector Marketing, 12*(2), 149–158.

12

❖

Cause-Related Marketing and Other Collaborations With the Business Sector

Learning Objectives

On completion of this chapter, the reader will

- Understand the role of collaborating with the business sector in helping an organization achieve its objectives

- Describe the different types of business-nonprofit relationships

- Understand the potential risks and benefits of collaborating with a company

> ## Learning Objectives (Continued)
>
> - Describe the challenges of managing a collaboration with a business
>
> - Understand the factors that influence consumer reactions to campaigns generated from the relationship with a business

Opening Vignette: Share Our Strength

Share Our Strength (SOS) is a nonprofit organization founded in Washington, DC, in 1984 by Bill Shore to fight hunger (you may visit its website at www.strength.org/). Bill Shore realized that to make a difference in reducing hunger, his organization had to grow substantially and needed to attract resources. The conservative administration of President Ronald Reagan (1981–1989) advocated less government support for social welfare organizations, making it unlikely that SOS could grow if it depended on government support. Instead, SOS made a strategic decision to foster relationships with corporate partners to garner resources and publicity in order to make a difference in reducing hunger.

SOS began a Taste of the Nation event featuring a small number of volunteer chefs who would cook for fund-raising events. Taste of the Nation fund-raising events were held in various cities and proved successful. SOS attracted the attention of American Express, which wanted to demonstrate its corporate responsibility by supporting a worthy cause. Furthermore, American Express wanted to increase its card usage in the restaurant sector. SOS and American Express developed a program in which American Express donated 3% of cardholder charges during the November and December holiday season. The campaign was called Charge Against Hunger. The program was successful in obtaining favorable publicity for American Express, and restaurant card patronage increased substantially. American Express decided to continue the campaign. Between 1993 and 1996, the company contributed $21 million to SOS from its Charge Against Hunger campaign.

Not only did SOS obtain financial support through its collaboration with the business sector; it also gained widespread public recognition of its mission. SOS grew from a local to a regional to a national organization as a result of its ability to attract corporate support for its cause. Furthermore, the advertisement campaigns of companies like American Express put SOS before a national audience. Since its humble beginnings in 1984, SOS has raised more than $180 million and has funded more than 1,100 local, state, federal, and international antihunger programs.

Importance of Collaborating With the Business Sector

According to Business for Social Responsibility, an international consultancy helping businesses become more socially responsible (www.bsr.org), **cause-related marketing (CRM)** refers to a commercial activity in which companies and nonprofit organizations form alliances to market an image, product, or service for mutual benefit. Although

CRM began in the United States in the 1980s, as the opening vignette illustrates, it has spread worldwide. Companies are getting involved with nonprofit organizations in ways that also provide business benefits.

Growth in Business-Nonprofit Relationships

Nonphilanthropic business involvement with nonprofit organizations received much attention in the early 1980s, when American Express developed CRM campaigns to support the Statue of Liberty restoration in addition to Share Our Strength. A decade later, 63% of the largest U.S. corporations and charities were familiar with CRM, and 52% of U.S. corporations reported some involvement with CRM. Two decades after American Express's CRM campaign, one survey showed that 91% of managers believed that CRM can enhance their brand's image or their company's reputation. In another survey, 12,000 consumers in 12 European countries reported buying a product because of its link to a good cause. Two other studies found that consumers are familiar with CRM campaigns and would be willing to switch to a CRM brand if price and quality of alternatives were equivalent. In other recent surveys, 85–92% of corporations and 65% of nonprofit organizations reported participation in some form of CRM (Wymer & Samu, 2003b). Therefore, business and nonprofit partnering has become more common, and consumers are becoming used to advertising campaigns featuring a business and its chosen cause. To understand this trend, it is useful to discuss the benefits partners hope to receive from these partnerships.

Costs and Benefits

Obviously, nonprofit organizations and businesses have incentives that motivate them to develop partnerships. However, in addition to potential benefits, there are potential costs associated with these relationships. The costs and benefits of these collaborations will be discussed first from the perspective of nonprofit organizations, then from the perspective of businesses.

Nonprofits' Perspective

Financial Contributions. The primary motivation for nonprofits to develop a relationship with a company is financial (Figure 12.1). In a climate of shrinking public funding and an increasing number of nonprofit organizations, revenue from collaborating with the business sector is attractive.

Publicity. Nonprofits may have additional objectives. Partnering with a major corporation gives the nonprofit's cause credibility and recognition. Partnering with a business with a strong reputation can increase customer trust in the nonprofit, even if the nonprofit is championing an unpopular cause. It can also lead to increased support for the cause and higher evaluations of the cause's importance.

Risks. Partnering with a company is not without risk. In many cases, businesses enter into relationships with nonprofit organizations, not just from a sense of social responsibility, but also from a desire to further business objectives. Some companies feel little obligation or commitment toward the nonprofit organizations with which

❖ **Figure 12.1** Costs/Benefits: Nonprofits' Perspective

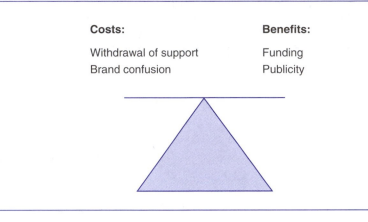

Costs:	Benefits:
Withdrawal of support	Funding
Brand confusion	Publicity

they collaborate. Corporate partners can discontinue their support with little warning. Therefore, nonprofit organizations experience uncertainty of future business support. For example, in 1988, Kodak decided to cut its contributions to nonprofit organizations from $20 million to $13 million.

Another risk that nonprofit organizations face when entering into highly publicized associations with corporations is that public attitudes may change and even become negative. While greater recognition may help the cause, many nonprofit managers are concerned that public contributions will decline. When individuals learn that major corporations are supporting a nonprofit organization with millions of dollars, they may feel that the nonprofit does not need their comparatively smaller contributions. Declining contributions from the public can lead to serious problems.

Perhaps the greatest risk advocacy groups face when entering into alliances with businesses is loss of credibility and integrity if the public perceives the partnership as compromising the nonprofit's objectivity.

If nonprofit managers have a better appreciation of the motives of businesses for supporting of a cause, they can respond more effectively to corporate managers' expectations.

Businesses' Perspective

Businesses may obtain benefits from their association with nonprofit organizations in addition to the satisfaction of supporting a worthy cause (Figure 12.2). Businesses can have various types of relationships with nonprofit organizations, and the type of relationship partially determines the benefits. Among the various benefits businesses may gain are increased sales; brand differentiation; new and deeper community connections; improved public reputation; enhanced brand image; enhanced managerial skills; improved employee recruitment, morale, and retention; a demonstration of shared values with a target market; and enhanced government relations.

Image Enhancement. Supporting an important cause is a way for a business to demonstrate its social responsibility to the public. The business wants the public,

❖ **Figure 12.2**   Costs/Benefits: Businesses' Perspective

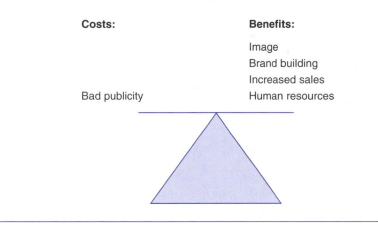

policy makers, and its customers to have a positive impression of the company and its brands. Publicly supporting a popular cause or a respected nonprofit organization is a way for the company to develop good will. Studies show that consumers feel companies ought to support important causes.

Brand Management. Brand managers understand the impact of customer perception of a brand on the marketability of the brand. The 2004 Cone Corporate Citizenship Study reported that brands associated with worthy causes evoke positive attitudes from consumers. Furthermore, while consumers may not select a brand that represents an inferior value, they will allow the brand's support of a cause to be a tiebreaker in cases in which price and quality are equivalent.

Increased Sales. In one type of business-nonprofit relationship, CRM, the business agrees to donate a percentage of a product's sales, usually up to a predetermined maximum. Numerous companies have increased sales using CRM promotions. This is especially true for a competitive brand linked to a popular cause. However, many factors influence consumer responses to these promotions, and managers must be cautioned not to be overly optimistic in their sales forecasts for CRM promotions.

Human Resources Benefits. Many employees like working for a company that supports worthy causes. Employee morale increases as a company's community involvement increases. One study found recruiting recent college graduates was easier for companies that were well-known supporters of worthy causes.

For a company to realize human resources benefits, it must meaningfully support a cause that is important to its employees and reflects their values. The CEO of a company may personally want to support the local symphony, but if the company's employees do not also feel supporting the symphony is important, the support will not yield substantial human resources benefits. One company found that many of its employees were parents of school-age children and had difficulty being involved with their children's teacher and school because teacher-parent conferences were scheduled during the workday. The company started supporting the local school with donations, created a space at the factory for school counselors to meet with parents, and allowed its employees to meet with counselors during working hours to discuss issues concerning their children. Employee morale and satisfaction rose substantially in this example.

Many companies encourage their managers and employees to get involved in their communities through volunteering. Those companies that allow personnel to choose where they wish to volunteer and that provide them with a specified amount of paid time off to volunteer have been shown to increase employee community involvement (Graff, 2004).

Risks. While supporting nonprofits offers many benefits for businesses, there are also risks. Although a primary motivation for entering into a relationship with a nonprofit organization is to enhance public relations, public relations may actually be damaged from the alliance. AT&T, for instance, supported Planned Parenthood for several years. At one time, Planned Parenthood was viewed positively as supporting family planning and helping young women. However, over time, Planned Parenthood became identified with the pro-choice side of the abortion debate. Responding to pressure as the public debate over abortion grew, AT&T withdrew its support from Planned Parenthood. In response, Planned Parenthood bought a full-page ad in the *New York Times* denouncing the company (Himmelstein, 1997). From this experience, corporations learned that they may find it difficult or even disastrous to end relationships with nonprofits.

Companies must choose their nonprofit associates carefully. They must have a social vision and must make sure that initiatives benefiting business do not harm society. Working with the National Parks Conservation Association, Coca-Cola established a CRM promotion in which it would plant a tree in California's Redwood National Park when consumers mailed in proofs of purchase from Minute Maid products and $.75. The promotion was criticized for hypocrisy by several environmental groups because of Minute Maid's packaging, which they considered very unfriendly to the environment (Himmelstein, 1997). Companies need to carefully select their alliances to avoid embarrassing publicity.

Similarly, business-nonprofit relationships that provide a direct benefit to the business (e.g., increased sales) may diminish the company's public credibility. For example, if a gun manufacturer were to partner with the National Rifle Association to lobby against gun control and for constitutional rights, the result might backfire if the alliance were viewed as actually an attempt to protect the company's financial interests.

Different Types of Relationships With Businesses

The following discussion will present the most common types of relationships between the business community and the nonprofit community. Previously, general risks and benefits were discussed. As each type of business-nonprofit relationship is presented, risks and benefits that are specific to that type of relationship will also be discussed. This will help the reader understand the similarities and differences among the various relationships.

Corporate Philanthropy

Business support of causes or nonprofit organizations in the form of monetary or nonmonetary (i.e., in-kind) contributions is **corporate philanthropy**. Usually the support is financial. Some large companies allocate funds to a corporate philanthropy budget, have a manager oversee the disbursement of funds, and claim these disbursements as tax-deductible charitable contributions. Corporate philanthropy also includes allowing employees to volunteer (known as corporate volunteering) for local nonprofit organizations while the volunteers receive compensation from their companies (in contrast to companies who encourage employees to volunteer without compensation).

Most moderate-size and large companies engage in some level of corporate philanthropy. For example, Walt Disney Company once donated $70,000 to Habitat for Humanity for the construction of a townhouse in Burbank, California, and Mentadent has donated $250,000 to Imus Ranch, which provides recreational experiences for children with cancer.

Corporate-sponsored philanthropy is a tax-deductible charitable contribution. Corporations may give away up to 5% of their pretax profits as charitable contributions. Corporate philanthropy supports worthy events and organizations, usually in the localities of company facilities, and maintains community relations.

In corporate philanthropy, the business's interest in the relationship is in supporting a nonprofit organization and its mission. Since the business is disbursing funds where it wishes, it maintains a good measure of power in this type of relationship. Compared with other types of business-nonprofit relationships, corporate philanthropy requires the least commitment in terms of business resources and managerial involvement. In addition to supporting a worthy cause, a business may also wish to help its target markets and its employees identify with it by supporting causes they care about. The primary benefit to the participating business is favorable publicity, enhanced public goodwill, and greater public awareness of the business or its brand. Any subsequent increase in sales would be an indirect effect of the relationship because the link between the product and the sale is mediated by the effects of customer recognition of the business-nonprofit relationship.

A primary motivation for recipient nonprofit organizations is additional funding. In some instances, announcing large funding from major corporations is prestigious, publicly demonstrating the worthiness of one's cause, and may improve the ability of the nonprofit to raise funds from other sources in the future.

All the business-nonprofit relationships described in this article have a degree of risk associated with them. A chief risk is that a partner will behave in a scandalous manner, sullying (by association) the reputation or image of the innocent partner(s). A potential risk for the corporate partner is that employees or shareholders may resent its philanthropy during periods of declining valuation of the corporation's stock. Similarly, employees may resent corporate giving during business cycles that result in pay freezes or layoffs.

For nonprofit recipients of corporate philanthropy, the potential risk of collaborating with businesses may be even greater than for the corporate partner. For example, the ability of the nonprofit to raise funds from private donors (usually a nonprofit's major source of funding) may be greatly reduced as a result of any damage to its reputation, threatening the nonprofit's survival. Another risk faced by the nonprofit is an unexpected withdrawal or reduction of funding from its corporate partner. When corporations are merged or acquired, nonprofit organizations typically receive reduced funding. For example, after Gillette acquired Duracell in 1996, Gillette slashed the battery manufacturer's contributions budget by more than half.

Corporate Foundations

The **corporate foundation** (or corporate-sponsored foundation) is a nonprofit entity created by a company to manage its philanthropy objectives. Corporate-sponsored foundations file Form 990-PF with the Internal Revenue Service, as other private foundations do. As in corporate philanthropy, this type of corporate involvement with the nonprofit sector emphasizes the nonprofit's mission or cause. The corporate partner maintains control through its surrogate, the foundation. The foundation is responsible to trustees who are usually corporate officers. In most cases, the foundation establishes a directive that specifies the types of causes the foundation is seeking to fund. Potential grantees submit competitive grant proposals to the foundation, which awards grants based on the merits of the proposals and the available funds.

Foundations are usually created by large corporations. For example, the AOL Foundation was created by AOL and has launched several national grant initiatives, including the Interactive Education Initiative, which offers grants, online networking, and other types of support to teams of educators with innovative ideas for using technology to enhance student learning. Lucent Technologies created the Lucent Technologies Foundation, whose program is known as the Lucent Peer Collaborative Initiative, a multimillion-dollar, multiyear initiative aimed at creating a new model for fostering collaboration between teachers with the ultimate goal of improving the learning environment for students. In another example of foundation giving, the Delta Air Lines Foundation donated $500,000 to the Atlanta Symphony Orchestra in 1998.

Although supporting worthy causes is the primary motivation of corporate foundations, they may also wish their good works to be noticed by their target markets and their employees. The risks and motivations of foundations are similar to those of corporate philanthropic programs, but the creation of a foundation reduces the risk of shareholder and employee resentment during periods of business down cycles. A corporate foundation, unlike corporate philanthropy, allows a company to put aside more money than it donates in good times and donate more than it puts aside in bad times. It is also possible for a foundation to establish an endowment, which can compensate for fluctuations in business cycles and therefore reduce stockholder and employee resentment of corporate giving during periods when stockholders' stock values are not increasing and employees are experiencing austerity measures.

For nonprofits seeking grants from corporate foundations, funding and publicity would be key motivations, and they would face little risk of reputation damage and little risk of the unexpected withdrawal of corporate support. This is very similar to the motivations and risks associated with corporate philanthropy and illustrates the similarities between the two types of business organizations.

Licensing Agreements

In this type of business-nonprofit relationship, a nonprofit organization allows a corporation to use its name and logo in return for a flat fee or a royalty. Businesses seek licensing agreements with nonprofit organizations that have strong, favorable images (e.g., names, brands) in the minds of important market segments.

A typical company is primarily interested in generating sales through its licensing agreements with nonprofits. Frequently, the partnering business also seeks the favorable publicity common in business-nonprofit relationships. Therefore, the business's focus is primarily on itself and secondarily on the nonprofit or its cause. Business managers view licensing agreements as business decisions, not good works.

A business will typically have a great deal of operational control in this type of relationship. The business must perform the marketing activities necessary to generate sales from the licensing agreement. A nonprofit organization's control is generally limited to how its name is presented.

There are numerous examples. To mention just two, both SmithKline Beecham (mentioned in Chapter 2) and the Florida Department of Citrus established licensing agreements to use the American Cancer Society's logo. The drug manufacturer used the logo to help promote its nicotine patch for smoking cessation, and the state of Florida used it to promote the role of orange products in preventing cancer.

The risks licensing agreements pose for nonprofits are possible damage to reputation and image, reduced funding, and withdrawal of corporate support. The licensing partnership does expose the nonprofit to risk of reputation damage because such an agreement implies that the nonprofit *endorses* the product. When a product has been linked to a nonprofit, the public believes the nonprofit has evaluated the product. If the product happens to be of poor quality or even harmful to consumers, the nonprofit's reputation can be especially tarnished.

For the corporate partner, a licensing agreement represents, in addition to the expenses associated with the formation of the agreement, a possible investment in merchandise as well as in marketing, distribution, and other expenses associated with promoting the licensed items. A nonprofit scandal may lead to a loss of sales in addition to harming the company's reputation.

Affinity Cards. Affinity cards are an example of a licensing agreement. They generally take the form of a major credit card printed with the image, brand, or logo of an institution of particular interest to a target group. For example, a university would enter into an agreement with a credit card company to produce credit cards printed with a photo representing the university. The university would receive a nominal percentage of sales charged with the card (e.g., 0.5–1.0%). The university would provide the credit card issuer with a list of alumni or students and endorse the association. Then the card issuer would solicit customers using direct marketing tactics. For example, MBNA America (a large credit card issuer) entered into an affinity card program with the National Education Association (NEA). The affinity card is offered to NEA members.

Members are offered attractive interest rates and a series of credit card benefits, and a percentage of sales goes to support the NEA.

In an affinity card arrangement, businesses use the nonprofit's favorable image to attract new customers by leveraging the loyalty that exists within the nonprofit's sphere of influence. Businesses place more emphasis on the marketing aspects of this business-nonprofit relationship. Nonprofits use the licensing agreement as a revenue source and benefit in terms of increased funding, greater publicity, and recognition.

The Internal Revenue Service has challenged nonprofits' claim that revenue from affinity card agreements is royalties and not subject to federal income tax. The Internal Revenue Service has argued in tax court that nonprofits are subject to unrelated business income tax on affinity card revenue. The nonprofit community has prevailed. In one case (Sierra Club v. Commissioner, T.C. Memo 1999-86, 3/23/99), the Sierra Club successfully defended its claim that affinity card revenue is royalty income.

The Sierra Club's arguments were bolstered in tax court because it was able to prove it had very few responsibilities in the affinity card agreement. Under the Sierra Club program, the Club authorized a credit card company to issue its members a card bearing the Club's name and logo. The Club retained the right to approve the marketing program and agreed to cooperate in the solicitation and to encourage its members to use the program. The Club president signed a letter endorsing the program, which the card company mailed (improperly using the Club's nonprofit mailing permit) to members. The card company maintained all records and agreed to pay the Club 0.5% of total purchases, plus half of the fees received by the credit card company above 1% of total purchases.

Sponsorships

In licensing agreements, a business pays a nonprofit for using the nonprofit's image in the business's advertisements, packaging, and so forth. In **sponsorships**, the business pays the nonprofit a sponsorship fee for using the business's brand in the nonprofit's advertisements or other external communications. There are two components of sponsorships: (a) the sponsor pays the nonprofit a fee for the sponsor's right to associate itself with the activity sponsored and (b) the sponsor advertises the sponsorship. Both activities and their associated expenses are necessary if the sponsorship is to be a meaningful investment.

A business participating in sponsorships is primarily interested in promoting its brand or company name, although sponsors are also obviously interested in funding and promoting the event. Nonprofits are concerned about protecting their favorable public image and will generally have the preponderance of control about how a sponsor advertises its sponsorship. Sponsors, however, have paid for the right to associate their name with the event and will exercise some power in the relationship as well.

Examples abound. Honda Motor Company, Acura, Saucony, and Tylenol were some of the corporate sponsors of the 13th Annual Los Angeles Marathon. The event attracted 40,000 participants and 1 million spectators. Insight.com, Blue Cross Blue Shield of Arizona, and MicroAge were some of the corporate sponsors for the Fiesta Bowl National Band Championship, the MicroAge Fiesta Bowl Parade, and the Insight .com Tucson Fiesta Bowl Football Classic.

There are several types of business-nonprofit sponsorships: sports sponsorships, book sponsorships, exhibitions, education sponsorships, expeditions, cultural activities, local events, and documentary films.

Sponsorships between businesses and nonprofits have experienced a sharp rise in corporate marketing budgets. While businesses are motivated primarily by the opportunities to present their names and brands before target markets and the public in a favorable light, nonprofits are motivated to enter into sponsorship agreements to generate funding. The funding may be sought to support the event (e.g., Special Olympics), or the sponsored event may be a fund-raiser for the nonprofit (e.g., Race for the Cure).

CRM

In CRM, the level of corporate contributions to its nonprofit partners is dependent on consumer purchases of designated corporate brands. Usually the company specifies a maximum amount it will contribute to the cause. A key characteristic of CRM is that a business's contribution to the nonprofit is linked to and is proportional to sales.

CRM became popular in 1983, when funds were being solicited to restore the Statue of Liberty. American Express created a campaign and contributed a few cents each time its customers used their American Express cards in a transaction. Because of the favorable publicity and increased sales American Express experienced, other companies developed their own CRM programs, and CRM programs have since become common. For example, in 1995, Nabisco produced a special edition of its Barnum's Animal Crackers, donating $0.05 from the purchase of each box, up to $100,000, to the American Zoo Aquarium Association.

CRM is controlled primarily by the corporate partners. Besides contributing money to the nonprofit, businesses promote their association with the cause through promotional and advertising activities. Businesses may spend much more on advertising their association with a favorable cause than they actually contribute to the cause. Businesses that participate in transaction-based promotions may be interested in supporting the cause, but they are also interested in exposing market segments to favorable images of the company and its brands.

The benefits of transaction-based promotions to participating businesses are publicity, public relations, customer or employee goodwill, and increased sales. The benefits to nonprofit organizations are increased funding and expanded publicity and recognition.

CHAPTER INSIGHT **CRM in the United Kingdom**

Business in the Community found that in the United Kingdom in 2003, £58.2 million was raised by 67 businesses benefiting 64 charities and good causes through 82 cause-related programs. This level represented a 15% increase compared to 2002 figures (Business in the Community, 2004).

Joint Issue Promotions

In **joint issue promotions**, nonprofit organizations and businesses work together to support a cause. Instead of a business's giving money to a nonprofit to support its activities, businesses engage directly in activities to further the cause. A characteristic of joint issue promotions is that the business and nonprofit partners are jointly involved in advancing the cause. The contribution of participating businesses is generally promotional and operational. Corporate partners are often involved in the nonprofit's programmatic operations (Andreasen, 1996). The following example should clarify this point.

Hand in Hand was a program created to better educate women about breast cancer. The American College of Obstetricians, the American Health Foundation, and the National Cancer Institute were the nonprofit partners, and *Glamour* Magazine and Hanes Hosiery were the corporate partners. The educational objectives of Hand in Hand were achieved through the distribution and advertisement of educational materials. While *Glamour* and Hanes wanted to support a worthy cause, they also wanted to place their names before their target markets in a meaningful and positive manner.

In this type of nonprofit and business relationship, nonprofits have a preponderance of control. However, corporate partners can exercise varying levels of power themselves, depending on the agreement forming the joint issue promotion. Businesses may contribute resources and expertise that allow for substantial power in the relationship.

Joint issue promotions can be prominent when the partnering organizations are well known, the business's mission and its nonprofit partner's cause have some linkage, and the publicity is performed over mass media. While supporting a worthy cause is the business's primary motive for entering into this relationship, a secondary motive is generating favorable publicity directed toward a desirable market segment. The publicity is more strategically directed than in other types of business-nonprofit relationships. By participating in joint issue promotions, businesses are hoping to be perceived as champions of a cause that is important to their customers. In the Hand in Hand example, *Glamour* and Hanes Hosiery's customers are women, who are most concerned about and most affected by breast cancer.

Nonprofits are motivated to join this relationship because it is directed at achieving their goals and objectives. By tapping into the resources and capabilities of companies, nonprofits are able to bring much greater awareness to their cause than would otherwise be possible. Control and coordination among participating organizations is not great, but it is greater than in other types of business-nonprofit relationships simply because partnering organizations are mutually involved in the promotion.

CHAPTER INSIGHT   **European Consumers Support CRM**

In a 2000 survey of 12,000 consumers in 12 European countries, CSR Europe reported that, in a 1-year period, two in five consumers bought a product because of its links with good causes or a product labeled as social, ethical, or environmental. One in five consumers said they would pay more for such products. (The interested reader can order the report online at www.csreurope.org/publications/europeansurvey/)

Joint Ventures

A business-nonprofit **joint venture** is a new nonprofit entity created by the partnering organizations to achieve mutually desirable objectives. For example, environmental groups educate the public about environmental hazards and socially irresponsible business practices. Environmental groups seek policy remedies from the government in the form of new restrictions, regulations, and laws. Historically, the business sector viewed environmental groups as adversaries. Now, some progressive companies are discovering that cooperating with advocacy nonprofits by forming joint ventures produces more favorable results than opposing them.

Some businesses are forming joint ventures with former nonprofit adversaries. The purpose is to evaluate certain aspects of the businesses' formerly criticized operations. Typically, the joint venture is responsible for developing standards, for monitoring business compliance, and for managing a certification program. Responsible businesses that operate in compliance with standards are given the right to place certification logos on their product packaging to signal to the public their social responsibility and goodwill.

Businesses generally enter into these agreements after a policy shift from opposing a nonprofit's efforts to cooperating with them. The companies' motivations for changing their tactics include more favorable relations with their target markets and the public at large (which influences legislators). Human resources benefits may also accrue as the company develops a more favorable public image. Companies may see these cooperative arrangements as a means of differentiating themselves from their competition. The risks to partnering businesses are similar to those previously discussed, namely being associated with a partner that misbehaves and attracts negative publicity.

Nonprofits enter into these agreements as a means of accomplishing their goals. In cases in which advocacy groups find it impractical to garner public or government support to accomplish their goals, negotiating with a targeted industry or corporation may be an attractive means of achieving progress. For example, the Nature Conservancy and Georgia Pacific created a joint venture through which the Nature Conservancy was able to preserve valuable forestland owned by Georgia Pacific that would have been very difficult to preserve through normal advocacy methods. Furthermore, the Nature Conservancy, through its relationship with Georgia Pacific, has access to many more resources than it would have otherwise.

Nonprofit partners of businesses forming joint ventures face special risks. It is possible for a watchdog group to alienate itself from part of its constituency as well as from other advocacy groups agitating for similar reforms. Some members of advocacy groups may be idealistic or hold extreme positions, viewing pragmatic cooperation with corporations as a total defeat instead of a partial victory. Other advocacy groups may feel the partnering nonprofit is compromising its values and integrity. Joint venturing nonprofits, therefore, may risk losing the support of some of their membership and being ostracized by other advocacy groups. To ameliorate these risks, they will have to promote heavily the potential benefits of cooperation to their community and then continue to communicate the successes achieved through cooperation instead of agitation.

| CHAPTER INSIGHT | Mexican Consumers Support CRM |

The first CRM campaign in Mexico was conducted in 1993. Six years later, a survey of Mexican consumers found the following:

- As many as 68% of consumers believe companies have a responsibility to help solve social problems.
- 74% of consumers are likely to switch brands if they know the new brand supports a cause (when price and quality are equal).
- 74% of consumers are likely to change stores if they know the new store supports social causes.
- 54% will pay between 5% and 10% more for a product that supports a social cause.

Setting Objectives

For relationships between nonprofit organizations and businesses to be successful, partners must establish clear and realistic goals and communicate their expectations to each other. These relationships may fail for several reasons, such as unrealistic expectations of benefits from the relationship. One partner's expected outcomes may be inconsistent with the expected outcomes of the other partner. The following discussion will examine goal setting from the perspective of business and then from the perspective of the nonprofit organization.

Business Perspective

Managers should be cautioned against establishing objectives that (a) predict business returns in a relatively brief time and (b) benefit the business more than the cause it is supporting. Although it is quite acceptable to provide support for a cause for a limited period, businesses accrue benefits proportional to their commitment. Businesses that expect rapid benefits from their support, especially in the form of swift improvements in sales, are often disappointed. If managers fail to realize that the cause of the disappointing outcome was inappropriate objectives, they may come to believe that supporting causes in general is not worthwhile.

Managers need to understand their own values as well as the values of their company's employees, shareholders, and customers. Then those managers need to find a cause to support that reflects these values. Managers also need to understand what to expect in terms of direct benefits (i.e., benefits that can be directly correlated with program expenses, such as sales), indirect benefits (such as goodwill, brand recognition, and enhanced company reputation), and societal benefits (the satisfaction of benefiting society by supporting a worthy cause). The primary caution to managers is that they should recognize they have been trained to set objectives that provide direct, measurable benefits to the business. Collaborating with a nonprofit organization to support a cause is a different type of business activity and requires different planning.

If, in addition to supporting a worthy cause, management desires increased sales, the forecast improvement in sales should be modest until the campaign has sufficient history to make refinements in forecasting and program tactics. Sometimes, managers will provide optimistic sales forecasts to generate corporate support. However, if top management can be persuaded to support a cause only by high expectations of improved sales, then it may be best to find another cause or to delay involvement with any cause until the corporate culture has changed.

If a company has selected a cause to support that is important to its target markets, employees, and so forth, it can expect the indirect benefits stated above. When planning to support a cause, it would be appropriate to set objectives that reflect these expectations. If the appropriate partner has been selected and the company is willing to support the cause in a meaningful way, it can set objectives that relate to improved company reputation, brand image, employee morale, and so forth. Even though these variables are not as easily measured as sales, they nevertheless may be measured, usually through market research techniques (e.g., surveys). It would be best to establish a current level of these variables, predict modest increases as the relationship with the nonprofit organization develops, and adjust future predictions over time.

A company's objectives (i.e., what the company hopes to get out of its support of a cause) will influence the type of relationship that develops. An increase in sales will be achieved most directly through a CRM program. Company goals aimed at building company or brand image are more likely to result in a sponsorship, joint venture, or joint issue promotion. Companies more interested in demonstrating corporate social responsibility are more likely to choose to support a cause through corporate philanthropy or a corporate foundation.

In general, establishing goals for a company's support of a cause is difficult for business managers because it usually does not relate directly to the business's primary task of making profits. Managers are used to relating their decisions to the potential impact on profits. Table 12.1 summarizes some useful guidelines to follow instead.

Nonprofit Perspective

From nonprofit managers' perspectives, setting objectives for collaborative programs with businesses is a more straightforward task. The business managers have to set objectives for supporting another organization, but the nonprofit managers have to set objectives related to their own organization's mission.

If, for example, the nonprofit organization's mission is to educate women about breast cancer prevention, then, knowing the corporate support level, the nonprofit manager can estimate how many women will receive its educational materials. If its mission is to reduce hunger, the nonprofit can estimate how many meals will be provided from its corporate support. Table 12.2 lists characteristics of good objectives.

Finding a Corporate Partner

There are generally two ways for nonprofit managers to locate corporate support. They can use a consultant to recruit a corporate supporter, or they can recruit a corporate partner themselves.

❖ **Table 12.1**   Business Guidelines for Cause Marketing Planning

1. Set objectives relating to the targeted cause. For example, if the company chose to support breast cancer awareness, it could set an objective such as, "For each of the next two years, our company's support of this cause will result in 200,000 more women being educated about the risks and prevention of breast cancer."
2. Avoid overly optimistic projections to win support from your company. Unrealistic objectives will decrease your probability of successful outcomes and reduce future support of causes.
3. Avoid projecting substantial short-term benefits. Until benchmarks are established through collaborative experiences with nonprofit organizations, it is unwise to expect quick returns.
4. Keep projected sales increases from cause-related marketing programs modest until you have enough experience to accurately anticipate increases in sales from cause-related marketing programs.
5. Objectives that predict improvements in indirect benefits should be measurable. Take initial measurements of variables of interest in order to have a benchmark to determine the level of improvement over time. Be aware that other factors can also influence indirect benefits and be sensitive to their impact on the variables you are measuring.

❖ **Table 12.2**   Characteristics of Good Objectives

- They are related to the nonprofit's mission.
- They are measurable in order to assess outcome success.
- They are realistic but challenging.

Using Consultants

Consultants have two characteristics that enable them to be very useful in recruiting corporate support. First, they have corporate contacts. Established consultants will have extensive corporate and nonprofit connections. Resource One, for example, located in Lansing, Michigan, has a database of more than 4,000 corporate and nonprofit contacts. Second, consultants have experience. Cone Communication, for instance, has been tracking CRM trends in national surveys for years and is one of the leading sources of information about cause marketing.

Consultants build their own name recognition and develop contacts by attending and making presentations at national meetings of groups interested in corporate philanthropy, foundations, sponsorships, nonprofit management, and so forth. Some consultants have developed useful websites. Some consultants produce newsletters. Therefore, locating a consultant may be as easy as talking with colleagues in other nonprofit organizations, searching the Internet, or attending nonprofit conferences. There are several notes of caution, however, in finding a consultant.

Look for a consultant who specializes in helping nonprofit organizations and corporations form relationships. This may be a consultant who specializes exclusively in business-nonprofit relationships or a consultant who has a major division devoted to business-nonprofit relationships.

Look for a consultant who has sufficient experience. A good choice would be a consultant with several years' experience, one who has developed an extensive database of contacts in the business and nonprofit sectors. It is useful to have a consultant with enough experience to have learned from past successes and failures.

As discussed previously, corporations and nonprofit organizations can enter into several types of relationships. If you are unsure of which type of relationship with a corporation is best for your nonprofit organization, then select a consultant who is creative in developing innovative types of business-nonprofit associations. If you know the type of corporate support you want, then select a consultant who specializes in it.

Use a consultant to find a suitable corporate partner but not to manage the relationship. The purpose of the consultant is to bring suitable partners together in a manner that facilitates successful outcomes for all parties. If the relationship is developed properly at its inception, the partners can manage the relationship themselves. Having the partners manage their own relationship helps promote open communication, which enables partners to adjust expectations, discover shared values, and develop future collaborations.

Recruiting Your Own Corporate Partner

Nonprofit managers may encounter difficulties locating a suitable consultant, or they may simply prefer to locate their own corporate supporters. In either case, nonprofit managers will have to devote considerable time and energy to locating a corporate partner and developing the relationship. This process is manageable if done properly. You can find your business supporter in one of two ways: serendipitously or purposefully.

Serendipity. Nonprofit managers relying on serendipity are hoping that a fortunate accident will bring a corporate partner to their notice. Nonprofit managers might find a corporate partner by recruiting from the nonprofit's board, by making a presentation at a local Rotary Club meeting, or by asking colleagues. While this method does sometimes result in success, the next process will improve the odds of success.

Partner Recruitment Process. A good process is needed for three reasons. First, it helps nonprofit managers clarify their own perceptions, expectations, goals, and objectives for the relationship. Second, it works within the consensus-building culture of most nonprofit organizations. Third, it improves the probability of finding the best-suited corporate partner, increasing the odds of successful outcomes for the business and the nonprofit. The process is discussed below.

Step 1. Evaluate the reasons you want to develop a relationship with a business. What do you want from the relationship?

Step 2. What are your goals? Are you looking for financial contributions, publicity, in-kind donations, marketing expertise?

Step 3. Match your mission with a business's target market. If your mission is to educate men about prostate cancer, then you may be attractive to a business that markets to men in general or older men in particular. If your mission is to reduce child abuse, then you may be attractive to a business marketing to parents. This step is particularly important because there are many good causes, and you will be most successful in recruiting a business that perceives you as offering it a means of identifying with its target market. This step also helps you focus on businesses most likely to value collaborating with you.

Step 4. List the benefits a business will receive from collaborating with you. Keep in mind that although most businesses want to support a good cause, they will find most compelling a cause that meshes with their values, a cause of importance to their target markets, and a cause that will provide some business returns. Businesses spend enormous sums advertising to their target markets to improve the recognition and image of their brands. Therefore, it is easier for businesses to justify using resources to promote their brands favorably than to justify giving money away to charities. When *Glamour* Magazine and Hanes Hosiery gave money to help educate women about breast cancer, they were pleased to support a worthy cause. However, they were able to justify using their resources in this way because the education campaigns put their brands before their target markets, adult women, in a favorable way.

Step 5. Approach the business. Steps one through three help build a list of prospective corporate partners. Step four helps screen the list a bit; the business that would benefit the most from associating with your nonprofit is usually the best choice as a partner. Step four also helps you formulate the message you will use in persuading the business to collaborate.

Schedule a meeting with the highest-ranking officer of the business if possible. It would be best to meet with the CEO. It is likely that the vice president of marketing will also be involved. Keep in mind that corporate culture is different from the cultures of most nonprofit organizations. Business managers tend to make decisions relatively quickly and with relatively few people involved. The business emphasis is on efficiency and productivity. In nonprofit organizations, consensus building is very important among board members, other managers, and resource providers, creating a slower pace of decision making.

During the meeting with the corporate officer, it is important to discuss the mission of the nonprofit and its importance. However, the nonprofit manager needs to demonstrate an awareness of the business manager's perspective by discussing what benefits the business can hope to obtain from the relationship. There are two major dimensions of the presentation to the prospective corporate partner: first, persuading the prospective partner that supporting your cause is a worthwhile thing for the business to do and allowing the business to demonstrate its social responsibility; and second, persuading the prospective partner that your cause is important to the business's customers, potential customers, and employees. It is the convergence of these two factors that is most attractive to the business. If the nonprofit manager discovers that the prospective corporate partner is not interested in supporting the cause, it would be better to look for another partner.

Once a suitable corporate partner has been recruited, the nonprofit manager's attention must be directed at managing the relationship. Collaborating with a corporate partner demands a considerable amount of the nonprofit manager's time. Many nonprofits fail to appreciate the time required by these relationships. The manager's time represents a cost to the nonprofit organization and should be taken into consideration. It may be best for the nonprofit to designate someone to work with the corporate supporter.

Managing the Relationship

The nonprofit organization must communicate to its corporate partner what the primary use of the contributed resources will be. The business should communicate to the nonprofit organization what outcomes it would like to see. The business should discuss these outcomes in terms of the cause it is supporting as well as anticipated business benefits. Once expectations are communicated, managers should develop the type of relationship that will best meet their mutual objectives (e.g., sponsorship, joint issue promotion, etc.). It is also important for partners to establish a time frame for the relationship, that is, when the relationship will begin and when it will end. If appropriate to the situation, managers should develop a strategy for the dissolution of the relationship when it comes to its natural termination.

The nonprofit manager should keep in mind that businesses, especially those businesses not experienced in supporting a cause, are initially reluctant to commit their resources in a long-term relationship. Businesses may prefer a specified period of support in order to allow them the option of termination if the collaboration produces disappointing outcomes. Successful relationships with business supporters can evolve over time to deeper levels of commitment and longer duration.

Both nonprofit managers and business managers must be sensitive to each other's culture in order to facilitate successful and transparent communication. In one of its programs supporting a cause, Microsoft funded and developed computer labs in select public libraries. The relationships with the selected public libraries were tested because of cultural differences. Microsoft's teams were used to making quick decisions and working long days in order to complete a project. Employees in the public libraries, however, took a long time to make decisions and worked a strict 8-hour day. While neither partner changed its culture during the experience, communication improved as each group gained an appreciation for the other.

It is important that partners' expectations and responsibilities be clarified and committed to in writing, perhaps even in a contract, so that when misunderstandings occur, the partners can refer to their written agreement. Obviously, a written understanding of partners' responsibilities should be as clear as possible to reduce the chances of differing interpretations.

Communication between organizations should occur frequently and at several levels of the organizations. Diffusing the accountability and communication throughout the organizations will reduce the chance of the relationship's stalling if a key person leaves an organization.

Even though multilevel communication is desirable, top-level support is crucial. Top managers need to perceive common values with the nonprofit organization and need to believe in the importance in the cause. In long-term relationships, it is not unusual for the corporate leader to serve on the nonprofit's board, even as chairperson.

❖ **Figure 12.3** Consumers' Responses to Business Support of Cause

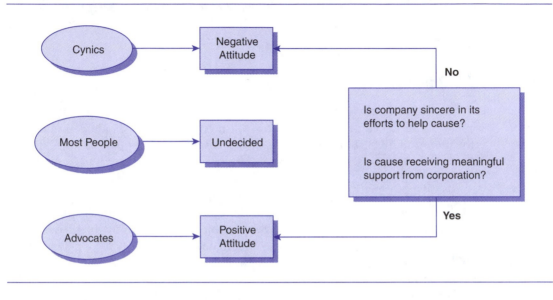

The business needs to actively help the nonprofit organization achieve its goals. Nonprofit managers need to help the business realize benefits from its support. Nonprofit managers need to help their corporate partners obtain favorable publicity for their support and should express appreciation in creative ways when they have the opportunity.

Model of Consumer Responses to Campaign

Consumer Attitudes Toward Businesses

Surveys have repeatedly found that, in general, consumers feel companies should support worthy causes. Consumers generally have favorable attitudes toward companies that actively support their communities and worthy causes. However, consumer attitudes toward companies that support nonprofit organizations are somewhat more complex than they may at first appear.

As Figure 12.3 shows, a small number of consumers are cynics. They are distrustful of business in general, and their negative attitudes are not altered by advertising or other forms of communication featuring a business supporting a cause. Other consumers are staunch advocates of the cause. They appreciate a business's helping their cause, and their attitudes toward the company become more favorable as a consequence.

The largest number of consumers is undecided and will allow their perceptions of the company's motives for supporting a cause to influence their attitudes. If undecided consumers believe the business's support of the cause is self-serving, their attitudes toward the business will not improve. Consumers will believe the company's support of the cause is genuine if they perceive the company's support to be honest and its level of support meaningful.

Consumers perceive company support of a cause to be honest if there is a consistency between the company's products or services and the nonprofit's mission. A cigarette company's support of the American Lung Association would likely be perceived to be dishonest because the company's product is at odds with the nonprofit's mission. Pepsi Cola's support of adult literacy would likely be perceived has having neutral honesty: There is neither a negative nor a positive relationship between the company's product and the cause. Consumers would likely perceive Kraft Foods' support of an antihunger cause to be honest because there is a clear connection between a food producer and a cause that seeks to feed hungry people.

Three factors generally influence consumers' perceptions of the meaningfulness of corporate support for a cause. First, the company must actually give money or in-kind donations to the nonprofit. Managers can bolster this factor by periodically releasing information regarding the accumulated company support to date. Second, the amount of money or other support the company is giving to the cause must not be trivial. When a company pledges to give a nonprofit a few cents per consumer purchase, the amount on a per-transaction basis may seem negligible to consumers. Managers need to disclose accumulated totals, which may be substantial sums, providing a clearer picture of the real levels of support. Third, the resources expended promoting the company's support of the cause have to appear reasonable in relation to its actual support of the cause. If a large corporation spends $20 million on a national advertising campaign to promote its support of a cause, but the campaign results in only $1 million for the cause, consumers may remain skeptical. However, nonprofit managers can communicate to the public the value to the nonprofit of the company's contributions.

In general, if businesses want to receive favorable publicity and identify with their target markets, they need to make sure they are supporting causes that are important to their target markets. They need to make sure that the manner in which they are supporting the cause appears not self-serving but genuine, honest, and meaningful.

Consumer Purchase Intentions

In CRM, the business bases its level of support on consumer purchases. Corporate managers often choose CRM campaigns as a means of simultaneously supporting a cause and increasing product sales. Managers should understand the factors that influence the sale of products featured in a CRM program. Some consumers are very loyal to a brand and cannot be persuaded to switch to a competitor's brand. Figure 12.4 depicts the remaining consumers, those who are not strictly loyal to a specific brand.

The cynics represent a small group of consumers who are skeptical of the business's motive for supporting the cause. Cynics are unlikely to support the CRM program with their purchases.

Advocates really care about the cause and will buy the featured brand to support the company helping their cause.

❖ **Figure 12.4** Consumers' Purchase Intentions

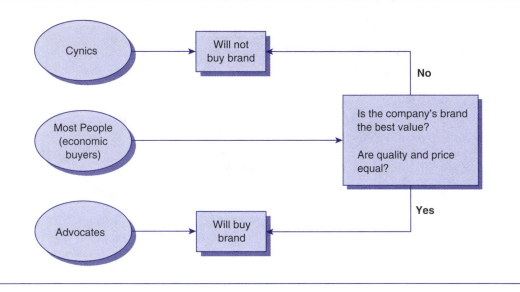

The majority of consumers believe the company's support of the cause is a good act. While their attitudes toward the company may be positive, they are unlikely to let the brand's connection to a cause influence their normal economic buying behavior. Consumers will normally buy the brand they perceive to offer the best value. However, a brand's support of a cause can serve as a tiebreaker between equivalent alternatives. If the featured brand is about the same quality and price as the competitor's brand, then consumers will likely buy the featured brand if it supports a cause they care about.

Public Response to Nonprofit

Most nonprofit organizations are dependent on a favorable public image to further their missions. Nonprofit organizations having wide public appeal need a modest amount of support from a large general public. Nonprofit organizations appealing to smaller groups of supporters must attract deeper levels of commitment. In either case, recruiting new supporters while retaining existing supporters is crucial. Therefore, a nonprofit manager must be concerned about the response of individual supporters to its collaboration with a corporation.

Assuming that the corporate partner will not do anything that could be considered scandalous, nonprofit managers have two major concerns. First, nonprofit managers need to consider whether individual supporters will reduce their support on learning that a corporation is supporting their cause. Individual donors may feel that their contributions are meager (and therefore less important) compared with the contribution of a corporation. It may be that the publicity generated by the business-nonprofit collaboration will result in wider public recognition of the cause and produce more individual donors. This is especially true for small, little-known nonprofit organizations. Nonprofit managers need to communicate to current donors the importance of their donations and specifically that, in the aggregate, their contributions far exceed corporate support.

Second, nonprofit managers need to consider whether key supporters will perceive corporate support as a compromise of integrity. This is a particular concern among advocacy nonprofit organizations. Supporters of a cause promoting reform may view a corporate partnership as "selling out" or commercializing the cause.

During a period of growing government conservatism, when policy makers are unlikely to place restrictions on the business sector, advocacy groups may find it easier to collaborate with an opponent than to agitate for reform. Furthermore, companies may find it favorable to their public images to cooperate with an advocacy group rather than receive continuous negative publicity. Recently, the Nature Conservancy, a conservation advocacy group, and Georgia-Pacific, the largest corporate owner of nature preserves in the United States, agreed to a joint-venture relationship to protect and manage some particularly sensitive and untouched preserves. Through this collaboration, the Nature Conservancy furthered its mission by protecting some pristine areas, and Georgia-Pacific was able to demonstrate its social responsibility without substantially reducing its key resources.

Nonprofit managers need to define their organizations in terms of the desired results (e.g., protecting wilderness areas) rather than in terms of tactics (e.g., lobbying for government regulation of industry). Framed this way, nonprofit managers can take advantage of tactical opportunities to achieve strategic successes. Nonprofit managers also need to avoid demonizing opponents. While demonizing opponents may help raise funds in the short term, it can create an adversarial culture that can prevent beneficial and necessary compromises.

Gender Differences

Three separate studies have found that women are more responsive to CRM appeals than men are. Women tend to be more willing to participate in the programs (e.g., purchase featured brands). They tend to have better attitudes toward the programs and the participating organizations. Women are more receptive to CRM appeals and are more persuaded by them.

The reasons women are more responsive than men to business-nonprofit collaborations are not well understood. Some propose that girls are taught to express helping, nurturing behaviors whereas nurturing behavior is not encouraged in boys. Men are also thought to be more action oriented and individualistic rather than nurturing and communal.

This is not to suggest that men are not good target markets for business-nonprofit programs. They are. However, women may be slightly more responsive to the programs.

Managerial Issues

The following issues are relevant for nonprofit managers:

1. **Collaborating with a business.** Business support may create a new revenue source for a nonprofit organization. Furthermore, the business may contribute other resources, such as marketing expertise, volunteers, or product donations.

2. **Exchange relationship.** While the business may believe it is good to support a worthy cause, it also needs to partially justify its support as a good business decision. Through associating with the nonprofit, a business may obtain favorable publicity, demonstrate social responsibility, identify with its target markets, improve employee morale, and possibly increase sales.

3. **Exclusivity.** Some businesses may want to be the exclusive corporate supporter of a nonprofit. It is advantageous for a business to be the only corporation identified with an important cause. However, the nonprofit must weigh this consideration against possible disadvantages. Large, well-know nonprofit organizations are in a better negotiating position than are smaller, relatively little-known nonprofits. It may be useful for the nonprofit manager to visit a comparable nonprofit's website to discover the number of corporate supporters that are publicized.

4. **Experience curve.** Attracting business supporters and managing the relationships and resulting programs require considerable time, attention, and skill. For the nonprofit manager new to these relationships, it is advisable to begin modestly in order to learn what is most effective for the nonprofit organization.

Summary

The nonprofit marketing issues presented in this chapter are summarized here according to the chapter learning objectives they meet.

Understand the role of collaborating with the business sector in helping an organization achieve its objectives. Nonprofit organizations are increasingly looking to the business sector for an additional resource stream. This trend is occurring at a time of declining government support of the nonprofit sector, increasing competition among a growing number of nonprofit organizations, and soaring competitiveness in the business sector.

Describe the different types of business-nonprofit relationships. There is a variety of ways businesses can collaborate with and support nonprofit organizations. The type of collaboration the partners develop is usually influenced by their own objectives. Among the various types of relationships are corporate philanthropy, corporate foundations, joint issue promotions, transaction-based promotions (CRM), sponsorships, and joint ventures.

Understand the potential risks and benefits of collaborating with a company. Scandalous behavior by a partner is rare but, if it were to occur, could damage collaborators' reputations. Also, partners that have unrealistic expectations or that poorly manage the collaborative program are at risk of failing to meet the goals that motivated the formation of the relationship.

Nonprofit organizations may find that more resources are needed to manage the relationship than they anticipated. They may grow dependent on corporate support, only to find it withdrawn because of a merger, acquisition, or declining business period.

Describe the challenges of managing a collaboration with a business. Partners need to become familiar with each other's cultural norms and decision-making processes. Goal setting should be a joint exercise to help each organization understand the other's perceptions and to develop realistic goals. Frequent, open communication at various levels of the organizational hierarchy is important. Developing a detailed program and committing assigned tasks and responsibilities to writing will help avoid conflicts over misunderstandings later. Nonprofit managers should work to help their business supporters achieve benefits from their support.

Understand the factors that influence consumer reactions to campaigns generated from a relationship with a business. Under favorable circumstances, marketing campaigns can be effective in influencing positive target market attitudes and consumer purchases. Campaigns can have a positive effect on consumer attitudes if the business does not appear to be self-serving. In terms of influencing consumer purchase behavior, CRM campaigns can serve as tiebreakers if price and quality are nearly the same as those of competing products.

Glossary

Cause-related marketing (CRM). A business marketing program in which a specified amount is advertised to be donated to a charity or cause for each consumer purchase made. There is usually a specified maximum limit on total donations.

Corporate foundation. Also called company-sponsored foundation; a private foundation whose assets are derived primarily from the contributions of a for-profit business. While a company-sponsored foundation may maintain close ties with its parent company, it is an independent organization with its own endowment and as such is subject to the same rules and regulations as other private foundations.

Corporate philanthropy. Sometimes called corporate giving or grant making; involves monetary or other types of contributions (e.g., products, personnel, publicity) to a nonprofit organization, charity, or cause. Large companies may have a department devoted to managing their philanthropy programs.

Joint issue promotion. A type of collaboration between business supporters and nonprofit organizations in which materials for an education program are developed and disseminated to a target audience.

Joint venture. In the context of nonprofit management, a new nonprofit entity created by the partnering businesses and nonprofit organizations to achieve mutually desirable objectives.

Licensing agreement. In this type of business-nonprofit relationship, nonprofit organizations allow corporations to use their names and logos in return for a flat fee or a royalty.

Sponsorship. A type of collaborative relationship between a business and a nonprofit organization in which the business sponsor pays a sponsorship fee to the nonprofit organization to support its program. The sponsoring business obtains the right to associate its corporate name or brand with the sponsored program. In many cases, businesses spend more promoting their association with the sponsored program through advertising than they spend supporting the program.

QUESTIONS FOR REVIEW

1. Define *cause-related marketing*.

2. Define *corporate foundation*.

3. Define *corporate philanthropy*.

4. Define *joint issue promotion*.

5. Define *joint venture*.

6. Define *licensing agreement*.

7. Define *sponsorship*.

8. Describe two sources a nonprofit manager can use to find a corporate supporter.

QUESTIONS FOR DISCUSSION

1. Why are nonprofit managers increasingly looking for support from the business sector?

2. What benefits can nonprofit managers expect from corporate support?

3. What benefits do corporate managers expect from supporting a cause?

4. What are the risks nonprofit managers face when partnering with a corporation?

5. Describe guidelines a corporate manager should use in setting objectives for a program with a nonprofit organization.

6. What guidelines should a nonprofit manager follow in setting objectives for a collaborative program with a corporate supporter?

7. What characteristics should a nonprofit manager look for when searching for a consultant to help find a corporate partner?

8. Describe the process a nonprofit manager can use to recruit a business supporter.

9. Describe factors that influence consumers' attitude change when they are exposed to CRM appeals.

10. Describe factors that influence consumer purchase intentions toward a brand-associated CRM program.

INTERNET EXERCISES

1. Enter www.pfdf.org/collaboration/challenge/, then look over the worksheets as if you are a nonprofit manager interested in forming alliances with businesses. This activity should give you an idea of the range of planning involved.

2. Enter www.cavill.com.au/pages.asp?area=9&page=55. Review how the business sector's involvement with the nonprofit sector has evolved over the past 20 years.

3. Enter www.charityvillage.com/cv/research/rcaus.html and read the series of short articles.

4. Enter www.conenet.com/Pages/cause_brand.html and read how corporations can benefit from collaborating with nonprofit organizations.

TEAM EXERCISES AND ROLE PLAYING

1. Enter www.ibm.com/ibm/ibmgives/ and examine IBM's position on supporting the nonprofit sector. What are IBM's motives? What benefits do you think IBM receives from its involvement in supporting causes? Compare IBM's program with that of Cisco (www .cisco.com/web/about/ac48/about_cisco_community_and_philanthropy_home.html). Which corpration's program is likely to be more successful? Why?

2. Create four teams. Each team represents a management team for a nonprofit organization whose mission is reducing teenage suicide. Each team should develop a plan for attracting a corporate supporter, identify a potential corporate supporter, and prepare a list of arguments to present to the corporation explaining why it should collaborate with the nonprofit organization.

MINICASE: Teens-USA

Kelli Michaels is the national executive director of Teens-USA, a national nonprofit organization dedicated to improving conditions of America's teenagers. Teens-USA has a number of target programs aimed at helping teens: (a) reducing drug abuse, alcohol abuse, and cigarette smoking; (b) reducing violence and sexual abuse of teens at school and at home; (c) improving school performance; (d) reducing teen pregnancy and sexually transmitted diseases; and (e) reducing the suicide rate among teens.

Founded in 1960, Teens-USA was initially funded by government grants. From 1960 to 1980, donations from individual contributors gradually rose to equal the amount from government grants. From 1980 to 2003, the federal government continually reduced the grants it gave to social welfare organizations. By 2003, government grants represented only 15% of Teens-USA's total

funding, corporate foundations and corporate philanthropic giving represented 5% of total funding, and individual donations accounted for 80% of total funding.

Among the programs of Teens-USA, reducing teen pregnancy and sexually transmitted diseases has been the most controversial. From 1960 to 1975, Teens-USA developed educational programs that plainly discussed the need for contraception. Teens-USA helped school systems develop family life curricula. It provided teens with brochures and counseling about contraception and sexually transmitted diseases. From its offices, it distributed condoms to teens on request. Beginning in 1975, the abortion debate began to polarize Americans on the issue of teen sexuality. Since Teens-USA did not provide abortion services, it could avoid committing to a side in the abortion debate more easily than some other similar organizations could.

However, in the mid-1980s, First Lady Nancy Reagan promulgated the Just Say No campaign to dissuade illegal drug use. This promotion spread to the abortion debate, emphasizing total sexual abstinence as the solution to teen pregnancy and sexually transmitted diseases. The pro-choice side opposed the promotion of abstinence as the solution to teen pregnancy and sexually transmitted diseases. The pro-choice group believed the Just Say No campaign was not effective in changing teen behavior and questioned the motives of the campaign (i.e., whether it was really intended to help teens or to win support of religious conservatives). Teens-USA began to include abstinence in its educational materials, but the organization continued to promote contraceptive and disease-preventing behavior to teens. This stance alienated many conservatives who supported the Just Say No abstinence position.

Michaels has two major issues to deal with. First, revenues have increased little over the past 5 years. Revenues have remained near $15 million annually, although government reductions have been replaced by individual contributions. Second, the organization has never allocated much money for marketing purposes. Funds that were not needed for operating expenses were used in the target programs. As a result, Teens-USA is not very well known.

As Michaels plans for another year, she realizes that government funding continues to decline and individual donations are not growing.

Perhaps attracting a corporate supporter will help. A large, multinational corporation has approached Michaels, offering to contribute $1.5 million each year for 5 years. In return for this level of support, Michaels must agree to allow the corporation to use Teens-USA's name and logo in its advertising. Furthermore, Teens-USA must guarantee that the corporation will be its exclusive corporate supporter.

As Michaels considers this offer, she has several concerns. The multinational corporation has several divisions. One division markets alcoholic beverages. Another division markets tobacco products. Will seeing Teens-USA's logo on a beer commercial send a mixed message to teen viewers? Will the partnership between Teens-USA and the corporation reduce individual donations?

Questions for the Case

1. Should Michaels accept the corporation's offer? Why or why not?

2. Should Michaels make a counteroffer? If so, what should it be?

3. What companies would be attractive partners for Teens-USA?

4. What benefits would a corporate partner receive?

5. What benefits would Teens-USA receive from collaborating with a corporation?

References and Bibliography

Amery, E. A. (2002). *Trends: Creating win-win relationships through cause-related marketing. Insidegiving.com,* Retrieved November 21, 2005, from www.onphilanthropy.com/bestpract/bp2001-08-22i.html

Andreasen, A. R. (1996). Profits for nonprofits: Find a corporate partner. *Harvard Business Review, 74*(Nov/Dec), 47–59.

Austin, J. E. (1999). Strategic collaboration between nonprofits and businesses. *Nonprofit & Voluntary Sector Quarterly, 29*(supplemental), 69–97.

Austin, J. E. (2000). *The collaborative challenge: How nonprofits and businesses succeed through strategic alliances.* San Francisco: Jossey-Bass.

Barone, M. J., Miyazaki, A. D., & Taylor, K. A. (2000). The influence of cause-related marketing on consumer choice: Does one good turn deserve another? *Journal of the Academy of Marketing Science, 28*(2), 248–262.

Basil, D. Z. (2002). *Cause-related marketing and consumer attitudes: The effects of balance and fit on cognitive processing.* Doctoral dissertation, University of Colorado.

Berger, I. E., Cunningham, P. H., & Drumwright, M. E. (1999). Social alliances: Company/nonprofit collaboration. *Social Marketing Quarterly, 5*(3), 49–53.

Berger, I. E., Cunningham, P. H., & Kozinets, R. V. (1998). Consumer persuasion through cause-related advertising. *Advances in Consumer Research, 26*(October), 1–7.

Billitteri, T. J. (2000, June 15). Venturing a bet on giving. *Chronicle of Philanthropy,* 1.

Blum, D. E. (2000, June 15). 9 out of 10 companies have charity marketing deals. *Chronicle of Philanthropy,* 39.

Bronn, P. S., & Vrioni, A. B. (2001). Corporate social responsibility and cause-related marketing: An overview. *International Journal of Advertising, 20*(2).

Business in the Community. (2004). *2003 cause related marketing tracker.* Retrieved November 21, 2005, from www.bitc.org.uk/resources/research/research_publications/crmtracker2003.html

Cavicchio, C. (2001). *Analysis: Corporate philanthropy in the new millennium.* insidegiving.com, Retrieved November 21, 2005, from www.onphilanthropy.com/tren_comm/tc2001-08-22k.html

Cone Corporate Citizenship Study. (2004). Retrieved November 21, 2005, www.coneinc.com/ Pages/pr_30.html

Cone/Roper. (1999). *Cause related trends report.* Boston: Cone Communications.

Cone/Roper benchmark study. (1993). Boston: Cone Communications.

Creyer, E. H., & Ross, W. T. (1997). The influence of firm behavior on purchase intention: Do consumers really care about business ethics? *Journal of Consumer Marketing, 14*(6), 421–432.

Crimmins, J., & Horn, M. (1996). Sponsorship: From managerial ego trip to marketing success. *Journal of Advertising Research, 36*(4), 11–21.

Dahl, D. W., & Lavack, A. M. (1995). Cause-related marketing: Impact of size of corporate donation and size of cause-related promotion on consumer perceptions and participation. In D. W. Stewart & N. J. Vilcassim (Eds.), *1995 AMA winter Educators' Conference: Marketing theory and applications: Vol. 6* (pp. 476–481). Chicago: American Marketing Association.

Dreessen, E. (2001). What we should know about the voluntary sector but don't. *Canadian Journal of Policy Research, 2*(2), 11–19.

Drumwright, M. E., Cunningham, P. H., & Berger, I. E. (2000). *Social alliances: Company/nonprofit collaboration* (report no. 00–101). Cambridge, MA: Marketing Science Institute.

Farquarson, A. (2000, November 15). Marketing campaigns impact on consumer habits. *Guardian.* Retrieved November 15, 2005, from society.guardian.co.uk/voluntary/story/0,7890, 397881,00.html

García, I., Gibaja, J. J., & Mujika, A. (2003). A study of the effect of cause-related marketing on the attitude towards the brand: The case of Pepsi in Spain. *Journal of Nonprofit & Public Sector Marketing, 11*(1), 111–135.

Graff, L. (2004). Making a business case for employer-supported volunteerism. *Volunteer Canada.* Retrieved November 21, 2005, from www.volunteer.ca/volunteer/pdf/ESVThinkPiece.pdf

Himmelstein, J. L. (1997). *Looking good and doing good: Corporate philanthropy and corporate power.* Indianapolis: Indiana University Press.

Independent Sector. (2002a). *Facts & figures on corporate philanthropy and cause-related marketing.* Retrieved November 14, 2005, from www.independentsector.org/mission_market/facts _figures.htm

Independent Sector. (2002b). *Motivations for partnering.* Retrieved November 15, 2005, from www.independentsector.org/mission_market/Motivations.htm

Johar, V., & Pham, M. T. (1999). Relatedness, prominence, and constructive sponsor identification. *Journal of Marketing Research, 36*(August), 299–312.

Levy, R. (1999). *Give and take: A candid account of corporate philanthropy.* Boston: Harvard Business School Press.

McDaniel, S. (1999). An investigation of match-up effects in sport sponsorship advertising: The implications of consumer advertising schemas. *Psychology and Marketing, 16*(2), 163–184.

Morton, C. R. (1999). *Corporate social advertising's effect on audience attitudes toward company and cause.* Doctoral dissertation, University of Texas at Austin.

Pringle, H., & Thompson, M. (1999). *Brand spirit: How cause related marketing builds brands.* Chichester, UK: Wiley.

Reed, P. B., & Selbee, L. K. (2001). Canada's civic core. *Canadian Journal of Policy Research, 2*(2), 28–33.

Ross, J. K., III, Patterson, L. T., & Stutts, M. A. (1992). Consumer perceptions of organizations that use cause-related marketing. *Journal of the Academy of Marketing Science, 20*(1), 93–97.

Sagawa, S., & Segal, E. (2000). *Common interest, common good: Creating value through business and social sector partnerships.* Boston: Harvard Business School Press.

Smith, C. (1994). The new corporate philanthropy. *Harvard Business Review, 72*(May-June), 105–116.

Spethmann, B. (1999, February). Brands benefit from cause-based promotions as much as the nonprofits they support. *PROMO Magazine,* 31–36.

Strahilevitz, M., & Myers, J. G. (1998). Donations to charity as purchase incentives: How well they work may depend on what you are trying to sell. *Journal of Consumer Research, 24*(March), 434–446.

Till, B. D., & Nowak, L. I. (2000). Toward effective use of cause-related marketing alliances. *Journal of Product & Brand Management, 9*(7), 472–484.

Webb, D. J., & Mohr, L. A. (1998). A typology of consumer responses to cause-related marketing: From skeptics to socially concerned. *Journal of Public Policy & Marketing, 17*(2) 226–238.

Weeden, C. (1998). *Corporate social investing: The breakthrough strategy for giving and getting corporate contributions.* San Francisco: Berrett-Koehler.

Welsh, J. C. (1999). Good cause, good business. *Harvard Business Review, 77*(5), 21–23.

Wymer, W. W., Jr., & Samu, S. (2003a). Dimensions of business and nonprofit collaborative relationships. *Journal of Nonprofit & Public Sector Marketing, 11*(1), 3–22.

Wymer, W. W., Jr., and Samu, S. (Eds.). (2003b). *Nonprofit and business sector collaboration: Social enterprises, cause-related marketing, sponsorships, and other corporate-nonprofit dealings.* Binghamton, NY: Best Business Books.

Index

About the Authors

Walter Wymer, Jr., is Associate Professor of Marketing in the School of Business at Christopher Newport University (CNU), in Newport News, Virginia. He earned his D.B.A. from Indiana University in 1996, taught one year at Jacksonville University, and joined the faculty of CNU in 1997. His area of research expertise is nonprofit marketing. He has published peer-reviewed articles and given presentations on volunteer marketing, cause-related marketing, direct marketing, social marketing, and fundraising. He is a former president of the Atlantic Marketing Association. He is editor of the *Journal of Nonprofit & Public Sector Marketing* and North American editor of the *International Journal of Nonprofit & Voluntary Sector Marketing.*

Patricia Knowles is Associate Professor in the Department of Marketing, College of Business and Behavioral Science, Clemson University, Alabama, where she teaches courses in nonprofit marketing, promotional strategy, consumer behavior, and marketing principles. She joined the marketing faculty in the fall of 1991. Her academic research is concerned with issues in nonprofit marketing, marketing strategy analysis (such as product portfolio matrices), perceptions of promotional tools, and B2B advertising. She has published in the *Journal of Nonprofit and Public Sector Marketing, Journal of the Academy of Marketing Science, Marketing Education Review, Journal of Marketing Education, Marketing Management Journal, Journal of Service Research, Journal of Marketing Management, Journal of Personal Selling & Sales Management, Journal of Services Marketing, Journal of Business and Industrial Marketing, Journal of Education for Business, Journal of Teaching in International Business, Psychological Reports,* and *Journal of International Consumer Marketing,* as well as in specialized journals in the field of psychology. In addition, she has numerous national conference proceedings and has made many presentations. She is also coauthor of the textbook *Business Marketing,* published by McGraw-Hill/NTC in 2001. Her degrees include a B.A. in psychology, an M.A. in experimental psychology, and a Ph.D. in experimental/physiological psychology. In addition, she completed postdoctoral study at the University of Georgia in marketing.

Roger Gomes is Associate Professor in the Department of Marketing, College of Business and Behavioral Science, Clemson University, Alabama, where he teaches courses in international marketing, business-to-business marketing, and M.B.A. strategic analysis. He joined the marketing faculty in the fall of 1987. Previously, he had been technical manager and later a division marketing manager for first-tier suppliers to the automotive, copier, and computer industries. His academic publications span logistics, leadership, and e-commerce as they relate both to business and to nonprofit marketing. He has published in the *Journal of Nonprofit and Public Sector Marketing, Journal of the Academy of Marketing Science, Marketing Education Review, Journal of Marketing Education, Journal of Marketing Management, Journal of Segmentation in Marketing, Transportation Journal, Journal of Business Logistics, Journal of Current Issues and Research in Advertising, Industrial Marketing Management,* and *International Journal of Physical Distribution and Materials Management.* In addition, he has numerous national conference proceedings and has made many presentations. In addition to being on the editorial review boards of leading journals, he has twice been elected an officer and national executive board member of the Academy of Marketing Science, president of the regional Council of Logistics Management, and executive board member of the regional National Association of Purchasing Management. He is also coauthor of the textbook *Business Marketing,* published by McGraw-Hill/NTC in 2001. His degrees include a B.S. in mechanical engineering, an M.B.A. in management, and a Ph.D. in marketing.

Barry O'Mahony is a Senior Lecturer and Course Director for the Bachelor of Business in Events Management at Victoria University, Melbourne, Australia. He has extensive experience in the hospitality industry and has been in the field of education since 1988, first as an advanced skills teacher within the technical and further education sector and in his current position at Victoria University. He has acted as an adviser to a number of international organizations on the design, implementation, and maintenance of quality systems and is currently a registered auditor for AS/NZ ISO9001 (1994) Quality Systems.

Michael Polonsky is the Melbourne Airport Chair in Marketing in the School of Tourism, Hospitality and Marketing at Victoria University in Melbourne, Australia. Prior to taking up this position, he was an Associate Professor at the University of Newcastle and has also taught at Charles Sturt University (Australia), Massey University (New Zealand), the University of the Witwatersrand (South Africa), and Temple University (United States). He has a Ph.D. from the Australian Catholic University, two master's degrees (Rutgers University—Newark and Temple University), and a B.S. from Towson State University. His areas of research include environmental marketing and management, stakeholder theory, ethical and social issues in marketing, cross-cultural studies, and marketing education. He has published extensively across these areas, having coedited three books, one of which was recently translated into Chinese; authored or coauthored 11 book chapters; authored or coauthored 70 journal articles; and presented more than 100 presentations at national and international conferences. Some of his works have appeared in the *Journal of Market Focused Management, Journal of Marketing Communications, European Journal of Marketing, Business Horizons, Journal of Marketing Theory and Practice, Journal of Business Ethics, Journal of Macromarketing, Journal of Marketing Management, International Journal of Nonprofit and Voluntary Sector Marketing, Business Strategy and the Environment, International Journal of Retailing & Distribution Management, Journal of Organizational Change Management, Journal of Business and Industrial Marketing, International Marketing Review, International Journal of Advertising,* and *Journal of Advertising Research.*